VISUAL QUICKSTART GUIDE

FrameMaker 7

FOR WINDOWS AND MACINTOSH

Victoria Thomas

Peachpit Press

Visual QuickStart Guide
FrameMaker 7 for Windows and Macintosh
Victoria Thomas

Peachpit Press

1249 Eighth Street
Berkeley, CA 94710
510/524-2178
800/283-9444
510/524-2221 (fax)

Find us on the World Wide Web at: http://www.peachpit.com
To report errors, please send a note to errata@peachpit.com

Peachpit Press is a division of Pearson Education

Copyright © 2003 by Victoria Thomas

Editor: Becky Morgan
Production Coordinator: Connie Jeung-Mills
Copyeditor: Judy Ziajka
Compositor: Owen Wolfson
Indexer: Victoria Thomas
Cover Design: The Visual Group
Cover Production: Nathalie Valette

ISBN 0-321-15947-0

9 8 7 6 5 4 3 2 1

Printed and bound in the United States of America

Dedication

This book is dedicated to my parents,
Nance Thomas and Jack Thomas,
and to my sisters, Gai and Sandra.

Acknowledgments

I first want to thank Rebecca Gulick, a former colleague, who suggested me for this project. Thank you, Rebecca!

Working with Becky Morgan, my editor at Peachpit, has been a pleasure; I appreciate her insight about what users want and need and her straightforward and flexible attitude. Thank you also to Connie Jeung-Mills and Judy Ziajka.

I couldn't have managed working at home without the help and support of my husband, Marc Morris. (Although there were times when I had to be satisfied with the standard IT response to a call for help: "Well, it works for me. I don't know what you're doing wrong.")

Thank you to Eric Lopatin, a former colleague, who is currently working in the interoperability group at Adobe Systems. Eric contributed to this book in many ways, including: showing up at my house with a replacement keyboard the day after I splashed water on mine!

Thank you to Susan Frahm Modlin and Simon Bate, who wrote the excellent chapter on XML publishing, having had the opportunity to work with a beta version of FrameMaker 7.0.

Thank you to my former colleagues at Electronics for Imaging (EFI), with whom I worked for over six years. We did the impossible day in and day out and pushed FrameMaker to the extreme doing so.

Thank you to my colleagues at Blue Martini Software, who made it possible for me to take vacation days to work on the book at home.

Finally, thank you to the four founders of Frame Technology and creators of FrameMaker: Charles Corfield, Steve Kirsch, David Murray, and Vickie Blakeslee.

FOREWORD

I went to work as a technical editor at Frame Technology in June of 1990, several years before it was acquired by Adobe Systems.

Prior to 1990, I worked for several years at Addison-Wesley, an educational publisher, first as a copyeditor and then as a production editor. When the first computers arrived in the Secondary Math department, they were sequestered, along with a laser printer, off in a corner office for the desktop publishing group, a sort of electronic typing pool.

Developmental editors put their typed or hand-written copy into the in box and collected the computer printouts a couple of days later. But very quickly it became clear to the editors, if not to management, that there was something wrong. They endured typos and copy and paste errors (the best one was a math problem that started out with, "Twelve students were laid face down on a cafeteria table...," which they finally decided probably started out as, "Twelve playing cards were laid face down...").

The editors marched into the managing editor's office and demanded that the computers be distributed among the editors, who would use them to prepare their own manuscripts. *That* was the beginning of desktop publishing at Addison-Wesley.

After several years there, I had an opportunity at Frame Technology. But the position was put on hold and the hiring manager suggested I take a class in UNIX. I had no idea what UNIX was, but obediently enrolled in an intensive 18-week class at a local community college.

The UNIX class seemed to go on forever. People moved, babies were born, the seasons changed, and I kept going every Tuesday and Thursday. It made me more and more determined to launch myself into the age of desktop publishing.

When the call from Frame came, I was just about to give up hope and accept a job at Addison-Wesley. I had an agonizing weekend trying to decide what to do. On the one hand, I felt the call to devote my life to the generally underpaid, but noble, profession of educational publishing. On the other hand, high tech was singing its swan song. Frame was a startup, the salary was princely in comparison, and yes, I would be using a desktop publishing application to help create user manuals.

My first day at Frame went by in a blur. By then I knew that FrameMaker was a desktop publishing application. But I discovered that as a Technical Editor, I would not actually work in FrameMaker but would edit printed drafts. It was a major blow, but things looked better several months later when I moved to the Training group, where there was a great need for training materials—authored in FrameMaker. Working in FrameMaker was a joy and a delight, and I loved the task at hand, creating training for new users.

I've never developed any religious fervor for any one machine or OS. Since leaving a mainly UNIX environment at Frame, I've functioned in both Windows and Macintosh environments, and they both work for me. At Frame I fell madly in love with FrameMaker, however, and have never felt any different in the intervening years.

When Adobe Systems acquired Frame Technology and FrameMaker, we were all somewhat nervous. Would Adobe abandon FrameMaker in favor of (gulp) PageMaker? Lisa Kelly, a colleague and technical writer extraordinaire, said that she would continue to use FrameMaker even if she had to take the code in house and learn how to program to keep things going. That's how we all felt.

As I've moved into different positions in software and hardware companies, the truth is that today I work more in other applications. But I still roam around cubicles listening for someone who might want a little help with FrameMaker. I drop everything else to help and advise. My heart beats faster when I hear of someone in another group who's decided to use FrameMaker.

So, after all this time, I say thanks to Frame Technology for hiring me, thanks to Adobe Systems for embracing FrameMaker and making it even better, and most importantly, thanks to everyone I've ever worked with who knows and loves FrameMaker.

Victoria Thomas
vthomas5@earthlink.net
December 2002

TABLE OF CONTENTS

INTRODUCTION

Welcome to the *FrameMaker 7 for Windows and Macintosh: Visual QuickStart Guide.*

FrameMaker, the foremost application for creating technical documents, was released first for UNIX and soon after for Mac OS and then for Windows. Along the way, Frame Technology added SGML authoring with FrameMaker+SGML and HTML capabilities.

Now, FrameMaker has added XML authoring to its rich feature set. FrameMaker 7.0 is truly a powerful, enterprise-class authoring and publishing solution. Although the focus of this book is not on the authoring of structured documents, you will be introduced to the structured interface and associated concepts.

This book also shows you that FrameMaker can be a great choice for most of the documents you need to create. Simple reports, letters, and slide presentations are just as easy to create in FrameMaker as in most other desktop publishing applications.

Why Choose FrameMaker?

Your choice of FrameMaker depends on

◆ The kind of work you do

◆ The types of documents you want to create

◆ Whether and how you need to repurpose content

Among FrameMaker users are book authors (this book was authored in FrameMaker), technical writers, course developers, corporate knowledge workers, and information architects.

The types of documents you can create include content-driven documents, such as books and manuals, online help, and content-rich eBooks. But once you feel comfortable working in FrameMaker, you'll want to use it for all the corporate documents you create.

And FrameMaker has a fun side too. Look at the clip art provided with the program or import your own GIF and JPEG files to create more personal invitations and presentations (**Figure i.1**).

FrameMaker is adept at repurposing content with features such as conditional text, variables, import of templates that control document layout, size, and formatting—and powerful PDF, HTML, XML, and SGML export file types (**Figure i.2**).

Whether you're working in fully-formatted templates that ship with FrameMaker 7.0, using corporate or other templates, or creating your own templates, you can work quickly and effectively (**Figure i.3**). FrameMaker formatting is so efficient, you can focus on developing and organizing content, adding illustrations, and when you're ready, creating a PDF or other format file to share with others or publish.

Figure i.1 You can use the clip art that comes with FrameMaker in all kinds of documents.

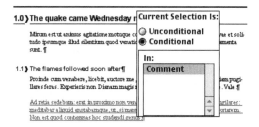

Figure i.2 A document can include conditional text, which appears in one or more versions and can be hidden or shown, as in this example. Text with the Comment condition is red and underlined.

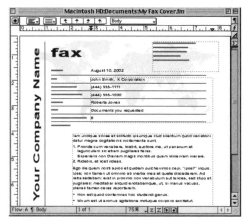

Figure i.3 Start by using FrameMaker templates; then try modifying them to create your own customized templates.

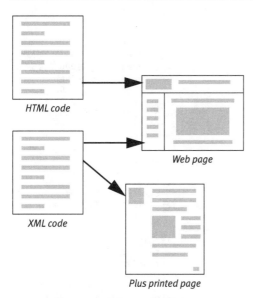

HTML code

Web page

XML code

Plus printed page

Figure i.4 HTML code describes how to display information on a Web page, but XML can also be used for printed output as well as Web content.

Figure i.5 The Element Catalog in the Structured FrameMaker interface looks much like the Paragraph Catalog and the Character Catalog.

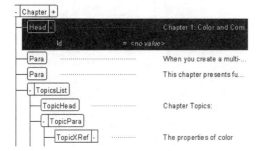

Figure i.6 The Structure View gives you an outline view of your document.

New Features in FrameMaker 7.0

In general, when Adobe releases a new version of FrameMaker, the features you know and love are still there, along with new features, including the release-defining features described in the following sections. As well as providing support for export to HTML via WebWorks Publisher, FrameMaker 7.0 takes advantage of the power of XML (**Figure i.4**).

Powerful XML capabilities

FrameMaker 7.0 provides powerful XML round-trip capabilities.

◆ Easily create and edit valid XML. Use FrameMaker's context-sensitive styling language to format your documents with EDDs (Element Definition Documents). Define read-write rules to automatically map XML elements to headings, lists, tables, graphics, and so on, using the Element Catalog (**Figure i.5**), the Structure View (**Figure i.6**), and continuous validation.

◆ Open, edit, and save XML files and DTDs. FrameMaker writes well-formed and valid code so that you can open an XML document in Structured FrameMaker and save it back out to XML—known as a a round trip—and have confidence that the code is compliant.

◆ Structured FrameMaker supports namespace usage for all elements in an XML document. When you import an XML document, all namespaces are preserved; and you can view, edit, add, or delete namespaces.

◆ Cascading Style Sheets (CSS) help preserve the look of a FrameMaker document when you export to HTML. When you save a document as HTML, a standardized .css file is automatically created. It contains formatting specifications that duplicate the look and feel of the original document.

◆ FrameMaker ships with three sample industry-standard structured applications (see page 342) for structured authoring: DocBook 4.1, xDocBook 4.1.2, and XHTML.

◆ Unicode (UTF-8 and UTF-16) characters in XML files are now automatically mapped to the appropriate fonts for printing from FrameMaker.

✔ Tips

■ A namespace is a collection of related XML element names identified by a unique namespace name, so that your globally declared element names won't clash with the same element names in someone else's document if your documents are combined. Namespaces also tell other applications which tags and attributes to process in an HTML or XML document.

■ Cascading Style Sheets let you assign font properties to all elements with a particular tag in an HTML or XML document (**Figure i.7**). You could always do this individually for each element, but using styles makes the task much easier. And of course, if you change your mind, you need to make the change in only one place and the change will be applied consistently throughout the document. Finally, you can use the same styles for different documents, thus enforcing styles across documents.

```
}
LI.Tip {
            display: block;
            text-align: left;
            text-indent: -13.500000pt;
            margin-top: 6.000000pt;
            margin-bottom: 0.000000pt;
            margin-right: 0.000000pt;
            margin-left: 13.500000pt;
            font-size: 10.000000pt;
            font-weight: bold;
            font-style: Regular;
            color: #000000;
            text-decoration: none;
            vertical-align: baseline;
            text-transform: none;
            font-family: "Kepler MM";
}
LI.Tip-Head {
            display: block;
            text-align: left;
            text-indent: 0.000000pt;
            margin-top: 6.000000pt;
            margin-bottom: 0.000000pt;
            margin-right: 0.000000pt;
            margin-left: 0.000000pt;
            font-size: 12.000000pt;
            font-weight: medium;
            font-style: Regular;
            color: #000000;
            text-decoration: none;
            vertical-align: baseline;
            text-transform: none;
            font-family: "Meta Plus Bold"
}
```

Figure i.7 Snippet of a .css file showing the mapping of Tip and Tip Head paragraph formats in FrameMaker to HTML elements.

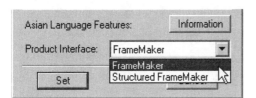

Figure i.8 You can change the interface in the File > Preferences dialog box.

File Info

Author:	Douglas Adams
Title:	Hitchhiker's Guide to the Galaxy
Subject:	An odyssy to find the meaning of the universe and everything else...
Keywords:	Humor, philosophy, space travel, aliens, other worlds, mathematics
Copyright:	Pocket Books
Web Statement:	Text only version of a very popular book, made into a television series in the UK by the BBC
Job Reference:	ISBN: 0671701592; (July 1982)
Marked:	Yes

Create Date: 1998-09-26T03:45:28.0Z
Modify Date: 2002-08-10T18:58:42.0Z
Metadata Date: 2002-08-10T18:58:42.0Z

Set (No Undo)   Cancel

Figure i.9 Metadata is descriptive information about the document that can be searched and processed by a computer.

Combined product

Previously FrameMaker and FrameMaker+ SGML were separate products, but now they are combined. When the product first launches, you can choose to work in the standard FrameMaker interface or in Structured FrameMaker. At any time you can change from one interface to the other by making a choice in the Preferences dialog box. Choose File > Preferences to display the Preferences dialog box (**Figure i.8**).

✔ Tip

■ To make the interface change take effect, Exit (Windows) or Quit (Mac OS) and then restart FrameMaker.

Improved and expanded multichannel publishing

Although FrameViewer (Windows) and FrameReader (Mac OS) are no longer supported in the current product, you can output documents from FrameMaker to many different formats depending on the ultimate destination of the document.

◆ Recent versions of FrameMaker integrate with Adobe Acrobat, which has become an industry standard on both Windows and Mac OS platforms. The latest version of Acrobat Distiller is bundled with FrameMaker. You can either export to "standard" PDF 1.4 or print to file and distill the resulting PostScript file.

◆ FrameMaker 7.0 now supports the XMP (eXtensible Metadata Platform) standard for describing document properties for work with content management systems, such as knowledge databases. Metadata is descriptive file information that can be searched and processed by a computer (**Figure i.9**). By embedding metadata tags in documents you make documents easier to track, manage, and retrieve.

NEW FEATURES IN FRAMEMAKER 7.0

◆ Using WebWorks Publisher Standard Edition 7.0, bundled with FrameMaker 7.0, you can create Web-ready HTML documents. You can use the HTML templates included with WebWorks Publisher., or you can use your own templates to tailor your Web pages.

WebWorks Publisher automatically converts any graphics format you use in a FrameMaker document to Web-safe GIF, JPG, and PNG versions. You can import SVG graphics and automatically rasterize them (convert them to bitmap format) at a chosen resolution.

◆ New features in WebWorks Publisher Standard Edition include:

▲ SVG image support

▲ Microsoft Reader and Palm Reader Standard Edition Templates

▲ AltText support, which allows you to add an alternate text description of an illustration as an attribute of the anchored frame that contains the illustration (**Figure i.10**)

▲ (Internet Explorer only) Support for display of Rubi characters in HTML and XML

▲ Improved online help, which uses the new WebWorks Help 3.0 format, with an auto-scrolling index, faster and better search, and easier navigation

◆ Create eBooks from FrameMaker documents by saving your books as tagged PDF files, which are readable with the Adobe eBook Reader and with the Acrobat Reader for Palm and Windows CE devices. You can specify PDF setup, bookmarks, tags, and links in the PDF Setup dialog box (**Figure i.11**).

✔ Tip

■ See your screen reader documentation for information on installation and use with FrameMaker or Acrobat documents.

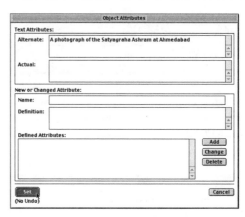

Figure i.10 Add alternate text (altText) descriptions for graphics in the Object Attributes dialog box.

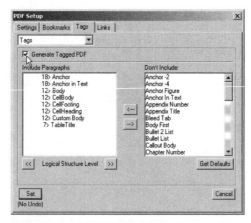

Figure i.11 In the PDF Setup dialog box, you can specify tags setup for eBooks.

New buttons

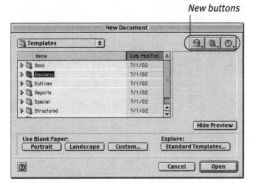

Figure i.12 The New Document dialog box.

Figure i.13 To save documents so that they can be opened in FrameMaker 6.0, choose Format > Documents 6.0 in the File > Save As dialog box.

Enhanced authoring tools

FrameMaker's authoring features have always been some of its greatest assets. Adobe has enhanced several of them as follows:

◆ You can associate specific paragraph tags (styles) on body pages with master pages of your choice. So for example, if you use the Chapter Title paragraph format on the first page of a new chapter, FrameMaker automatically uses a First custom master page.

◆ You can now rearrange master pages, whereas in previous versions they appeared in the order you added them.

◆ FrameMaker offers an expanded selection of layout options when you open a new document, and also a richer set of sample documents. The Mac OS New Document dialog box (**Figure i.12**) provides three new buttons at the top right: Shortcuts, Favorites, and Recents.

◆ Documents can be saved in FrameMaker 6.0 format for backward compatibility (**Figure i.13**).

◆ You can import new graphics file formats, including SVG format, placed PDF 1.4, and native Illustrator 9.0 and 10 files.

◆ FrameMaker 7.0 provides an updated set of text import filters for Microsoft Office.

NEW FEATURES IN FRAMEMAKER 7.0

Collaboration features

FrameMaker 7.0 now supports WebDAV protocol for workgroup management, a version-control process for passing documents from one collaborator to another (**Figure i.14**). Because this process works over Web-accessible networks, group members can share files no matter where they are physically located.

✔ Tip

■ To use the workgroup management features in FrameMaker, you must be able to connect to a WebDAV server. Once connected, you must specify a URL for each document For more information about WebDAV, see www.webdav.org.

Accessibility enhancements (Windows only)

FrameMaker 7.0 uses system colors to draw window backgrounds, text, and other graphics. Users who have trouble discerning different colors or variations in contrast or who have low visual acuity can set high-contrast color schemes and custom text and background colors in the Windows Control Panel to make the information in the FrameMaker interface easier to view.

✔ Tip

■ (Windows only) In addition to the FrameMaker built-in cursors, you can use custom system cursors. Locate the maker.ini file in the FrameMaker 7.0 folder and open it in a text editor. Change the value of UseSystemCursor to On, save the maker.ini file, and restart FrameMaker.

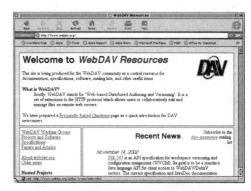

Figure i.14 A WebDAV Web page can be a valuable tool in a workgroup setting.

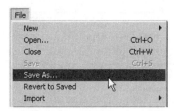

Figure i.15 Choose File > Save As or, in other words, "From the File menu, choose Save As."

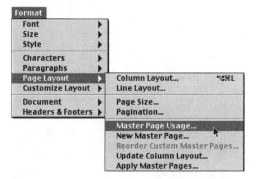

Figure i.16 Choose Format > Page Layout > Master Page Usage or, in other words, "From the Format menu, choose Page Layout and then Master Page Usage."

Using This Book

This book is similar to other Visual QuickStart Guides from Peachpit Press. Each chapter is divided into short sections that deal with specific topics. Each of the sections briefly introduces the topic and then presents procedures associated with the topic.

For example, in the chapter about tables, you find out how to insert a table, how to navigate within tables, how to add and delete table titles, and so on.

Platform-specific information

As with most Adobe applications, FrameMaker is almost identical on both Windows and Mac OS platforms. Places where it looks or works differently are called out in the text. In general Windows screen captures alternate with Mac OS screen captures.

Sidebars

Sidebars are used in this book to highlight or expand on material important to the chapter or anecdotal information that you might find interesting, but not vital. You can find them easily—they have a light gray background.

Menu commands

This book sometimes uses a shorthand to describe menu commands. For instance, the instruction "Choose Page Layout from the Format menu and then choose Master Page Usage" (**Figure i.15**) may be more succinctly stated as, "Choose Format > Page Layout > Master Page Usage" (**Figure i.16**).

Other actions

You will also see the following instructions:

◆ *Click* means press the left mouse button (Windows) or mouse button (Mac OS) and then release it. You click buttons and tools icons, you select radio buttons and check boxes, and you click in a document to place the cursor. Sometimes you double-click (**Figure i.17** and **Figure i.18**); or even triple-click (**Figure i.19**).

◆ *Press* usually means hold down a mouse button or a keyboard key.

◆ *Type* means enter text from the keyboard. You may be instructed to type your name, for example, or you may be give something very specific to type, for example, type My Document.

Screen captures

Screen captures are sometimes shown fully and sometimes a portion of the interface is shown. In the previous **Figure i.15**, for example, the File menu is longer than is shown, but the point is well illustrated without showing the entire menu. Sometimes settings are highlighted with a black oval.

Keyboard shortcuts

FrameMaker uses some of the universal platform shortcuts for each platform. For example, to copy selected text you can press Ctrl-C (Windows) or Command-C (Mac OS).

When two keyboard shortcuts are included for the same command, the first is generally for Windows and the second is for Mac OS, even when they are not explicitly identified as such.

A hyphen indicates that each key must be pressed simultaneously. For example, Ctrl-Z means to press the Control and Z keys at the same time. If the key sequence does not contain a hyphen, then press one key after

Figure i.17 In the FrameMaker document window, double-click a word to select it.

Figure i.18 Double-click a cross-reference or variable in the document window to open the Cross-Reference or Variable dialog box.

Figure i.19 Triple-click a paragraph to select it.

the other. For example, Esc space T means to press the Escape key, then the spacebar, then the T key.

Letter keys are always shown in uppercase; if you need to press the Shift key, it will be stated explicitly. For example, Ctrl-B means to press the Control key and the letter "b" at the same time, but not to hold down the Shift key.

In addition to common shortcuts, FrameMaker has keyboard shortcuts for almost every task you need to perform while you're working. Superusers work almost exclusively from the keyboard, and the number of keyboard shortcuts they know is staggering. Many are "secret" shortcuts they've gleaned from developers or user groups!

For a list of keyboard shortcuts, see Appendix A, "Keyboard Shortcuts."

Special characters

FrameMaker allows you to enter most of the special characters you need using keyboard shortcuts. I'm partial to em dashes and could not function well without knowing the keyboard shortcut, which is Control-Q Shift-Q (Windows) or Shift-Option-hyphen (Mac OS).

For a list of keyboard shortcuts for entering special characters, see Appendix B, "Special Characters."

Other references

This book does not document exhaustively every option on every menu or in every window or dialog box. Its goal is to show you what you need to do to perform basic and intermediate tasks. If you want to know about a feature or task in greater detail, consult the *FrameMaker 7.0 User Guide* or FrameMaker online help (see *Using Online Help* on page 20).

GETTING STARTED

You may already have FrameMaker 7.0 installed on your computer. As long as you have the components listed on *What to Install* on page 2, you'll be able to follow all of the procedures in this book.

System Requirements

Adobe lists the following system requirements for FrameMaker 7.0.

Windows

◆ Intel Pentium processor

◆ Microsoft Windows 98, Windows Millenium Edition, Windows 2000, Windows NT, or Windows XP

◆ 64 MB of RAM (128 MB recommended)

◆ 140 MB of available hard disk space (200 MB recommended)

◆ CD-ROM drive

◆ Video card capable of displaying 256 colors recommended

◆ Adobe PostScript, PCL, or GDI printer (Adobe PostScript printer recommended)

Mac OS

◆ PowerPC processor that supports the Energy Saver control panel (G3 or G4 recommended)

◆ Mac OS 9.0, 9.1, 9.2, or Mac OS X v.10.1 Classic

◆ 128 MB of RAM (256 MB recommended)

◆ 180 MB of available hard disk space (320 MB recommended)

◆ 800x600 VGA monitor (1,024x768 recommended)

◆ CD-ROM drive

◆ Macintosh compatible printer (Adobe PostScript printer recommended)

◆ Support for Adobe Type Manager (ATM) and TrueType

✔ Tip

■ It's hard to say whether you should go with the minimum or recommended RAM or hard disk space. If you plan to work with relatively small documents that are not graphics intensive, then the minimum requirements should work for you. But if you routinely work on long technical documents and often need to generate books with multiple files, your system needs to meet the recommended requirements.

What to Install

For both Windows and Macintosh versions of FrameMaker, you should install the following components.

FrameMaker 7.0 software

Unlike previous versions of FrameMaker, this version combines both FrameMaker (unstructured mode) and FrameMaker+ SGML (structured mode) in one product.

The first time you start the program, you can choose which interface you want to use (FrameMaker is chosen by default). At any time you can switch to the other interface by selecting it in the Preferences dialog box (see page 5).

✔ Tip

■ Fonts are not included with FrameMaker 7.0 for Windows. Fonts included with the Mac OS version are Arial, Euro Mono, Euro Sans, Euro Serif, Times New Roman, and Heisei.

International dictionaries

FrameMaker dictionaries are text files used for spell checking and hyphenation. When you specify a US English installation, US English dictionaries are installed. If you are going to be working with text in other languages supported by Adobe, you can install additional dictionaries. You can edit the dictionary files manually or just let FrameMaker edit them automatically when you spell check a document (see page 40).

Adobe Acrobat Distiller 5.0

You need to have Acrobat Distiller installed to save FrameMaker documents in PDF format, and you need Adobe Reader to view and print PDF files. Adobe Acrobat Reader 5.0 is installed with Acrobat Distiller; you do not need to install it separately. FrameMaker does not, however, include the full-featured Acrobat application.

✔ Tips

■ If you already have Acrobat Reader installed on your computer, you should upgrade it with this installation when you are prompted to do so.

■ (Windows only) FrameViewer support is discontinued in FrameMaker 7.0. In nearly all cases, you can transition from FrameViewer to Acrobat Reader.

WebWorks Publisher Standard Edition

You should install WebWorks Publisher if you need to convert FrameMaker files to any of the following onine formats:

◆ HTML

◆ HTML with Cascading Style Sheets (CSS)

◆ Microsoft Reader

◆ Palm Reader

◆ XML with CSS

◆ XML with eXtensible Stylesheet Language (XSL)

✔ Tip

■ You cannot create customized templates or modify existing templates with the Standard Edition. However, you can use templates created or modified in WebWorks Publisher Professional Edition with the Standard Edition.

Documentation

FrameMaker 7.0 comes with printed documentation, online manuals, and HTML-based online help system, which you can access with a standard Web browser.

Printed documentation

In addition to the Adobe FrameMaker 7.0 CD, you'll find the following documents in the FrameMaker box:

◆ *User Guide*

This reference manual contains detailed information about FrameMaker tools and commands.

◆ *Adobe FrameMaker Quick Reference Card* for Version 7.0

Keep this card near your computer. Once you get going with FrameMaker, you'll definitely want to explore keyboard shortcuts. On the back of the card is a list of keystrokes for entering special characters.

◆ WebWorks Publisher Standard Edition *Getting Started* booklet

Online help

Of course, the easiest way to access FrameMaker documentation while you're working is via the HTML-based help system.

To display FrameMaker online help, from the Help menu, choose Help Topics. Help opens in your default browser window. For more about using the help system, see page 20.

Online manuals

To access online manuals, go to the following location:

◆ Windows:
`D:\apps\Adobe\FrameMaker7.0\`
`OnlineManuals`
or

◆ Mac OS:
`Adobe FrameMaker 7.0:`
`OnlineManuals`

There, you'll find a number of manuals in PDF format, including the following. As you can see, they're specialized manuals and for the most part not geared toward a beginner or intermediate user.

◆ (Mac OS only) AppleScript_Reference.pdf
This document provides enough information to start you writing AppleScript scripts for FrameMaker products. You may want to use this manual in conjunction with a general-reference book on AppleScript.

◆ Character_Sets.pdf
This document lists the character sets used for FrameMaker 7.0 documents using Western fonts, and shows how to type each character in the set.

◆ Chinese_and_Korean_Features.pdf
FrameMaker supports Simplified Chinese, Traditional Chinese, and Korean features. You can display, enter, print, search and replace, import, and export Chinese and Korean text. using this manual as a guide.

◆ Customizing_Frame_Products.pdf
This document describes how to customize FrameMaker by changing settings in initialization files and creating custom menu configurations.

DOCUMENTATION

- Docbook_Starter_Kit.pdf
  The DocBook DTD is a commonly used DTD that defines markup for technical books and other computer documentation. FrameMaker provides a starter kit for the DocBook DTD that allows you to translate between XML documents using that DTD and FrameMaker documents.

- Filters.pdf
  This document describes and documents the filters that come with FrameMaker: document filters, text filters, and graphics filters.

- MIF_Reference.pdf
  MIF (Maker Interchange Format) is a group of ASCII statements that create an easily parsed, readable text file of all the text, graphics, formatting, and layout constructs that FrameMaker understands. Because MIF is an alternative representation of a FrameMaker document, it allows FrameMaker and other applications to exchange information while preserving graphics, document content, and format.

- MML_Reference.pdf
  MML (Maker Markup Language) is a markup language that you can use with any text editor to create simple, unstructured FrameMaker documents. Later, you can open the MML file as a FrameMaker document or import it into a FrameMaker template.

- Multiple_Platforms.pdf
  This document is primarily for those who use FrameMaker on different platforms and move documents among the platforms. It also covers issues of compatibility among different system configurations and upgrade versions.

- Structure_Dev_Guide.pdf
  This document is for anybody who develops structured FrameMaker templates and XML or SGML

applications. It is not for end users who author structured documents that use such templates and applications.

- XHTML_Starter_Kit.pdf
  XHTML is a reformulation of the HTML 4 document types as applications of XML. FrameMaker provides a starter kit for the XHTML DTD that you can use to translate between XML documents using that DTD and FrameMaker documents. This starter kit is an XML structure application. You can use the application as is or modify it to suit your organization.

- XMLcss.pdf
  The XMLcss plug-in examines the actual formatting used in a FrameMaker document and produces a CSS that ties element names to the actual formatting of these elements. Context-based formatting rules are also handled correctly.

✔ Tip

- A new manual, the *XML Cookbook* is available to help you learn to work in the structured authoring environment. To access this manual, go to:

  ▲ Windows:
  ```
  C:\Program Files\Adobe\
  FrameMaker7.0\XML Cookbook
  ```

  ▲ Mac OS:
  ```
  Adobe FrameMaker
  7.0:XMLCookBook
  ```

The *XML Cookbook* gives you a jump-start at implementing a structured authoring system for your documentation. It guides you through the development, authoring, and publishing stages—from creating a structured authoring template to importing and exporting XML. It contains examples, illustrations, and short tutorials to help you build your skills with Structured FrameMaker 7.0.

DOCUMENTATION

Using Adobe Online

Adobe Online provides access to up-to-the-minute information about services, products, and tips for using FrameMaker and other products.

To access the Adobe Web site for your region:

1. Go to www.adobe.com.

2. Click the Adobe Worldwide link and choose your geographical region.

To use Adobe Online:

1. In FrameMaker, choose Help > Adobe Online.

2. If it is your first time on the Web site, click Yes or No to automatic weekly checks.

   or

   Click Tell Me More to open a Web page describing the Adobe Online features.

3. Click Updates to open the Adobe Product Updates dialog box.

To set Adobe Online preferences:

1. Choose File > Preferences > Adobe Online.

2. From the pop-up menu, specify how often to check for new product updates.

✔ Tip

■ You must have an Internet connection and an Internet browser installed to use Adobe Online.

Register!

As with all software there are advantages and practically no disadvantages to registering your software. You can register in several different ways as listed in the *Technical Support, Upgrades, and Special Offers* booklet that comes with FrameMaker 7.0:

◆ Online

   You can register online when you first start the application after you choose the interface that you want to use. You need to be connected to the Internet to register online. You can also register at any time by choosing Help > Registration.

◆ Via the Web

   Go to www.adobe.com.

◆ By fax

◆ By mail

   The registration card is actually the back cover of the booklet, and it has your serial numbers for FrameMaker and (Quadralay) WebWorks already affixed at the bottom.

✔ Tip

■ If you live outside the United States or Canada, you'll need to find the label that represents the Adobe registration card processing center nearest your location and affix it on the front of the card to cover the address already printed there.

THE
DOCUMENT WINDOW

2

The best way to work with FrameMaker is to have the document window open on a full screen. Since I'm working on files that are part of a book file, I have the book open at the top left of the monitor and the documents open to the right of the book window.

A document window opens when you open a document—one for each document you have open on the screen. A window shows the document with its text formatted, its graphics and other content in place, and everything laid out in a page design.

All the illustrations in this chapter show simple FrameMaker, that is, FrameMaker without the SGML/XML interface.

✔ Tips

- ■ Regardless of the structure status of the document you open, FrameMaker opens in the interface you last chose. For example, you can open a document created in FrameMaker+SGML, but you won't see the structure views. And conversely, you can open a FrameMaker document in FrameMaker+SGML.

- ■ If you are using FrameMaker for the first time, to open a document for practice, from the File menu, choose New > Document. In the dialog box that appears, click Portrait at the bottom left.

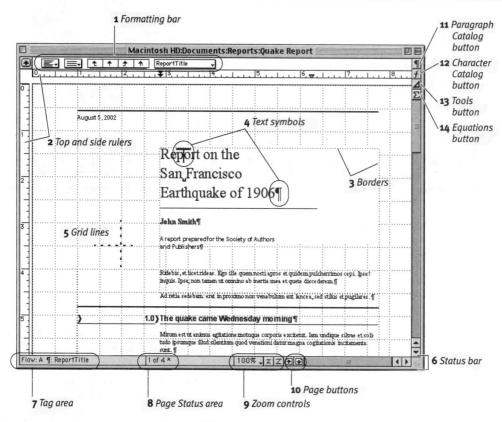

1 *Formatting bar*

11 *Paragraph Catalog button*

12 *Character Catalog button*

13 *Tools button*

14 *Equations button*

4 *Text symbols*

2 *Top and side rulers*

3 *Borders*

5 *Grid lines*

6 *Status bar*

7 *Tag area*

8 *Page Status area*

9 *Zoom controls*

10 *Page buttons*

Figure 2.1 The document window showing all View options on.

The Document Window

The document window (**Figure 2.1**) includes menus, tools, and settings you'll use when you work in FrameMaker.

1. *Formatting bar*

The formatting bar at the top of the document window contains text formatting controls including alignment, line spacing, tab stops, and paragraph tags. See *Using the formatting bar* on page 16.

2. *Top and side rulers*

The top ruler contains paragraph indent (upside-down triangles) and tab stop (arrows pointing up) symbols. When you draw, move, or resize an object, the object's position is shown on the rulers at the top and side.

3. *Borders*

Borders define text frames, graphic frames (anchored and unanchored), and imported objects that sit directly on the page.

4. *Text symbols*

Text symbols, such as paragraph or end-of-flow symbols, are nonprinting symbols you should have turned on as you work.

5. *Grid lines*

A visible square grid helps guide you if you're drawing or arranging objects.

6. *Status bar*

The status bar at the bottom of the document contains information about the document.

7. *Tag area*

The tag area on the far left of the status bar shows the following in order from left to right:

▲ Conditional text tag in parentheses (if present)

▲ Current flow (or nothing if the text flow is untagged)

▲ Paragraph format preceded by a paragraph symbol (¶)

▲ Character format preceded by a character symbol (*f*) (optional)

An asterisk (*) appears by the tag name if the tag contains a formatting override; it goes away when the document is saved.

8. *Page Status area*

The Page Status area displays the current page number and the total number of pages in the document. For files that are part of a book:

▲ The number on the left shows the page number in the book.

▲ The page number and total number of pages in parentheses refer to the document file only.

For example, if "11 (3 of 10)" appears in the Page Status area, the current page in the book is page 11, but the current page in the current document is page 3 out of a total of 10 pages in that document.

An asterisk (*) appears if the document has been changed since it was last saved; it goes away when the document is saved.

9. *Zoom controls*

Zoom controls display the current zoom percentage and include buttons for zooming in and out.

10. *Page buttons*

The page buttons take you to the previous or next page.

11. *Paragraph Catalog button*

The Paragraph Catalog button displays a palette of predefined paragraph text formats, or styles.

12. *Character Catalog button*

The Character Catalog button displays a palette of predefined text formats, or styles for paragraph format overrides.

13. *Tools button*

The Tools button displays the Tools palette, which contains drawing and graphics formatting tools.

14. *Equations button*

The Equations button displays the Equations palette, which contains commands for inserting, filling in, and manipulating equations.

This book does not include directions for working with equations and math symbols.

THE DOCUMENT WINDOW

Zooming

There are two ways to change the zoom setting of a document (**Figure 2.2**):

◆ Choose from the Zoom pop-up menu at the bottom of the window.

◆ Click the Zoom In or Out button at the bottom of the window.

To zoom in or out:

◆ From the Zoom menu at the bottom of the document window, choose a value greater or smaller than the current value.

or

Click the Zoom In or Zoom Out button. FrameMaker will zoom in to the next greater or next smaller value on the Zoom menu.

When you zoom in or out, FrameMaker automatically resizes the document window to fit the new size. If more than one page fits in the window, you can "shrink" the window around just the current page by choosing Fit Window to Page from the Zoom pop-up menu.

Although the values on the menu, 25%, 50%, and so on, will probably serve your purposes, if you wish you can customize the percentages on the Zoom menu.

To set new zoom values:

1. From the Zoom menu, choose Set (**Figure 2.3**).

   The Zoom Menu Options dialog box appears.

2. Change any of the percentage values in the boxes (**Figure 2.4**).

3. Click Set.

   You will see your new values the next time you display the Zoom menu. FrameMaker reorders values in ascending order.

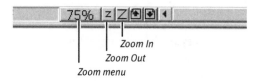

Zoom In
Zoom Out
Zoom menu

Figure 2.2 Choose from the Zoom pop-up menu or click the Zoom Out or Zoom In button.

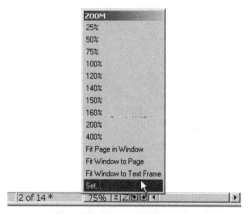

Figure 2.3 Choose a percent from the Zoom menu or choose Set to set new zoom values. To resize the window to fit the current page, choose Fit Window to Page.

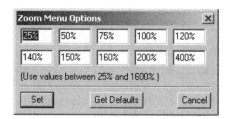

Figure 2.4 Change any of the values in the Zoom Menu Options dialog box, and FrameMaker automatically reorders them on the menu.

ZOOMING

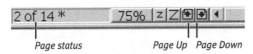

Page status   Page Up   Page Down

Figure 2.5 Click in the Page Status area to go to a particular page, or use the Page Up and Page Down buttons at the bottom right.

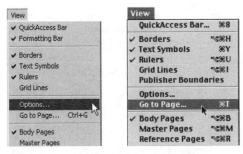

Figure 2.6 To set options such as the display units of rulers, from the View menu, choose Options (left). To go to a particular page, choose Go to Page (right).

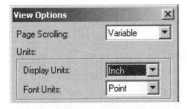

Figure 2.7 These are good default settings in the View Options dialog box.

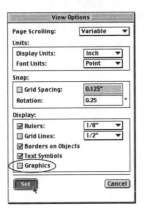

Figure 2.8 You turn on or off display of graphics in the View Options dialog box.

Navigating

There are a number of ways to navigate in a FrameMaker document besides using the scroll bars at the right and bottom.

To go to a particular page:

1. Click in the Page Status area (**Figure 2.5**).

   or

   From the View menu, choose Go to Page (**Figure 2.6**).

2. Type the page number in the Go to Page dialog box that appears.

To page up and down:

◆ Click the Page Up or Page Down button (**Figure 2.5**).

To set page scrolling:

1. From the View menu, choose Options (**Figure 2.6**).

2. In the View Options dialog box, choose an option from the Page Scrolling menu at the top (**Figure 2.7**).

   To display as many pages as will fit in the window from left to right, choose Variable, the most practical option. You can also choose Vertical or Horizontal. Choose Facing Pages to display pages two at a time, side by side.

✔ Tips

■ To go to the first or last page in a document, hold down the Shift key and click the Page Up or Page Down button.

■ To navigate in a document more quickly, turn off the display of graphics. From the View menu, choose Options to display the View Options dialog box (**Figure 2.8**), where you can turn off graphics. Anchored frames will behave as if they're empty and pages will draw faster on the screen. Whenever you wish, you can turn on graphics again.

NAVIGATING

View Options

You should have borders, text symbols, and rulers (**Figure 2.9**) turned on when you're working in a FrameMaker document.

◆ Borders (**Figure 2.10**) allow you to see the boundaries of text and graphics frames and imported graphics.

◆ With text symbols on (**Figure 2.11**), you'll avoid accidentally deleting markers, such as cross-reference, index, and conditional text markers. When you copy and paste text, you can see whether the text has an index marker, for example, that you may need to delete or change.

◆ The top ruler shows you the first, left, and right margin symbols and the type and location of tab stops.

If you wish, you can also work with visible grid lines on, as shown in **Figure 2.1**. But many users find grid lines distracting, and so do I unless I'm creating an illustration in FrameMaker.

To turn rulers on or off:

◆ From the View menu, choose Rulers.

To turn borders on or off:

◆ From the View menu, choose Borders.

To turn text symbols on or off:

◆ From the View menu, choose Text Symbols.

You can also turn on or off rulers, borders, and text symbols in the View Options dialog box (see page 14).

Figure 2.9 To work efficiently and effectively, work with these View options on.

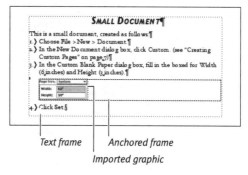

Text frame   Anchored frame
Imported graphic

Figure 2.10 Work with borders on so you can see all of the elements in the document window.

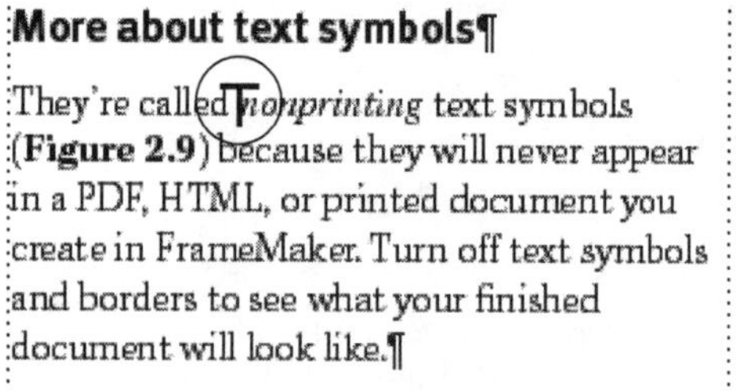

More about text symbols¶

They're called *nonprinting* text symbols (**Figure 2.9**) because they will never appear in a PDF, HTML, or printed document you create in FrameMaker. Turn off text symbols and borders to see what your finished document will look like.¶

Figure 2.11 In this illustration, if you drag to select the word "nonprinting" and cut and paste it elsewhere without the index marker displayed, you risk leaving the index marker stranded in its original location.

Report on the
San Francisco
Earthquake of 1906¶

John Smith¶

A report prepared for the Society of Authors
and Publishers¶¶

Figure 2.12 FrameMaker has very fine text formatting controls, including the ability to keep words together, in the example above, with a nonbreaking space between the words "San" and "Francisco."

More about text symbols

Text symbols are called nonprinting because they never appear in a PDF, HTML, or printed document you create in FrameMaker. Turn off text symbols and borders to see what your finished document will look like.

Symbols for the following appear in the document window when you turn on text symbols: paragraph and end-of-flow, tab, anchor, marker, forced (soft) return, nonbreaking space (**Figure 2.12**), discretionary hyphen, and suppress hyphenation.

✔ Tip

■ If you have conditional text in your document, you must work with text symbols on to avoid accidentally deleting *hidden* conditional text, shown by the presence of a marker symbol (see **Figure 10.9** on page 190).

Borders and Grids

Borders appear around text frames, graphic frames, and imported objects when the Borders view option is on. You work with borders on, as shown in **Figure 2.10**, so you can see the boundaries of, for example, an anchored frame.

You should turn off borders when you want to see what your final document will look like when it's printed. In addition, when you're using a graphics frame to crop an image, you should zoom in and turn off borders so you can see exactly how much of the image appears in the document.

For example, when I display the *Small Document* that I created especially for this book, I don't want to take up page real estate to show the title banner. Once I've imported the graphic, I turn off borders and then microposition the graphic (see page 116) inside its anchored frame (see page 150) so that just the right amount of the document window shows at the top.

There are two types of grids to help you draw and align objects:

◆ Visible grid, shown in **Figure 2.13**.

◆ Invisible snap grid, which attracts objects to it as you draw, rotate, resize, or drag objects, including indent and tab stop symbols on the top ruler.

   For more information about indents and tab stops, see *Changing Basic Paragraph Properties* on page 64. For more about using the snap grid for drawing and resizing, see *Using Grids* on page 105.

I work with Snap turned off most of the time but I use this feature for repetitive tasks in which I want to do *exactly* the same thing every time. I use the visible grid when drawing or sometimes when positioning objects. Set grid spacing for both grids in the View Options dialog box (**Figure 2.14**).

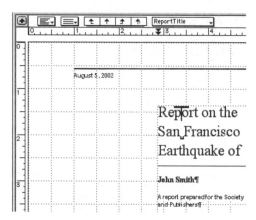

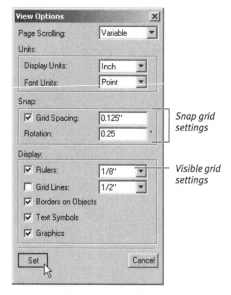

Figure 2.13 The visible grid appears in the document window, but it doesn't appear when you print the document.

Figure 2.14 Turn on Snap and specify the spacing between grid lines in the Grid Spacing text box. Choose a value from the Grid Lines menu to specify the space between grid lines for the visible grid.

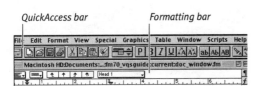

QuickAccess bar   Formatting bar

Figure 2.15 The QuickAccess bar includes both common document commands such as Print and text formatting commands such as Bold and Italic.

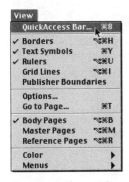

Figure 2.16 Choose View > Quick Access Bar.

Orientation   Commands

Figure 2.17 You can change the vertical or horizontal orientation of the QuickAccess bar; you can also display any of four groups of commands.

Using Toolbars

In addition to the status bar at the bottom of the document window, there are two toolbars (**Figure 2.15**):

◆ The QuickAccess bar

◆ The formatting bar

Unless your monitor has significant real estate issues, you should work with the formatting bar displayed at the top of the window. You can also work with the QuickAccess bar displayed.

Using the QuickAccess bar

The QuickAccess bar provides a versatile and easy way to access common file commands such as New, Open, Save, and Print with a simple click. It also includes editing commands such as Cut, Copy, Paste, and Clear and special commands such as Anchored Frame, Footnote, and Insert Table. You can change the orientation of the QuickAccess bar from vertical to horizontal and back.

✔ Tip

■ All the commands on the QuickAccess bar are shown on the front of the *Quick Reference Card*.

To display the QuickAccess bar:

◆ From the View menu, choose the first option, QuickAccess Bar (**Figure 2.16**).

To change the orientation of the QuickAccess bar:

◆ Click the Orientation button (**Figure 2.17**). The QuickAccess bar toggles between horizontal and vertical orientation.

To display a different set of commands:

◆ Click the up or down button in the middle of the QuickAccess bar (**Figure 2.17**).

The small chart icon shows you which group of commands you have displayed.

To close the QuickAccess bar:

◆ (Windows) From the View menu, choose QuickAccess bar.

(Mac OS) Click the close box on the bar.

Using the formatting bar

Formats in a FrameMaker document are stored in three catalogs:

◆ Paragraph Catalog (see page 62)

◆ Character Catalog (see page 88)

◆ Table Catalog (see page 203)

A Structured FrameMaker document also has an Element Catalog (see page 328).

In addition to using the Paragraph Catalog to format text, you can also format paragraphs from a menu on the formatting bar.

To display or hide the formatting bar:

◆ (Windows) From the View menu, choose Formatting Bar (**Figure 2.18**).

(Mac OS) Click the arrow at the top left of the document window (**Figure 2.19**).

The arrow points up when the toolbar is displayed and down when it's hidden. You must have rulers turned on to display the formatting bar.

You can specify a number of settings on the formatting bar (**Figure 2.20**):

◆ Alignment of paragraphs in a text frame.

◆ Line spacing between lines of text in a paragraph or between paragraphs.

Figure 2.18
(Windows only) Choose
View > Formatting Bar.

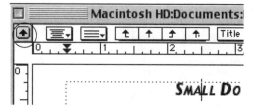

Figure 2.19 (Mac OS only) The arrow at the top left toggles display of the FrameMaker formatting bar at the top of the document window.

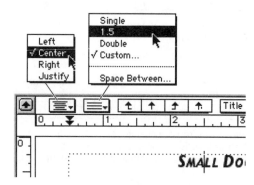

Figure 2.20 With the insertion point in a paragraph or with multiple paragraphs selected, choose from the Alignment or Spacing pop-up menu on the formatting bar. To set the spacing between paragraphs, you must select two paragraphs.

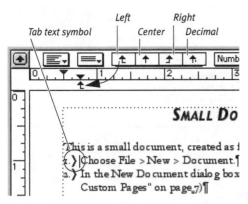

Figure 2.21 With the insertion point in a paragraph, you can drag a tab stop from the toolbar into the top ruler in the document window. The toolbar has four types of tab stops: Left, Center, Right, and Decimal.

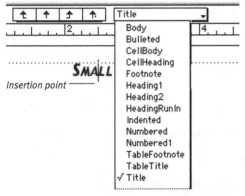

Figure 2.22 Choose a paragraph format from the pop-up menu to apply to the current paragraphs.

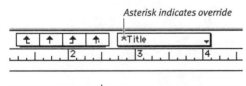

Figure 2.23 An asterisk (*) at the beginning of the paragraph tag indicates that the current paragraph is different from the paragraph format stored in the Catalog.

◆ Tab stops in the top ruler (**Figure 2.21**). For more about tabs, see page 82.

◆ Paragraph (format) tags in a pop-up menu For more about applying formats, see below.

✔ Tip

■ Changing or creating tabs is a two-step process:

▲ Define a tab stop.

▲ Press the Tab key in the document to move the insertion point to the defined tab stop.

For example, in **Figure 2.21** you can see the tab stop on the rule at the 3/4-inch mark and the tab text symbol in the paragraph itself.

To apply a paragraph format from the formatting bar:

◆ With the insertion point in a paragraph or with several paragraphs selected, choose a paragraph tag from the pop-up menu (**Figure 2.22**).

The format you chose is applied to the paragraphs.

To update all paragraphs from the formatting bar:

1. Make any changes you want to make to the current paragraph in the Paragraph Designer (see page 63).

   The paragraph format menu displays the format of the paragraph that contains the insertion point. An asterisk appears in front of the format (**Figure 2.23**).

2. From the pop-up menu on the formatting bar, choose Update All.

   The Update Paragraph Format dialog box appears.

   (continues on next page)

USING TOOLBARS

3. Click Update (**Figure 2.24**).

The new paragraph format settings are applied to all paragraphs that have the same tag, and are then stored in the Paragraph Catalog.

The asterisk disappears from the paragraph tag to indicate that the paragraph no longer has a format override applied.

To add a new paragraph format to the Catalog from the formatting bar:

1. Make any changes you wish to make to the current paragraph in the Paragraph Designer (see page 63).

2. From the pop-up menu on the formatting bar, chose New Format (**Figure 2.25**).

3. In the New Format dialog box, type a name for the new format (**Figure 2.26**).

4. Click Create.

The new format is stored in the Paragraph Catalog and applied to the current paragraphs. It now appears in the pop-up menu on the formatting bar (**Figure 2.27**).

✔ Tip

■ Make paragraph format names, or tags, meaningful. In this book, for example, the paragraph format with the title of each chapter is called Chapter Title. Paragraphs that are steps in procedures are called Number List.

By using meaningful names, you'll find it easier to work in your documents over time, when you may forget the function of the formats you've created. And if another person has to work in the document, that person's life will be easier too.

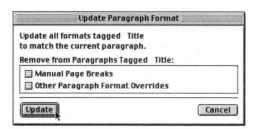

Figure 2.24 When you make changes to a paragraph format, choosing Update All from the Paragraph menu on the formatting bar to display the Update Paragraph Format dialog box.

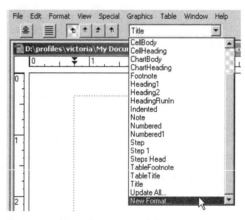

Figure 2.25 From the paragraph format pop-up menu, choose New Format.

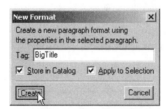

Figure 2.26 Type a name for the new format in the New Format dialog box.

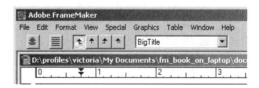

Figure 2.27 The new format appears in the menu.

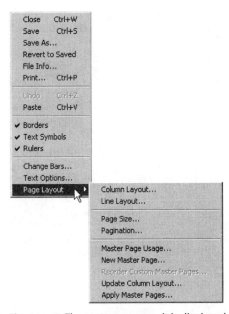

Figure 2.28 The context menu as it is displayed in the margin of a document window, outside a text column (Windows).

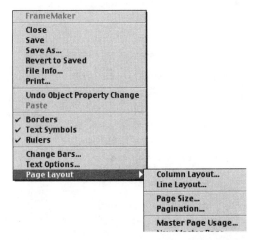

Figure 2.29 The context menu as it is displayed in the margin of a document window, outside a text column (Mac OS).

Using Context Menus

Context menus contain commands that change depending on the focus of the pointer. For example, the commands on the context menu are different when the pointer is:

◆ In the margin of a document

◆ Over text (see page 60)

◆ Over a graphic (see page 168)

◆ Over a table (see page 240)

To display a context menu:

◆ (Windows) Right-click (**Figure 2.28**).
or
(Mac OS) Control-click or right-click if you have a two-button mouse (**Figure 2.29**).

The context menu displayed in the margin of a document window, outside any text columns, includes commands from the File menu, the Format menu, and the View menu—commands that affect your work in the document as a whole. It provides a quick and easy way to change view options in the document window, for example.

Using Online Help

FrameMaker provides a comprehensive, HTML-based online help system.

To launch online help:

◆ From the Help menu, choose Help Topics (**Figure 2.30**).

or

Press F1 or the Help key.

✔ Tip

■ You need Netscape Communicator 4.0 or later or Microsoft Internet Explorer 4.0 or later to view online help.

You can use the Contents and Index links on the left to find general information, and the Search link to look up specific words or phrases. It may take a little more time to wait for the search database to load the first time, but it will help you if you're unfamiliar with FrameMaker features and terminology.

In addition to using the table of contents or index, you can search for a topic.

To search online help:

1. Click the Search link at the top left of the window (**Figure 2.31**).

2. Type a word or phrase in the text box.

3. Click the Search button.

A list of links to relevant topics appears under the Search button (**Figure 2.32**).

Figure 2.30 Help comes up in your default browser window.

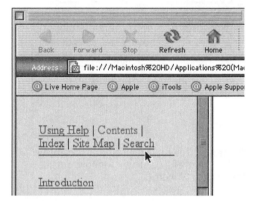

Figure 2.31 To search onlne help, click the Search link at the top left of the window.

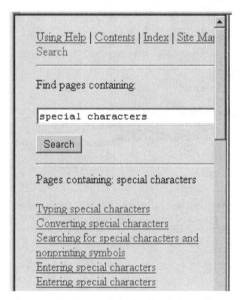

Figure 2.32 This search looked for information on typing special characters into dialog boxes.

Figure 2.33 Choose the product interface in the Preferences dialog box.

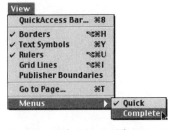

Figure 2.34 The View quick menu; to display the complete menu, choose View > Menus > Complete.

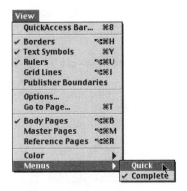

Figure 2.35 The View complete menu; to display the quick menu, choose View > Menus > Quick.

Changing the Interface

FrameMaker 7.0 includes both FrameMaker and Structured FrameMaker (formerly called FrameMaker+SGML). When you start FrameMaker for the first time, you will be prompted to choose an interface. FrameMaker is chosen by default.

To change the product interface:

1. From the File menu, choose Preferences > General.

   The Preferences dialog box appears.

2. From the Product Interface menu at the bottom of the dialog box, choose FrameMaker or Structured FrameMaker (**Figure 2.33**).

3. Click Set.

Restart FrameMaker to make the change take effect.

You can display a full set of menu commands in the main menus at the top of the document window or just subsets of the menu commands, called quick menus.

To display quick or complete menus:

◆ From the View menu, choose Menus > Complete (**Figure 2.34**) or Menus > Quick (**Figure 2.35**).

✔ Tips

■ If you are working in Structured FrameMaker, the FrameMaker interface may have been customized to show and hide menu commands to take advantage of templates and workflow at your site using the Frame Developer's Kit (FDK), a separate product that provides tools for developers to use to customize the FrameMaker interface.

■ If you don't see all of the menu commands described in this book, you may have quick menus displayed.

ADDING AND EDITING TEXT

Adding and editing text in FrameMaker is much like editing text in other authoring applications—but much, much better and easier. Features such as Smart Spaces and Smart Quotes and powerful search and cross-reference capabilities make every user a power user.

Smart Spaces prevent you from typing more than one space in a row; Smart Quotes automatically substitute curvy quotation marks when you type straight quotation marks. Of course, if you prefer not to use them, they can be turned off.

In the Find/Change window, in addition to searching for text, you can search for markers, unresolved cross-references, and even paragraph and character formats. You can then change the text you find to text or you can paste text from the Clipboard.

And be sure to look at the special copy options in FrameMaker: you can copy paragraph and character formats, conditional text settings, and table column widths.

Selecting Text

FrameMaker gives you a number of options for selecting text:

◆ Drag to select.

◆ To select a word, double-click it.

◆ To select a paragraph, triple-click it.

◆ To select a range of text, click at the beginning (or double-click the first word) and Shift-click at the end.

◆ To select all of the text in a text flow, with the insertion point in a text frame, from the Edit menu, choose Select All in Flow (**Figure 3.1**).

Here are some keyboard shortcuts for selecting text:

◆ To select a single character, press Esc H C (highlight character). FrameMaker selects the first character to the right of the insertion point (**Figure 3.2**).

◆ To select a sentence, with the insertion point in the sentence, press Esc H S (highlight sentence) (**Figure 3.3**).

✔ Tips

■ It's generally better to double-click and triple-click instead of dragging to select words and paragraphs. It's more accurate and you won't accidentally leave behind the first or last characters or include leading and trailing spaces you don't want to include.

■ If you try to choose Select All in Flow and instead you see the command Select All on Page, the insertion point is not in a text flow. Click in a text flow and try again.

■ Use the Esc H C shortcut to select markers, which can be notoriously difficult to select, rather than trying to drag to select them.

Figure 3.1 With the insertion point in a text frame in your document, choose Edit > Select All in Flow.

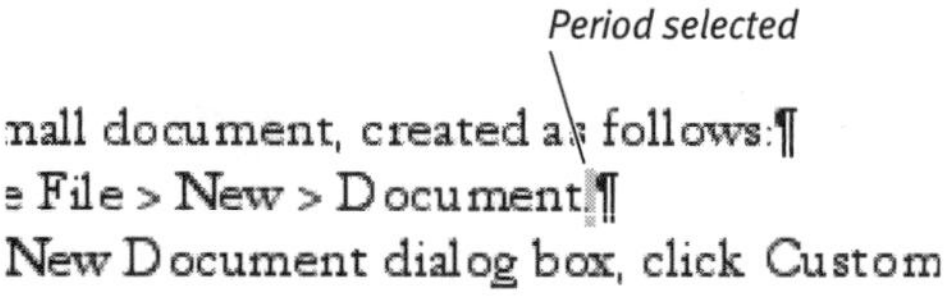

Period selected

Figure 3.2 Use the keyboard shortcut Esc H C to select a single character, such as a period.

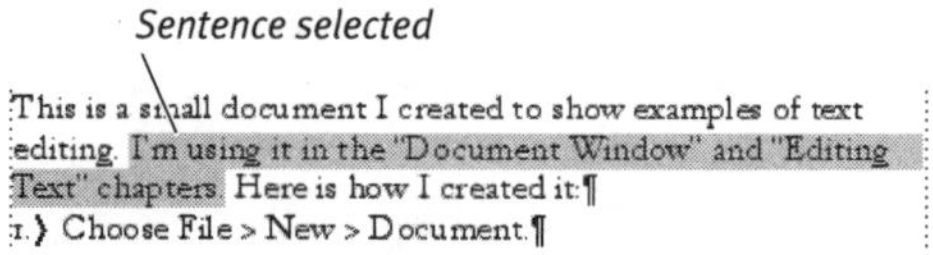

Sentence selected

Figure 3.3 Make your selection more accurate by using the keyboard shortcut Esc H S to select a sentence. You can then extend your selection by Shift-clicking farther along.

Figure 3.4 When you choose Cut, the selected text is deleted, but when you choose Copy, it stays in place.

Figure 3.5 If nothing is selected, the Cut and Copy commands are dimmed (unavailable).

Copying, Moving, and Deleting Text

On both Windows and Mac OS platforms, you copy, paste, and delete pretty much the same as in other applications. You can copy and paste text:

- ◆ Between documents

- ◆ Into a dialog box

To copy selected text:

- ◆ From the Edit menu, choose Copy (**Figure 3.4**).

    or

    Press Esc E C or Ctrl-C or Command-C.

    The selected text is copied to the Clipboard, where it stays until you copy or cut text again.

To cut selected text:

- ◆ From the Edit menu, choose Cut.

    or

    Press Ctrl-X or Command-X.

    You can also use the Esc E X shortcut.

    The selected text is deleted and copied to the Clipboard, where it stays until you copy or cut text again.

If nothing is selected, the Copy and Cut commands are dimmed on the menu (**Figure 3.5**). For special copy options that allow you to copy text formats, see pages 84 and 91.

To paste text from the Clipboard:

- ◆ From the Edit menu, choose Paste.

    or

    Press Esc E P or Ctrl-V or Command-V.

✔ Tip

■ Text on the Clipboard always retains its character format. For example, if you copy and paste text from one paragraph into a paragraph, with a different format, it retains the paragraph font properties of the paragraph it came from (**Figure 3.6**). Select the text and apply the Default ¶ Font character tag (**Figure 3.7**) to format this text to match the surrounding text (**Figure 3.8**).

If you include a paragraph symbol (¶) with the text you copy or cut, when you paste the selection, the paragraph format is also pasted.

You can also move text without first copying it to the Clipboard as long as the original and new locations are both in the document window.

To copy and paste text without using the Clipboard:

1. Put the insertion point where you want to paste the copied text (**Figure 3.9**).

2. (Windows) Hold down the Alt key and select the text you want to copy and paste (**Figure 3.10**).

   or

   (Mac OS) Hold down the Command and Control keys and select the text you want to copy and paste.

   The copied text appears at the insertion point (**Figure 3.11**).

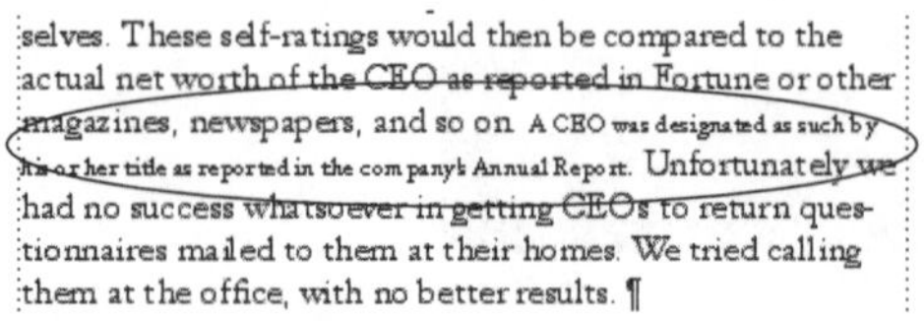

selves. These self-ratings would then be compared to the actual net worth of the CEO as reported in Fortune or other magazines, newspapers, and so on. A CEO was designated as such by his or her title as reported in the company's Annual Report. Unfortunately we had no success whatsoever in getting CEOs to return questionnaires mailed to them at their homes. We tried calling them at the office, with no better results. ¶

Figure 3.6 When you paste text from one paragraph into another, the text retains its format.

Figure 3.7 Click the Character Catalog button to display the Character Catalog.

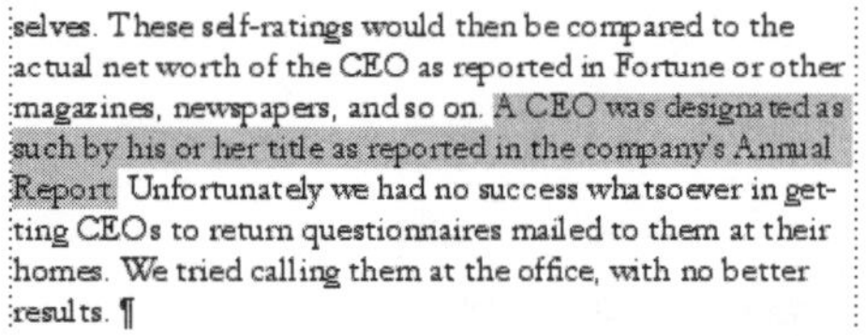

selves. These self-ratings would then be compared to the actual net worth of the CEO as reported in Fortune or other magazines, newspapers, and so on. A CEO was designated as such by his or her title as reported in the company's Annual Report. Unfortunately we had no success whatsoever in getting CEOs to return questionnaires mailed to them at their homes. We tried calling them at the office, with no better results. ¶

Figure 3.8 Default ¶ Font character format changes text to the default font properties of its paragraph format.

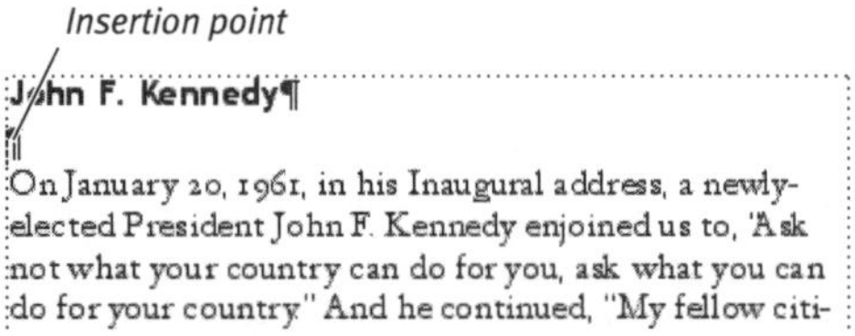

Insertion point

John F. Kennedy¶

On January 20, 1961, in his Inaugural address, a newly-elected President John F. Kennedy enjoined us to, "Ask not what your country can do for you, ask what you can do for your country." And he continued, "My fellow citi-

Figure 3.9 Although it seems backward, first click where you want to copy the text ...

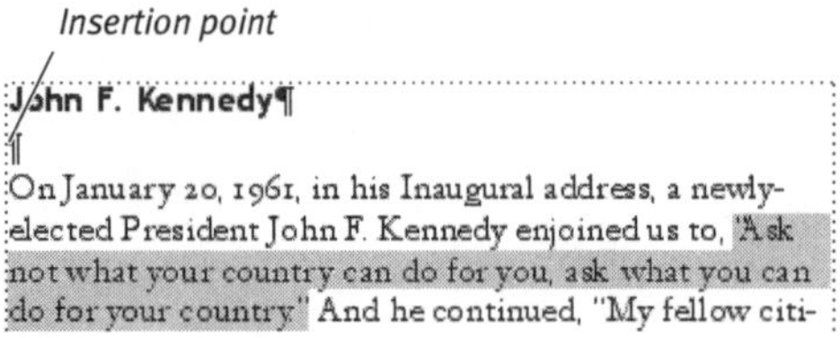

Insertion point

John F. Kennedy¶

On January 20, 1961, in his Inaugural address, a newly-elected President John F. Kennedy enjoined us to, "Ask not what your country can do for you, ask what you can do for your country." And he continued, "My fellow citi-

Figure 3.10 ... then hold down keys while you select the text you want to copy and paste.

John F. Kennedy¶

"Ask not what your country can do for you, ask what you can do for your country."¶

On January 20, 1961, in his Inaugural address, a newly-elected President John F. Kennedy enjoined us to, "Ask not what your country can do for you, ask what you can do for your country." And he continued, "My fellow citi-

Figure 3.11 The selected text is pasted at the insertion point.

Figure 3.12 The Undo command can be a life saver when you're moving text around.

Edit

Undo	⌘Z
Cut	⌘X
Copy	⌘C
Paste	⌘V
Clear	~W
Copy Special	▶
Select All in Flow	⌘A

Figure 3.13 You cannot go back to the text that was overwritten on the Clipboard by undoing a copy.

To delete selected text:

◆ Press Back Space, Delete, or Esc E B.

or

From the Edit menu, choose Clear.

To undo an edit:

◆ Immediately after you cut, paste, or clear, from the Edit menu, choose Undo (**Figure 3.12**).

The command is undone.

✔ Tips

■ FrameMaker has only one level of undo. Also, you cannot undo the Copy command and go back to text that was on the Clipboard before you copied the last selection. If you try to choose Undo after copying text, the command will be dimmed on the menu (**Figure 3.13**).

■ If you copy and paste text that includes an index or cross-reference marker and then you change some details of the text, be sure to delete the cross-reference marker and revisit the index marker text (see page 281) to ensure that it's still relevant.

■ If text you copy and paste contains hidden conditional text, the conditional text will be copied and pasted along with the text you intend to copy and paste, even though you can't see it. If this is not your intention, then you need to display the hidden conditional text and delete it

Better yet, when a document contains conditional text, work with all text showing, including conditional text (see page 189).

COPYING, MOVING, AND DELETING TEXT

Formatting Text

Text formats, or styles, are specified in the Paragraph and Catalog Designers and stored in the Paragraph and Character Catalogs. Unless you are building templates or modifying formats in FrameMaker templates, you will be applying predefined formats. (For details about creating or modifying formats, see Chapter 4 and Chapter 5.)

The name of the format is called a "tag" and Paragraph and Character Catalogs provide a list of tags for formats that have been defined in a template or by a document designer.

To display the Paragraph Catalog:

◆ Click the Paragraph Catalog button at the top right of the document window (**Figure 3.14**).

or

Choose Format > Paragraphs > Catalog.

or

Press Ctrl-M or Command-M.

The Catalog appears (**Figure 3.15**).

To display the Character Catalog:

◆ Click the Character Catalog button.

or

Choose Format > Characters > Catalog.

or

Press Ctrl-D or Command-D.

The Catalog appears (**Figure 3.15**).

When you apply a *paragraph* format, it affects the current paragraph (the one with the insertion point) (**Figure 3.16**) or multiple selected paragraphs (**Figure 3.17**).

When you apply a *character* format, which changes just a portion of the text in a paragraph, you must first select the text (**Figure 3.18**). Character formats are also used to format text lines (see page 127).

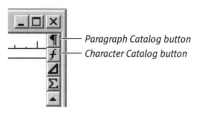

Paragraph Catalog button
Character Catalog button

Figure 3.14 Click the Paragraph Catalog or Character Catalog button to display the Catalog.

Figure 3.15 Paragraph and Character Catalogs are floating palettes, which you can resize or move.

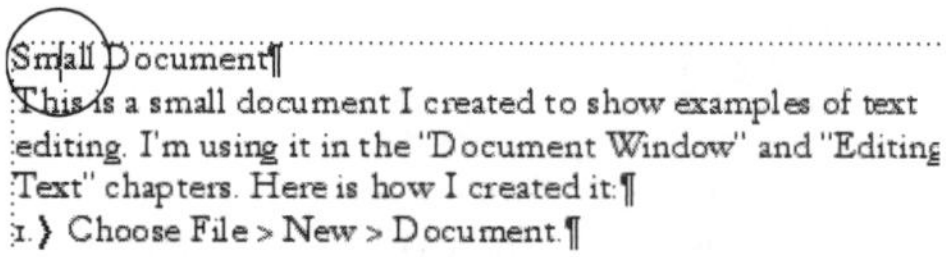

Figure 3.16 To select a paragraph to format, either put the insertion point in the paragraph ...

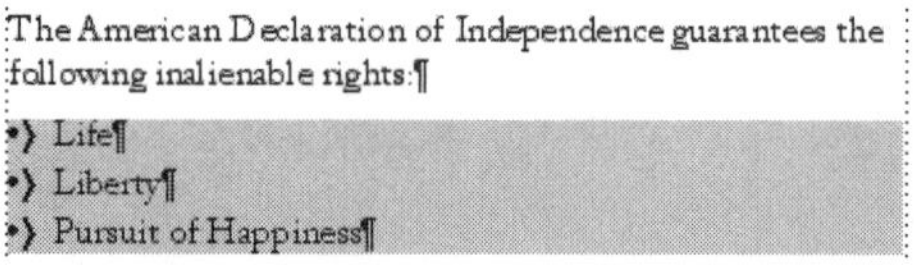

Figure 3.17 ... or select one or more paragraphs.

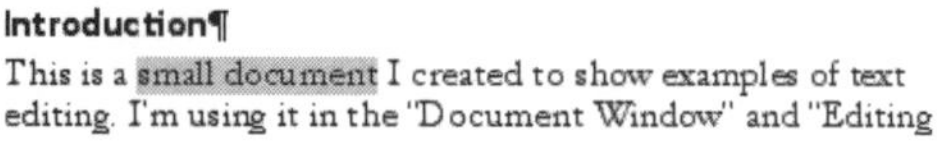

Figure 3.18 Select text in a paragraph to apply a character format, which overrides the paragraph's format stored in the Paragraph Catalog.

FORMATTING TEXT

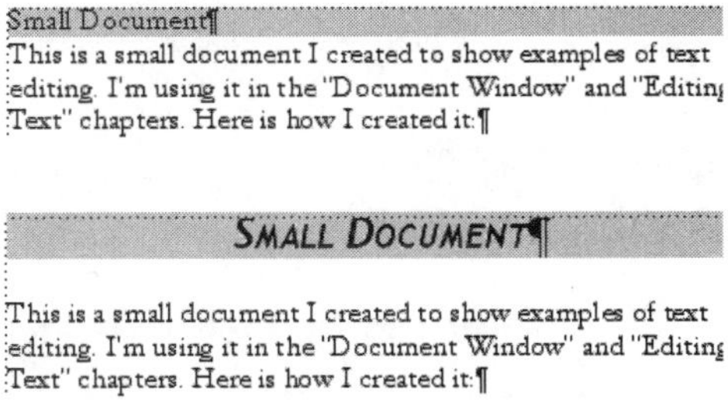

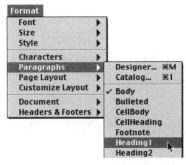

Figure 3.19 Before (top) and after (bottom) applying the Title paragraph format from the Paragraph Catalog.

Figure 3.20 Formats stored in the Catalog also appear on the Format > Paragraphs menu.

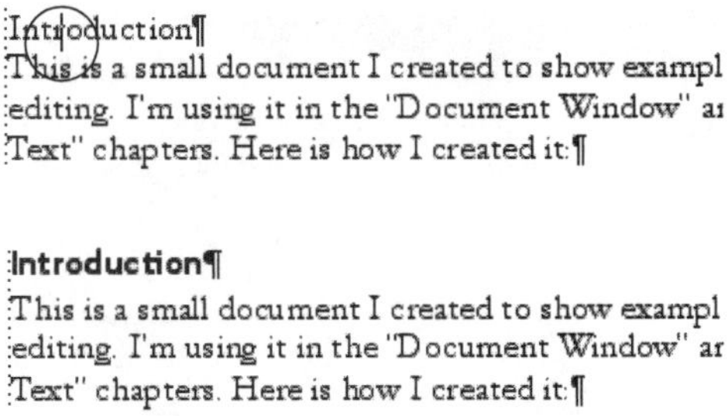

Figure 3.21 Before (top) and after (bottom) applying a paragraph format.

Figure 3.22 Type the paragraph tag until it appears in the Tag area or use the up and down arrow keys.

Applying paragraph formats

You can apply a paragraph format by choosing from the menu on the formatting bar at the top of the document window (see page 17). Here are some other ways.

To apply a paragraph format from the Catalog:

◆ Put the insertion point in a paragraph or select one or more paragraphs and click a tag in the Paragraph Catalog.

The format is applied to the current paragraphs (**Figure 3.19**).

To apply a paragraph format from the Format menu:

◆ Put the insertion point in a paragraph or select one or more paragraphs, and from the Format menu, choose Paragraphs and then choose a tag from the submenu (**Figure 3.20**).

The format is applied to the current paragraphs (**Figure 3.21**).

To apply a paragraph format using a keyboard shortcut:

1. Select one or more paragraphs.

2. Press Ctrl-9 or Control-9.

The tag area at the bottom left of the document window reverses to black (**Figure 3.22**).

3. Start typing the tag, or name, of the format you want to apply.

You can use the up and down arrows to cycle through the formats.

4. When the correct format appears in the Tag area at the bottom left of the document window, press Enter or Return.

The format is applied to the current paragraphs.

If you change your mind, click in the document to continue working without applying the format.

FORMATTING TEXT

29

Applying character formats

You can apply character formats from the Catalog or the Format > Characters menu, and you can also use the QuickAccess bar (see page 15). When you apply a character format to selected text, the character tag appears to the right of the paragraph tag in the Tag area of the status bar (**Figure 3.23**).

To apply a character format from the Catalog:

◆ Select text in a paragraph or a text line or select the text line as a graphic object (see page 106), and then click a tag in the Character Catalog.

To apply a character format from the Format menu:

◆ Select text in a paragraph or a text line or select the text line as a graphic object, and from the Format menu, choose Characters, and choose a tag from the submenu (**Figure 3.24**).

To return select text to its default character formatting:

◆ Select text and in the Character Catalog, click Default ¶ Font or from the Format menu, choose Characters > Default Paragraph Font.

The selected text returns to the default font of the paragraph.

To apply a character format using a keyboard shortcut:

1. Select one or more paragraphs or text in a paragraph or text line.

2. Press Ctrl-8 or Control-8.

The current format appears in the tag area on the status bar at the bottom left of the document window (**Figure 3.25**).

If you change your mind, click in the document to continue working without applying the format.

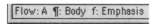

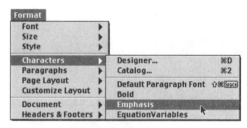

Figure 3.23 Examples of Bold and Emphasis (italic) character format overrides in a Body paragraph.

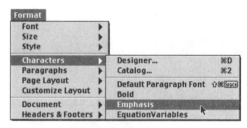

Figure 3.24 Choose a format from the Format > Characters menu.

Figure 3.25 Type the character tag until it appears in the Tag area or use the up and down arrow keys.

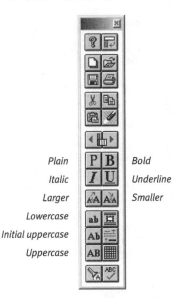

Plain	P B	Bold
Italic	I U	Underline
Larger	A A	Smaller
Lowercase	ab	
Initial uppercase	Ab	
Uppercase	AB	

Figure 3.26 Although the QuickAccess bar is displayed with a horizontal orientation, this illustration shows it with a vertical orientation (see page 15).

1.) Choose File > New > Document.¶
2.) In the New Document dialog box, click Custom.
(see "Creating Custom Pages" on page 7).¶

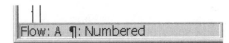

Flow: A ¶: Numbered

Figure 3.27 Example of an underline character format override applied to the word "Custom" from the QuickAccess bar or via a keyboard shortcut.

3. Start typing the tag, or name, of the format you want to apply.

   You can use the up and down arrows to cycle through the formats.

4. When the correct format appears in the Tag area at the bottom left of the document window, press Enter or Return.

   The format is applied to the current paragraphs.

To apply character formats from the QuickAccess bar:

1. Select one or more paragraphs or text in a paragraph or text line.

2. Click a format such as plain, bold, italic, underline, uppercase, or lowercase (**Figure 3.26**).

   Plain format removes character formatting from selected text.

   When you format selected text from the QuickAccess bar or via a keyboard shortcut, it is called an ad hoc text format override and has no character tag (**Figure 3.27**).

✔ Tips

- If you accidentally apply the wrong character format from the Catalog, while the text is still selected, click Default ¶ Font in the Catalog before trying again. This removes the character format you just applied. If you click Bold when you mean Emphasis and don't go back to the Default ¶ Font, the Bold format could stick, and you may end up with Bold plus the Emphasis format.

- If you apply the Default ¶ Font character format to return selected text to the default font properties of its paragraph format and you still see the character formatting, reapply the paragraph's paragraph format.

Smart Spaces and Special Spaces

When you're working in a document, type one space between sentences. You don't need to type two spaces as you might have done in other applications, because this one proportional space is right for the font you're using. With Smart Spaces on, even if you type more than one consecutive space, only one space appears. You should work with Smart Spaces turned on, so that you won't accidentally add extra, unneeded spaces.

To turn Smart Spaces on or off:

1. From the Format menu, choose Document > Text Options.

2. In the Text Options dialog box, click the check box for Smart Spaces (**Figure 3.28**).

3. Click Apply.

   Smart Spaces are now on or off and will remain so until you make another change.

If you want to make sure that a pair of words or numbers stay together, use another kind of space, a nonbreaking space (**Figure 3.29**).

To add a nonbreaking space:

◆ Type Esc spacebar H.

There are a number of other fixed-width spaces you can add to control the amount of space between words, as shown in **Table 3.1**.

✔ Tips

■ Text options are associated with the document, not the session, so they persist from session to session.

■ Although with Smart Spaces on you can type only one consecutive space, you can type as many fixed-width, or special, spaces as you wish.

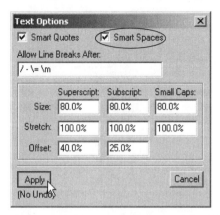

Figure 3.28 When you open a FrameMaker blank document, Smart Spaces are off by default. Turn them on in the Text Options dialog box.

Report on the San Francisco Earthquake of 1906¶

Figure 3.29 Adding a nonbreaking space ensures that even if text is added, the words stay together.

Table 3.1

Keyboard Shortcuts for Special Spaces		
Space	Width	Type
Em space	Same width as font's point size	Esc spacebar M
En space	Half of an em space	Esc spacebar N
Numeric space	Same width as font's o (zero) character	Esc spacebar 1 (one)
Thin space	1/12 width of an em space	Esc spacebar T

ɪ, in his Inaugural address, a newly-
ohn F. Kennedy enjoined us to, "Ask
ɪtry can do for you, ask what you can
ɪ" And he continued, "My fellow citi-
ɪsk not what America will do for you,
we can do for the freedom of man."

Figure 3.30 Curved quotation marks are proper for most types of written communication.

Furnished Apartment For Rent!		
Room	**Floor**	**Area Rug**
Living Room	16' x 14'	10' x 12'
Dining Room	14' x 12'	8' x 10'
Kitchen	12' x 12'	n/a
Bathroom	10' x 8'	4' x 6'
Master Bedroom	14' x 10'	8' x 10'
Guest Bedroom	10' x 16'	5' x 9'

Figure 3.31 There are times when you'll want to type a number of straight quotation marks.

Figure 3.32 If you want to type more than a few straight quotes to express inches or feet, it's easier to turn off Smart Quotes and then turn it back on when you're finished.

Table 3.2

Keystrokes for Straight Quotes		
To type	Windows	Mac OS
Single straight quotation mark (')	Ctrl-'	Control-'
Double straight quotation mark (")	Esc "	Control-"

Smart Quotes

When you type a single or double quotation mark in the documents you're working on, you usually want to see curved quotation marks (**Figure 3.30**). You could always type them as special characters (see page 386), but that would be pretty tedious. With Smart Quotes on, whenever you type a straight single or double quotation mark from the keyboard, FrameMaker makes it a curved quotation mark.

To turn Smart Quotes on or off:

1. From the Format menu, choose Document > Text Options.

2. In the Text Options dialog box, select Smart Quotes.

3. Click Apply.

   Smart Quotes are now on or off and will remain so until you make another change.

Unlike Smart Spaces, Smart Quotes are on in most FrameMaker templates. But if you want straight quotes to express inches or feet (**Figure 3.31**), you can go to the Text Options dialog box and turn them off (**Figure 3.32**). Then turn them back on when you're finished, or you can type them as special characters.

To type straight quotation marks when Smart Quotes are on:

◆ To type a straight single or double quotation mark, use the keystrokes shown in **Table 3.2**.

✔ Tip

■ Smart Quotes don't apply to text typed in dialog boxes, even though you might want to use curved quotation marks in a cross-reference, for example. To find out how to type curvy quotation marks in dialog boxes, see *Typing in Dialog Boxes* on page 388.

Adding Tabs

FrameMaker has four types of tabs you can use: Left, Center, Right, and Decimal. You need to do two things in FrameMaker to add tabs to a paragraph:

◆ Define a tab stop in the top ruler (**Figure 3.33**) or in the Paragraph Designer.

◆ Press the Tab key in the document to add a tab text symbol (>) and move the insertion point to the defined tab stop.

A tab symbol is inserted in text every time you press Tab even if the paragraph doesn't have tab stops—you'll see them if Text Symbols are on (**Figure 3.34**).

To add a tab stop in the ruler:

1. Drag a tab stop from the formatting bar down to the top document ruler (**Figure 3.35**).

   You can drag as many tab stops as you wish into the document ruler, but they won't take effect until you also press the Tab key for each stop.

2. When you have the text looking the way you want, click Apply in the Paragraph Designer.

✔ Tip

■ In the example here (**Figure 3.36**), the tab stop is shown at the 1-3/4-inch mark on the top ruler, but in the Tab Stops area of the Paragraph Designer, the value is displayed as 1.0 inch. That's because the top ruler measures from the left side of the document window, but in the Paragraph Designer, the measurement is displayed relative to the left border of the text frame that contains the paragraph. The text frame is 3/4 inch from the left side of the document window.

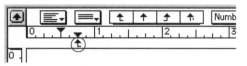

Figure 3.33 A left tab stop is defined in the ruler.

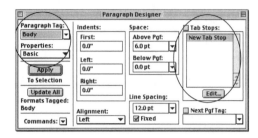

Tab symbol in document

Figure 3.34 The first line contains three tabs made by pressing the Tab key. But because there are no tab stops in the paragraph format, the insertion point doesn't move.

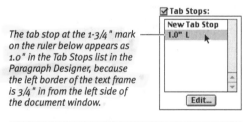

Figure 3.35 Drag the left tab stop from the formatting bar (top) down into the top ruler.

The tab stop at the 1-3/4" mark on the ruler below appears as 1.0" in the Tab Stops list in the Paragraph Designer, because the left border of the text frame is 3/4" in from the left side of the document window.

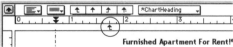

Figure 3.36 The ruler and the Paragraph Designer show different measurements for tab stops.

Figure 3.37 You can add tab stops in the Edit Tab Stops dialog box as many times as you wish until the text looks the way you want it to.

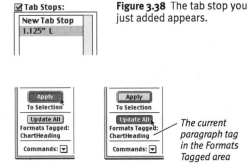

Figure 3.38 The tab stop you just added appears.

The current paragraph tag in the Formats Tagged area

Figure 3.39 To apply the new tab stops, click Apply or Update All.

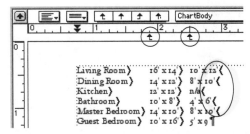

Figure 3.40 With text symbols on, you can see the forced return symbols at the end of each line in the chart except the last one.

To add a tab stop in the Paragraph Designer:

1. From the Format menu, choose Paragraphs > Designer to display the Paragraph Designer.

   The first time you display the Paragraph Designer in a session, it opens with Basic properties showing. After that, it opens showing the same properties as the last time.

2. In the Tab Stops area, click Edit.

3. In the Edit Tab Stop dialog box, type a number in the New Position text box (**Figure 3.37**).

4. Click Continue.

   The new tab stop appears in the Tab Stops list (**Figure 3.38**).

5. Click Apply to apply the tab stops to the current paragraph.

   or

   Click Update All to apply the tab stops to all paragraphs in the document with the same tag (**Figure 3.39**).

✔ Tip

■ If you want to line up multiple lines of text to create a simple chart such as the one shown in **Figure 3.40**, use a forced return (Shift-Enter or Shift-Return) between lines. Because all of the lines are part of the same paragraph, they line up.

   Then, if you want to change alignment, just put the insertion point in the paragraph and move the tab stop once. As you move the tab stop in the ruler, the entire column moves to help you decide where to position the tab stop.

ADDING TABS

Finding and Replacing Text

Once you've been using FrameMaker for a while, you'll find yourself searching for much more than just text (**Figure 3.41**). For instance, here are some of the items you might search for:

◆ Index markers (see page 281)

◆ Unresolved cross-references (see page 51)

◆ Variables (see page 170)

In this section you'll see how to find and replace text and explore find and change options. For a wider discussion of the items you can search for and how to use wildcard characters, see the *Adobe FrameMaker 7.0 User Guide.*

To find text:

1. From the Edit menu, choose Find/Change (**Figure 3.42**).

   or

   Press Ctrl-F or Command-F.

   The Find/Change window appears.

2. Type or paste the text you want to find in the Find Text box (**Figure 3.43**).

3. Select one or more of the following search options:

   ▲ Select Consider Case if, for example, you want to search for "an" but not "An" (**Figure 3.44**).

   ▲ Select Whole Word if, for example, you want to search for the word "an" but not the letters "an" where they are embedded in another word, such as "man."

   FrameMaker begins searching at the insertion point in the type of page you are working in, for example, body pages, but not master or reference pages. It searches multiple text flows one after the other. At

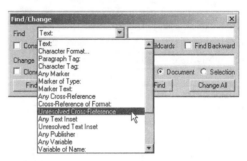

Figure 3.41 The Find pop-up menu displays all of the items you can search for in the document.

Figure 3.42 Choose Edit > Find/Change.

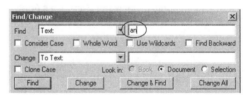

Figure 3.43 In addition to typing text, you can also paste text into the text box.

Figure 3.44 Choose options to narrow your search.

Figure 3.45 FrameMaker searches forward unless you click the Find Backward check box.

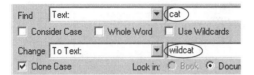

Figure 3.46 FrameMaker considers case when it replaces the text, so when it finds "Cat" it replaces it with "Wildcat" and not "wildcat."

Figure 3.47 Be sure you've thought through the change you're making before you click Change All.

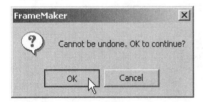

Figure 3.48 FrameMaker checks to make sure this is really what you want to do.

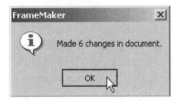

Figure 3.49 The report tells you how many changes were made.

the end of the document, it starts again at the beginning.

4. To search backward from the insertion point or current file, select Find Backward (**Figure 3.45**).

5. Select one of the following options:
   ▲ To search all the files in the active book, click Book.
   ▲ To search the current document, click Document.
   ▲ To limit the search to selected text, click Selection.

6. Click Find.
   FrameMaker searches for text as you've specified.

To find and change text:

1. In the Find/Change window, type the text you want to find in the Find Text box.

2. Type the text you want to replace the original text with in the Change To Text box.

3. If you want FrameMaker to replace "Cat" with "Wildcat" and not "wildcat," for example, click Clone Case (**Figure 3.46**).

4. Click Find.

5. When FrameMaker selects the text that you want to change, click Change.
   Find and replace text quickly by clicking Change and Find instead of Change.

6. If you are certain that this is the change you want to make, click Change All (**Figure 3.47**).
   A warning message appears.

7. Click OK (**Figure 3.48**).
   FrameMaker finds all occurrences of the text in the document, book, or selected text and replaces them. A message tells you how many changes were made (**Figure 3.49**).

You can also find and replace text with the contents of the Clipboard if you change by pasting.

To change by pasting:

1. Copy the replacement text onto the Clipboard.

2. From the Change pop-up menu, choose By Pasting (**Figure 3.50**).

   The selected text is replaced by the text you copied to the Clipboard.

✔ Tips

■ After the first instance is found, choose Edit > Find Next or press Ctrl-G or Command-G.

■ *This is a mission-critical tip:* Before using any of the powerful Find/Change options, such as Change All, save your document. If for some reason you make unintentional changes, you can revert back to the saved version (**Figure 3.51**). While I was working on this book, I accidentally deleted every occurrence of the lowercase letter "o." Because I had saved the file, I was able to revert to the last saved version and didn't lose any work.

■ Use the Whole Word option when you're finding and changing text with a word like "cat" that can appear as part of words such as "catalog" and "catch." Without the Whole Word option on, FrameMaker would change "catalog" to "wildcatalog" and "catch" to "wildcatch."

■ To find out how many times text appears, type the text in the Find Text text box, copy and paste exactly the same text into the Change To Text text box, and select Clone Case (**Figure 3.52**). Then Click Change All. A message box tells you how many changes were made, or how many times the text appears in the document or book (**Figure 3.53**).

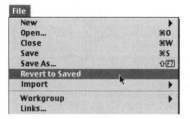

Figure 3.50 FrameMaker pastes the contents of the Clipboard.

Figure 3.51 The Revert to Saved command can be a life saver.

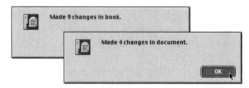

Figure 3.52 Copy text from the Find Text box to the Change To Text box to be 100 percent sure that the text in both boxes is same.

Figure 3.53 When you click Change All, FrameMaker displays the number of changes that were made.

■ If you get an unexpectedly low number of changes, check to see whether the text appears correctly in the Find Text box or whether you've used the correct search options. The same advice applies if you get an unexpectedly large number of changes,.

■ Be careful when you use the Change By Pasting command. Once a writer accidentally pasted her friend's e-mail address into a technical manual!

About FrameMaker Dictionaries

When you spell check a document, FrameMaker compares each word with the words in the following dictionaries:

◆ **Main dictionary.** A standard dictionary with hyphenation rules that is installed when you install FrameMaker; you can't add or delete words from the main dictionary.

◆ **Site dictionary.** A list of words, usually technical terms, FrameMaker adds to the main dictionary for spell checking. You can add words common to your site or workgroup, for example, the company name and product, and distribute it to the group. The site dictionary is normally in dict\site.dict (Windows) or FrameMaker Dictionaries:Site Dictionary (Mac OS).

◆ **Document dictionary.** A list of words used for spell checking no matter who is working on the document. Add a word to the document dictionary in the Spelling Checker window by clicking Allow in Document; delete a word from the document dictionary by clicking Unlearn. The document dictionary is part of the document rather than a separate file.

◆ **Personal dictionary.** A dictionary for words *you* use often and to be used by FrameMaker when *you* spell check a document, words that are neither document nor site specific, for example, your name. Add a word to your personal dictionary in the Spelling Checker window by clicking Learn; delete a word by clicking Unlearn.

Spell Checking

FrameMaker's spell checking capabilities are more robust than those found in other applications. It uses four dictionaries every time you spell check a book or document. You can add or remove words from the site, document, and personal dictionaries. You can share the site dictionary among members of your workgroup.

FrameMaker also checks for repeated words, unusual hyphenation or capitalization, extra spaces, and so on. No matter what you are spell checking, FrameMaker checks only the type of pages you are viewing, for example, body pages, but not master or reference pages.

You can open the Spelling Checker window from a document or book. If you open the Spelling Checker window from a document that is not part of a book, you can check the entire document or the current page. To spell check the page that contains the insertion point, click the Current Page radio button.

If a document is part of a book, you can check all files in a book at the same time either from a document or from the book window.

(continues on next page)

Running the spelling checker

You can spell check from your current document or from the active book.

To spell check from a document:

1. From the Edit menu, choose Spelling Checker.

   or

   Press Esc E S or Command-L.

2. Do one of the following:

   ▲ To start in the current document and then continue checking other documents in the book, click Book (**Figure 3.54**).

   ▲ To limit checking to the current document, click Document (**Figure 3.55**).

   ▲ To limit checking to the page with the insertion point, click Current Page.

3. Click Start Checking.

   FrameMaker starts checking, displays the first suspect word in the Misspelling area (**Figure 3.56**), and selects the word in the document. The suggested correction appears in the text box and alternative corrections in the scroll list. If the issue is not a misspelling, a different issue appears at the top left (**Figure 3.57**).

4. Do one of the following:

   ▲ To accept the suggestion in the Correction text box, click Correct.

   ▲ For an alternate suggestion, select from the scroll list.

   ▲ Type your own correction in the Correction text box (**Figure 3.58**).

   ▲ To add the word to your personal dictionary, click Learn (**Figure 3.59**).

   ▲ To add the word to the document dictionary, click Allow in Document (**Figure 3.59**).

   ▲ To leave the word unchanged, do nothing.

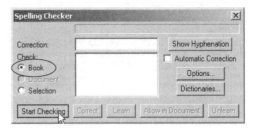

Figure 3.54 If the document is part of a book, you can spell check all the files in the book.

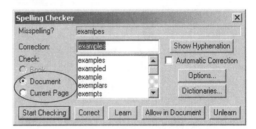

Figure 3.55 You can limit spell checking to the current document or to just the current page.

Misspelling   *Suggested correction*

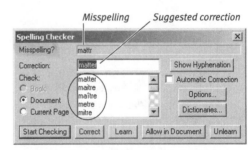

Figure 3.56 FrameMaker suggests a correction for a misspelled word and provides alternative corrections in the scroll list below.

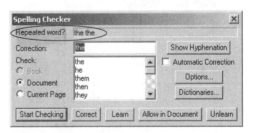

Figure 3.57 In addition to spelling errors, FrameMaker can find other common typing errors, such as repeated words.

Figure 3.58 You can always type a correction in the Correction text box.

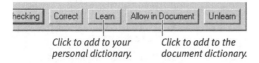

Click to add to your personal dictionary.   *Click to add to the document dictionary.*

Figure 3.59 You can add words to your personal dictionary or to the document dictionary.

Figure 3.60 "QuickStart" would be a good candidate for the Peachpit Press site dictionary.

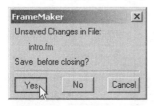

Figure 3.61 FrameMaker prompts you to save changes before closing the file.

Figure 3.62 A message tells you FrameMaker has finished spell checking the book.

5. Click Start Checking.

If you are checking a document, FrameMaker starts checking at the insertion point and continues until it reaches the end of the document, and then starts again at the beginning. Words added to one of your dictionaries will not be questioned again.

If you are checking a book, FrameMaker starts checking in the active document and continues until all documents in the book have been checked.

To spell check from a book:

1. From the Edit menu in the book window, choose Spelling Checker.

or

Press Esc E S or Command-L.

2. Click Start Checking.

When FrameMaker encounters the first suspect word, it opens the document, selects the word, and displays the word in the Misspelling area (**Figure 3.60**). At this point the checking options are the same as they are for spell checking a document: Book, Document, and Current Page.

3. Perform one of the actions listed in the previous task and click Start Checking.

If you've made a correction in the file open for checking, you'll be prompted to save your change(s) before FrameMaker closes the file (**Figure 3.61**).

4. Click Yes.

When the last document in the book has been checked, a message appears to let you know (**Figure 3.62**).

5. Click OK.

(continues on next page)

✔ Tips

- FrameMaker does not spell check hidden conditional text. To check conditional text, first display the text (see page 189) and then spell check.

- FrameMaker does not spell check text that has been manually micropositioned.

- FrameMaker does not spell check marker text. To check marker text, you need to generate a file with marker text (see page 280) and spell check that file.

- To skip a paragraph or text in a paragraph, in the font properties, set Language to None (**Figure 3.63**).

  If you choose a language other than English from the Language menu in the font properties, FrameMaker will use the dictionary for that language when it spell checks that paragraph or selected text.

Spell checking options

You can turn a number of options on and off to specify what to check for during spell checking.

To set spell checking options:

1. In the Spelling Checker window, click the Options button (**Figure 3.64**).

   The Spelling Checker Options dialog box appears (**Figure 3.65**).

2. Turn options on or off.

   For example, you might work with Smart Quotes on and use straight quotes only occasionally. In that case, you could safely turn off the Straight Quotes option.

   However, even though you may occasionally type a space in front of a period intentionally, you may decide to keep a period in the Space Before list so that FrameMaker will catch extra spaces in front of periods at the end of sentences.

3. Click Set.

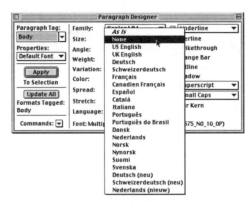

Figure 3.63 Choose None from the Language pop-up menu to specify no spell checking.

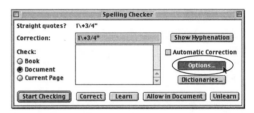

Figure 3.64 Click the Options button to display the Spelling Checker Options dialog box.

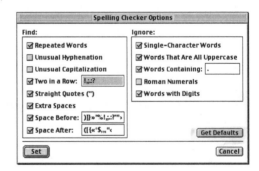

Figure 3.65 These are the Framemaker default spelling checker options.

Figure 3.66 Click Get Defaults to retrieve the default spelling checker options.

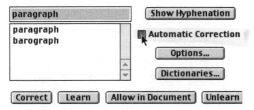

Figure 3.67 In the Spelling Checker window, click Automatic Correction and then Correct.

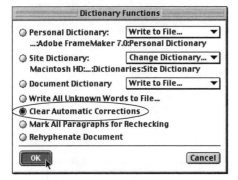

Figure 3.68 Click Clear Automatic Corrections and then OK.

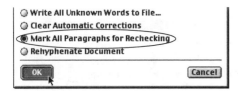

Figure 3.69 Mark paragraphs for rechecking in the Dictionary Functions dialog box.

To restore default spell checking options:

◆ In the Spelling Checker Options dialog box, click Get Defaults (**Figure 3.66**).

You can have FrameMaker automatically correct future occurrences of errors, but think carefully to make sure that you don't make a correction behind the scenes that you don't really intend.

To automatically correct future occurrences of errors:

1. When FrameMaker questions a word or other error during spell checking, click Automatic Correction (**Figure 3.67**).

2. Click Correct.

To stop making automatic corrections:

1. In the Spelling Checker window, click Dictionaries.

2. In the Dictionary Functions dialog box, click Clear Automatic Corrections (**Figure 3.68**).

3. Click OK.

If you add spelling checker options, you may want to spell check again after telling FrameMaker to mark all paragraphs for rechecking. (FrameMaker normally checks only paragraphs that have been edited since the last check.)

To mark all paragraphs for rechecking:

1. In the Spelling Checker window, click Dictionaries.

2. In the Dictionary Functions dialog box, click Mark All Paragraphs for Rechecking.

3. Click OK (**Figure 3.69**).

    You need to run the spelling checker after marking all paragraphs for rechecking.

SPELL CHECKING

Using the Thesaurus

A thesaurus gives you synonyms, related words, and antonyms to enhance your writing and help you find *exactly* the right word. Although technical writers strive for consistency of expression—they don't want users to have to wonder why it's one way here and another way there—in general the more specific a word the better. If you can't quite find the right word, try using the thesaurus that comes with FrameMaker.

To look up a selected word:

1. Select a word (**Figure 3.70**) and from the Edit menu, choose Thesaurus.

   or

   Press Ctrl-Shift-T or Command-Shift-T. The Thesaurus window appears. In this example, information for the word "notion" takes up two screens (**Figure 3.71**).

2. If you like one of the synonyms or related words, click it (**Figure 3.72**).

   Clicking the word "concept" takes you to the Thesaurus information for that word.

   FrameMaker keeps track of the last 10 words you looked up in the Word pop-up menu at the top left (**Figure 3.73**).

3. When you get to the right word, click Replace (**Figure 3.74**).

   FrameMaker replaces the original word selected with the new word (**Figure 3.75**).

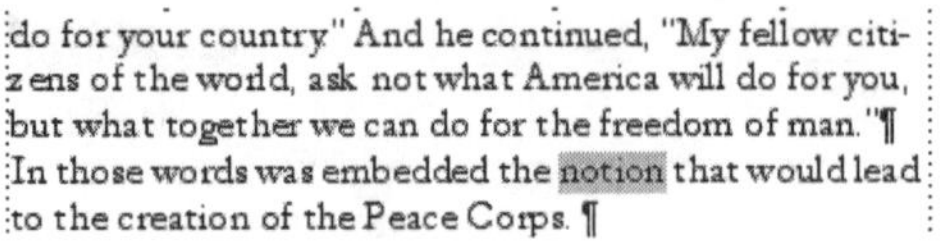

do for your country" And he continued, "My fellow citizens of the world, ask not what America will do for you, but what together we can do for the freedom of man." In those words was embedded the notion that would lead to the creation of the Peace Corps.

Figure 3.70 You can select only one word at a time.

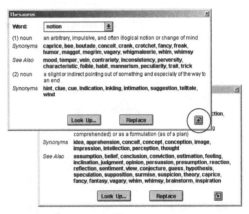

Figure 3.71 In the Thesaurus window, you can click the arrow in the bottom-right corner to see the next or previous screen.

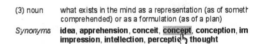

Figure 3.72 Click another word in the Thesaurus window to look it up.

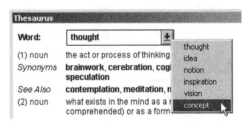

Figure 3.73 You can go to any of the last 10 words you looked up by choosing the word from the Word menu.

Figure 3.74 When you find the right word, click Replace.

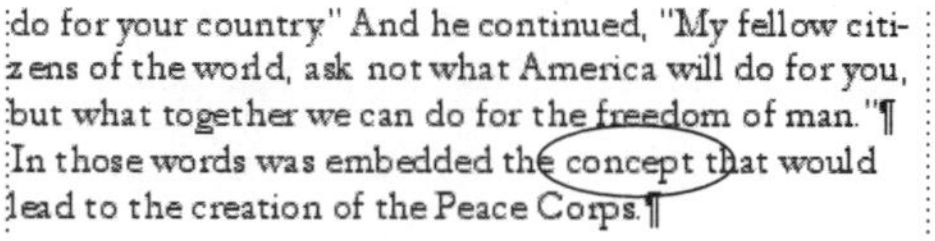

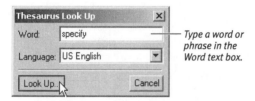

Figure 3.75 The word "notion" is replaced by the new word "concept."

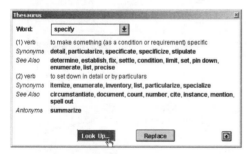

Figure 3.76 Click Look Up to look up the word or phrase in the Word text box.

Figure 3.77 To go back to the Look Up dialog box, click Look Up in the Thesaurus window.

Figure 3.78 The thesaurus has no information for the phrase "make a fuss."

You can use the thesaurus to look up any word without selecting it in a document.

To look up any word:

1. Make sure nothing is selected in the document window, and from the Edit menu, choose Thesaurus.

   The Thesaurus Look Up dialog box appears.

2. Type a word into the Word text box, and click Look Up (**Figure 3.76**).

   The Thesaurus window displays the information for the word you looked up (**Figure 3.77**).

To look up a phrase:

1. Make sure nothing is selected in the document window, and from the Edit menu, choose Thesaurus.

   The Thesaurus Look Up dialog box appears.

2. Type a phrase, including hyphens, into the Word text box, and click Look Up.

   The Thesaurus window displays the information for the phrase you looked up. If FrameMaker has no entry for the phrase, a message is displayed (**Figure 3.78**).

✔ Tip

■ FrameMaker uses either the language of the currently selected text or, when nothing is selected, the language of the interface. To specify a different language, enter a word in the Thesaurus Look Up dialog box and choose a language from the Language pop-up menu.

USING THE THESAURUS

Inserting Page Breaks

Page breaks in a FrameMaker document are all part of a paragraph's Pagination properties, including all of the following:

◆ Start settings: Anywhere, Top of Column, Top of Page, Top of Left Page, Top of Right Page

◆ Keep With settings: Next Paragraph, Previous Paragraph

◆ Widow/Orphan Lines set to a value greater than 1

In the case of Head 1 paragraphs in this book (**Figure 3.79**), all three properties are set to ensure that

◆ Every Head 1 paragraph starts at the top of a column.

◆ The heading always stays with the next paragraph.

◆ If a heading breaks over two or more lines, at least two of the lines stay together.

Unless you apply a page break and then update all paragraphs with the same format, a page break represents a paragraph format override.

To specify the Start property from the Special menu:

1. From the Special menu, choose Page Break (**Figure 3.80**).

   The Page Break dialog box appears.

2. To remove the page break override, click Wherever It Fits.

   or

   To insert a page break, choose from the At Top of Next Available pop-up menu (**Figure 3.81**).

3. Click Set.

   A page break property is removed from or applied to the paragraph.

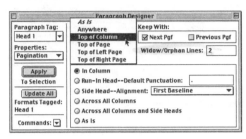

Figure 3.79 This Head 1 paragraph format demonstrates all three ways to control page breaks: Start, Keep With, and Widow/Orphan Lines.

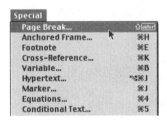

Figure 3.80 With the insertion point in the paragraph you want to move, choose Special > Page Break.

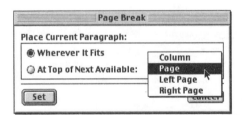

Figure 3.81 A page break applied to a Body paragraph from the Page Break dialog box becomes an override to the paragraph's format.

The first paragraph in this column is set to start at Top of Column.

Figure 3.82 Text was deleted from the text column on the left, so the next paragraph is stranded at the top of the right text column—leaving unwanted empty space in the text column on the left (circled).

Figure 3.83 Set Widow/Orphan Lines to a very large number.

Asterisk indicates format override

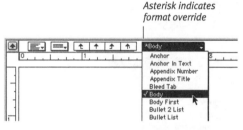

Figure 3.84 To remove any override, including a page break override, reapply its paragraph format.

✔ Tips

■ In practice, you may want to use hard page breaks sparingly, because the other two methods are as effective and much less intrusive. For example, what if you add a page break to a Body paragraph to bring it to the top of a column, and then later you add text in the text flow. Now there is unwanted white space at the bottom of the previous column (**Figure 3.82**). If you had used the Keep With Next Paragraph setting instead, you might have avoided this situation.

■ If you want to create a format such that a paragraph, no matter how long, would never break over a column or page, set Widow/Orphan Lines to a very large number (**Figure 3.83**).

■ The easiest way to remove an override quickly is to reapply its paragraph format from the menu on the formatting bar (**Figure 3.84**).

■ If paragraphs are behaving mysteriously and you can't figure out why, check the Pagination settings in the Paragraph Designer.

The Tip Head Format Example

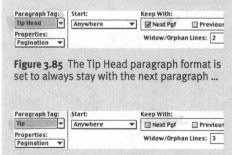

Figure 3.85 The Tip Head paragraph format is set to always stay with the next paragraph ...

Figure 3.86 ... but the Tip paragraph format, the one that follows it, is not set to stay with the previous paragraph.

The Tip Head (**Figure 3.85**) and Tip (**Figure 3.86**) paragraph formats in this book provide an example. Keeping the first tip with its heading is controlled by the Tip Head's Keep With Next Paragraph setting. But in Tip paragraphs, there isn't a Keep With setting because Tip paragraphs shouldn't necessarily stay together.

However, to be sure that one or two lines of a tip won't break over to the top or be stranded at the bottom of a column, the Widow/Orphan Lines is set to 3.

Using Cross-References

Adding cross-references to a document (**Figure 3.87**), which can become links in Web documents, is relatively easy in FrameMaker. With the insertion point indicating where you want a cross-reference to appear, specify

- ◆ The document with the source

- ◆ The location of the source itself, identified either as a specific paragraph or by a cross-reference marker

- ◆ The cross-reference format

The source of the cross-reference can be in the current document or another document in the book if the current document is part of a book. FrameMaker keeps track of the source of a cross-reference, and although they are not updated dynamically as you work, you can manually update cross-references in a document or a book.

The source of a cross-reference can be either a specified paragraph or a cross-reference marker you insert manually.

To add a cross-reference to a paragraph:

1. If you are cross-referencing another document, make sure that document is open.

2. Click where you want to add a cross-reference (**Figure 3.88**).

3. From the Special menu, choose Cross-Reference (**Figure 3.89**).

   or

   Press Esc S C or Command-K.

   The Cross-Reference dialog box appears.

4. Make sure Current is chosen from the Document pop-up menu, and from the Source Type menu, choose Paragraphs (**Figure 3.90**).

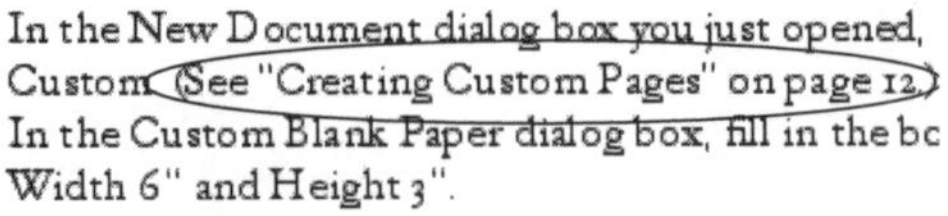

In the New Document dialog box you just opened, Custom (See "Creating Custom Pages" on page 12.) In the Custom Blank Paper dialog box, fill in the bo Width 6" and Height 3".

Figure 3.87 FrameMaker makes it easy to create complex cross-references and ensure that formats are consistent across files in a book.

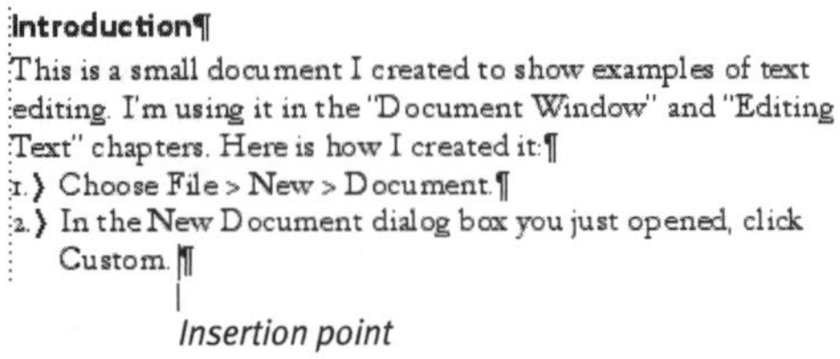

Figure 3.88 You can insert a cross-reference anywhere in a text frame, but not in a text line.

Figure 3.89 Choose Special > Cross-Reference.

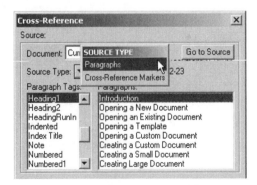

Figure 3.90 In this example the source of the cross-reference is a Heading 1 paragraph.

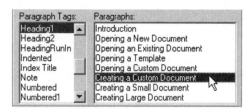

Figure 3.91 Select the text of the paragraph that is the source of the cross-reference.

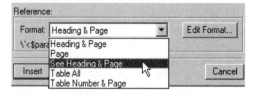

Figure 3.92 Predefined formats appear in the Formats pop-up menu.

Figure 3.93 The definition of the current format appears below it.

Introduction¶
This is a small document I created to show examples of text editing. I'm using it in the "Document Window" and "Editing Text" chapters. Here is how I created it:¶
1.) Choose File > New > Document.¶
2.) In the New Document dialog box you just opened, click Custom. See "Creating a Custom Document" on page 10.¶

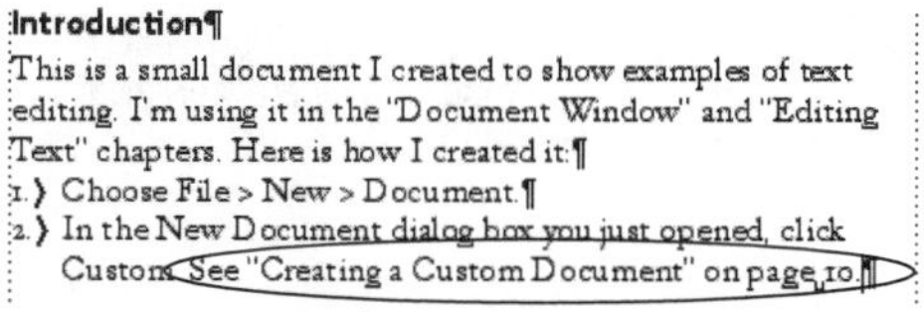

Figure 3.94 In this example the entire sentence with the cross-reference is specified in its format.

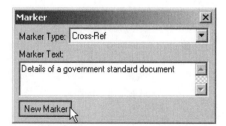

Figure 3.95 The description in the Marker Text box should uniquely identify the marker.

5. In the Paragraph Tags list, select the *tag* of the source paragraph.

6. In the Paragraphs list, select the *text* of the source paragraph (**Figure 3.91**).

7. From the Format menu, choose a format for the cross-reference and click Insert (**Figure 3.92**).

   The definition of the format appears below it (**Figure 3.93**).

   The new cross-reference appears at the insertion point in the document (**Figure 3.94**) and a cross-reference marker is inserted at the source.

In the previous task, you specified a particular paragraph as the source of the cross-reference. You can also insert a cross-reference marker as the source, for example, in a situation where a long paragraph breaks across two pages and you specifically want to refer to the beginning of the paragraph or to the end of the paragraph, which may be on the following page.

To insert a cross-reference marker:

1. With the insertion point at the source for the cross-reference, from the Special menu, choose Marker.

   or

   Press Esc S M or Command-J.

   The Marker window appears.

2. From the Marker Type pop-up menu, choose Cross-Reference.

3. Type a description for the marker in the Marker Text box (**Figure 3.95**).

4. Click New Marker.

   FrameMaker inserts a cross-reference marker at the insertion point.

✔ Tips

■ If you can't find a predefined cross-reference in your document, you can create a new format.

■ When you specify a paragraph as the source of a cross-reference, FrameMaker inserts the cross-reference marker at the beginning of the paragraph (**Figure 3.96**). You may want to copy and paste this marker to a location in the paragraph where you can see it better, so you won't accidentally delete it as you're editing text (**Figure 3.97**).

■ The Marker window displays the marker type of the last marker selected in the document. For example, if you're inserting index markers and then select a cross-reference marker, and after that go back to inserting index markers, remember to go back to index markers. If you don't, you'll find yourself adding the wrong type of marker without realizing it.

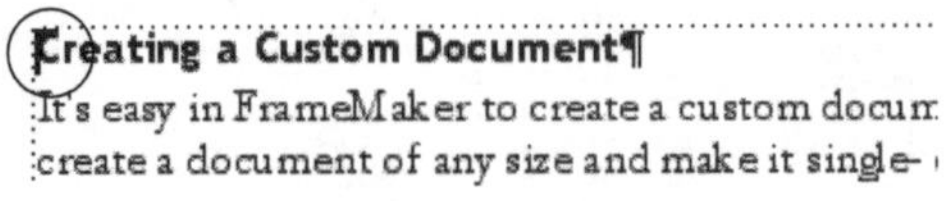

To add a cross-reference to a cross-reference marker as the source:

1. Insert a cross-reference marker.

2. From the Special menu, choose Cross-Reference.

3. In the Cross-Reference dialog box, from the Source Type pop-up menu, choose Cross-Reference Markers (**Figure 3.98**).

4. In the Cross-Reference Markers list to the right, select the description you entered in the Marker window when you added the cross-reference marker (**Figure 3.99**).

5. From the Format pop-up menu at the bottom of the dialog box, choose a format.

6. Click Insert.

   The cross-reference appears at the insertion point.

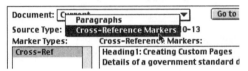

Figure 3.96 A marker symbol looks like an uppercase letter "T."

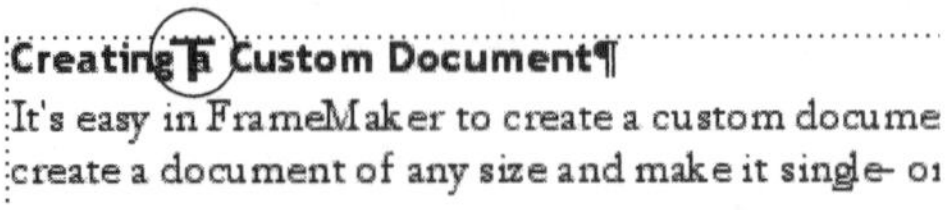

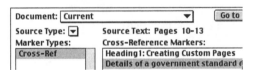

Figure 3.97 Copy and paste the marker in a different location so you can see it better.

Figure 3.98 Choose a cross-reference marker as the source.

Figure 3.99 The Cross-Reference Markers list includes both markers inserted by FrameMaker and ones you inserted manually.

USING CROSS-REFERENCES

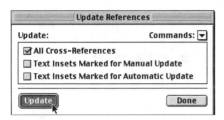

Figure 3.100 Select All Cross-References in the Update References dialog box.

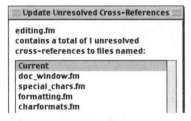

Figure 3.101 This message tells you that the current file contains one unresolved cross-reference. You can search for it in the Find/Change window.

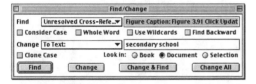

Figure 3.102 Choose Edit > Find/Change to display the Find/Change window.

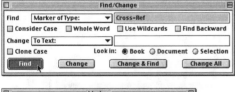

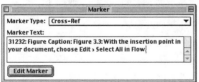

Figure 3.103 With both windows visible on the screen, you can see the text for each cross-reference marker found in the Marker Text box.

When you're editing a document, you move text and illustrations and they often end up on different pages than where they started. If the document is part of a book, when you update the book, you can update cross-references. Or you can update the cross-references in the current document manually.

To update cross-references in a document:

1. From the Edit menu, choose Update References.

   or

   Press Ctrl-U or Command-U.

2. In the Update References dialog box, select All Cross-References, and click Update (**Figure 3.100**).

   If the document you're updating contains any unresolved cross-references, a message appears (**Figure 3.101**).

3. In the Find/Change window, find the unresolved cross-reference (**Figure 3.102**) and resolve it in the Cross-Reference dialog box.

✔ Tip

■ Selecting markers is difficult, and you may want to select and copy a marker to delete it or to paste it at a different location:

   ▲ Zoom in so that the document is at 150 percent or greater. Then click just to the left of the marker and use the keyboard shortcut Esc H C to select the marker.

   ▲ In the Find/Change window, choose Marker of Type from the Find pop-up menu and type Cross-Ref in the text box. Display the Marker window and position it so that both windows are visible on the screen (see page 351). Search until you find the marker you want to select (**Figure 3.103**).

Counting Words

FrameMaker has a number of utilities, such as word count. If you're preparing a document or a book to go out for translation, for example, it's useful to know how many words might have to be translated to estimate the cost.

In Asian-language documents with multibyte characters, the count report lists the number of single-width characters, the number of double-width characters, and the total of both.

To count the number of words or characters in a document:

1. From the File menu, choose Utilities > Document Reports.

   The Document Reports dialog box appears (**Figure 3.104**).

2. To count the number of words in a document, choose Word Count.

   or

   To count the number of characters in a document, choose Asian Character Count.

3. Click Run.

   The report lists the number of words (**Figure 3.105**) or the number of characters (**Figure 3.106**).

   In a non-Asian document, the report lists the number of alphanumeric characters in the document.

✔ Tips

■ Although you cannot generate a report for the number of words in a book, you can do so for each document in the book and then add up the counts.

■ To find out the number of pages in a book, select the last file in the book window and look at the page count (**Figure 3.107**). Add the number of any front matter pages numbered separated.

Figure 3.104 Click Run to display the report.

Figure 3.105 The report displays the number of words in the document.

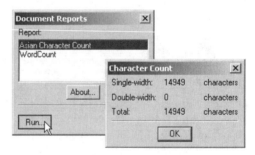

Figure 3.106 In a document with non-Asian text, Asian Character Count displays the number of alphanumeric characters.

These are the page numbers for the last file in the book (selected).

Figure 3.107 This book has 414 pages, excluding front matter, which is numbered separately.

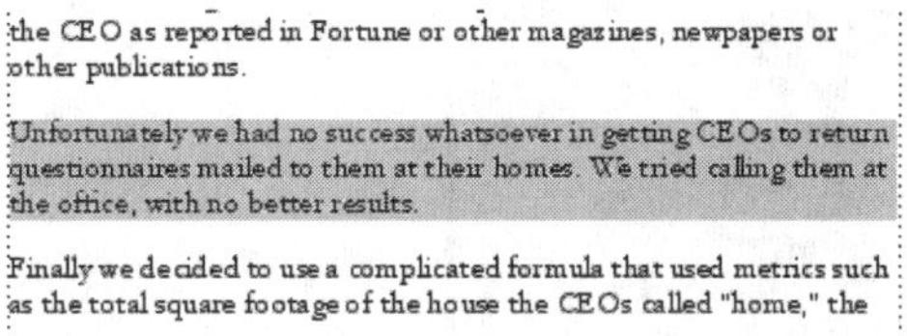

the CEO as reported in Fortune or other magazines, newpapers or other publications.
Unfortunately we had no success whatsoever in getting CEOs to return questionnaires mailed to them at their homes. We tried calling them at the office, with no better results.
Finally we decided to use a complicated formula that used metrics such as the total square footage of the house the CEOs called "home," the

Figure 3.108 Select the paragraph you want to flag.

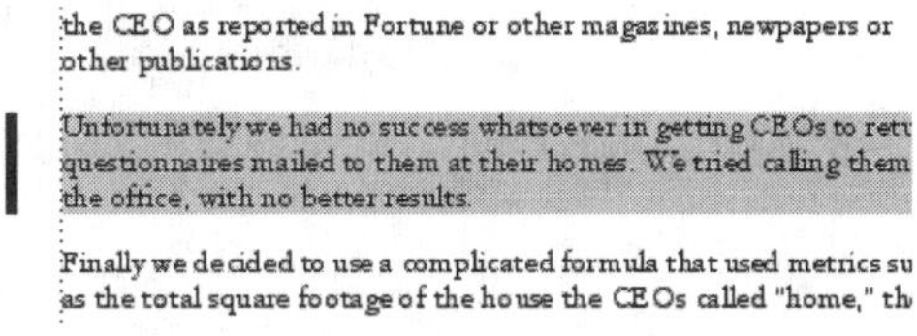

the CEO as reported in Fortune or other magazines, newpapers or other publications.
Unfortunately we had no success whatsoever in getting CEOs to retu questionnaires mailed to them at their homes. We tried calling them the office, with no better results.
Finally we decided to use a complicated formula that used metrics su as the total square footage of the house the CEOs called "home," th

Figure 3.109 A change bar indicates to reviewers or others in the workgroup that content has been added or changed.

Character Designer
Character Tag:
Apply
To Selection
Update All
Characters...
Commands:
Family: Kepler MM
Size: 10.0 pt
Angle: Regular
Weight: 275 Light
Variation: 575 Normal 1
Color: Black
Spread: 0.0%
Stretch: 100.0%
Language: US English
Underline
Overline
Strikethrough
Change Bar
Superscript
Small Caps
Pair Kern

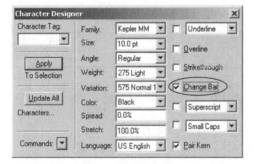

Figure 3.110 In the Character Designer you can apply a Change Bar to selected text.

Paragraph Designer
Basic
Default Font
Pagination
Numbering
Advanced
Table Cell
Paragraph Tag:
Body
Properties:
Default Font
Apply
To Selection
Update All
Formats Tagged:
Body
Commands:
Family: Kepler MM
Size: 10.0 pt
Angle: Regular
Weight: 275 Light
Variation: 575 Normal 10 0
Color: Black
Spread: -0.75%
Stretch: 100.0%
Language: US English
Underline
Overline
Strikethrough
Change Bar
Superscript
Small Caps
Pair Kern

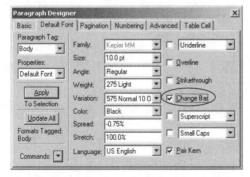

Figure 3.111 In the Paragraph Designer, you apply a Change Bar format to selected text.

Tracking Changes

When you make changes, you often want to be able to track the changes, that is, flag them so you or someone else can see what's changed. Tracking changes in a FrameMaker document can be as simple as manually applying a change bar, a vertical line in the margin that identifies new or changed text.

To add and remove change bars manually from the Format menu:

1. Select the text you want to flag.

   You can select text in a paragraph or select one or more paragraphs (**Figure 3.108**).

2. From the Format menu, choose Style > Change Bar.

   or

   Press Esc C H or Command-Shift-Y.

   A change bar appears next to the text you marked (**Figure 3.109**).

3. To remove the change bar, repeat step 2.

   The change bar disappears.

To add change bars manually by applying a format:

1. Select the text you want to flag or select one or more paragraphs.

2. Display the Character Designer or the Paragraph Designer.

3. For selected text, in the Character Designer, turn on Change Bar, and click Apply (**Figure 3.110**).

   or

   In the Paragraph Designer, go to Default Font Properties, turn on Change Bar, and click Apply (**Figure 3.111**).

   A change bar appears next to the selected text or paragraph(s).

To turn change bars on or off automatically:

1. In the current document or in the book window with selected documents, from the Format menu, choose Document > Change Bars (**Figure 3.112**).

2. In the Change Bar Properties dialog box, change the appearance of the change bars if you wish (**Figure 3.113**).

   Although the default thickness is 2 points, you may prefer to set the thickness to 4 points to make a thicker, more noticeable change bar.

3. Select Automatic Change Bars.

   or

   If the Automatic Change Bars check box is checked, click it again to turn it off.

4. Click Set.

   When you start editing the document, change bars flag changes you make.

   Automatic change bars do not detect a change in graphics imported by reference unless the filename or formatting changes.

Turning off automatic change bars means only that no additional change bars will be added. To remove existing change bars, you need to clear them.

To clear existing change bars:

1. In the current document or in the book window with selected documents, from the Format menu, choose Document > Change Bars.

2. In the Change Bar Properties dialog box, click Clear All Change Bars (No Undo).

3. Click Set (**Figure 3.114**).

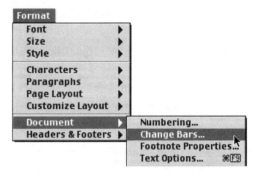

Figure 3.112 Choose Format > Document > Change Bars to turn on or off automatic change bars.

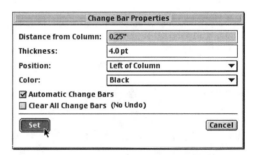

Figure 3.113 Turn on automatic change bars in the Change Bar Properties dialog box. You can specify the location and color of change bars.

Figure 3.114 To remove existing change bars, you need to clear them.

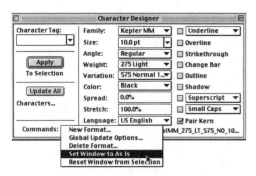

Figure 3.115 From the Commands menu, choose Set Window to As Is.

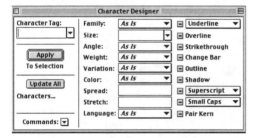

Figure 3.116 All settings in the Character Designer set to As Is.

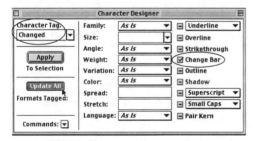

Figure 3.117 Type a character tag in the text box and turn on Change Bar.

You can create a character format that adds change bars. That way, you can select text to flag and then just apply the format.

To create a character format to add change bars:

1. Display the Character Designer.

2. From the Commands menu at the bottom left, choose Set Window to As Is (**Figure 3.115**).

   All settings are changed to As Is (**Figure 3.116**).

3. In the Character Tag text box, type a name for the new format, in this example, Changed, and click the Change Bar check box to turn it on (**Figure 3.117**).

4. Click Update All to add the new character format to the Catalog.

   Now when you want to flag changed text, you can select it and apply the Changed format.

To remove character format change bars:

◆ Select the text and apply the Default ¶ Font character format.

✔ Tip

■ If you apply the Default ¶ Font character format and the character formatting doesn't go away, reapply the paragraph's paragraph format.

TRACKING CHANGES

Comparing Documents

FrameMaker has the capability to compare two versions of a document and tell you whether they are the same or different. If they are different, FrameMaker can generate:

- A composite document, a conditional document that combines content from both documents.

- A summary document that lists and described the differences between the two documents.

Comparing documents is not very useful if the content of the two documents is radically different, for example, if chunks of content have been moved around, because it generates too many bogus changes.

In addition to added, changed, and deleted text, FrameMaker can detect changes in

- Anchored frames

- Cross-references

- Text insets (text imported by reference)

- Imported graphics

- Tables

To compare documents:

1. Open both versions of the document and make the newer version active (**Figure 3.118**).

2. From the File menu, choose Utilities > Compare Documents (**Figure 3.119**).

3. In the Compare Documents dialog box, from the Older Document pop-up menu, choose the older version of the documents you want to compare.

4. If you don't need a composite document, click Summary Document Only (**Figure 3.120**).

Figure 3.118 You need to start with two versions of the same document open on the desktop.

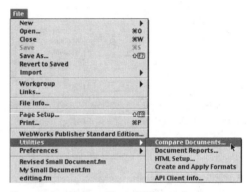

Figure 3.119 Choose File > Utilities > Compare Documents.

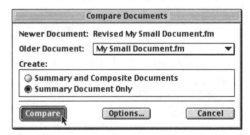

Figure 3.120 The Newer Document specified is the active document and you choose the document to compare it to from the Older Document menu.

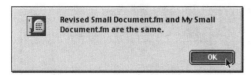

Figure 3.121 If the contents of the two versions of the document are identical, this message appears.

Document Comparison Summary

Documents

	Name	Modification Date
Newer Document:	Revised My Small Document.fm	September 15, 2002 11:48 pm
Older Document:	My Small Document.fm	August 27, 2002 6:55 pm

Number of Changes

Type	Insertions	Deletions	Changes
Text Content	1	1	1
Tables	0	0	1
Anchored Frames	0	0	1
Cross-References	0	0	1

Figure 3.122 In the summary document, changes are grouped in sections, such as Text Content Changes and Table Changes.

5. Click Compare.

If the content of the two versions of the document are identical, a message appears (**Figure 3.121**).

If there are differences between the two documents, a new document appears, the summary document (**Figure 3.122**).

6. If you want to save the summary document, from the Edit menu, choose Save.

The document is saved as Summary.fm.

✔ Tip

■ Every time you compare document, the summary document is named Summary.fm. If you don't want to overwrite the last summary document you created, give the current summary document a different name.

Comparing Autosave Documents

If your system shuts down unexpectedly, FrameMaker creates autosave documents for all open documents. When your system is back up and running and you try to open one of these documents, FrameMaker lets you know that an autosave document is available and asks if you want to open it.

Use Document Compare to see if the autosave file is the same as or different from the active file and then do one of the following:

◆ If the autosave file is the same, then ignore it and use the active file.

◆ If the autosave file is different, check the summary file to see if it, in fact, contains your most recent changes. If it does not, then use the active file. If it does, then open the autosave file and save it with the active filename to overwrite the "older" file.

To be on the safe side, rename the active file before you save the autosave file with the active filename so as *not to overwrite the active file.*

Importing Text from Another File

You can import formatted or unformatted text from another document. Unformatted text contains only the words; formatted text contains information on fonts, indents, spacing, autonumbering, and so on. Importing by copying makes it easy to transfer the imported material from one location to another, but it increases the document size. In addition, if you make changes to the source material, you must reimport it to update the document with the latest version.

Text imported by reference into a FrameMaker document is called a text inset. A text inset is linked to the source document and can't be edited outside of that source document. A common use of text insets is for legal verbiage in the front matter of technical manuals that needs to be used by all members of a workgroup (**Figure 3.123**).

Importing unformatted text

When you import the text from a text file, you specify whether to import it by copying or by reference and how to treat lines in the text file.

To import a text file by reference:

1. Click where you want to insert the text (**Figure 3.124**).

2. From the File menu, choose Import > File. The Import File dialog box appears.

3. Navigate to the text file you want to import, and select it in the Documents list.

4. Choose Import by Reference (**Figure 3.125**).

   Importing by reference keeps the imported text or graphics linked to the source file for automatic or manual updating.

Figure 3.123 In this example the text file contains copyright statements from the legal group.

Figure 3.124 Click where you want to insert text.

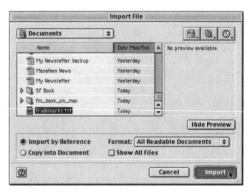

Figure 3.125 Select the text file to import and how to import it.

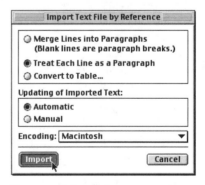

Figure 3.126 Specify how to treat the imported text and whether to update automatically or manually.

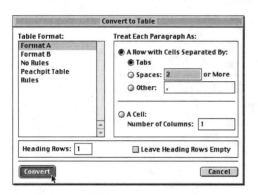

Figure 3.127 Specify how to convert the text.

Figure 3.128 The text inset appears at the insertion point.

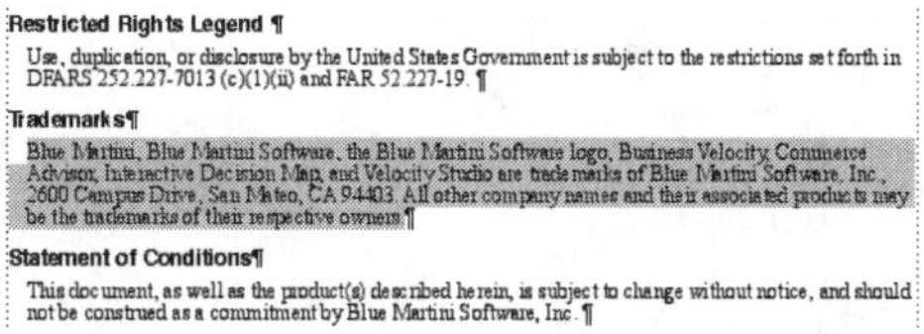

Figure 3.129 Double-click a text inset to display the Text Inset Properties dialog box.

Figure 3.130 To manually update a text inset, click Update Now.

5. Click Import.

   The Import Text File by Reference dialog box appears (**Figure 3.126**).

6. Specify how to treat the imported text:

   ▲ To break the text into paragraphs only at blank lines, click Merge Lines into Paragraphs. Use this option for a paragraph-oriented text file, such as a file containing document text.

   ▲ To break the text into paragraphs at the end of each line, click Treat Each Line As a Paragraph. Use this option for a line-oriented text file, such as a file containing computer code.

   ▲ To convert the imported text to a table, click Convert to Table. Specify a table format and other settings. Use this option only if the file contains delimited text, such as text output from a database program.

7. If you are importing the text by reference, specify how to update the text inset:

   ▲ To update the text inset whenever you open the document, click Automatic.

   ▲ To update only when you specify, click Manual.

8. Accept the default value in the Text Encoding pop-up menu and click Import.

   If you selected Convert to Table, the Convert To Table dialog box appears (**Figure 3.127**). (For information about the settings in the Convert to Table dialog box, see page 237.)

   The imported text takes on the character and paragraph formatting used at the insertion point (**Figure 3.128**).

To update a text inset manually:

1. Double-click the text inset (**Figure 3.129**).

2. In the Text Inset Properties dialog box, click Update Now (**Figure 3.130**).

   The text inset is updated with changes from the imported text file.

Using a Context Menu over Text

The context menu that is displayed when text is selected or when the pointer is over text, includes commands from the Edit menu, the Format menu, and the Special menu—commands you are likely to need when you're editing text.

To display a context menu:

◆ (Windows) Right-click (**Figure 3.131**).

or

(Mac OS) Control-click or right-click if you have a two-button mouse (**Figure 3.132**).

The context menu that appears over text has a number of submenus for the FrameMaker special copy commands and for text formatting.

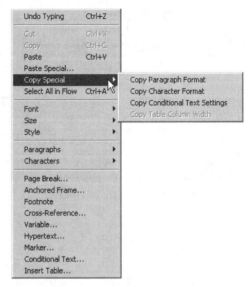

Figure 3.131 The context menu as it is displayed when text is selected or the pointer is over a text column (Windows).

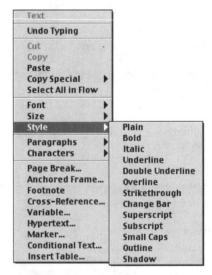

Figure 3.132 The context menu as it is displayed when text is selected or the pointer is over a text column (Mac OS).

FORMATTING PARAGRAPHS

Our original plan called for a questionnaire to be sent to the CEOs of Fortune 1000 companies to ask them to rate themselves. These self-ratings would then be compared to the actual net worth of the CEO as reported in Fortune or other magazines, newspapers, and so on.

Figure 4.1 This side heading paragraph is created in the Paragraph Designer and then saved in the Paragraph Catalog for future use.

In Chapter 2, you saw how to apply predefined paragraph formats from the formatting bar and paragraph and character formats from the Catalogs. In Chapter 3, you saw the Pagination properties and how they control page breaks and the Change Bar setting in the Default Font properties.

In fact, everything about a paragraph, such as the side heading paragraph in **Figure 4.1**, is specified in its format: its position relative to the text frame, its font properties, where it starts, the format you get for the next paragraph when you press Enter or Return, whether or not it allows hyphenation, if it has any tabs—even what language to use for spell checking.

In this chapter, you see how to change paragraph properties in the Paragraph Designer, how to create a new format and add it to the Paragraph Catalog, and how to delete a format from the Catalog.

About Paragraph Formatting Terms

FrameMaker uses a number of terms in relation to paragraph formatting (most of which can also be applied to character formats, discussed in the next chapter):

◆ A *paragraph format* is a set of properties that define the paragraph: its appearance and where it appears relative to other text.

◆ A *paragraph tag* is the name of a paragraph format, for example, Anchor, Body, Chapter Number, and Chapter Title.

◆ The *Paragraph Catalog* is a small floating palette that contains a list of paragraph tags for formats that have been defined and stored in the Catalog. You can display the Catalog and then click a tag to apply a format to one or more paragraphs (**Figure 4.2**).

◆ Formats are created and changed in the *Paragraph Designer*, a special window with pages, or panes, for each set of properties that define a format (**Figure 4.3** and **Figure 4.4**). You can change a property and then apply it to the current paragraph or to all paragraphs with the same tag.

On Windows, you can navigate the Paragraph Designer either by clicking tabs or by choosing from the Properties menu. On Mac OS, choose from the Properties pop-up menu.

Figure 4.2 Click a Catalog icon to display the Paragraph Catalog (left) and Character Catalog (right).

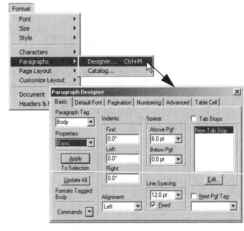

Figure 4.3 Choose Format > Paragraphs > Designer to display the Windows Paragraph Designer.

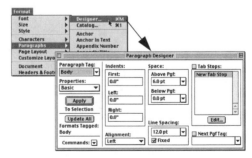

Figure 4.4 Choose Format > Paragraphs > Designer to display the Mac OS Paragraph Designer.

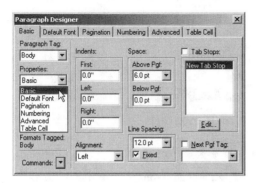

Figure 4.5 The Windows Paragraph Designer.

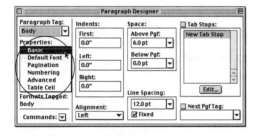

Figure 4.6 The Mac OS Paragraph Designer.

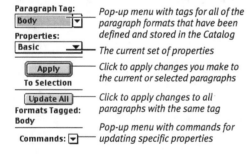

Figure 4.7 The left side of the Designer looks the same no matter which set of properties is displayed on the right.

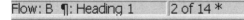

Figure 4.8 The tag of the current paragraph is displayed in the Tag area of the status bar.

The Paragraph Designer

You change existing formats and create new ones in the Paragraph Designer (**Figure 4.5**). In this chapter you'll see that paragraph formats are made up of several sets of properties, as follows (**Figure 4.6**):

◆ Basic—Indents, Space Above and Below, Tab Stops, Alignment, Line Spacing, and Next Paragraph Tag

◆ Default Font—Font related properties, including Color and Language; looks the same in both the Paragraph and Catalog Designers

◆ Pagination—Start, Keep With Next and Previous Paragraph, Widow/Orphan Lines, and heading Format

◆ Numbering—Autonumber Format, Building Blocks and Character Format and Position

◆ Advanced—Hyphenation, Word Spacing, and Frame Above and Below Paragraph (a frame allows you to add a graphic)

◆ Table Cell—Cell Vertical Alignment and Cell Margins

You specify property settings on the right side of the window and you apply them selectively on the left (**Figure 4.7**).

✔ Tips

■ Paragraph formats affect *the entire paragraph*; to format selected text in a paragraph, use a character format.

■ When you are changing paragraph properties, a best practice is to first apply the change to the current paragraph(s) and then if you like what you see, update all other paragraphs with the same tag.

■ If multiple paragraphs are selected, the first paragraph's tag appears in the Tag area (**Figure 4.8**) and the formatting bar.

THE PARAGRAPH DESIGNER

63

Changing Basic Paragraph Properties

You might find yourself happily using *predefined* paragraph formats, choosing them from the formatting bar at the top of the document window or clicking them in the Paragraph Catalog. But it won't be long before you'll want to change something about a paragraph's format.

To display the Paragraph Designer:

◆ From the Format menu, choose Paragraphs > Designer (**Figure 4.9**).

   or

   Press Ctrl-M or Command-M.

The first time you display the Paragraph Designer, you see the Basic properties. After that, you go directly to the set of properties last displayed.

Wherever possible, FrameMaker gives you the option of choosing from a menu or typing in a text box. For example, in the Basic properties, you can choose from a menu of available paragraph tags (**Figure 4.10**) or you can type a tag into the text box. You can choose a value from the Space Above Paragraph menu (see **Figure 4.25** later in the chapter) or you can type in the text box.

✔ Tip

■ Although you may work in a corporate environment and have to follow strict formatting and layout guidelines, if you think you don't have a format you need to make information flow well, go to your manager or production person and ask for what you need. You'll usually find that there's a good reason why you can't do what you want or more likely, that other people in your group also need this new format. In the latter case, chances are good that the format will be added to your template and distributed to the group.

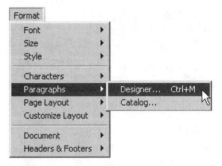

Figure 4.9 Choose Format > Paragraphs > Designer.

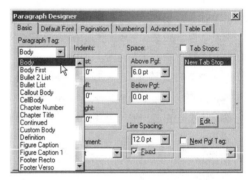

Figure 4.10 Choose a paragraph tag from the menu to display its Basic properties. This choice will not be applied to the current paragraph until you click Apply.

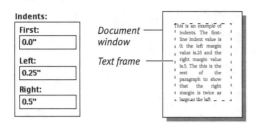

Figure 4.11 In this example, the first line of the paragraph has no indent. The left side of the paragraph is 0.25" from the left edge of the text frame. The right side of the paragraph is 0.5" from the right edge of the text frame.

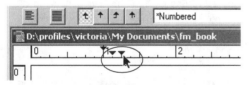

Figure 4.12 The First, Left, and Right indent symbols on the top ruler.

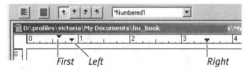

Figure 4.13 Drag the indent symbol to its new location on the ruler.

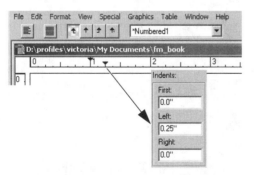

Figure 4.14 Although the Left indent symbol is at the 1-3/4" mark on the ruler (measured from the left side of the document window), the value in the Paragraph Designer is 0.25" measured from the left edge of the text frame.

Changing paragraph indents

Paragraph indents are measured from the left and right edges of the *text frame*, not from the left and right sides of the document window (**Figure 4.11**). A text frame is a rectangular frame that controls placement of the document text, also called a text column.

The First indent refers to the first line of a paragraph, the Left indent to the rest of the lines, and the Right indent to the right side of the paragraph.

To change paragraph indents:

1. Click in a paragraph or select paragraphs.

2. Drag the First, Left, or Right indent symbol (**Figure 4.12**) to a new location on the ruler at the top of the document window (**Figure 4.13**).

   When you change an indent in the top ruler, the value for that indent is updated in the Paragraph Designer (**Figure 4.14**).

   or

   In the Basic properties of the Paragraph Designer, type new values in the First, Left, or Right text boxes.

3. To apply the new indents to the selected paragraphs, click Apply.

4. To apply the new indents to all paragraphs with the same tag and store them in the Catalog, click Update All.

✔ Tips

■ If you want indents to be uniformly spaced, you should work with Snap on and set grid spacing to a relatively small value, such as 1/8-inch intervals (see page 105).

(continues on next page)

CHANGING BASIC PARAGRAPH PROPERTIES

■ When you move indents on the ruler, the change is applied immediately to selected paragraphs, but it represents a format override of the paragraph's format unless you update all paragraphs to the new indents in the Paragraph Designer.

■ You can change the unit of measure displayed in the top and side rulers and in dialog boxes. From the View menu, choose Options. In the View Options dialog box, choose from the Display Units pop-up menu (**Figure 4.15**).

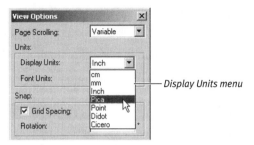

Display Units menu

Figure 4.15 Choose a value from the Display Units menu to specify units of measure for rulers and values in dialog boxes and windows, such as the Paragraph Designer.

Changing paragraph alignment

In general, text is easier to read if the text is left aligned. The unevenness of the right side of left-aligned text is called rag. Text that is left aligned and not justified is described as ragged right.

Lines of text in formal invitations are often center aligned, as are titles and sometimes even first-level headings. If you want paragraphs to form a rectangular block, with even left and right edges, then use justified alignment.

To change paragraph alignment:

1. Click in a paragraph or select paragraphs.

2. In the Paragraph Designer, choose from the Alignment pop-up menu and click Apply (**Figure 4.16**).

   or

   In the formatting bar, choose an option from the Alignment pop-up menu (**Figure 4.17**).

   The new alignment is applied to the selected paragraphs as an override and an asterisk appears in front of the format in the Tag area of the status bar at the bottom left of the document window (**Figure 4.18**).

3. To apply the new alignment to all paragraphs with the same tag and store it in the Catalog, click Update All (**Figure 4.19**).

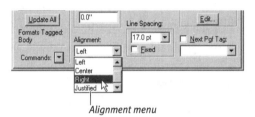

Alignment menu

Figure 4.16 Choose from the Alignment menu in the Basic properties of the Paragraph Designer.

Alignment menu

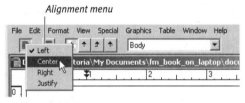

Figure 4.17 Choose from the Alignment pop-up menu on the formatting bar.

Figure 4.18 Format override in the Tag area of the status bar.

Figure 4.19 Click update All to apply the new alignment to all paragraphs with the same tag.

Spacing pop-up menu

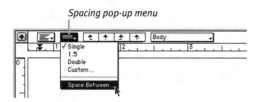

Figure 4.20 Select two paragraphs and choose Space Between.

Figure 4.21 Select a space above option (left), or enter a custom value in the text box (right).

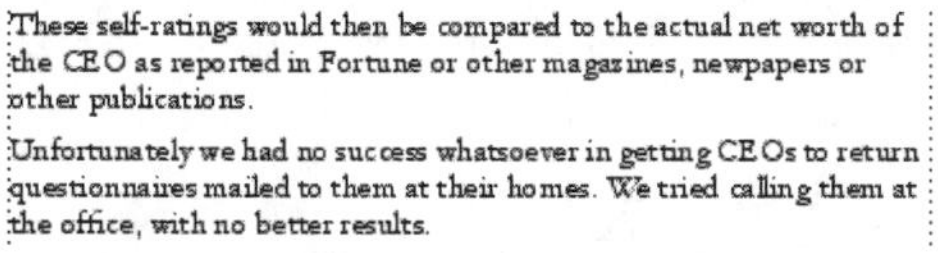

These self-ratings would then be compared to the actual net worth of the CEO as reported in Fortune or other magazines, newpapers or other publications.

Unfortunately we had no success whatsoever in getting CEOs to return questionnaires mailed to them at their homes. We tried calling them at the office, with no better results.

Figure 4.22 In this example, the custom space above the second paragraph is 6 points.

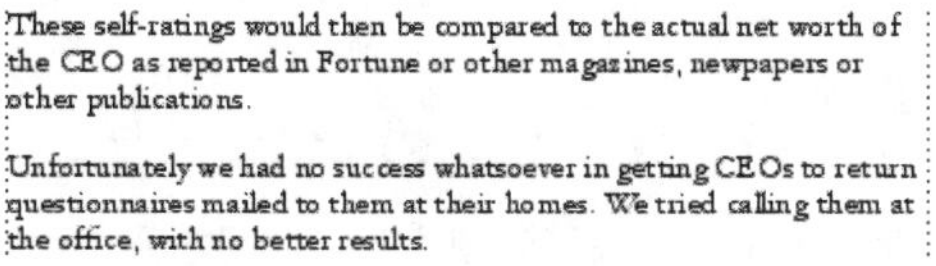

These self-ratings would then be compared to the actual net worth of the CEO as reported in Fortune or other magazines, newpapers or other publications.

Unfortunately we had no success whatsoever in getting CEOs to return questionnaires mailed to them at their homes. We tried calling them at the office, with no better results.

Figure 4.23 Here, the custom space is 1 Line, or 12 points.

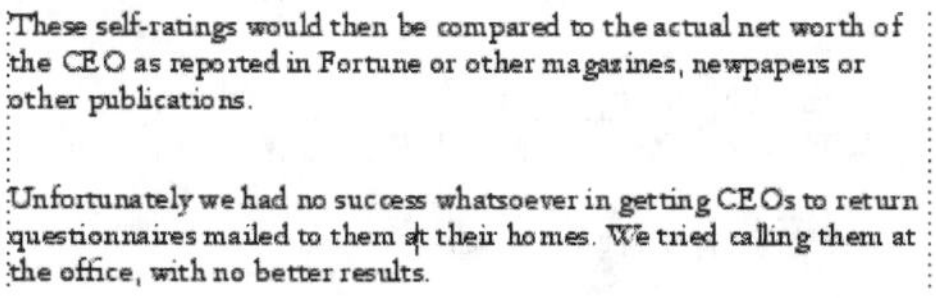

These self-ratings would then be compared to the actual net worth of the CEO as reported in Fortune or other magazines, newpapers or other publications.

Unfortunately we had no success whatsoever in getting CEOs to return questionnaires mailed to them at their homes. We tried calling them at the office, with no better results.

Figure 4.24 Here the custom space is 2 Lines, or 24 points.

Changing paragraph spacing

The space between paragraphs in a FrameMaker document is controlled by Space Above Paragraph and Below Paragraph and Space Between Paragraphs settings.

To change the space between paragraphs from the formatting bar:

1. Select two paragraphs.

2. In the formatting bar, from the Spacing pop-up menu, choose Space Between (**Figure 4.20**).

3. In the Space between Paragraphs dialog box (**Figure 4.21**), select None, 1 Line (to add 12 points above the second paragraph), or 2 Lines (to add 24 points above the second paragraph), or enter a value in the Custom dialog box.

4. Click Set.

   The new space above is applied to the *second* paragraph as an override.

5. To apply the new space above to all paragraphs with the same tag, in the Paragraph Designer, click Update All.

A good space above is half of the line spacing value. For example, for a Body paragraph with 12-point line spacing, a comfortable space above is 6 points (**Figure 4.22**). Another common setting is 1 Line (**Figure 4.23**); as you can see in **Figure 4.24**, the 2 Lines setting may leave more space between paragraphs than you want or need for readability.

CHANGING BASIC PARAGRAPH PROPERTIES

To change space above and space below in the Paragraph Designer:

1. Click in a paragraph or select paragraphs.

2. Choose a value from the Space Above Paragraph (**Figure 4.25**) or Space Below Paragraph pop-up menu (**Figure 4.26**).

   or

   Type a value in one or both of the text boxes.

3. To apply the new values to the current paragraphs, click Apply.

4. To update all paragraphs with the same tag, click Update All.

✔ Tips

- To determine the space between paragraphs, FrameMaker looks at the
  - ▲ Space Below Paragraph setting for the first paragraph
  - ▲ Space Above Paragraph setting for the second paragraph

  FrameMaker then uses the larger value.

- In most cases you can format a document using only the Space Above Paragraph setting. An exception to this general rule is when you want to add space between a title or heading and the *first* body paragraph that follows it (**Figure 4.27**).

- If a paragraph appears at the top of a text column, the Space Above setting is ignored (**Figure 4.28**); if it falls at the bottom of a text column, the Space Below setting is ignored.

- You should never need empty paragraphs in a FrameMaker document. Always use the Space Above and Below settings to add space between paragraphs and always use Pagination properties to insert a page break.

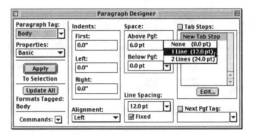

Figure 4.25 Space above a paragraph is added to the line spacing.

Figure 4.26 The Space Below setting is most often used for title or heading paragraphs to leave more space before the first paragraph of text following the title or heading (shown below).

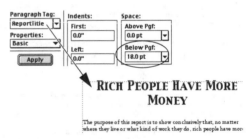

Figure 4.27 Adding 18 points of space below the Report Title paragraph format means that wherever you use this format, you will see more space between the title and the following paragraph of text.

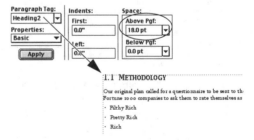

Figure 4.28 The Space Above setting is ignored if the paragraph appears at the top of a text column.

Changing line spacing in a paragraph

In addition to controlling the space between paragraphs of text, you can also control the spacing between lines of text in a paragraph.

To change line spacing:

1. Click in a paragraph or select paragraphs.
2. In the Paragraph Designer, choose a value from the Line Spacing pop-up menu or type a value in the text box (**Figure 4.29**).

   or

   In the formatting bar, choose an option from the Spacing pop-up menu (**Figure 4.30**).

   The new spacing is applied to the selected paragraphs as an override (**Figure 4.31**).

   When you change the font size, FrameMaker automatically recalculates the line spacing to an appropriate value. To prevent this, you need to specify fixed line spacing.
3. To make the new value apply even if the font size is changed, select Fixed (**Figure 4.32**).
4. To apply the new value to the selected paragraphs, click Apply.
5. To update all paragraphs with the same tag, click Update All.

Line Spacing:
12.0 pt
Fixed
Single (13.0 pt)
1.5 (19.5 pt)
Double (26.0 pt)

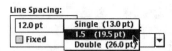

Figure 4.29 Choose from the Line Spacing menu or type a value in the text box.

Body
√ Single
1.5
Double
Custom...
Space Between...
Introduction¶
This is a small document I created to show examp
editing. I'm using it in the "Document Window" a
Text" chapters. Here's how I created it:¶

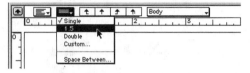

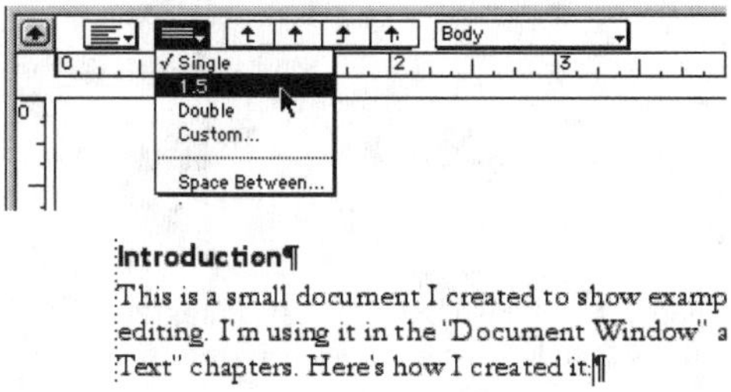

Figure 4.30 Choose an option from the Spacing menu ...

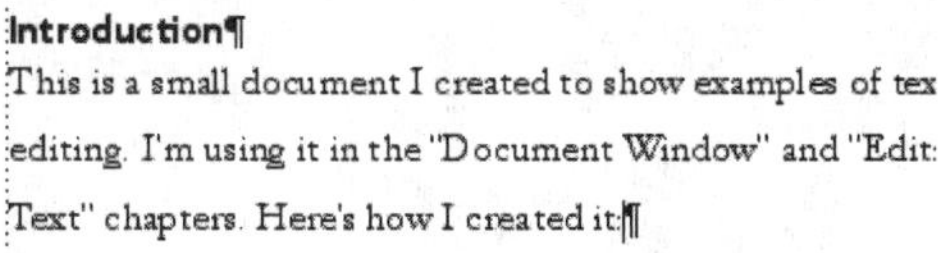

Introduction¶
This is a small document I created to show examples of tex
editing. I'm using it in the "Document Window" and "Edit:
Text" chapters. Here's how I created it:¶

Figure 4.31 ... to apply the format immediately and create a format override.

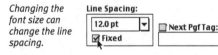

Changing the font size can change the line spacing.

Line Spacing:
12.0 pt
Fixed
Next Pgf Tag:

Figure 4.32 Select Fixed to keep line spacing constant even if the font size is changed.

Specifying a format for the next paragraph

When you press Enter or Return for a new paragraph, FrameMaker gives you the same paragraph format for the new paragraph as for the preceding one unless you specify a different paragraph tag. But in most documents, for example, you know that after every first-level heading paragraph you're going to need a body paragraph. In that case, you should use the Next Paragraph Tag setting (**Figure 4.33**) in the Basic properties.

To specify a format for the next paragraph:

1. Click in a paragraph or select paragraphs.

2. Choose a paragraph tag from the Next Paragraph Tag pop-up menu, or type a tag in the text box.

3. To apply the new value to the selected paragraphs, click Apply.

4. To update all paragraphs with the same tag, click Update All.

   In this example (**Figure 4.34**), when you come to the end of a Tip Head paragraph and press Enter or Return, the next paragraph will be a Tip paragraph.

✔ Tip

- Even if you have specified a paragraph format for the next paragraph, you can always override it by applying a different format.

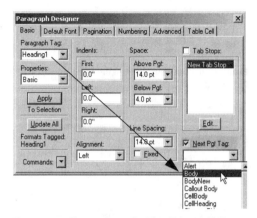

Figure 4.33 Choose from the Next Paragraph Tag pop-up menu.

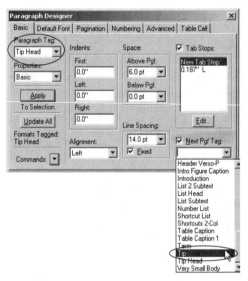

Figure 4.34 When you press Enter or Return in a Tip Head paragraph, the next paragraph will always be a Tip paragraph.

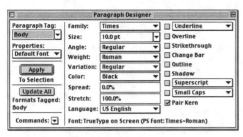

Figure 4.35 The Default Font properties in the Paragraph Designer look exactly like properties in the Character Designer.

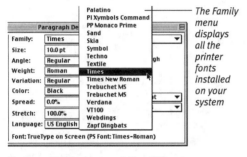

Figure 4.36 Windows and Mac OS systems handle fonts differently. Consult your system documentation for details.

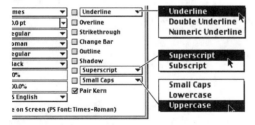

Figure 4.37 Menu choices for style options.

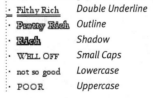

Figure 4.38 Each bullet in this list has the default font setting listed at the right.

Working with Font Properties

Everything related to the appearance of the font itself is included in the Default Font properties (**Figure 4.35**) in the Paragraph Designer.

The font itself determines the Angle, Weight, and Variation options that are available (**Figure 4.36**). For example, some font families use the term Oblique or Obliqued in the Angle menu for an italic (slanted) style. The Weight menu may display terms such as Medium, Bold, Bolded, or Black for different weights. In some fonts both Bold and Black are choices; in others only one or the other is available.

The following properties can be set to create special effects, but you could work in FrameMaker for a long time before you would ever need to change the defaults:

◆ Spread, sometimes called tracking, adds or subtracts space between characters expressed as a percentage (0 percent is normal).

◆ Stretch specifies the width of the character shapes expressed as a percentage (100 percent is normal).

Many of the Default Font properties such as Underline and Strikethrough should already be familiar to you (**Figure 4.37**). And you've already seen how to apply Change Bars to selected paragraphs (see page 53).

✔ Tips

■ Use font properties such as Outline or Shadow (**Figure 4.38**) sparingly and rarely in a corporate context. In general, they tend to reduce readability.

■ Pair kerning adjusts the visual space between any two characters in the same

(continues on next page)

word. Pair kerning also turns on ligatures, such as "fi" and "fl" (Mac OS only). The kerning pairs and the ligatures are defined in the font itself. The only time you might want to turn Pair Kern off is when you are using monospace fonts, such as Courier, or when you want to emulate a monospace font in a proportional font.

- FrameMaker can skip spell checking in a paragraph if Language is set to None (see page 42).

Text is only one of the items for which you can specify a color from a standard set plus custom colors you've defined. You can also add color to graphics, conditional text, and table formats.

To add color to text:

1. Click in a paragraph or select paragraphs.

2. From the Color pop-up menu in the Default Font properties of the Paragraph Designer, choose a standard color or a custom color (**Figure 4.39**).

   The Color menu displays a list of standard colors and predefined custom colors.

3. To apply the new value to the current paragraphs, click Apply.

4. To update all paragraphs with the same tag, click Update All.

To create reverse text (light on dark):

1. In a text frame, work with the font, size, and weight until it looks the way you want.

2. Create a dark color shape that completely covers the text you want to reverse (see page 108), taking into account any space you want as a border around the text.

3. Send the dark shape to the back behind the text frame with the text (see page 119).

4. Change the paragraph font to a light color (**Figure 4.40**).

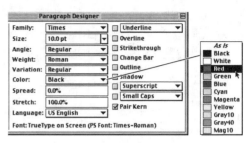

Figure 4.39 The Color menu displays a list of standard colors, such as red, green, and blue, and custom colors that have been defined, in this example, Gray10, Gray40, and so on.

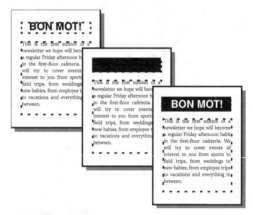

Figure 4.40 Use light color text on a dark background for reverse text.

Text frame

Text line ——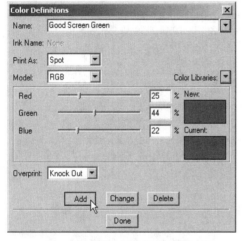

Figure 4.41 You can use a text frame (top) or a text line (bottom) for a single line of reversed text, but if you want to reverse more than one line of text, you should use a text frame.

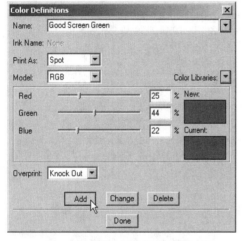

Figure 4.42 Define a new custom color and experiment to find a readable green (Windows).

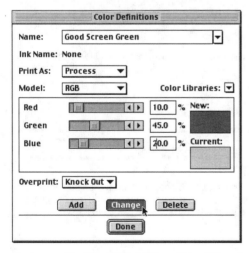

Figure 4.43 The Mac OS definition will be different.

✔ Tips

■ You can also use a *text line* instead of a text frame for reverse text and use a light color in the character format (**Figure 4.41**).

■ The following standard colors keep text readable on the screen: red, blue, and magenta. The following standard colors are extremely difficult, if not impossible, to read on the screen: green, cyan, and yellow.

  If you want to use green on the screen, for example, you should create a new color and experiment until you find a version of the color that is readable on the screen (**Figure 4.42**). On a Mac OS computer, screen color (RGB) definitions will be different (**Figure 4.43**).

  For information on how to create a new color, see page 141.

■ If you want to use a percentage tint for text, 70 percent blue, for instance, you need to first define and name the tint, and then choose it from a Color menu.

WORKING WITH FONT PROPERTIES

Run-In and Side Headings

In this book, the headings are all In Column headings, that is, they come in between other paragraphs and each sits on its own line (**Figure 4.44**). Run-in headings work well as third- or fourth-level headings in a document (**Figure 4.45**). Side headings are a little more complicated, because they involve a significant change in page layout: adding a column in addition to the main text column to accommodate the side heading (**Figure 4.46**).

To create a run-in heading:

1. Click in the paragraph you want to change and display the Pagination properties of the Paragraph Designer.
2. Click the Run-In Head radio button and specify punctuation to appear at the end of the run-in heading (**Figure 4.47**).

   or

   For no punctuation, delete the contents of the Default Punctuation text box and type a space.
3. Click Apply or Update All.

   The paragraph after the heading paragraph moves up to occupy the same line (**Figure 4.48**).

   But these are still two separate paragraphs, as you can see by the end-of-paragraph symbols. If you specified punctuation, it appears at the end of the run-in heading.

✔ Tip

- Creating run-in headings in the Paragraph Designer, rather than just applying a bold character format to the introductory words in a paragraph, enables you to include them in tables of contents and running headers and footers and to make them a source of cross-references.

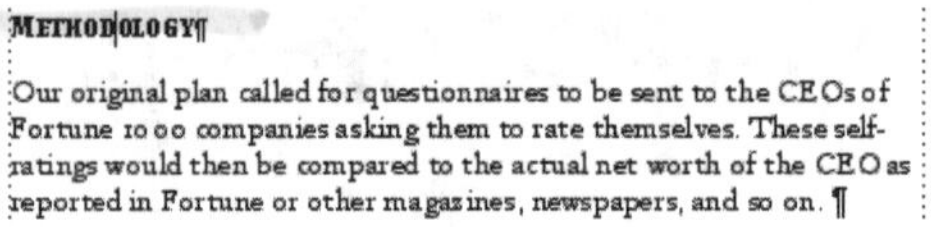

METHODOLOGY¶
Our original plan called for questionnaires to be sent to the CEOs of Fortune 1000 companies asking them to rate themselves. These self-ratings would then be compared to the actual net worth of the CEO as reported in Fortune or other magazines, newspapers, and so on. ¶

Figure 4.44 the most common type of heading is In Column.

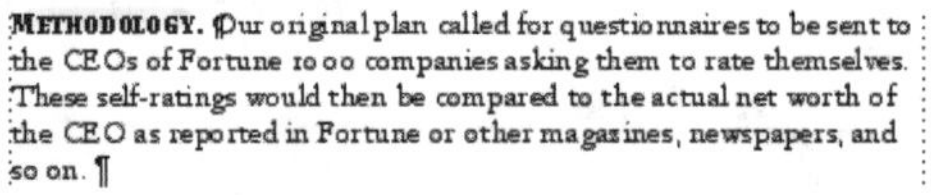

METHODOLOGY. Our original plan called for questionnaires to be sent to the CEOs of Fortune 1000 companies asking them to rate themselves. These self-ratings would then be compared to the actual net worth of the CEO as reported in Fortune or other magazines, newspapers, and so on. ¶

Figure 4.45 A run-in heading sits on the same line as the paragraph that follows, but the heading is usually distinguished by a larger or bolder font, or both.

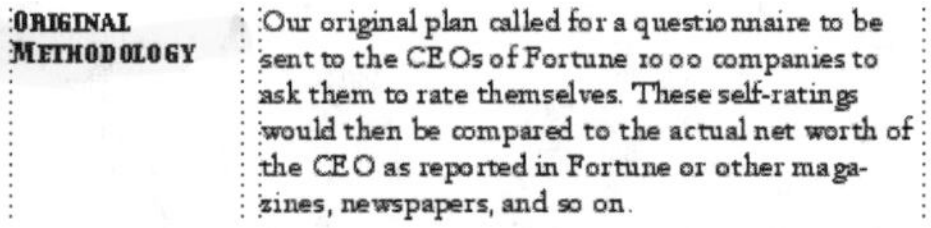

ORIGINAL METHODOLOGY
Our original plan called for a questionnaire to be sent to the CEOs of Fortune 1000 companies to ask them to rate themselves. These self-ratings would then be compared to the actual net worth of the CEO as reported in Fortune or other magazines, newspapers, and so on.

Figure 4.46 Side headings occupy their own side heading column to the left or right of the main text column.

Format:
In Column
Run-In Head--Default Punctuation:
.
Side Head--Alignment:
First Baseline
Across All Columns
Across All Columns and Side Heads
As Is

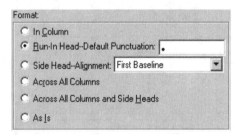

Figure 4.47 You can use a period (.) at the end of a run-in heading, but it's not absolutely necessary.

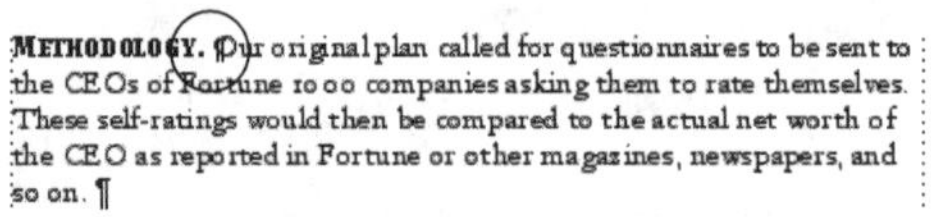

METHODOLOGY. Our original plan called for questionnaires to be sent to the CEOs of Fortune 1000 companies asking them to rate themselves. These self-ratings would then be compared to the actual net worth of the CEO as reported in Fortune or other magazines, newspapers, and so on. ¶

Figure 4.48 The heading paragraph still ends with an end-of-paragraph symbol, but the next paragraph starts on the same line.

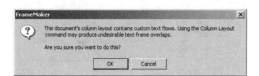

Figure 4.49 If your document contains custom text flows, this warning appears when you choose Format > Page Layout > Column Layout.

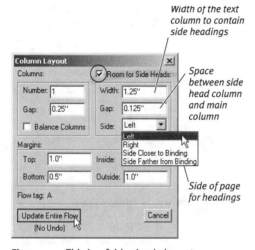

Width of the text column to contain side headings

Space between side head column and main column

Side of page for headings

Figure 4.50 This is a fairly simple layout with one main text column—appropriate for adding a side heading column.

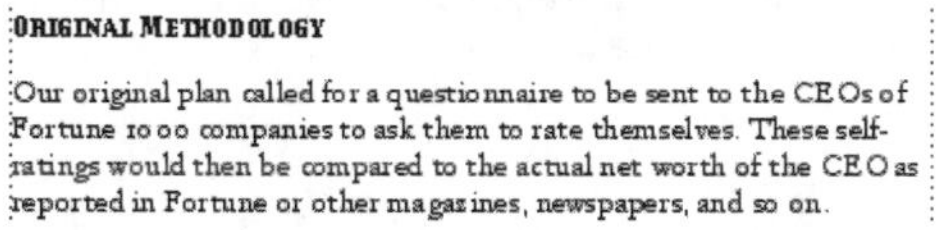

ORIGINAL METHODOLOGY

Our original plan called for a questionnaire to be sent to the CEOs of Fortune 1000 companies to ask them to rate themselves. These self-ratings would then be compared to the actual net worth of the CEO as reported in Fortune or other magazines, newspapers, and so on.

Figure 4.51 Making room for side headings is the first thing you need to do.

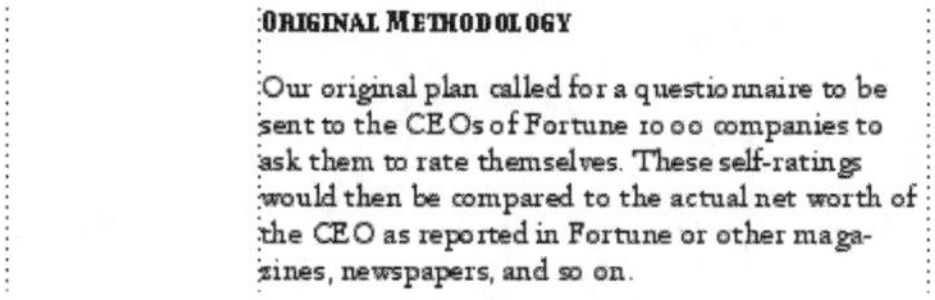

ORIGINAL METHODOLOGY

Our original plan called for a questionnaire to be sent to the CEOs of Fortune 1000 companies to ask them to rate themselves. These self-ratings would then be compared to the actual net worth of the CEO as reported in Fortune or other magazines, newspapers, and so on.

Figure 4.52 FrameMaker moves all paragraphs not designated as side headings to the main text column.

Before you create a side heading paragraph format, you need to add a side heading column for the entire flow.

To make room for side headings:

1. From the Format menu, choose Page Layout > Column Layout.

   If a body page contains a text flow (text in a series of connected text frames) not found on its corresponding master page, a warning message appears (**Figure 4.49**), In this case, you might want to reconsider your decision to create a text column for side headings. If you still want to go ahead, click OK.

   The Column Layout dialog box appears.

2. Select the Room for Side Heads check box at the top right (**Figure 4.50**).

3. Specify the following:
   - ▲ Width for the side heading column
   - ▲ Gap between the side heading column and the main text column
   - ▲ Side of the page for the side heading column

4. Click Update Entire Flow.

   The layout of the entire document changes from the original format (**Figure 4.51**) to allow for a second text column for the side headings on the side you specified in the Column Layout dialog box (**Figure 4.52**).

To create a side heading:

1. Click in the paragraph you want to change to display the Pagination properties of the Paragraph Designer.

2. Click the Side Head radio button.

3. Choose from the Alignment pop-up menu (**Figure 4.53**):

   ▲ First Baseline aligns the baseline of the first line of the heading with the first line of the following paragraph.

   ▲ Top Edge aligns the top edge of the first line of the heading with the top edge of the following paragraph.

   ▲ Last Baseline aligns the baseline of the last line of the heading with the baseline of the last line of the following paragraph.

4. Click Apply or Update All.

   The heading now moves into the side heading column you created (**Figure 4.54** and **Figure 4.55**).

✔ Tip

■ If you are a template designer using side headings with multiple text columns or multiple text flows, make sure you set up and test everything carefully. The way things work will be mysterious to your users and they will be frustrated if everything doesn't work as advertised.

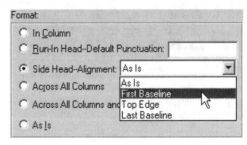

Figure 4.53 In the Pagination properties, choose an option for aligning the baseline of the side heading.

ORIGINAL METHODOLOGY — Our original plan called for a questionnaire to be sent to the CEOs of Fortune 100 companies to ask them to rate themselves. These self-ratings would then be compared to the actual net worth of the CEO as reported in Fortune or other magazines, newspapers, and so on.

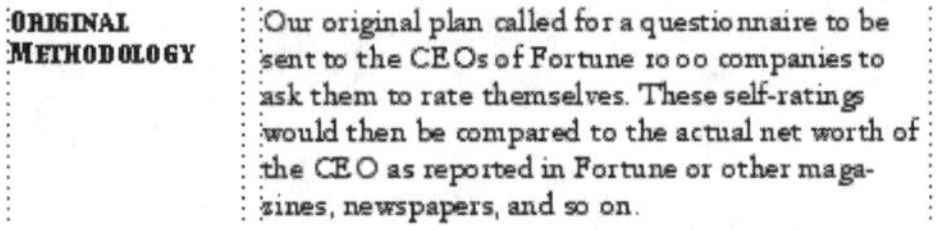

Figure 4.54 The heading paragraph moves into the side heading column.

ORIGINAL METHODOLOGY — Our original plan called for a ... sent to the CEOs of Fortune ... ask them to rate themselves. ... would then be compared to tl ... the CEO as reported in Fortu ... zines, newspapers, and so on.

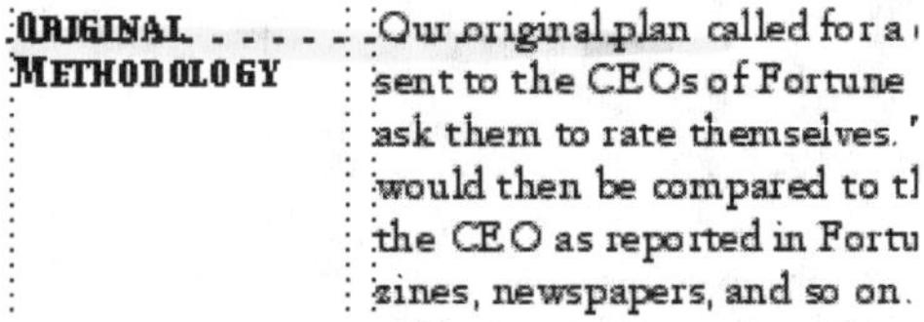

Figure 4.55 Looking a little closer, you can see that the baseline of the first line of the side heading is aligned with the baseline of the first line of the paragraph beside it.

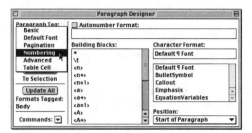

Figure 4.56 Go to the Numbering properties in the Paragraph Designer to let FrameMaker keep track of chapter numbers, numbered steps, and much more.

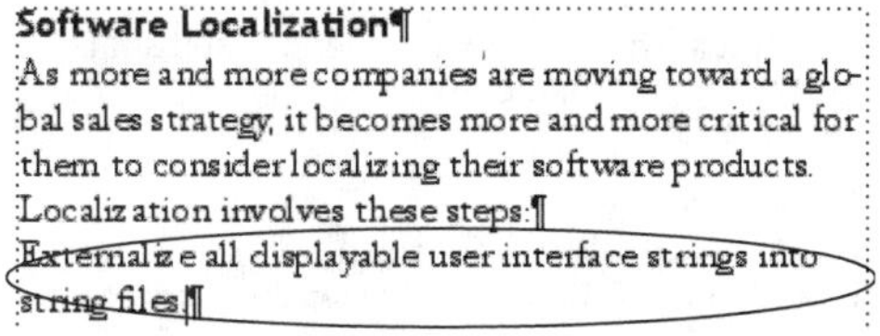

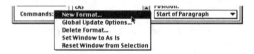

Figure 4.57 Start with a plain body text paragraph.

Figure 4.58 Choose Commands > New Format.

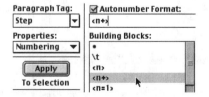

Figure 4.59 The Step tag is applied to the current paragraph and appears in the Paragraph Tag text box in the Paragraph Designer.

Figure 4.60 When you select from the Building Blocks list, your selection appears in the Autonumber Format text box.

Using Numbering Paragraph Properties

You'll use FrameMaker's Numbering properties (**Figure 4.56**) most commonly in numbered steps and bulleted lists. You'll also use them to number chapters and appendixes.

Autonumbering paragraphs

To create a numbered step paragraph format:

1. Click in a paragraph you want to convert to a numbered step (**Figure 4.57**).

2. In the Numbering properties of the Paragraph Designer, from the Commands pop-up menu at the bottom left, choose New Format (**Figure 4.58**).

   The New Format dialog box appears.

3. Type a name for the format in the Tag text box and click Create (**Figure 4.59**).

   The new name is applied to the paragraph and appears in the Paragraph Tag box in the Paragraph Designer. But the paragraph looks the same as before.

4. From the Building Blocks list, select <n+> (**Figure 4.60**).

   The Autonumber Format check box is turned on and <n+> appears in the box.

5. Type a period (.) and then a space (**Figure 4.61**).

   When you use the Step format, the autonumber will be followed by a period and a space.

6. Click Update All to apply the autonumber to the current paragraph and to store the format in the Catalog (**Figure 4.62**).

   Every time you press Enter or Return at the end of a Step paragraph, FrameMaker gives you the next step ready for typing (**Figure 4.63**).

You cannot create a new paragraph format if the same tag is already stored in the Paragraph Catalog. You can either change and save the properties of the existing format or delete the format from the Catalog and start again.

To delete a format from the Catalog:

1. In the Paragraph Catalog, click Delete at the bottom of the window.

   or

   In the Paragraph Designer, from the Commands pop-up menu, choose Delete Format (**Figure 4.64**).

2. In the Delete Formats from Catalog dialog box, select the formats to delete from the scroll list and click Delete.

   You can delete as many formats as you wish (**Figure 4.65**).

3. When you've finished, click Done.

   FrameMaker deletes the selected formats from the Catalog.

✔ Tips

■ If you are deleting a number of formats from the Catalog and accidentally delete a format you didn't intend to, click Cancel; the deletions don't take effect until you click Done. You will have to start again, so it really pays to go slowly and carefully when you're deleting a number of formats.

■ Paragraphs with deleted tags have a format override. To add a format back to the Catalog, click in the paragraph with the deleted format and in the Paragraph Designer, click Update All.

■ If a paragraph format is no longer used, delete it from the Catalog so no one will inadvertently use it.

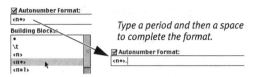

Figure 4.61 You create an autonumber format by selecting building blocks and typing in the text box.

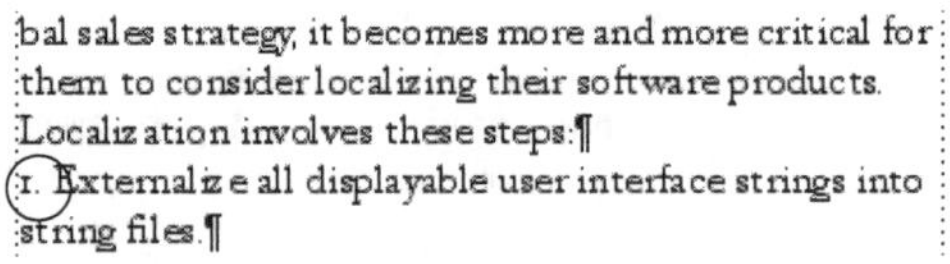

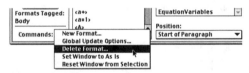

Figure 4.62 The autonumber, period, and space appears in front of the text.

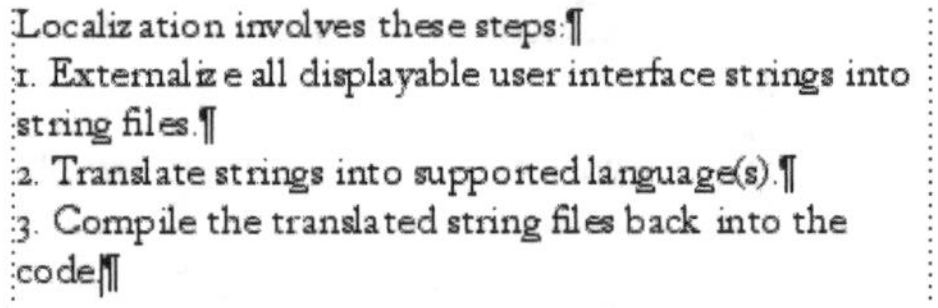

Figure 4.63 Every time you press Enter or Return, FrameMaker gives you an incremented step number.

Figure 4.64 You can delete a format from the Paragraph Catalog or from the Paragraph Designer.

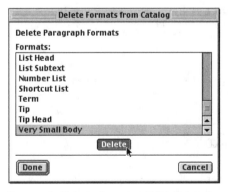

Figure 4.65 Select a format and click Delete for each format you want to delete from the Catalog.

Resetting Counters

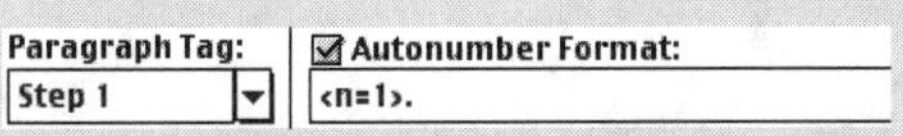

Paragraph Tag: | ☑ **Autonumber Format:**
Step 1 | ‹n=1›.

Figure 4.66 Hard coding the counter means that no matter where this paragraph appears, it will be numbered 1.

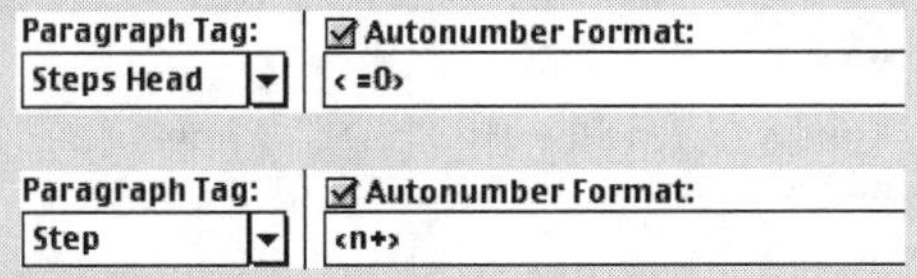

Paragraph Tag: | ☑ **Autonumber Format:**
Steps Head | ‹ =0›

Paragraph Tag: | ☑ **Autonumber Format:**
Step | ‹n+›

Figure 4.67 This format resets the "n" counter to 0 (top), and the next Step paragraph increments it to 1 (bottom), and so on.

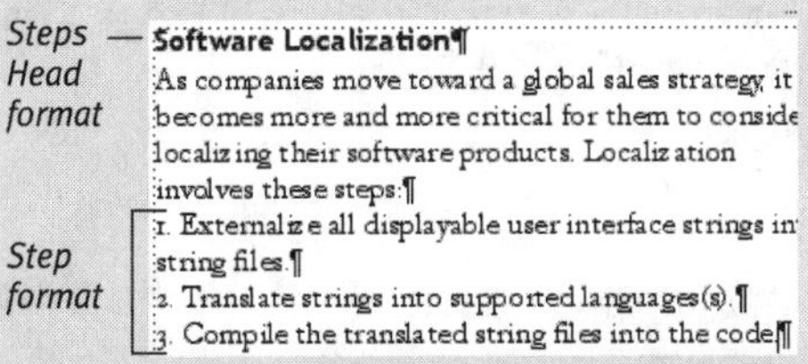

Steps — **Software Localization**¶
Head
format   As companies move toward a global sales strategy, it becomes more and more critical for them to conside localizing their software products. Localization involves these steps:¶

Step   1. Externalize all displayable user interface strings in string files.¶
format   2. Translate strings into supported languages(s).¶
   3. Compile the translated string files into the code.¶

Figure 4.68 As long as the Steps Head format always occurs between sets of numbered steps and never occurs in numbered steps, it can reset the autonumber counter. The counter gets incremented in the first Step paragraph and in each subsequent Step paragraph in the list.

Autonumbered paragraphs are numbered consecutively in a text flow. For example, in this book, the figure numbering increments independently of the procedures numbering, because they are in different text flows. Also, figures number from the beginning to the end of a chapter and numbered steps need to restart at the beginning of each procedure.

One way to accomplish this is to create a paragraph format (you could call it Step 1) and hard code the number "1" (**Figure 4.66**). But this method is error prone and undermines the automatic aspect of autonumbering. You shouldn't have to remember to use a Step 1 format for the first step in a procedure.

A more satisfactory method is to reset the autonumbering counter in a paragraph somewhere *between* procedures. A heading that describes the procedure is perfect for resetting the counter (**Figure 4.67**). FrameMaker can reset a counter without displaying its value. The following procedure describes how to reset a simple counter, but the same principle applies to complex numbering as well.

To reset the autonumber counter:

1. Choose a paragraph format that always occurs between procedures but *never inside a procedure.*

2. In that paragraph format, add an autonumber format as follows: < =0>. Remember to include a space after the left angle bracket (<).

3. Click Update All.
   Every time you add a new procedure, the Steps Head paragraph resets the counter (**Figure 4.68**).

Adding text to autonumbers

You can combine literal text with an autonumber counter if, for example, instead of just numbering steps in a procedure, you want to add the word "Step" in front of the autonumber.

To include text in an autonumber format:

1. Click in a numbered step paragraph.
2. In the Numbering properties of the Paragraph Designer, click on the left side of the Autonumber Format text box, in front of the autonumber counter (**Figure 4.69**).
3. Type the text you want to appear in front of the number, including punctuation and spaces (**Figure 4.70**).
4. Click Update All to add the text in front of the number in all Step paragraphs (**Figure 4.71**).

You can use only text without autonumber counters, in note or alert paragraphs, for example. In the following section, you'll use text only in the autonumber format without any actual numbering.

To create a note format:

1. Go to the Numbering properties in the Paragraph Designer, and from the Commands menu, choose New Format.
2. In the New Format dialog box, type a tag for the new paragraph format (**Figure 4.72**).
3. In the Paragraph Designer, in the Autonumber Format text box, type the text you want to introduce the note.

   In this example, the word "NOTE" is followed by a colon and a period.
4. Click Update All.

   The autonumber text appears (**Figure 4.73**).
5. Type the note itself (**Figure 4.74**).

Paragraph Tag:
Step
Properties:
Autonumber Format:
<n+>.

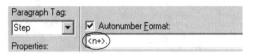

Figure 4.69 Step paragraphs already have an autonumber counter in this example.

Paragraph Tag:
Step
Properties:
Autonumber Format:
Step <n+>.

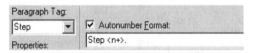

Figure 4.70 Type the word "Step" in front of the autonumber and add a space.

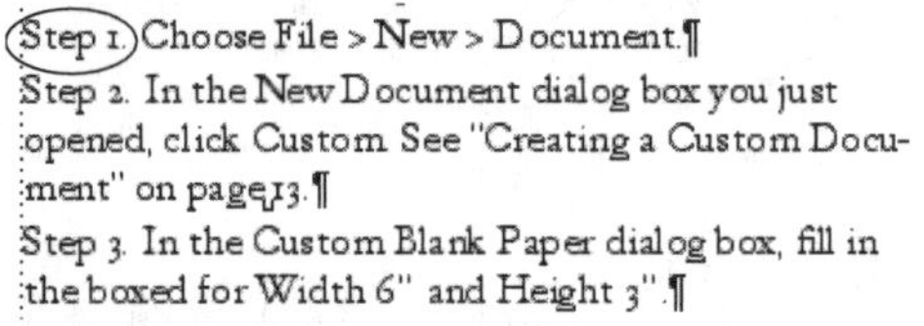

Step 1. Choose File > New > Document.¶
Step 2. In the New Document dialog box you just opened, click Custom. See "Creating a Custom Document" on page 13.¶
Step 3. In the Custom Blank Paper dialog box, fill in the boxed for Width 6" and Height 3".¶

Figure 4.71 Update all Step paragraphs.

New Format
Create a new paragraph format using the properties in the Paragraph Designer.
Tag: Note
Store in Catalog
Apply to Selection
Create
Cancel

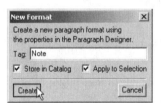

Figure 4.72 Type a name for the new format in the Tag text box.

Paragraph Tag:
Note
Properties:
Autonumber Format:
NOTE:
2. Translate strings into supported lan
3. Compile the translated string files.¶
NOTE: ¶

Figure 4.73 Even though you haven't typed anything yet, the autonumber text appears.

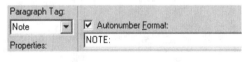

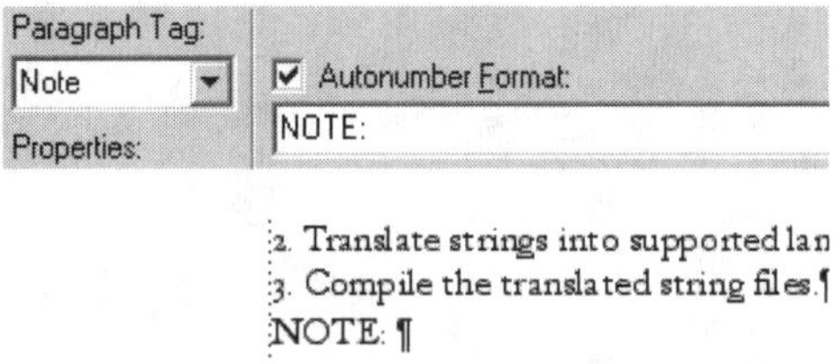

2. Translate strings into supported languages(s).¶
3. Compile the translated string files.¶
NOTE: Translation can be done in house or by third party localization vendors.¶

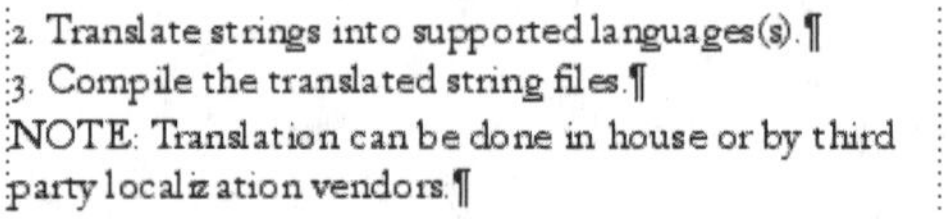

Figure 4.74 Because you stored the format in the Catalog, you can use it elsewhere in the document ...

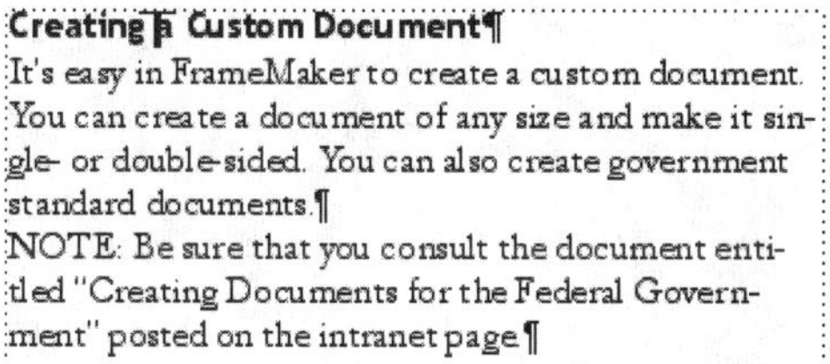

Creating a Custom Document¶
It's easy in FrameMaker to create a custom document. You can create a document of any size and make it single- or double-sided. You can also create government standard documents.¶
NOTE: Be sure that you consult the document entitled "Creating Documents for the Federal Government" posted on the intranet page.¶

Figure 4.75 ... and be sure it's formatted in exactly the same way.

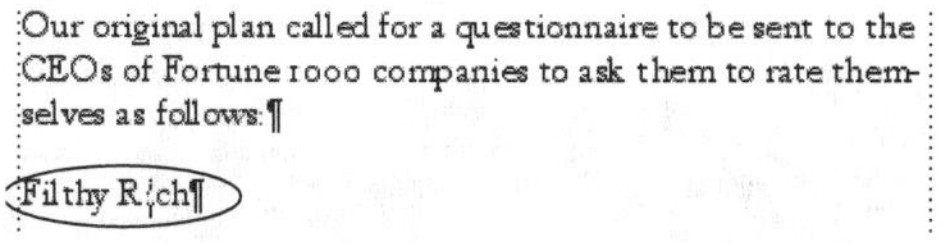

Our original plan called for a questionnaire to be sent to the CEOs of Fortune 1000 companies to ask them to rate themselves as follows:¶
Filthy Rich¶

Figure 4.76 Start with a plain body text paragraph.

New Format
Create a new paragraph format using the properties in the Paragraph Designer.
Tag: Bullet List
Store in Catalog
Apply to Selection
Create
Cancel
Paragraph Tag:
Bullet List
Properties:
Numbering

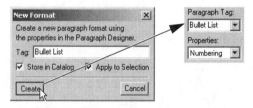

Figure 4.77 The Bullet List tag is applied to the current paragraph and appears in the Paragraph Tag text box in the Paragraph Designer.

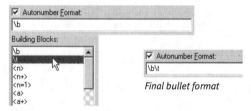

Autonumber Format:
\b
Building Blocks:
\b
\t
<n>
<n+>
<n=1>
<a>
<a+>
Autonumber Format:
\b\t
Final bullet format

Figure 4.78 Select the bullet, then the tab \t from the Building Blocks scroll list.

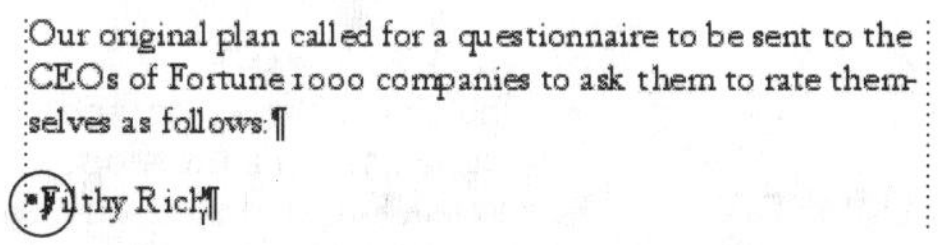

Our original plan called for a questionnaire to be sent to the CEOs of Fortune 1000 companies to ask them to rate themselves as follows:¶
•Filthy Rich¶

Figure 4.79 A bullet and a tab symbol are added to the paragraph, but because there is no tab stop in the paragraph, the text doesn't move.

The advantage of creating a format for the introductory text (in this example, "NOTE: ") and storing it in the Catalog is that you can use if elsewhere in the document, and it will look exactly the same, thus enforcing format consistency (**Figure 4.75**).

Creating formats for bullet lists

You can use an autonumber format to add a bullet or other character in bullet lists. And although you can create bullet paragraphs without using a tab, you will mostly likely want to add a little breathing space between the bullet and the beginning of the text. Remember that adding a tab is a two-step process. (See *Adding Tabs* on page 34.)

To create a bullet list paragraph format:

1. Click in a paragraph you want to change to a bullet paragraph (**Figure 4.76**).
2. In the Numbering properties of the Paragraph Designer, from the Commands pop-up menu, choose New Format.
3. In the New Format dialog box, type a name for the format in the Tag text box (**Figure 4.77**).

   The new name is applied to the paragraph and appears in the Paragraph Tag box. But the paragraph still looks the same as it did before.
4. From the Building Blocks list, select \b (Windows) or the bullet symbol (Mac OS) and then \t.

   The Autonumber Format check box is turned on and a bullet symbol and tab (\t) appear in the box (**Figure 4.78**). The format is now complete.
5. Click Update All to apply the autonumber to the current paragraph and to store the format in the Catalog for future use (**Figure 4.79**).

You've specified the bullet to appear at the beginning of bullet list items, but you still need to add the tab stop.

To add a tab stop to a bullet format:

1. With the insertion point still in the Bullet List paragraph, go to the Basic properties in the Paragraph Designer (**Figure 4.80**).

   You'll find this easier if you turn on Snap before you drag the tab down into the ruler.

2. Drag a Left tab from the formatting bar (**Figure 4.81**).

   The text moves over to the tab stop (**Figure 4.82**).

3. Click Update All.

   When you press Enter or Return at the end of a Bullet List paragraph, FrameMaker inserts a bullet and tab for the next item in the list (**Figure 4.83**).

You don't have to use plain bullets if you have the Zapf Dingbats font installed. FrameMaker allows you to assign a character format to just the autonumber part of the bullet paragraph (see page 96).

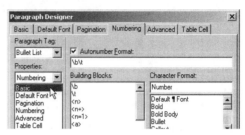

Figure 4.80 Go to the Basic properties to set the tab stop for the bullet paragraph.

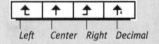

Figure 4.81 You can indent the beginning of the text 1/8" or 1/4".

Our original plan called for a questionnaire to be sent to the CEOs of Fortune 1000 companies to ask them to rate themselves as follows:¶

◦) Filthy Rich¶

Figure 4.82 The beginning of the text moves to the tab stop.

Our original plan called for a questionnaire to be sent to the CEOs of Fortune 1000 companies to ask them to rate themselves as follows:¶

•) Filthy Rich¶

•) Rich¶

•) ¶

Figure 4.83 Every time you press Enter or Return at the end of the paragraph, FrameMaker inserts a bullet and tab ready for you to type the next item.

About Tab Stops

FrameMaker uses four types of tab stops.

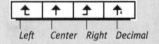

Tab stop symbols on the formatting bar

Left   Center   Right   Decimal

In the following illustration, each of the four lines has a different type of tab stop.

```
}              Left tab stop
}           Center tab stop
}      Right tab stop
}                 0.53847
```

A decimal tab stop can align on any character set in the Edit Tab Stop dialog box (**Figure 4.84**).

Alignment:
- ○ Left
- ○ Center
- ○ Right
- ● Decimal
- **Align On:** [.]

Figure 4.84 In the Basic properties in the Paragraph Designer, select a tab stop and click Edit to display the Edit Tab Stops dialog box.

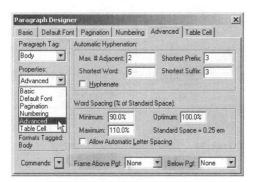

Figure 4.85 The Advanced Properties in the Paragraph Designer.

Finally we employed a complicated formula with metrics such as the total square footage of the house the CEOs called "home," the number of additional houses they owned, the number and model of their cars, and number of nannies they employed per child in their household (excluding children of former wives, unless they had custody of the children).

Figure 4.86 Without hyphenation, a justified paragraph can have holes, as in the first three lines here.

Finally we employed a complicated formula with metrics such as the total square footage of the house the CEOs called "home," the number of additional houses they owned, the number and model of their cars, and number of nannies they employed per child in their household (excluding children of former wives, unless they had custody of the children).

Figure 4.87 FrameMaker uses hyphenation rules to try to make lines the same length.

Automatic Hyphenation:

Max. # Adjacent:	2	Shortest Prefix:	3
Shortest Word:	5	Shortest Suffix:	3
☑ Hyphenate			

Figure 4.88 With hyphenation on, you can add finer controls such as the maximum number of hyphenated lines that can occur together.

Controlling Hyphenation

Hyphenation is set in the Advanced Properties (**Figure 4.85**). You'll rarely need to change most of the other Advanced properties, with the exception of the Frame Above and Below Paragraph properties at the bottom of the window (see page 260).

When FrameMaker hyphenates body text, it tries to make lines in a paragraph the same length. This is especially important in paragraph formats with justified text alignment. With hyphenation off, the paragraph has wide spaces between words, leaving holes in the text (**Figure 4.86**). The same paragraph with hyphenation on looks more even (**Figure 4.87**).

To control hyphenation:

1. Click in a paragraph or select several paragraphs.

2. In the Advanced Properties of the Paragraph Designer, select the Hyphenation check box to turn on hyphenation (**Figure 4.88**).

3. Set the following:
   ▲ To specify the maximum number of consecutive lines that can end with a hyphen, enter a value in the Maximum # Adjacent text box (the default is two lines).
   ▲ To specify the minimum length of a hyphenated word, enter a value in the Shortest Word text box (the default is five letters).
   ▲ To specify the minimum number of letters that can precede or follow a hyphen, enter values in the Shortest Prefix and Shortest Suffix text boxes (the default is three letters for both).

4. Click Apply or Update All.

Other Ways to Apply Paragraph Formats

FrameMaker has special copy options that allow you to copy and paste paragraph and character formats.

To copy and paste a paragraph format:

1. Click in a paragraph and from the Edit menu, choose Copy Special > Paragraph Format (**Figure 4.89**).

   or

   Press Ctrl-Alt-C or Command-Option-C.

   The paragraph format is pasted to the Clipboard.

2. Click in a paragraph or select paragraphs, and from the Edit menu, choose Paste.

   or

   Press Ctrl-V or Command-V.

   The paragraph format and tag are applied to the paragraph with the insertion point or to the selected paragraphs.

Once a paragraph format is copied to the Clipboard, you can use it to change formats selectively in the Find/Change window, as discussed in the next task.

To use the Find/Change window to apply a paragraph format:

1. From the Edit menu, choose Find/Change.

2. In the Find/Change window, from the Find pop-up menu, choose Paragraph Tag.

3. In the text box, type the paragraph tag you want to find (**Figure 4.90**).

4. Click Find.

   FrameMaker selects the next paragraph with the specified tag.

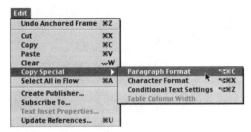

Figure 4.89 Choose Edit > Copy Special > Paragraph Format.

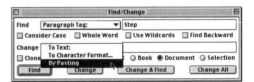

Figure 4.90 In the Find/Change window, from the Find menu, choose Paragraph Tag and type the format name in the text box.

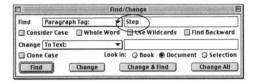

Figure 4.91 From the Change menu, choose By Pasting.

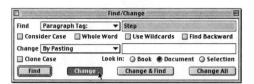

Figure 4.92 Click Change to paste the paragraph format on the Clipboard to the selected paragraph, or click Change and Find to change the selected paragraph and keep looking.

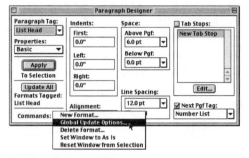

Figure 4.93 Start by choosing the destination tag from the Paragraph Tag menu in the Paragraph Designer, and then from the Commands menu, choose Global Update Options.

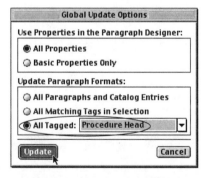

Figure 4.94 In this example, you'll change all Procedure Head paragraphs to List Head paragraphs.

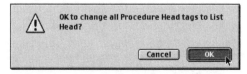

Figure 4.95 It's easy to get confused, so FrameMaker double-checks that this is really what you want to do.

5. From the Change menu, choose By Pasting (**Figure 4.91**) and click Change (**Figure 4.92**).

The paragraph format and tag on the Clipboard are pasted to the selected paragraph. (Remember that you are changing only the paragraph's format, not its content.)

You can use the global update options in the Paragraph Designer to change, for example, all Procedure Head paragraphs to List Head paragraphs.

To change all paragraphs of one format to another:

1. In the Paragraph Designer, from the Paragraph Tag menu, choose the format you want to update to.

2. From the Commands menu, choose Global Update Options (**Figure 4.93**). The Global Update Options dialog box appears.

3. Click the radio button next to All Properties, and from the All Tagged pop-up menu at the bottom of the dialog box, choose the paragraph format you want to update (**Figure 4.94**).

4. Click Update.

A warning message prompts you to confirm that it's OK to make the global change (**Figure 4.95**).

5. Click OK.

All the Procedure Head paragraphs are now updated to List Head paragraphs.

✔ Tips

■ If more than one paragraph is selected when you copy the paragraph format, the format of the first one is copied.

■ Copying and pasting a paragraph format does not create a format override. The format and the tag are both pasted.

Adding Footnotes

Although footnotes are more often used in formal documents, such as statistical reports or scholarly documents, they are easy to use in any FrameMaker document. Footnotes are autonumbered so that when you add, move, or delete footnotes, they are automatically renumbered.

To add a footnote:

1. Click the place in the text where you want to insert a footnote reference (**Figure 4.96**).

2. From the Special menu, choose Footnote.

   A footnote reference is inserted at the insertion point, and a footnote paragraph appears at the bottom of the text column (**Figure 4.97**).

3. Type the footnote text (**Figure 4.98**).

In order to copy, cut, or delete a footnote, you first need to select it. To select a footnote, you select the footnote reference in the text.

To select a footnote:

◆ Drag to select the footnote reference in the text.

   or

   Click in front of the footnote reference and press Esc H C.

   Both the footnote reference and the footnote are selected (**Figure 4.99**).

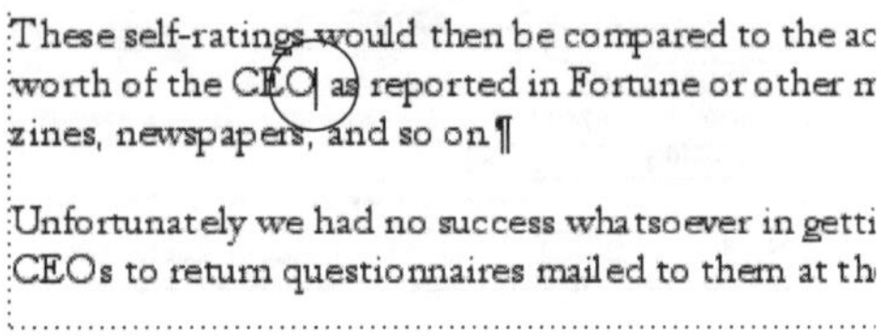

These self-ratings would then be compared to the ac worth of the CEO as reported in Fortune or other m zines, newspapers, and so on.¶

Unfortunately we had no success whatsoever in getti CEOs to return questionnaires mailed to them at th

Figure 4.96 The insertion point is where the footnote reference will be inserted.

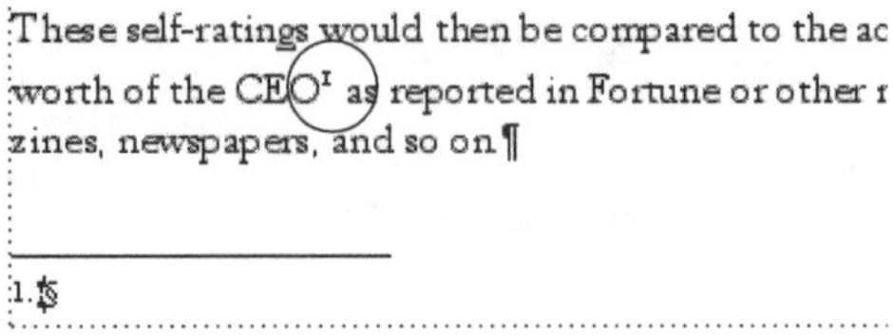

These self-ratings would then be compared to the ac worth of the CEO¹ as reported in Fortune or other r zines, newspapers, and so on.¶

1. §

Figure 4.97 A footnote reference is inserted at the insertion point. A footnote, including a footnote separator rule, appears at the bottom of the text column …

These self-ratings would then be compared to the actual net worth of the CEO¹ as reported in Fortune or other magazines, newspapers, and so on.¶

1.) A CEO was designated as such by his or her title as reported in the company's Annual Report§

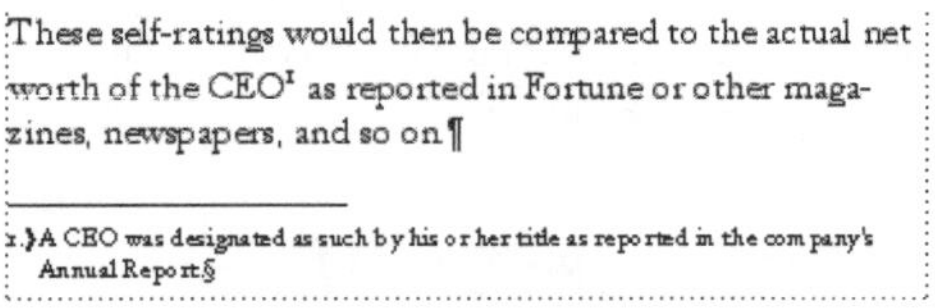

Figure 4.98 … ready for you to type.

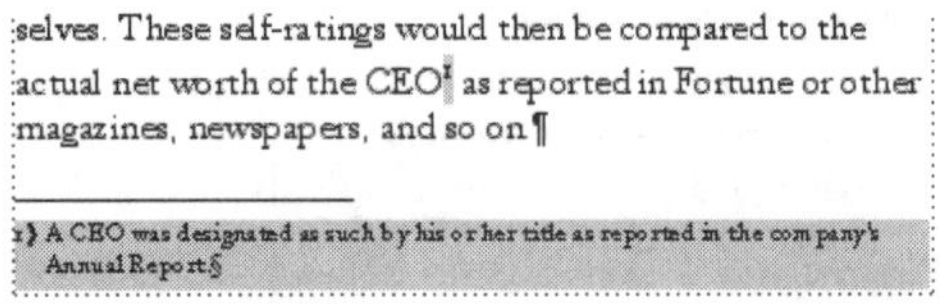

selves. These self-ratings would then be compared to the actual net worth of the CEO¹ as reported in Fortune or other magazines, newspapers, and so on.¶

1.) A CEO was designated as such by his or her title as reported in the company's Annual Report§

Figure 4.99 Select the footnote reference to copy, cut, or delete a footnote.

CHARACTER
FORMATTING

The boring fact about character formatting is this: It lets you select text in a paragraph and make it look different from its surrounding text. And if that were all you could do with character formats, that would be OK.

But FrameMaker character formatting also lets you do so much more. You can

◆ Copy and paste character formats

◆ Search for and replace character formats in the Find/Change window

◆ Format cross-references, variables, and index entries using character tags typed in dialog boxes or selected as building blocks

My personal favorite is the ability to create a character format and then apply it to the autonumber part of a paragraph (for instance, the bullets in this book are actually Zapf Dingbats).

For information on using character formats

◆ In cross-reference definitions, see page 99

◆ In variable definitions, see pages 174 and 180

◆ In index entries, see page 285

About Character Formatting Terms

FrameMaker uses a number of terms in relation to character formatting:

◆ A *character format* is a set of properties that describe selected text in relation to the text surrounding it (**Figure 5.1**).

◆ A *character tag* is the name of a character format.

◆ The *Character Catalog* is a small floating palette that contains a list of character tags for formats that have been defined and stored in the Catalog (**Figure 5.2**). You can display the Catalog and then click a tag to apply the format to selected text.

◆ Formats are created and changed in the *Character Designer*, a special window where you can change a property and then apply it to selected text or all text with the same tag (**Figure 5.3** and **Figure 5.4**).

FrameMaker uses three kinds of *character sets*: Dingbat for Zapf Dingbat font, Symbol for Symbol font, and Standard for all other fonts. Using these three character sets, you have access to a phenomenal number of special characters and dingbats.

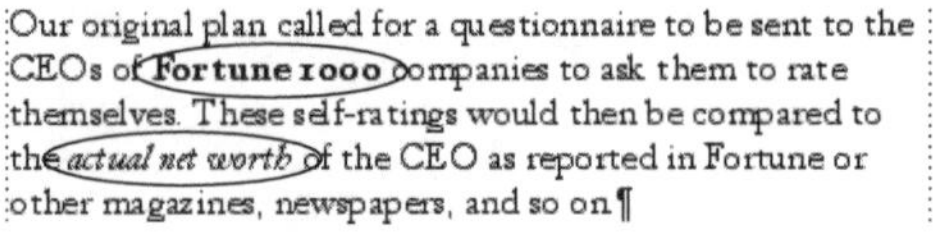

Our original plan called for a questionnaire to be sent to the CEOs of *Fortune 1000* companies to ask them to rate themselves. These self-ratings would then be compared to the *actual net worth* of the CEO as reported in Fortune or other magazines, newspapers, and so on.¶

Figure 5.1 This is a simple example of a Body paragraph with bold and italic character formats.

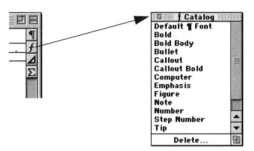

Figure 5.2 Click the Character Catalog icon to display the Character Catalog.

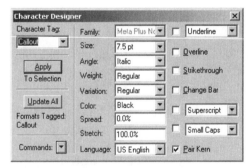

Figure 5.3 Choose Format > Characters > Designer to display the Windows Character Designer.

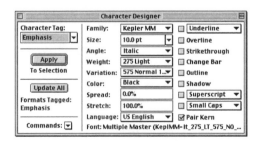

Figure 5.4 Choose Format > Characters > Designer to display the Mac OS Character Designer.

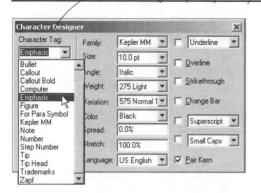

Figure 5.5 Here is a list of the character formats on the Character Tag menu in the Character Designer.

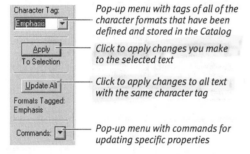

Figure 5.6 The left side of the Character Designer looks much the same as the left side of the Paragraph Designer.

Paragraph tag   Character tag

Figure 5.7 The tag of the current paragraph is displayed in the Tag area along with the character tag of selected text or text at the insertion point.

Working in the Character Designer

You change existing formats and create new ones in the Character Designer (**Figure 5.5**). The Character Designer mirrors the Default Font properties in the Paragraph Designer. You specify property settings on the right side of the window and you apply them selectively on the left (**Figure 5.6**).

The tag of the current paragraph and the character tag of selected text or text at the insertion point are displayed in the Tag area at the bottom left of the document window (**Figure 5.7**).

In addition to the predefined character formats, there is a character tag that you can't delete from the Catalog: Default ¶ Font. Use this format to return selected text to the Default Font paragraph properties of the surrounding text. You cannot use Default ¶ Font in the Character Designer, but it appears with character formats in other places, such as in the Catalog window.

For a discussion of properties in the Character Designer, see *Working with Font Properties* on page 71.

✔ Tips

■ Although you can format selected text in a number of different ways, the best approach is to create a character format and store it in the Catalog. Then the next time you need to format text for a similar purpose, you can just apply the format. The other people in your workgroup can easily see what you've done and what text has character formatting.

■ Paragraph formats affect the entire to paragraph; to format *selected text in a paragraph*, use a character format.

■ You delete character formats the same way you delete paragraph formats (see page 78).

Applying Character Formats

On pages 30 and 31, you saw how to

◆ Apply a format from the Format menu

◆ Apply a format from the Character Catalog

◆ Format selected text from the QuickAccess bar

◆ Choose a tag from the Character Tag menu in the Character Designer and click Apply or Update All

You can also format selected text by

◆ Using the Font, Size, and Style menus.

◆ Copying and pasting

To change font, size, and style from the Format menu:

1. Select the text you want to change.

2. From the Format menu, choose from the Font (**Figure 5.8**), Size (**Figure 5.9**), or Style (**Figure 5.10**) menu.

   The selected text is changed, but since you did not create a character format and store it in the Catalog, you will not see a character tag in the Tag area at the bottom left of the document window.

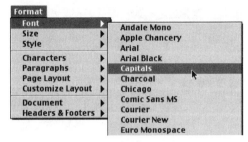

Figure 5.8 When you select text and use the Font, Size, and Style submenus, you will not see a character tag in the Tag area.

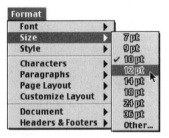

Figure 5.9 The Format > Size submenu.

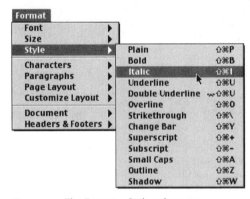

Figure 5.10 The Format > Style submenu.

APPLYING CHARACTER FORMATS

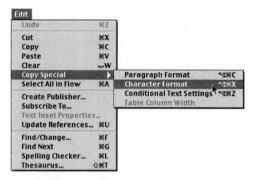

Figure 5.11 Choose Edit > Copy Special > Character Format to copy the selected character format to the Clipboard.

To copy and paste a character format:

1. Select text and from the Edit menu, choose Copy Special > Character Format (**Figure 5.11**).

— for Macintosh OS!

or

Press Esc E Y D or Command-Option-X.

The character format is pasted to the Clipboard. If the selected text has no character tag, then the Default Font paragraph properties of the selected text are copied.

2. Select text and from the Edit menu, choose Paste.

or

Press Ctrl-V or Command-V.

The character format is applied to the selected text.

✔ Tips

■ When you copy and paste a character format, if no tag is associated with the text you copied, no character tag is applied. If the text you copied has a character tag, the tag will be applied.

■ To remove all character formatting from selected text, from the Format menu, choose Style > Plain.

APPLYING CHARACTER FORMATS

Finding and Changing Character Formats

You can search for character formats in the Find/Change window.

To change character formats in the Find/Change window:

1. From the Edit menu, choose Find/Change.

2. In the Find/Change window, from the Find menu, choose Character Format (**Figure 5.12**).

3. In the Find Character Format dialog box (**Figure 5.13**), change settings to specify the format you want to find and click Set.

4. In the Find/Change window, click Find. FrameMaker selects the first text in the document that matches your specification.

5. If you want to use a character format you copied to the Clipboard, from the Change menu, choose By Pasting (**Figure 5.14**).

   or

   From the Change menu, choose To Character Format to display the Change to Character Format dialog box.

6. Specify the format you want to change and click Set (**Figure 5.15**).
   The dialog box closes.

7. In the Find/Change window, click Change or Change and Find.

   The character format is changed, and if you clicked Change and Find, the next instance of the character format you're searching for is selected.

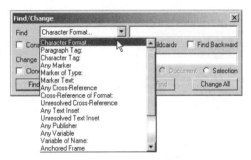

Figure 5.12 Choose Find > Character Format.

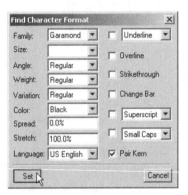

Figure 5.13 Specify the character format you want to change.

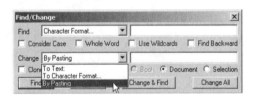

Figure 5.14 Choose Change > By Pasting.

Figure 5.15 The Change to Character Format dialog box.

Figure 5.16 Choose Commands > New Format.

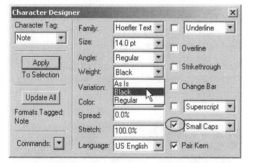

Figure 5.17 The Note character format is the same as the Note paragraph format except that it's bold and uses small caps.

Figure 5.18 The new character format appears in the Character Catalog, but the text at the insertion point doesn't change.

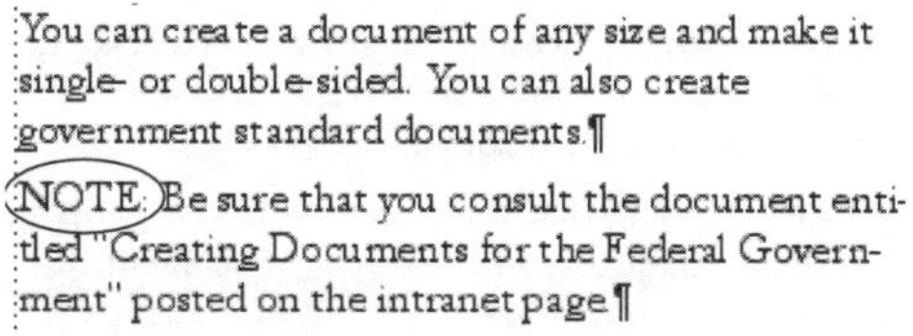

You can create a document of any size and make it single- or double-sided. You can also create government standard documents.¶

NOTE: Be sure that you consult the document entitled "Creating Documents for the Federal Government" posted on the intranet page.¶

Figure 5.19 This is the Note autonumber from the preceding chapter.

Creating and Using Character Formats

In the next sections you'll see how to create a number of character formats for different purposes: for example, to format autonumbers. Formatting autonumbers is a two-step process:

◆ Create a character format especially for the autonumber, in this example, Note.

◆ Associate the autonumber character format with the paragraph format.

To create a new character format:

1. Click in the note paragraph and from the Format menu, choose Characters > Designer to display the Character Designer.

   or

   Type Ctrl-D or Command-D.

   The Character Designer displays font properties of text at the insertion point.

2. In the Character Designer, from the Command menu at the bottom left, choose New Format (**Figure 5.16**).

3. In the New Format dialog box, type a name for the new format and click Create.

   The new tag appears in the Character Tag text box in the Character Designer. In this example, the new format is Note.

4. Make changes in the Character Designer and click Update All.

   In this example, the Note autonumber will have the same default font properties as the rest of the Note paragraph, except that it will be bold and use small caps (**Figure 5.17**).

   The new format appears in the Character Catalog (**Figure 5.18**), but the text remains unchanged (**Figure 5.19**). You need to go back to the Paragraph Designer to associate the new character format with the Note paragraph format.

To format autonumber text using a character format:

1. With the insertion point in the autonumbered paragraph, display the Paragraph Designer and go to Numbering Properties.

   All of the character formats that have been created and stored in the Character Catalog appear in the scroll list.

2. Select Note in the list (**Figure 5.20**).

   Because uppercase letters supersede small caps, in the next step you need to change NOTE to Note.

3. In the Autonumber Format text box, change NOTE to Note to enable the Smalls Caps setting in the character format (see **Figure 5.17** earlier in the chapter).

4. Click Update All (**Figure 5.21**).

   Now that you've associated the Note character format with the Note paragraph format, the autonumber is automatically formatted whenever you apply the Note paragraph format.

✔ Tips

■ In this example, both the paragraph and character formats were named Note, but they could have been named anything. In other words, they don't have to have the same tags. For example, you could use the Note character format in an Alert paragraph format, and it will match the Note autonumber format (**Figure 5.22** and **Figure 5.23**).

■ As a general rule, you should name a character format to describe its use, not its format. An exception is the use of a character format named after a font family, such as the Zapf character format on page 97, which uses the Zapf Dingbat equivalent for a standard character.

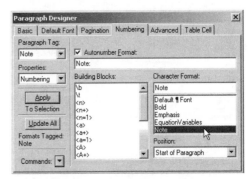

Figure 5.20 The Character Format scroll list displays all the character formats stored in the Catalog. Select Note in the list.

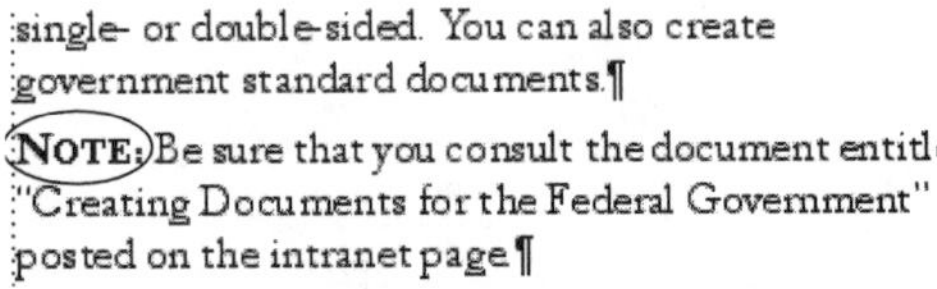

:single- or double-sided. You can also create :government standard documents.¶

(NOTE:)Be sure that you consult the document entitle "Creating Documents for the Federal Government" :posted on the intranet page.¶

Figure 5.21 The autonumber part of the note paragraph is now bold and uses small caps along with the initial uppercase letter.

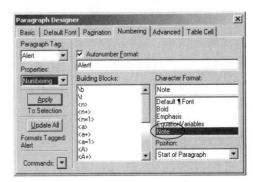

Figure 5.22 The Alert paragraph format uses a Note character format for its autonumber ...

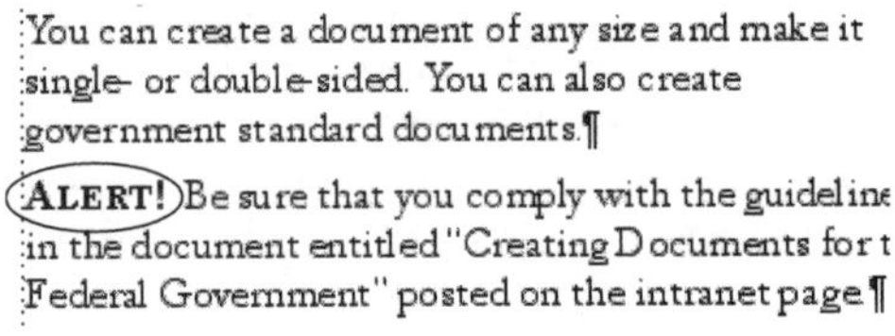

:You can create a document of any size and make it :single- or double-sided. You can also create :government standard documents.¶

(ALERT!)Be sure that you comply with the guideline :in the document entitled "Creating Documents for t :Federal Government" posted on the intranet page.¶

Figure 5.23 ... and it matches the Note autonumber format.

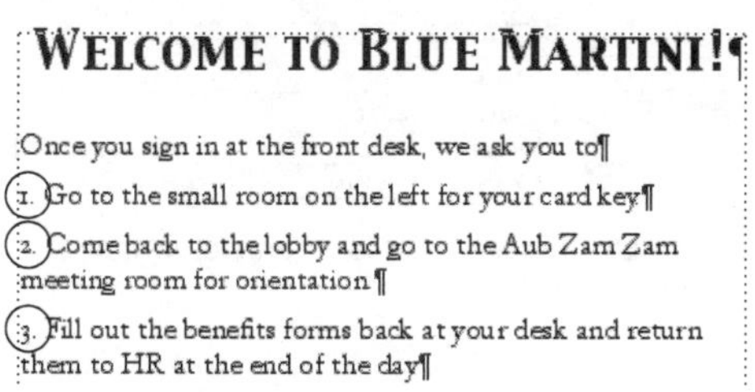

WELCOME TO BLUE MARTINI!¶
Once you sign in at the front desk, we ask you to¶
1. Go to the small room on the left for your card key¶
2. Come back to the lobby and go to the Aub Zam Zam meeting room for orientation.¶
3. Fill out the benefits forms back at your desk and return them to HR at the end of the day¶

Figure 5.24 The numbers have the same text format as the rest of the paragraph.

Character Designer
Character Tag:
Number
Apply
To Selection
Update All
Formats Tagged:
Number
Commands:
Family: Capitals
Size: 12.0 pt
Angle: Regular
Weight: Medium
Variation: Regular
Color: Black
Spread: 0.0%
Stretch: 100.0%
Language: US English
Underline
Overline
Strikethrough
Change Bar
Outline
Shadow
Superscript
Small Caps
Pair Kern
Font: TrueType on Screen (PS Font: CapitalsRegula...

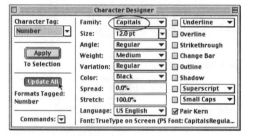

Figure 5.25 Capitals is a different font than the one used in the steps.

Paragraph Designer
Paragraph Tag:
Step
Properties:
Numbering
Apply
To Selection
Update All
Formats Tagged:
Step
Commands:
Autonumber Format:
Building Blocks:
Character Format:
Number
Callout
Emphasis
EquationVariables
Note
Number
Position:
Start of Paragraph

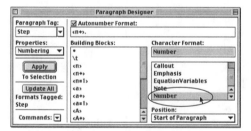

Figure 5.26 In the Numbering properties, select Number in the Character Format scroll list. Number then appears in the text box.

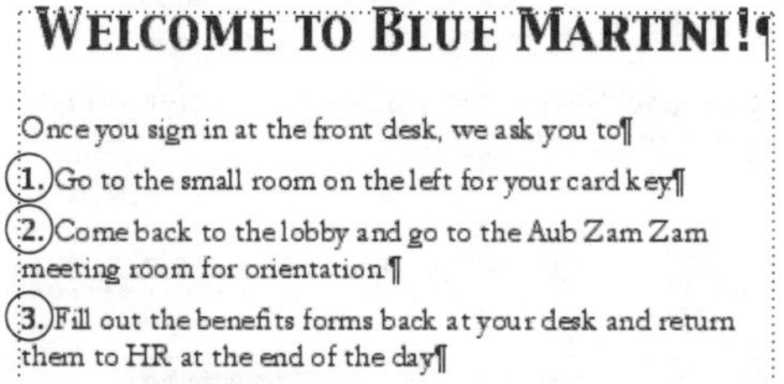

WELCOME TO BLUE MARTINI!¶
Once you sign in at the front desk, we ask you to¶
1. Go to the small room on the left for your card key¶
2. Come back to the lobby and go to the Aub Zam Zam meeting room for orientation.¶
3. Fill out the benefits forms back at your desk and return them to HR at the end of the day¶

Figure 5.27 Now the numbers look different from the rest of the Step paragraph and they match the title font.

Formatting autonumbers

You can also create a character format to use for autonumbers, such as the numbered steps in this book. The numbers are not only bold, they are also a different format from the rest of the paragraph. In this example, you will create the character format Number, which will format the step numbers so that they look different from the step text itself. At present they use the same format as the rest of the paragraph (**Figure 5.24**).

To use a character format for numbers in steps:

1. In the Character Designer, create a new character format and store it in the Catalog (**Figure 5.25**).

   In this example, it's called Number.
2. Click in a Step paragraph and display the Numbering properties in the Paragraph Designer.
3. In the Character Format scroll list, select the character format you just created.

   The format appears in the Character Format text box (**Figure 5.26**).
4. Click Update All.

   Now all Step paragraphs will have a different format for their autonumbers (**Figure 5.27**).

✔ Tips

- For the autonumbers, this example uses a serif font that matches the heading font. In general, sans serif, bold numbers are easier to read and stand out better from the rest of the paragraph.
- As in the previous example, the character tag is not important. You could have named it anything else. Now that you have the tag, you can use it wherever you want to format selected text, not just in autonumber formats.

Creating Bullet Symbol Formats

In addition to the regular bullet symbol (·) you can use any character in an installed font, including Zapf Dingbats. To do so, you need to

◆ Create a character format that uses Zapf Dingbat or any other installed font for the bullet autonumber (**Figure 5.28**).

◆ Use the standard character for the dingbat in the autonumber format (**Figure 5.29**).

◆ Associate the autonumber with the character format you created (**Figure 5.30** and **Figure 5.31**).

Table 5.1 shows some of the Zapf Dingbats (at 10 point size) you can use for bullets and the corresponding standard characters.

For the complete character sets, see the *FrameMaker Character Sets* online manual (see page 3).

✔ Tip

■ This book uses a number of Zapf Dingbats, including the tip heading used here, and they harmonize with the headings and body text. You should experiment to find the right dingbats to use in your document, ones that work well with the font size and style you're using—and as with all good things, don't overdo it!

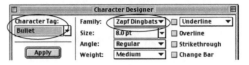

Figure 5.28 This is the Bullet character format as defined for this book.

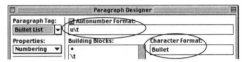

Figure 5.29 The standard character "u" is mapped to a filled-in diamond Zapf Dingbat.

Table 5.1

Zapf Dingbats as Bullets

Zapf dingbat	Standard character
☛	* (asterisk)
☞	1
◆▸	2
✓	3
✔	4
○	m
■	n
❑	o
❐	p
▲	s
▼	t
◆	u
❖	v
❦	Option-7

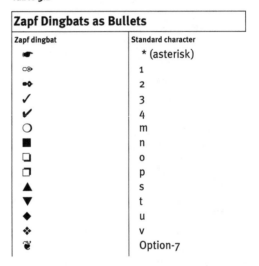

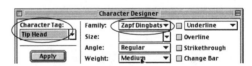

Figure 5.30 Here is the Tip Head character format used in this book ...

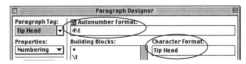

Figure 5.31 ... and the paragraph autonumber format, which uses the standard character 4.

Text box   Menu   Check box

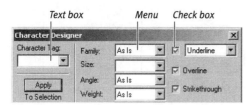

Figure 5.32 As Is on the Windows platform.

Text box   Menu   Check box

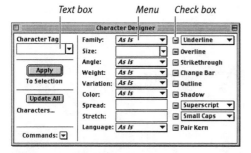

Figure 5.33 The Mac OS Character Designer shows different As Is settings for text boxes, menus, and check boxes.

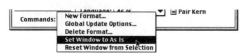

Figure 5.34 Choose Commands > Set Window to As Is.

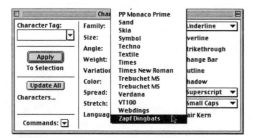

Figure 5.35 All fonts installed on your system appear on the Family menu.

Figure 5.36
This new format, Zapf, will use Zapf Dingbats to format standard characters.

Using the As Is Setting

The As Is setting appears in the Paragraph Designer and Catalog Designer, as well as in many dialog boxes. It looks a little different on Windows (**Figure 5.32**) and Mac OS (**Figure 5.33**) platforms. If the As Is setting appears in a window or dialog box, then the selected paragraphs or text has mixed settings. For example, if you selected two paragraphs with different fonts, the Family setting in the Character Designer would display As Is.

You use As Is as follows:

◆ To change some, but not all, of the properties displayed.

◆ To create character formats that selectively specify properties.

To create a character format using the As Is property:

1. In the Character Designer, from the Commands menu, choose Set Window to As Is (**Figure 5.34**).

2. From the Family menu, choose a font (**Figure 5.35**).
   In this example, the font is Zapf Dingbats.

3. From the Commands menu, choose New Format.

4. In the New Format dialog box, type a name for the new format and click Create (**Figure 5.36**).
   The new tag appears in the Character Tag text box in the Character Designer and it now appears in the Character Catalog for future use. When you apply the tag, the only property that is different is the font. The size and any other relevant settings stay the same.

Using the Euro Currency Symbol

Your operating system includes the Euro currency symbol (€) in its fonts for Windows 98 or later and for Mac OS 8.5 or later. Otherwise, you must install fonts that include the symbol. See your Windows system documentation to information about typing the Euro symbol on a Windows system.

If you plan to open a document on multiple platforms, you might want to consider one of Adobe's Euro font families (**Figure 5.37**).

To type the Euro currency symbol (Mac OS only):

1. In a text flow or text line, type Shift-Option-2.

The character might look like a nonsense character depending on the font in the surrounding text.

2. Select the character you just typed, and in the Character Designer, from the Family pop-up menu, choose a Euro font (**Figure 5.37**).

You can also choose Italic from the Angle menu or Bold from the Weight menu if you wish.

or

From the Format menu, choose Font, and then choose a Euro font (**Figure 5.38**).

The selected character is now the Euro symbol. Depending on which font you chose, it will look like this: € (Euro Mono), € (Euro Sans), or € (Euro Serif).

✔ Tips

■ The Adobe Euro fonts require Adobe Type Manager.

■ The three Euro fonts shown above come with the Mac OS version of FrameMaker. 7.0. They are also available on the Windows platform.

Figure 5.37 From the Family menu, choose a Euro font.

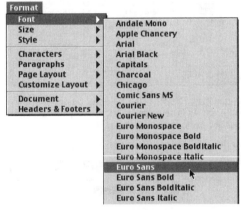

Figure 5.38 When you choose from the Format > Font submenu, you can choose to add bold, bold italic, or italic.

USING THE EURO CURRENCY SYMBOL

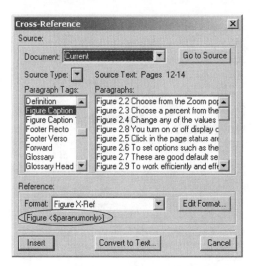

Figure 5.39 In the Cross-Reference dialog box, the current definition of the format chosen from the Format menu is displayed below the format.

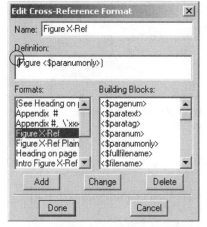

Figure 5.40 Click where you want the character format to start and then select a character format building block.

Formatting Text in Cross-References

You saw how to add a cross-reference to a FrameMaker document on page 48. When you add a cross-reference, you can also choose a format. Formats that have been defined and saved are available in the Format pop-up menu in the Cross-Reference dialog box.

A cross-reference format consists of a name and a definition. You build up the definition using any or all of the following:

◆ Building blocks for source information specify the wording and information contained in the cross-reference: for example, whether you want to see the text of a heading or just the page number.

◆ Literal text typed directly in the Definition text box.

◆ Character format building blocks.

In this example, you'll see how to add Bold Body character format to the part of the cross-reference inside the parentheses.

To add character formatting to a cross-reference definition:

1. From the Special menu, choose Cross-Reference.

or

Press Command-K.

The Cross-Reference dialog box appears (**Figure 5.39**). The current definition of the cross-reference format chosen from the Format menu appears under the format.

2. Choose a format to change from the Format pop-up menu and click Edit Format.

3. In the Edit Cross-Reference Format dialog box, click in the Definition text box where you want the character format to start (**Figure 5.40**).

(continues on next page)

4. Select a character format from the Building Blocks list (**Figure 5.41**).

The character format building block is added to the definition.

5. Click where you want to end the character format, and from the Building Blocks list, select <Default ¶ Font>.

The character format building block is added to the definition.

6. Click Change (**Figure 5.42**) to change the format definition, and click Done to close the Edit Cross-Reference Format dialog box.

7. In the Cross-Reference dialog box, click Done.

The Update Cross-References dialog box appears.

8. Specify how widely you want the change applied (the default setting updates all cross-references in the current document) and click Update (**Figure 5.43**).

9. In the Cross-References dialog box, click Done.

The cross-references are updated with the character formatting you just added (**Figure 5.44**).

More about cross-reference source building blocks

Building blocks for source information appear in angle brackets (< and >) and begin with a dollar sign ($). FrameMaker provides a comprehensive selection of building blocks. In many of the source building blocks, for example, <$paratext[*tag*]>, you replace the word "tag" with the actual paragraph tag of the paragraph that is the source for the cross-reference.

For example, if you want the cross-reference to display the text of a heading paragraph, then replace "tag" with "Head 1." The building block in the Definition text box would look like this: <$paratext[Head 1]>.

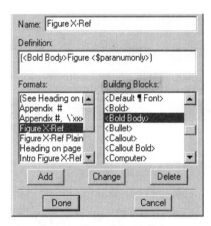

Figure 5.41 You'll need to scroll down so you can see the character format building blocks.

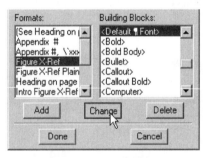

Figure 5.42 Click change to save the formatting changes you made.

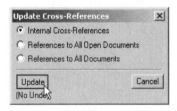

Figure 5.43 Select Internal Cross-References and click Update.

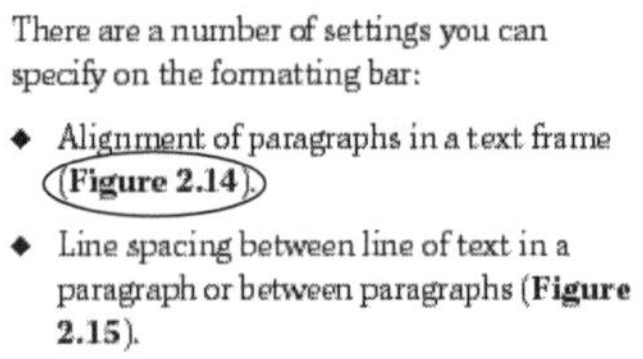

There are a number of settings you can specify on the formatting bar:

- ◆ Alignment of paragraphs in a text frame (**Figure 2.14**).

- ◆ Line spacing between line of text in a paragraph or between paragraphs (**Figure 2.15**).

Figure 5.44 All cross-references with the Figure X-Ref format are now bold.

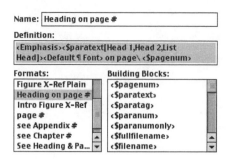

Name: Heading on page #

Definition:

<Emphasis><$paratext[Head 1,Head 2,List Head]><Default ¶ Font> on page\ <$pagenum>

Formats:	Building Blocks:
Figure X-Ref Plain	<$pagenum>
Heading on page #	<$paratext>
Intro Figure X-Ref	<$paratag>
page #	<$paranum>
see Appendix #	<$paranumonly>
see Chapter #	<$fullfilename>
See Heading & Pa...	<$filename>

Figure 5.45 This cross-reference format could be used to reference Head 1, Head 2, or List Head paragraphs.

You saw how to add a cross-reference to a FrameMaker document in *Adding Cross References* on page 48. You define and save cross-reference formats; available formats are displayed in the Format pop-up menu in the Cross-Reference dialog box.

Figure 5.46 This what the cross-reference format defined above looks like in the document.

There are a number of settings you can specify on the formatting bar:

◆ Alignment of paragraphs in a text frame (Figure 2.14).

◆ Line spacing between line of text in a paragraph or between paragraphs (Figure 2.14).

◆ Tab stops in the top ruler (Figure 2.15).

Figure 5.47 Without formatting, cross-references look the same as the surrounding text.

Edit Cross-Reference Format

Name: Figure X-Ref

Definition:

(<Bold Body>Figure <$paranumonly></>)

Figure 5.48 You can use </> to return to the default paragraph font.

If you want the format definition to include more than one heading paragraph, you type the list inside the square brackets with tags separated by commas (**Figure 5.45**). This definition means, "Insert the text of the source heading using Emphasis character format, and then go back to the default paragraph font. Insert the words 'on page' and then the page number of the cross-reference source. Keep the word 'page' and its page number together." The cross-reference in the document is formatted as specified (**Figure 5.46**).

For a complete list of building blocks and their meaning, see the *Adobe FrameMaker 7.0 User Guide* or online help.

✔ Tips

■ If you don't use character formatting in the cross-reference definition, FrameMaker uses the same format as the text at the insertion point (**Figure 5.47**). The character format you use in a cross-reference definition applies only to the cross-reference and not to any text that follows it in the document.

■ A cross-reference format definition, including building blocks, can be up to 255 characters long.

■ Never use angle brackets (< or >) in character tags. Angle brackets are reserved for building blocks, including character format building blocks.

Never use square brackets ([or]) in paragraph tags. Square brackets are reserved for building blocks.

■ As a shortcut, you can substitute </> for the <Default ¶ Font> building block, but since this tag isn't in the scroll list, you'll need to type it manually (**Figure 5.48**).

FORMATTING TEXT IN CROSS-REFERENCES

CREATING ILLUSTRATIONS

6

Using FrameMaker's drawing tools, you can create illustrations of amazing complexity. And if you *really* know how to draw, you can create even more amazing illustrations. Even if you can't draw at all, you can easily create simple diagrams and charts. This chapter includes some of FrameMaker's clip art so you can see great examples of what you can do with the drawing tools.

You can draw basic shapes, such as lines, rectangles, and circles and then edit and move them. You can group and ungroup objects, send them to the back and bring them to the front relative to other objects, align and distribute them, flip them upside down or left to right, and rotate and scale them. FrameMaker allows you to drag to resize, reshape, or reorient objects or to make precise changes using measurements.

You'll see the comparative advantages of using text lines or text frames for callouts. A much-requested feature in FrameMaker is runaround text, and you'll see how it works.

This chapter also shows you especially helpful shortcuts for graphics commands, and you'll see that they're very intuitive.

About the Tools Palette

If you're working in Windows, you have only one version of the Tools palette—the small version. If you're working in Mac OS, you can toggle between the small version (**Figure 6.1**) and a large version (**Figure 6.2**). If you're working intensely on illustrations using the drawing tools, you might want to display the large version, but the small version is often more convenient, especially if monitor real estate is an issue. This chapter assumes that you're working in the small palette.

The Tools palette includes:

◆ Selection tools for text and objects

◆ Drawing tools that include not only shapes but also text frames and text lines (**Figure 6.3**)

◆ Drawing properties, such as fill pattern, line width, and spot color (covered in the next chapter).

When you draw an object, it will have the current drawing properties displayed on the right side of the small Tools palette.

In general, you will draw in anchored frames (see page 150), so that when text is edited, illustrations stay put. You can place illustrations on any of the three types of pages in a FrameMaker document: body pages, master pages, or reference pages.

Click the Tools button at the top right of the document window or choose Graphics > Tools to display the Tools palette.

From now on in this chapter, the Mac OS Tools palette will be shown because it's easier to see which tool is selected.

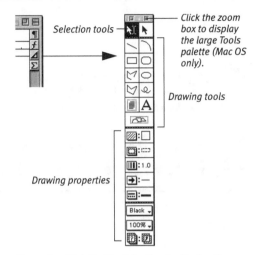

Figure 6.1 Click the Tools button to display the current (small or large) Tools palette.

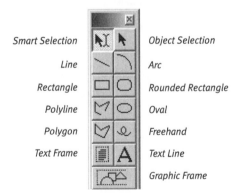

Figure 6.2 (Mac OS only) The large Tools palette includes commands from the Graphics menu.

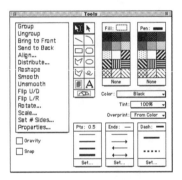

Figure 6.3 Click an individual selection or drawing tool to use it. The Smart Selection tool is active in this example.

Figure 6.4 Grid lines, like text symbols, never print.

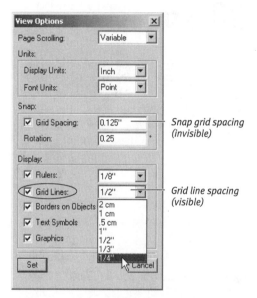

Snap grid spacing (invisible)

Grid line spacing (visible)

Figure 6.5 You set spacing for the snap grid in the Snap area and for the visible grid from the Grid Lines pop-up menu in the Display area.

Using Grids

Two types of grids are available when you're working in a FrameMaker document:

◆ Visible grid (**Figure 6.4**)—The visible grid is a nonprinting grid of dotted horizontal and vertical lines that is displayed in the document window to help you position and align objects.

◆ Invisible snap grid—The snap grid is an invisible grid that attracts objects to it as you draw, rotate, resize, or drag objects. In other words, objects "snap" to the grid lines even though you can't see the grid.

Depending on what you're doing, you may prefer working with the visible grid. None of the illustrations in this chapter shows a visible grid, so they don't look cluttered.

To turn the grids on or off:

◆ To turn on the visible grid, from the View menu, choose Grid Lines or press Esc V G.

or

To turn on the invisible snap grid, from the Graphics menu, choose Snap.

To change grid spacing:

1. From the View menu, choose Options. The View Options dialog box appears.

2. Do one or both of the following:

   ▲ In the Snap area, type a value in the Grid Spacing text box.

   ▲ In the Display area, choose from the Grid Lines pop-up menu (**Figure 6.5**).

3. Click Set.

   The grid lines in the document window display the new spacing.

✔ Tip

■ If you use the grids together, make the visible grid spacing a multiple of the snap grid interval so the grids coincide.

Selecting Objects

When an object is selected, small black rectangles, or selection handles, appear around each grouped or ungrouped object (**Figure 6.6**). As a general rule, all objects you select must be on the same page.

With the Smart Selection tool active ( ), you can select both text and objects.

◆ When the Smart Selection tool is over text, it becomes an I-beam ( ).

◆ When the Smart Selection tool is over an object, it becomes a hollow arrow ( ).

With the Object Selection tool active ( ), you can select *only objects*.

To activate a selection tool:

◆ Click a selection tool at the top of the Tools palette (**Figure 6.7**).

  After you draw an object, FrameMaker reverts to the Smart Selection tool. To keep the Object Selection tool active, Shift-click to select it.

To select an object:

◆ Click the object.

  If the object you want to select has a fill of None, you need to click its border.

  or

  To select a text line or text frame (see page 123) when the Smart Selection tool is active, Ctrl-click or Option-click it.

  Selection handles appear around the object (**Figure 6.8**).

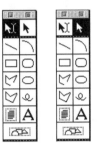

Figure 6.6 Graphics with selection handles around a grouped object (left), a rectangle (top right), and a text line.

Figure 6.7 When the Smart Selection tool is active (left), you can select both text and objects. When the Object Selection tool is active (right), you can select only objects, not text.

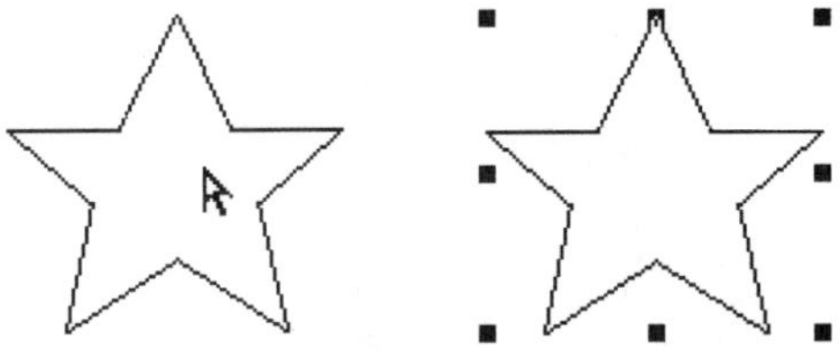

Figure 6.8 Click (left) an object to select it (right).

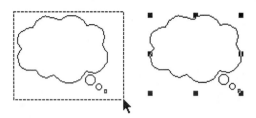

Figure 6.9 Drag a selection border completely around an object (left) to select it (right).

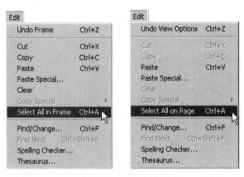

Figure 6.10 With one or more objects selected, hold down the Shift key and click to select an additional object.

Figure 6.11 To select all objects on a page or in a frame (when an anchored or graphic frame is selected), choose Edit > Select All in Frame (left). When nothing is selected, choose Edit > Select All on Page (right).

To select by dragging:

◆ Click outside any objects on the page or in a frame and drag diagonally to draw a selection border around the objects you want to select (**Figure 6.9**).

You must completely enclose an object to include it. Over a text column, you must have the Object Selection tool active.

To extend the selection:

◆ With one or more objects selected, Shift-click the next one (**Figure 6.10**).

To extend the selection to a text line or text frame when the Smart Selection tool is active, Shift-Ctrl-click or Shift-Option-click it.

To select all objects on a page or in a frame:

1. Click outside any object on the page or select a frame.

2. From the Edit menu, choose Select All in Frame or Select All on Page (**Figure 6.11**).

   or

   Click Ctrl-A or Command-A.

✔ Tips

■ If you click a text frame or a text line with the Object Selection tool active, the frame or line is selected as an object. To select the text itself, use the Smart Selection tool.

■ If you can't seem to select what you want, to or if you think something is selected and it appears not to be, the screen display may be corrupted. Try clicking outside everything on the page and starting again, or page up or down and back. To refresh the display, you can also press Ctrl-L or Command-L.

Drawing Simple Shapes

When you use FrameMaker drawing tools, remember that the current properties, shown on the right side of the properties area of the Tools palette, are used. You can change them afterward with the object still selected.

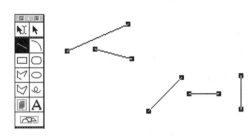

Figure 6.12 To constrain lines to horizontal, vertical, or 45 degrees, Shift-click or Shift-drag.

To draw a straight line:

1. Click the Line tool to select it.

   If you want to draw more than one line, Shift-click the tool.

   Raster Graphic! *Not precise on non-vertical/Horizontal.*

2. Click at the start and end of the line.

   or

   Drag from the start to the end of the line.

   To draw a horizontal or vertical line or a line at 45 degrees, Shift-click or Shift-drag (**Figure 6.12**).

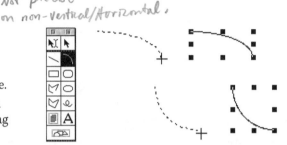

Figure 6.13 An arc is a curved line or a segment of the circumference of a circle.

To draw an arc:

1. Click the Arc tool to select it.

   If you want to draw more than one arc, Shift-click the tool.

   Can't modify arc angle (Try Graphics > Reshape)

2. Drag from the start to the end of the arc (**Figure 6.13**).

   To draw a circular arc, hold down the Shift key while you drag.

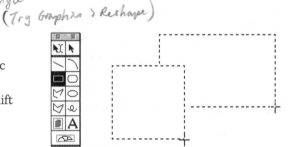

Figure 6.14 With the Rectangle tool selected, hold down the Shift key to draw a square.

To draw a rectangle or a square:

1. Click the Rectangle tool to select it.

   If you want to draw more than one shape, Shift-click the tool.

2. Click and then drag diagonally, releasing the mouse button when the rectangle is the right size.

   To draw a square, hold down the Shift key before you start drawing (**Figure 6.14**).

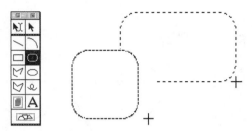

Figure 6.15 With the Rounded Rectangle tool selected, hold down the Shift key to draw a rounded circle.

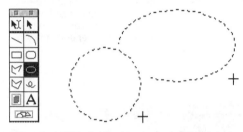

Figure 6.16 With the Oval tool selected, hold down the Shift key to draw a circle.

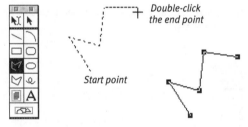

Figure 6.17 Click the start point and drag, click at each vertex, and double-click the end point.

Figure 6.18 To draw a horizontal or vertical segment or a segment at 45 degrees, Shift-click the end vertex for that segment.

To draw a rounded rectangle:

1. Click the Rounded Rectangle tool to select it.

   If you want to draw more than one rounded rectangle, Shift-click the tool.

2. Click and then drag diagonally, releasing the mouse button when the rounded rectangle is the right size.

   To draw a rounded square, hold down the Shift key before you start drawing (**Figure 6.15**).

To draw an oval or a circle:

1. Click the Oval tool to select it.

   If you want to draw more than one shape, Shift-click the tool.

2. Click and then drag diagonally, releasing the mouse button when the oval is the right size.

   To draw a circle, hold down the Shift key before you start drawing (**Figure 6.16**).

To draw a polyline:

1. Click the Polyline tool to select it.

   If you want to draw more than one polyline, Shift-click the tool.

2. Click and drag to draw the first segment; then click each vertex to draw subsequent segments (**Figure 6.17**).

   To draw a horizontal or vertical segment or a segment at 45 degrees, Shift-click the vertex (**Figure 6.18**).

3. At the end point, double-click.

DRAWING SIMPLE SHAPES

To draw a polygon:

1. Click the Polygon tool to select it.

   If you want to draw more than one polygon, Shift-click the tool.

2. Click and drag to draw the first segment; then click at each vertex.

   To draw a horizontal or vertical segment or a segment at 45 degrees, Shift-click the vertex.

3. At the end point, double-click (**Figure 6.19**).

To draw a regular polygon:

1. Draw a circle or a square a little bit larger than the polygon you want to create (**Figure 6.20**).

2. From the Graphics menu, choose Set # Sides.

3. In the Set Number of Sides dialog box, type a value into the Number of Sides text box and click Set (**Figure 6.21**).

   You can experiment to see what start angle you want, or you can rotate the polygon once it's drawn (see page 120).

   In this example, the polygon now has five sides of equal length.

To draw a freehand line:

1. Click the Freehand tool to select it.

   If you want to draw more than one freehand line, Shift-click the tool.

2. Click and drag where you want the line to go (**Figure 6.22**).

3. When you get to the end of the line, release the mouse button.

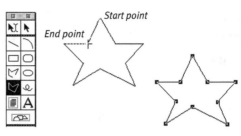

Figure 6.19 You don't need to go back to the starting point when you end a polygon.

Figure 6.20 You can draw either a circle or a square and use the Set # Sides command to convert it to a regular polygon.

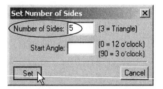

Figure 6.21 You can change the number of sides or the start angle.

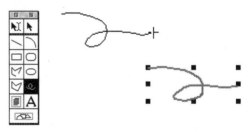

Figure 6.22 As in other applications, drawing with the Freehand tool takes practice to master.

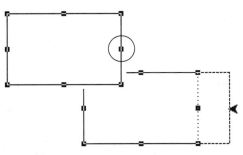

Figure 6.23 Drag one of the middle selection handles to make the selected object wider (as shown here) or taller.

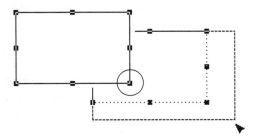

Figure 6.24 Hold down the Shift key and drag a corner selection handle to constrain proportions.

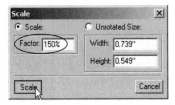

Figure 6.25 Select an object and choose Graphics > Scale; then enter a new scale factor.

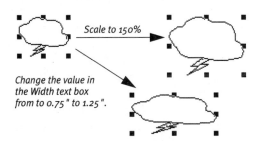

Scale to 150%

Change the value in the Width text box from to 0.75 " to 1.25 ".

Figure 6.26 To resize precisely, use the Scale dialog box.

Resizing Objects

You can select and resize an object by dragging one of its selection handles or by scaling.

To resize an object by dragging:

1. Select the object.

2. Do one of the following:
   ▲ To change the width or height, drag one of the middle selection handles (**Figure 6.23**).
   ▲ To change both the width and height, drag a corner selection handle.

   As you resize the object, you'll see marks in the top and side rulers to guide you.

   To constrain object proportions, hold down the Shift key while you drag (**Figure 6.24**).

To resize an object by scaling:

1. Select the object and from the Graphics menu, choose Scale.

   or

   Press Ctrl G O or Command G O.

2. In the Scale dialog box, change the value in the Factor text box and click Scale (**Figure 6.25**).

   or

   Change a value in the Width or Height text box, or both, and click Scale.

   The object is resized (**Figure 6.26**).

✔ Tip

■ In some applications, you can resize an object in a dialog box by changing either the width or the height and constraining proportions. FrameMaker does not have this feature, so you should *not* try to resize objects proportionally by using actual measurements in the Scale dialog box or in the Object Properties dialog box (see page 115).

Reshaping Objects

As well as resizing objects, you can reshape them in two other ways by using:

◆ Reshape handles

◆ Smooth/Unsmooth commands

Using reshape handles

Reshape handles (black handles) define an object's curve and control its location and its control points (white handles), which adjust the curvature. You can add and remove reshape handles to change the number of points that define the curve.

To display reshape handles:

◆ Select an object and from the Graphics menu, choose Reshape.

The selection handles are replaced by control points and reshape handles at points that define the curve (**Figure 6.27**).

You can reshape lines, polylines, polygons, curves, and arcs, but you will need to practice to gain precise control (**Figure 6.28**).

To reshape a curve:

1. Select a curve and from the Graphics menu, choose Reshape.

   Control points and reshape handles appear on and around the line.

2. Drag a reshape handle to define the curve or a control point to adjust the curvature.

   As you drag a reshape handle, the control points move as well to maintain a smooth curve (**Figure 6.29**).

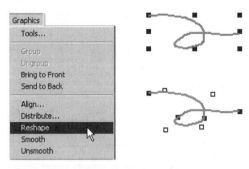

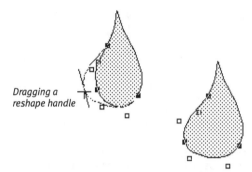

Figure 6.27 A freehand curve with selection handles (top) and with reshape handles (bottom).

Figure 6.28 Example of reshaping a filled polygon using a reshape handle.

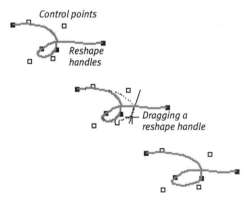

Figure 6.29 To reshape a freehand line, select it and choose Graphics > Reshape. Drag a reshape handle (middle) to reshape the curve (bottom).

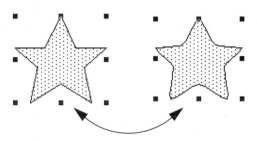

Figure 6.30 An example of a filled polyline unsmoothed (left) and smoothed (right).

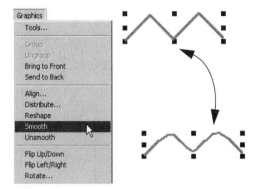

Figure 6.31 To smooth or unsmooth an object, select it and choose Graphics > Smooth or Unsmooth.

You can add and remove reshape handles to change the points that define the curve.

To add or remove a corner or reshape handle:

1. Display reshape handles.

2. (Windows) Ctrl-click the line where you want to add a reshape handle or the handle you want to remove.

   (Mac OS) With reshape handles displayed, Command-Option-click the line where you want to add a reshape handle or the handle you want to remove.

   Handles are added or removed, and the object shape changes accordingly.

Smoothing and unsmoothing

Smoothing means changing the angles of a closed shape or a polyline to smoothed curves (**Figure 6.30**). You can smooth and unsmooth polylines, polygons, rectangles, rounded rectangles, and freehand lines. When you smooth an object, you increase the curvature of its corners, and when you unsmooth, you decrease the curvature.

To smooth or unsmooth an object:

◆ Select the object and from the Graphics menu, choose Smooth or Unsmooth (**Figure 6.31**).

   If the selected object has not been smoothed and you choose Smooth, it will be smoothed. If the object has been smoothed, the command has no effect.

   If the selected object has been smoothed and you choose Unsmooth, the object is unsmoothed. If it has been unsmoothed or never smoothed, the command has no effect.

✔ Tip

■ If you want to draw a curvy line, but one that is somewhat regular, draw a polyline, which is easier to draw than a freehand line, and then smooth it.

RESHAPING OBJECTS

Arranging Objects

Besides repositioning, FrameMaker provides precise controls for arranging objects, such as grouping, aligning, and distributing.

Grouping and ungrouping objects

When you work with objects more complex than a simple shape or with multiple objects, then you'll need to be able to group and ungroup objects (**Figure 6.32**). You can also group grouped objects, and then when you ungroup them, they ungroup hierarchically (**Figure 6.33**).

To group objects:

1. Select objects you want to group.

2. From the Graphics menu, choose Group.

   or

   Press Esc G G (Graphics Group).

   A grouped object has one set of selection handles, as shown in **Figure 6.34**.

To ungroup a grouped object:

1. Select a grouped object.

2. From the Graphics menu, choose Ungroup.

   or

   Press Esc G U (Graphics Ungroup).

   A group of objects (ungrouped) has a set of handles for each object (**Figure 6.34**).

✔ Tips

- If you're working with an object and it seems to be behaving strangely, select it and check to see whether it's a grouped object. With the object selected, choose Graphics > Object Properties. Look at the top right of the Object Properties dialog box (**Figure 6.35**). You may need to ungroup the grouped object.

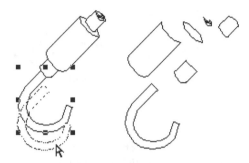

Figure 6.32 This drawing of a connector has six separate objects grouped.

Each object in an ungrouped object has its own set of selection handles.

Figure 6.33 Select a grouped object (left) and ungroup (middle). Select and ungroup again (right), and so on, to get to the basic shapes that make up the illustration.

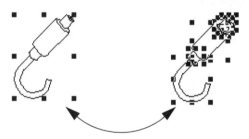

Figure 6.34 Select a grouped object (left) and choose Graphics > Ungroup, or select ungrouped objects (right) and choose Graphics > Ungroup.

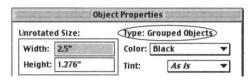

Figure 6.35 The Type field tells you whether the selected object is a grouped object.

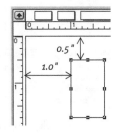

Figure 6.36 Select an object and choose Graphics > Object Properties. The top and left offset measurements of the rectangle on the right are shown in the Object Properties dialog box below.

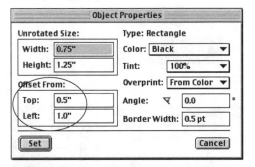

Figure 6.37 You can see the object type (at the top right), the object's size and location, and so on.

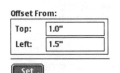

Figure 6.38 Reposition an object by changing one or both of its offset values.

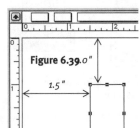

Figure 6.39 The object is repositioned relative to its offset from the top and left side of the document window.

■ If you're working on a document you know someone else will probably inherit, group objects in a rational manner so that the new owner can see what's going on. On the screen, a small line that's "escaped" from an illustration can be difficult to see.

Repositioning objects

You can copy, move, and arrange objects in many different ways including by selecting and dragging and by drag-copying.

To select and drag objects:

◆ Select one or more objects and drag them. Make sure your cursor looks like a hollow arrow ( ) before you start dragging.

To drag-copy:

◆ Hold down the Ctrl or Option key and drag the selected object.

To constrain movement to horizontal, vertical, or 45 degrees, hold down the Shift key.

✔ Tip

■ Group objects you want to drag-copy to make it easier to edit or reposition them. You can ungroup them later if you wish.

You can also reposition objects more precisely in the Object Properties dialog box, or you can microposition them using arrow keys.

To reposition an object using object properties:

1. Select an object and from the Graphics menu, choose Object Properties (**Figure 6.36**).

2. In the Object Properties dialog box (**Figure 6.37**), change values in the Offset From Top and Left text boxes; then click Set (**Figure 6.38**).

   The object is repositioned according to the offset values you changed (**Figure 6.39**).

To microposition a selected object:

◆ Hold down the Alt or Option key and use arrow keys to move the selected object up, down, left, or right.

✔ Tips

■ At a 100% zoom value, the object moves 1 point each time you press an arrow key.

■ For very precise positioning, zoom in to say, 200%; pressing an arrow key now moves an object 0.5 point.

■ To move an object 6 points at 100% zoom, hold down Shift-Alt or Shift-Option and then press an arrow key.

■ Sometimes when you copy and paste an object, it's pasted exactly on top of the object you copied, so you think that the Paste command didn't work. While the copied object is still selected, move or microposition it and you'll see that it was pasted correctly.

Aligning objects

The FrameMaker alignment commands are very useful—you'll find yourself using them constantly as you create and lay out illustrations. You can align objects as follows:

◆ Align all types of objects except graphic frames relative to each other.

◆ Align one object in an anchored frame or on a page relative to the frame or the page respectively.

To align objects:

1. Select objects you want to align.

   You can select objects and then extend the selection, or you can drag a selection frame around the objects you want to align (see page 107).

Figure 6.40 Select objects and choose Graphics > Align.

Figure 6.41 Objects align with the last object selected.

Figure 6.42 Select As Is to leave Left/Right alignment unchanged. Here objects are top aligned.

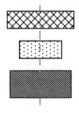

Figure 6.43 Select As is to leave Top/Bottom alignment unchanged, as shown in this example.

ARRANGING OBJECTS

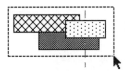

Figure 6.44 The same three objects selected with a selection border (left) align to the frontmost object, which is the smallest rectangle (right).

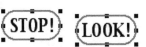

Figure 6.45 This example shows three grouped objects (rounded rectangles with text lines inside).

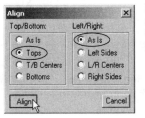

Figure 6.46 In the Align dialog box, align the tops of the grouped objects.

Figure 6.47 The grouped objects are top aligned.

2. From the Graphics menu, choose Align (**Figure 6.40**).

or

Press Esc G A (Graphics Align).

3. In the Align dialog box, select alignment in the Top/Bottom and Left/Right areas.

FrameMaker aligns all selected objects with the object selected last (**Figure 6.41**).

To leave alignment unchanged, select As Is (**Figure 6.42** and **Figure 6.43**).

These examples show alignment of objects that don't overlap; you can also align overlapping objects (**Figure 6.44**).

To align grouped objects:

1. Select two or more grouped objects (**Figure 6.45**).

2. From the Graphics menu, choose Align.

3. In the Align dialog box, select Tops and in the Left/Right area, select As Is (**Figure 6.46**).

The grouped objects behave as a single object and align to the last object selected (**Figure 6.47**).

✔ Tips

■ If the objects you want to align move in a way you didn't intend, immediately press Ctrl-Z or Command-Z to undo and then align again while objects are still selected. Or while they are still selected, just align them again.

■ If you select objects to align, FrameMaker aligns them with the last object you selected. But if you used a selection border, objects are aligned to the frontmost object or the last one added in the frame or on the page.

■ The Align dialog box always displays the last-used values, so if you need to use the same type of alignment over and over, align for all instances it at the same time.

ARRANGING OBJECTS

Distributing objects

You can distribute by using any of the following methods:

◆ Selecting equidistant centers so that the the middle points of selected objects are equidistant from each other.

◆ Selecting equidistant edges so that adjacent edges of objects are equidistant from each other.

◆ Specifying a value for the edge gap, that is, the gap between adjacent edges of objects. When objects are distributed with an edge gap value, all objects move except the one at the left or the top.

To distribute objects:

1. Select objects (**Figure 6.48**) and from the Graphics menu, choose Distribute.

   or

   Press Esc G D (Graphics Distribute).

2. In the Distribute dialog box, in the Horizontal Spacing or Vertical Spacing area, select Equidistant Centers or Equidistant Edges.

3. Click Distribute.

   The first and last objects stay in place and the remaining objects are distributed so that the space between their edges or centers is equal (**Figure 6.49**).

To specify an edge gap:

1. With the objects selected, from the Graphics menu, choose Distribute.

2. In the Distribute dialog box, in the Edge Gap text box, enter a new value and click Distribute (**Figure 6.50**).

   The edge gaps between adjacent objects are still equal, but the gap is the specified width (in this example, 0.125").

Figure 6.48 The objects are top aligned but not evenly distributed along a horizontal line.

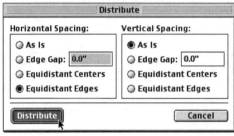

Edge gaps are equal

Figure 6.49 The first and last objects don't move, and the remaining objects are distributed so that the edges of adjacent objects are equidistant.

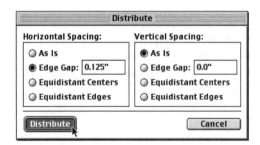

Edge gaps are the same and equal to 0.125"

Figure 6.50 Specifying an edge gap of 1/8" moves all objects except the leftmost one.

✔ Tip

■ To move objects together so that they just touch, distribute them with an edge gap of zero.

ARRANGING OBJECTS

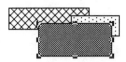

Figure 6.51 Select an object and choose Graphics > Send to Back.

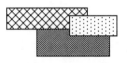

Figure 6.52 The selected rectangle moves to the bottom of the stack.

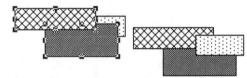

Figure 6.53 You can select more than one object (left) and send them all to the bottom of the stack (right).

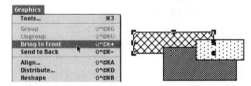

Figure 6.54 Select an object and choose Graphics > Bring to Front.

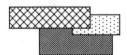

Figure 6.55 The selected rectangle moves to the top of the stack.

Reordering overlapping objects

Even when you're working with relatively simple objects, you often need to move overlapping objects to the top or bottom of a stack.

To send an object to the back:

1. Select the object you want to place at the bottom of the stack.

2. From the Graphics menu, choose Send to Back (**Figure 6.51**).

   or

   Press Esc G B (Graphics Back).

   The selected object moves to the bottom of the stack (**Figure 6.52**).

You can select more than one object and send all of the objects to the back (**Figure 6.53**), and you can select an object in the middle of the stack and send it to the back.

To bring an object to the front:

1. Select the object you want to place at the top of the stack.

2. From the Graphics menu, choose Bring to Front (**Figure 6.54**).

   or

   Press Esc G F (Graphics Front).

   The selected object moves to the top of the stack (**Figure 6.55**).

You can select more than one object to move to the top, and you can select an object in the middle to move to the top.

ARRANGING OBJECTS

Flipping and rotating objects

You can move and arrange objects for diagrams or illustrations in several ways, including flipping them across a vertical or horizontal axis and rotating them.

To flip objects:

◆ To flip an object across an imaginary horizontal line, select the object and from the Graphics menu, choose Flip Up/Down (**Figure 6.56**).

or

To flip an object across an imaginary vertical line, select the object and from the Graphics menu, choose Flip Left/Right (**Figure 6.57**).

You can rotate an object by dragging, or you can do it more precisely in the Rotate dialog box; you can rotate an object from its current position or from its original position.

To rotate an object by dragging:

1. Select the object.

2. Hold down the Alt or Command key and drag a handle.

   The pointer changes shape and a dotted shape shows you where the rotated object will be positioned (**Figure 6.58**).

   To constrain the rotation to 45-degree increments, hold down the Shift key.

✔ Tips

■ When you're just starting to rotate objects, the objects won't always end up where you envisioned. Save your document before you begin experimenting, or even better, work on the illustration to a scratch document and when it's ready to go, copy and paste it into an anchored frame in your document.

■ All objects except text lines rotate around their centers; text lines rotate around their alignment point set in the Object Properties dialog box (**Figure 6.59**).

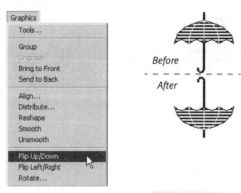

Figure 6.56 Choose Graphics > Flip Up/Down.

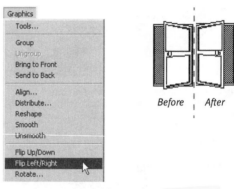

Figure 6.57 Choose Graphics > Flip Left/Right.

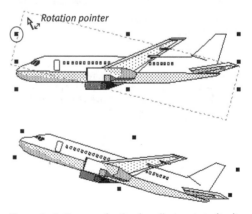

Figure 6.58 Drag a selection handle to rotate (top); stop dragging when the object is repositioned (bottom).

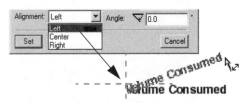

Figure 6.59 Text lines rotate around their alignment point (set in the Object Properties dialog box).

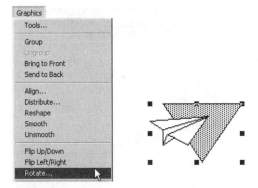

Figure 6.60 Choose Graphics > Rotate.

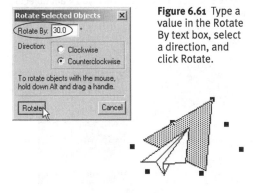

Figure 6.61 Type a value in the Rotate By text box, select a direction, and click Rotate.

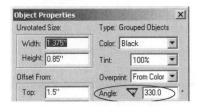

Figure 6.62 View and change the rotation angle in the Object Properties dialog box.

To rotate an object precisely:

1. Select the object and from the Graphics menu, choose Rotate (**Figure 6.60**).

2. In the Rotate Selected Objects dialog box, type a value into the Rotate By text box.

3. Select the direction and click Rotate (**Figure 6.61**).

   The object rotates the number of degrees specified clockwise or counterclockwise from its current position.

To unrotate or rerotate an object:

◆ To change an object to its unrotated position, select it and press Esc G 0 (zero). To then rerotate the object, press Esc G 1.

To view an object's rotation angle:

1. Select the object and from the Graphics menu, choose Object Properties.

   or

   Press Esc G O (Graphics Object).

2. In the Object Properties dialog box, view the value in the Angle text box (**Figure 6.62**).

   The angle value is relative to the object's original position, not its current position.

To rotate an object from its original position:

1. Select the object and from the Graphics menu, choose Object Properties.

2. In the Object Properties dialog box, type a value in the Angle text box and click Set.

   Any change you make is relative to the object's original position.

✔ Tip

■ Grouped objects rotate as a group, but individual objects each rotate individually.

Using gravity ∨ magnetic

When you create a diagram or an illustration, you will sometimes want to join lines or make objects touch. If you are working with the snap grid on (choose Graphics > Snap), objects are attracted to grid lines and you can ensure even, consistent shapes and placement of objects.

Even with micropositioning, you'll find it's difficult to position objects so that they just touch. The best approach in this case is to turn on Gravity. With Gravity on, objects attract each other when you draw, resize, or reshape them. Objects have different points of gravity, where the strongest pull is exerted (**Figure 6.63**).

To make objects attract each other:

1. From the Graphics menu, choose Gravity, if it isn't already on.

   Gravity is now on for the session in this document and in any others you might open until you turn it off.

2. Drag the handle of one of the objects you want to touch toward the other object, close to where you want them to touch (**Figure 6.64**).

   The handle "jumps" so that the two objects come together (**Figure 6.65**).

✔ Tips

- Gravity extends out 1 point regardless of whether zoom is at 100% or higher, so if you work at a higher zoom value, you'll be able to bring objects closer together without making them touch. This approach is helpful if you want to leave a very small space between objects.

- If Snap and Gravity are both on, Gravity takes precedence.

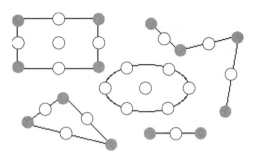

Figure 6.63 Gray circles on the various shapes show where gravity is strongest; white circles show where gravity exerts a weaker pull.

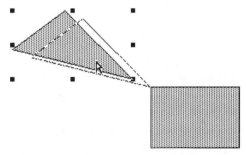

Figure 6.64 Turn on Gravity when you want objects to just touch.

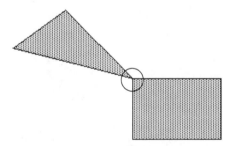

Figure 6.65 The point of the triangle is attracted to the corner of the rectangle.

ARRANGING OBJECTS

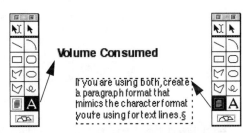

Figure 6.66 Text Line tool and example of text line (left); Text Frame tool and example of text frame (right).

Figure 6.67 Leave the settings as is and click Set.

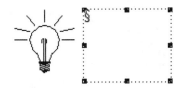

Figure 6.68 A new text frame is always selected.

Table 6.1

Text Lines versus Text Columns	
Text line	**Text frame**
Single lines	Multiple lines
Cannot use ¶ formats	Uses ¶ formats
No autonumbering	Uses Numbering properties of ¶ format
Space multiple lines manually	Uses Basic properties of ¶ format to control line spacing
Uses character format only	Can use character formats
Can select as object, even to apply character format	Can select text frame as object, but not text
Cannot be source of a cross-reference	Can contain cross-reference markers
Cannot contain variables	Can contain variables

Using Callouts

You can create callouts in illustrations by using either a text line or a text frame (**Figure 6.66**). In this book, text lines are used for single-line callouts and text frames for multiline callouts. You could use text frames for all callouts, but you might find that you prefer text lines, because they are easier to align, distribute, and so on. **Table 6.1** summarizes the differences.

Using text frames

Text frames contain all of the text in text flows in a FrameMaker document. In the following sections, text frames are used as callouts with illustrations.

To create a text frame:

1. Click the Text Frame tool to select it.

2. Drag diagonally where you want the text frame.

   The Create New Text Frame dialog box appears. Since you're drawing one text frame, you can leave the Columns Number and Gap text boxes as is (**Figure 6.67**).

3. Click Set.

   The text frame appears, and it's selected (**Figure 6.68**).

4. Click outside the frame to deselect it.

   (continues on next page)

USING CALLOUTS

5. Click at the top left (in front of the end-of-paragraph symbol) and start typing (**Figure 6.69**).

The paragraph format of text inside text frames is always Body by default. Once you click in the text frame to type, choose a different paragraph format if you wish (**Figure 6.70**).

If you're typing in a text frame and you see a black line at the bottom of the frame (**Figure 6.71**), you've overflowed the frame. For text frames used with callouts, the best approach is to increase the width or the height of the frame.

To resize a text frame:

◆ Select the frame and drag a handle (**Figure 6.72**).

Drag a middle handle to change the width or height and a corner handle to change both at the same time.

or

Select the frame and change its size in the Object Properties dialog box.

The solid black line disappears and you can see all the text you typed (**Figure 6.73**).

Figure 6.69
Click outside the frame; then click at the top left before typing.

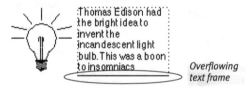

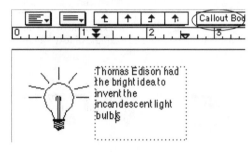

Figure 6.70 Create a different paragraph format for callout text, in this document it's Callout Body.

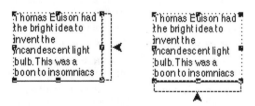

Overflowing text frame

Figure 6.71 A solid black line at the bottom of a text frame indicates that you're run out of space.

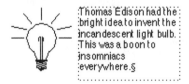

Figure 6.72 By dragging a selection handle, you can make the frame wider or taller...

Figure 6.73 ...or both to fit the text.

Figure 6.74
Here is an example of text that follows the object's contours.

Figure 6.75
The text column must be on top of the graphic.

Figure 6.76
Choose Graphics > Runaround Properties.

Figure 6.77
Specify the gap between the edge of the graphic and the adjacent edge of text.

Figure 6.78
The text runs around the contours of the graphic.

Using Runaround Text

An advantage of text frames when you use text with graphics is the ability to use runaround text. Objects that have runaround properties repel the text in a text frame if it gets close enough (it doesn't have to overlap). Text can follow the contours of the graphic (**Figure 6.74**), or it can align vertically at the edge of an imaginary box that bounds the graphic.

To create runaround text:

1. Position the graphic where you want it (normally in an anchored frame).

2. Create a text frame and position it close to the graphic or overlapping, as in this example (**Figure 6.75**).

   The text column must have a fill of None so you can see where it is positioned relative to the graphic.

3. Select the graphic and from the Graphics menu, choose Runaround Properties (**Figure 6.76**).

4. In the Runaround Properties dialog box, do one of the following:

   ▲ To have the text run around the contours of the object, select Run around Contour.

   ▲ To have the text run around an imaginary box bounding the graphic, select Run around Bounding Box.

   In this example, the text will run around the contours of the graphic.

5. Change the gap value and click Set (**Figure 6.77**).

   The text now runs around the graphic and follows its contours (**Figure 6.78**). If the text is too close or too far away, with the graphic still selected, display the Runaround Properties dialog box and change the gap.

USING RUNAROUND TEXT

To turn off object runaround properties:

1. Select a graphic and from the Graphics menu, choose Runaround Properties.

2. In the Runaround Properties dialog box, select Don't Run Around (**Figure 6.79**) and click Set.

   Text that's close to the graphic or overlapping is prevented from running around the graphic; the presence of the graphic no longer has any effect on the text in the text frame.

✔ Tips

- Although objects created in FrameMaker have runaround properties off by default, imported graphics have it on by default. If you see strange behavior, such as text in a text frame "shrinking" away from an imported graphic next to it (**Figure 6.80**), select the object, choose Graphics > Runaround Properties and turn off runaround properties in the dialog box; the problem is fixed (**Figure 6.81**).

- If you do want text to run around an imported graphic, make sure that the graphic is behind the text frame. Select the graphic and choose Graphics > Send to Back.

- For translation purposes, text from both text lines and frames is exported when you export the file to RTF (a common localization interchange format).

Figure 6.79 Select Don't Run Around to turn off Runaround properties.

Figure 6.80 Because imported graphics have Run around Contour set by default, if a text box is close to the graphic, text is repelled by the graphic.

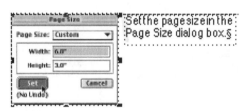

Figure 6.81 Turn off Runaround properties to fix the problem.

USING RUNAROUND TEXT

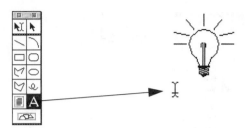

Figure 6.82 Select the Text Line tool and click where you want to text line to start.

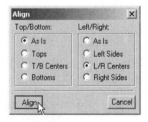

Figure 6.83 Type in the text line (left). Since text lines are one line only, every time you press Enter or Return, you will get another text line (right).

Figure 6.84 Select the text line and drag or use the arrow keys to microposition it.

Figure 6.85 You can also select the text line and then the illustration and align them.

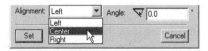

Figure 6.86 Specify the alignment of a text line in the Object Properties dialog box.

Using Text Lines

Text lines are objects that contain text. They are always one line, so when you press Enter or Return in a text line, you get a second text line. You can select and drag them; you can align and distribute them. They are used most often as labels, as in this example, or as callouts.

To add and reposition a text line:

1. Click the Text Line tool and then click where you want the line to start (**Figure 6.82**).

   A crossed I-beam appears.

2. Type the text (**Figure 6.83**).

   The line will be extended as you type until you reach the edge of the page. It will not wrap, and if you press Enter or Return, a new text line will be started. These two text lines are separate objects, and can selected, aligned, distributed, and so on.

   Clicking where you want the text line to start isn't a very accurate approach, so you may want to reposition the text line.

3. Ctrl-click or Option-click the text line to select it and then microposition it using the arrow keys (**Figure 6.84**).

4. If you want to align the text line with its accompanying illustration, select the text line and then the illustration and from the Graphics menu, choose Align.

5. In the Align dialog box, specify settings in the Top/Bottom or Left/Right area and click Align (**Figure 6.85**).

✔ Tip

■ You can left, right, or center align text in a text line. Select the line and choose Graphics > Object Properties. In the Object Properties dialog box, choose from the Alignment pop-up menu (**Figure 6.86**). If you subsequently edit text in the text line, it remains centered.

Using FrameMaker Clip Art

This chapter started by telling you that you don't need to know how to draw to create illustrations in FrameMaker. In fact, none of the illustrations used as examples throughout this chapter were drawn by the author. All of these drawings were found in the clip art files that comes with FrameMaker 7.0. You can access all this clip art and more in the file `Clipart.book` (**Figure 6.87**).

When you installed FrameMaker, you installed the clip art files. **Figure 6.88** and **Figure 6.89** show some examples from the clip art files. Most are grayscale, but some have spot colors (`Symbols.fm` and `Maps.fm` are a couple that do).

Since they're all created with FrameMaker's drawing tools, you can copy and paste them, ungroup them and just use part of the illustration, scale them, change their object properties, and so on.

Clip art files are located in:

◆ (Windows) `FrameMaker7.0\clipart`

◆ (Mac OS) `FrameMaker 7.0:ClipArt`

In the book file, double-click a clip art file to open it.

File > Open >
— Browse for Clipart book.

Figure 6.87 Open the Clipart.book file to access a complete set of clip art files.

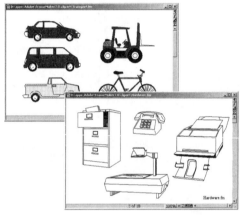

Figure 6.88 Cars, trucks, a bicycle, and the plane from page 120 are here.

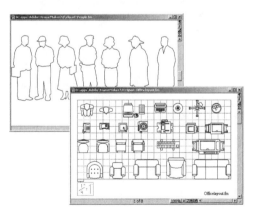

Figure 6.89 Lay out a new office suite and provide a workplace for the "shadow" people.

COLOR AND OBJECT PROPERTIES

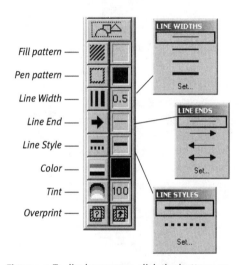

Fill pattern —
Pen pattern —
Line Width —
Line End —
Line Style —
Color —
Tint —
Overprint —

LINE WIDTHS
Set..

LINE ENDS
Set..

LINE STYLES
Set..

Figure 7.1 To display menus, click the buttons on the left side of the Tools palette.

In this chapter you'll explore FrameMaker's object drawing properties (**Figure 7.1**), which allow you, among other things, to fill all closed and some open shapes and specify their pen (border) pattern. You can set and choose line widths and arrow styles for one or both ends of a line, and you can use predefined arrow styles, or create your own by specifying the angle, tip angle, and length. In addition to a standard dotted or dashed line style option, you can specify other custom choices.

Using color and tint (a lightened version of a color), you can assign a wide variety of colors to lines and shapes. Any custom colors you create appear on Color menus, available to format text, table cells, change bars, and conditional text.

FrameMaker drawing tools and object properties work together so you can create many of the charts and illustrations you need for presentations, Web-ready documents, and printed pieces.

About Object Drawing Properties

Click the Tools button at the top right of the document window or choose Graphics > Tools to display the Tools palette (**Figure 7.2**).

In Mac OS only, you can use a large Tools palette (**Figure 7.3**), which displays selections for most of the object drawing properties conveniently on the palette. The Color, Tint, and Overprint menus are pop-up menus you display by clicking the appropriate button. All of the commands from the Graphics menu are displayed on the left side. This chapter assumes that you have the small Tools palette displayed on your screen.

For most of the drawing properties:

◆ On the left are pop-up menus that allow you to change the property of a selected object or specify choices.

◆ On the right are the current settings for any objects you may draw.

You can change any of the drawing properties before you draw an object, or you can select one or more existing objects and then change their properties. Once you change a property by choosing from a menu on the left, that value becomes the current setting and appears on the right side of the Tools palette.

You can customize lines as follows:

◆ You can specify widths for the four choices on the Line Widths menu.

◆ You can specify an arrow style for line ends.

◆ You can specify a style for the dotted or dashed line on the Line Styles menu.

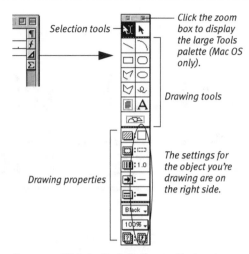

Figure 7.2 Click the Tools button to display the current (small or large) Tools palette.

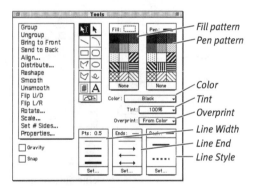

Figure 7.3 (Mac OS only) The large Tools palette displays object drawing property choices more expansively.

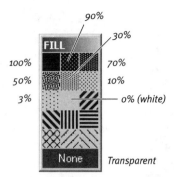

Figure 7.4 In addition to the stripe and cross patterns in the Fill and Pen menus are gray patterns with the tint percentages shown here.

Figure 7.5 Select an object to fill. In this example, only the large triangle is selected.

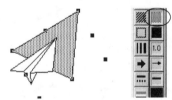

Figure 7.6 The fill pattern you choose from the pop-up menu (in this example, it's 30%) is applied and becomes the current setting.

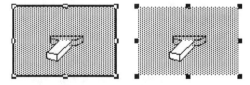

Figure 7.7 The selected rectangle (left) now has a pen pattern of 0%, or white (right).

Figure 7.8 Examples of other filled objects.

Applying Fill and Pen Patterns

← Border

The Fill and Pen menus look the same and provide gray patterns, a number of stripe and cross patterns, and a transparent option (**Figure 7.4**). You can fill any objects except lines and text lines.

To apply a fill pattern:

1. Select an object or objects to fill; you can also select grouped objects (**Figure 7.5**).

2. Choose a pattern from the Fill pop-up menu (**Figure 7.6**).

   The fill pattern is applied to the selected objects, and it becomes the current fill setting.

To apply a pen pattern:

1. Select an object or objects; you can also grouped objects.

2. Choose a pattern from the Pen pop-up menu.

   The pen pattern is applied to the selected objects (**Figure 7.7**), and it becomes the current pen setting.

✔ Tips

■ To make an object transparent, choose a fill pattern of None. Any objects behind this object will show through.

   If want an object to have a transparent border, choose a pen pattern of None.

■ If you don't want other objects behind to show through, choose a fill pattern of 0 percent (white).

■ You can "fill" the shapes created by objects other than closed shapes. In the example shown here, the arc (left), polyline (center) and freehand line (right) have a black pen pattern and different fill patterns (**Figure 7.8**).

Working with Lines

Drawing properties are the object properties that apply specifically to objects drawn in FrameMaker. Using drawing properties on the Tools palette, you can change a number of line properties, including:

◆ Line width

◆ Line end

◆ Line style

Setting line widths

As with the fill and pen patterns, the current property is displayed to the right of the pop-up menus. In the example in **Figure 7.9**, any line, arc, polyline, or freehand line you draw will be a solid line, 1 point wide, with an arrowhead at one end. Closed shapes, such as rectangles, rounded rectangles, ovals, and polygons will also be drawn with a 1-point, solid line; line ends have no effect on closed shapes (**Figure 7.10**).

To set values for the Line Widths menu:

1. From the Line Widths pop-up menu, choose Set (**Figure 7.11**).

The Line Width Options dialog box appears.

2. To retrieve FrameMaker's default values, click Get Defaults; the default values appear in the boxes (**Figure 7.12**).

or

To change any or all of the line width values in the four boxes, type a new value.

You can use any values between 0.015 and 360 points and enter them in any order.

3. Click Set.

Now when you choose a value from the Line Widths menu, you will be choosing among these values. FrameMaker orders the values you set from narrowest (top) to widest (bottom) on the menu.

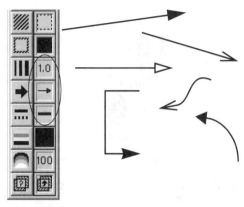

Figure 7.9 FrameMaker's arrow style choices include all the ones shown here.

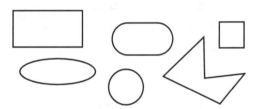

Figure 7.10 All shapes drawn with the drawing properties shown above will have the same line width and style.

Figure 7.11 From the Line Widths pop-up menu, choose Set to display the Line Width Options dialog box.

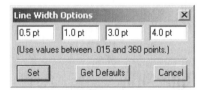

Figure 7.12 These are the FrameMaker line width default values.

WORKING WITH LINES

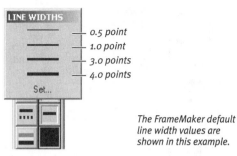

The FrameMaker default line width values are shown in this example.

Figure 7.13 Four lines are displayed; their width is set in the Line Width Options dialog box shown in Figure 7-12.

Figure 7.14 The new, and now current, line width appears to the right of the pop-up menu.

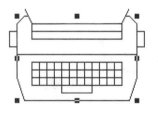

Figure 7.15 In this example, a polygon that is part of the drawing is selected.

Figure 7.16 The current value (and also the default value) of the third line in the menu is 3.0 points.

To specify a line width before you draw:

◆ From the Line Widths pop-up menu, choose one of the four lines (**Figure 7.13**).

The lines on the menu represent the current values in the Line Width Options dialog box.

The new line width appears to the right of the menu (**Figure 7.14**). Any line or shape you draw now will have the new line width setting.

To change the line width of an existing object:

1. Select any object (**Figure 7.15**) except a text line.

2. From the Line Widths pop-up menu, choose one of the four lines (**Figure 7.16**).

The line width of the selected object changes to the width you chose and this is now the current line width.

✔ Tips

■ When you change values on the Line Widths menu, none of the changes are applied automatically to existing objects. You need to select the object and apply the new line width as described in the preceding task.

■ If you have a number of shapes to draw with the same line width, draw them at the same time. Then you can set the current value, and all of the shapes will have the same line width.

■ You need to print pages to see how line widths will look when they're printed. If documents will eventually be printed commercially, you should send test files to the printer.

As a general rule, laser printed lines look thicker and blacker than the same lines printed on an offset press.

Setting line ends

You can apply a line end property to lines, arcs, polylines, and freehand lines. These are the choices on the Line Ends menu (**Figure 7.17**):

◆ No arrowhead

◆ An arrowhead at the beginning

◆ An arrowhead at the end

◆ Arrowheads at both ends

To specify a preset arrow style:

1. From the Line Ends pop-up menu, choose Set.

   The Line End Options dialog box appears (**Figure 7.18**).

2. Select a preset arrow style from among the eight available styles.

3. Click Set.

   The style you just set becomes the current style, and when you choose one of the arrowhead options from the Line Ends menu, FrameMaker will use that style.

To specify a line end before you draw:

◆ From the Line Ends pop-up menu, choose one of the four line ends (**Figure 7.19**).

   The lines on the menu represent the arrow styles set in the Line End Options dialog box.

   The new line end appears to the right of the menu (**Figure 7.20**). Any line that you draw now will have the new line end.

To change the line end of an existing line:

1. Select a line (**Figure 7.21**).

2. From the Line Ends pop-up menu, choose a different line end.

   The line end of the selected object changes to the option you chose (**Figure 7.22**) and this is now the current line end.

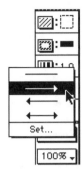

Figure 7.17 The menu choices specify the use of arrowheads. The menu choices, however, look the same no matter which style is current in the Line End Options dialog box.

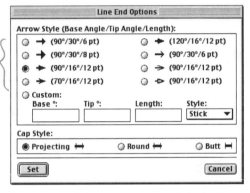

Figure 7.18 Select a preset arrow style in the Line End Options dialog box.

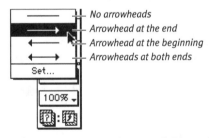

Figure 7.19 Four line ends are available on the Line Ends pop-up menu; the arrow style is set in the Line End Options dialog box.

Figure 7.20 The new, and now current, line end appears to the right of the pop-up menu.

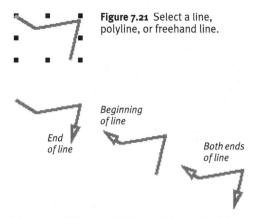

Figure 7.21 Select a line, polyline, or freehand line.

Figure 7.22 This example shows the results of the three arrow options available on the Line Ends menu.

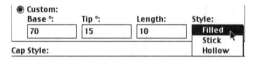

Figure 7.23 In the Line End Options dialog box, click Custom and design your own arrow style.

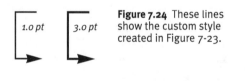

Figure 7.24 These lines show the custom style created in Figure 7-23.

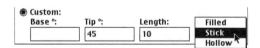

Figure 7.25 FrameMaker ignores the base angle value when you use a Stick custom style.

To create a custom arrow style:

1. From the Line Ends pop-up menu, choose Set.

2. In the Line End Options dialog box, select Custom.

3. Design your own arrow style by typing values in the Base, Tip, and Length text boxes, and choosing from the Style pop-up menu (**Figure 7.23**).

4. Click Set.

   The custom style you just created becomes the current style, and when you choose one of the arrowhead options, FrameMaker will use this style (**Figure 7.24**).

   Arrow styles looks different depending on line width, so you may have to experiment to see what works for you.

✔ Tips

■ When you change values on the Line Ends menu, none of the changes are applied automatically to existing lines. You need to select and apply the new line end as described above.

■ For custom arrow styles, FrameMaker ignores the base angle value when you choose Stick from the Style menu (**Figure 7.25**).

■ Since you cannot name and save arrow styles, if you come up with one that you especially like, make a note of it so you can use it again in future.

■ If you are part of a workgroup, implement a standard line width and arrow style for callout lines in shared documents. Use of a consistent format will make documents —whether destined for Web distribution, online viewing, or printing—look elegant and polished.

Setting line styles

The line styles apply to all objects you can draw in FrameMaker. These are the choices on the Line Styles menu:

◆ Solid line

◆ Dashed (and dotted) line

The style of a solid line, the first choice on the Line Styles menu, is controlled by the line width and line ends. You specify the style of a dashed line in the Dashed Line Options dialog box. The menu choices, however, look the same no matter which dashed line style is current in the Dashed Line Options box (**Figure 7.26**).

To specify a line style before you draw:

◆ From the Line Styles pop-up menu, choose a solid line or a dashed line.

The new line style appears to the right of the menu (**Figure 7.27**). Any line that you draw now will have the new line style.

To specify a dashed-line style:

1. From the Line Styles pop-up menu, choose Set.

   The Dashed Line Options dialog box appears (**Figure 7.28**).

2. Click a dashed-line option and click Set.

   The style you just set becomes the current line style for dashed lines you draw. The dashed-line option affects only dashed lines, not solid lines.

Figure 7.26 The menu choices specify a line style. The menu choices, however, look the same no matter which dashed line style is current in the Dashed Line Options dialog box.

Figure 7.27 The new, and now current, line end appears to the right of the pop-up menu.

Figure 7.28 Specify a dashed-line option for dashed lines.

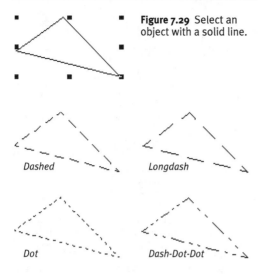

Figure 7.29 Select an object with a solid line.

Dashed

Longdash

Dot

Dash-Dot-Dot

Figure 7.30 These are examples of four different dashed lines.

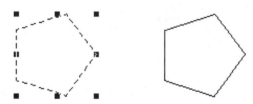

Figure 7.31 Before (left) and after (right) applying a solid-line style.

To change a solid line to a dashed line:

1. Select an object with a solid line (**Figure 7.29**).

2. From the Line Styles pop-up menu, choose the dashed line.

   The line is now dashed (**Figure 7.30**) and any objects you draw will have a dashed line.

To change a dashed line to a solid line:

1. Select an object with a dashed line.

2. From the Line Styles pop-up menu, choose the solid line.

   The line is now solid (**Figure 7.31**) and any objects you draw will have a solid line.

✔ Tip

■ When you change the current line style to a solid or dashed line, the change isn't applied automatically to existing object. You need to select and apply the new line style as described in the preceding tasks.

WORKING WITH LINES

Using Color

use Character Designer for colors

You can assign color to any object, except text and graphic frames, from the Tools palette (**Figure 7.32**). The Color menu displays both standard colors, which are predefined in all FrameMaker templates, and custom colors (see page 141).

To assign a color to a selected object:

1. Select an object (**Figure 7.33**).

2. From the Color pop-up menu, choose a color, and from the Tint pop-up menu, choose a tint percentage.

   The color and tint are assigned to the selected object (**Figure 7.34**), and they are now the current values.

You can also assign a tint value (100% is the default) to any color from the Tint pop-up menu. If you don't see the tint value you need, replace the 0% tint value with a custom value.

To add a tint value to the menu:

1. From the Tint pop-up menu, choose Other. The Tint Value dialog box appears (**Figure 7.35**).

2. Type a value in the Tint text box and click Set.

   The new value replaces the 0% value on the Tint pop-up menu, and it becomes the current tint value for objects you draw (**Figure 7.36**). It remains on the menu until you replace it with another value or end your session. When you restart, the program, FrameMaker reverts to the 0% value.

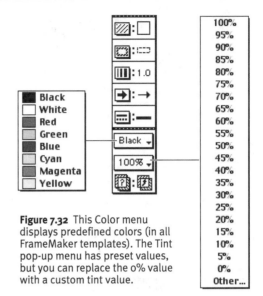

Figure 7.32 This Color menu displays predefined colors (in all FrameMaker templates). The Tint pop-up menu has preset values, but you can replace the 0% value with a custom tint value.

Figure 7.33 This object is a polyline, which has a fill as if it were a closed shape.

Figure 7.34 The black polyline is now magenta, both its fill and its pen pattern, and the new settings appear on the Tools palette.

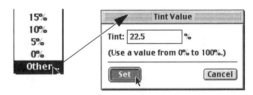

Figure 7.35 From the Tint pop-up menu, choose Other to set a custom tint.

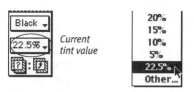

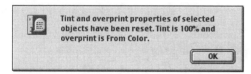

Figure 7.36 The new value replaces the 0% on the Tint pop-up menu.

Tint and overprint properties of selected objects have been reset. Tint is 100% and overprint is From Color.

OK

Figure 7.37 This message warns you that the Tint property has been resent to 100%.

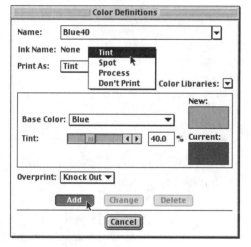

Figure 7.38 Apply a tint in the Color Definitions window.

To specify a color before you draw:

1. From the Color pop-up menu, choose a color.

When you change the color, the Tint setting reverts to 100%.

2. If you wish, from the Tint pop-up menu, choose a tint percentage.

Any line that you draw now will be assigned the new color. and tint.

✔ Tips

■ You cannot change the definition of a document's predefined colors: Black, White, Red, Green, Blue, Cyan, Magenta, and Yellow.

■ When you choose use the Tint pop-up menu, color is applied to both an object's fill and pen patterns.

■ If you assign a tint value of less than 100 percent to selected objects and then choose a color from the pop-up menu, even if it's the same color, an information box appears (**Figure 7.37**) and the value on the Tint menu is reset to 100%.

■ You can also apply a tint by:

   ▲ Using a fill pattern (see page 131)

   ▲ Defining a tint in the Color Definitions window (**Figure 7.38**)

More about tints

You can apply two types of tints:

◆ **Color-level tints**, which are named, defined, and saved in the Color Definitions window (**Figure 7.38**).

◆ **Object-level tints**, which are tints you apply to an object from the Tint pop-up menu on the Tools palette. You can also use the Tint menu in the Object Properties dialog box (see page 145).

USING COLOR

About Color Models and Color Libraries

FrameMaker allows you to create full-color documents that could ultimately be:

◆ Displayed on the screen in HTML or PDF format

◆ Printed on a color laser printer, called digital printing or desktop printing

◆ Printed on an offset press

If your document is destined for offset printing, you can prepare the files for one of the following:

▲ Use of one or more spot colors

▲ Four-color separation

To make the right choices about color, you need to understand a little about the color models FrameMaker uses to define color.

◆ **RGB** is for colors that will be viewed on a color monitor. Colors are created by combing red, green, and blue light.

◆ **HLS** is used to create colors by adjusting the hue (to control the color choice), lightness (to control the lightness and darkness of the color), and saturation (to control the amount of gray in the color). It is used in software color pickers and also in documents that will be viewed on a color monitor.

◆ **CMYK** is used when you plan to print on a color laser printer or create color separations for four-color process printing. A wide range of colors can be printed by laying down cyan, magenta, yellow, and black colored dots in toner or ink on top of each other in varying concentrations. These colors are also called process colors.

In contrast to process colors are spot colors, which are typically the colors added to a document and commercially printed with inks specified by a color matching system, or a color library. Typically, you pick a color from a vendor's swatch book, and that tells the printer what premixed ink to use or how to mix colors from that vendor to obtain a color that matches the color swatch.

The most common color matching system used in North America is the PANTONE Matching System, most often called just PANTONE or PMS. Your corporate logo is likely defined as a PANTONE color, so that whenever you print business cards, stationery, or a piece of marketing collateral, the logo color looks the same. Separate libraries are available for colors that will be printed on coated (shiny) or uncoated (matte) paper. The color you see on the screen is just an approximation of what the color will look like when it's printed. You can purchase PANTONE color swatches at many art supplies stores.

In other parts of the world, different color libraries are standard, for example, the TOYO color library is used in Japan.

FrameMaker comes standard with a number of color libraries, including PANTONE Coated and Uncoated. When you are defining and saving a color in the Color Definitions window using a color library, you should not alter the color's definition. To see what color libraries are present on your system, choose View > Color > Library to display the Color Definitions dialog box and then display the Color Libraries pop-up menu.

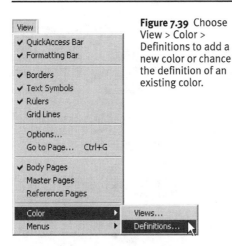

Figure 7.39 Choose View > Color > Definitions to add a new color or chance the definition of an existing color.

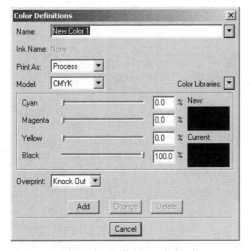

Figure 7.40 The Color Definitions dialog box appears, ready for you to add a new color.

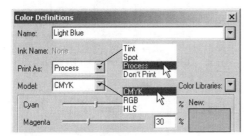

Figure 7.41 Type a name for the new color and then choose from the Print As and Model pop-up menus.

Defining and Changing Colors and Tints

Although you cannot change the definition of the eight standard FrameMaker colors, you can define, name, and save colors you want to use in your document for:

- ◆ Text, including text in tables
- ◆ Objects, including text lines
- ◆ Table cells (see page 222)
- ◆ Change bars
- ◆ Conditional text (see page 196)

The new colors appear on the Color menus of the Paragraph and Character Designers, Tools palette, Table Designer, Change Bar Properties dialog box, and Edit Condition Tag dialog box.

To add a new color:

1. From the View menu, choose Color > Definitions (**Figure 7.39**).

   The Color Definitions dialog box appears (**Figure 7.40**).

2. Type a name for the new color in the Name text box (**Figure 7.41**).

3. Specify how to print the color from the Print As pop-up menu as follows:

   ▲ Choose Tint to define a tint.

   ▲ Choose Spot Color to define a color that will be printed on a press with premixed inks or that uses a single printing plate.

   ▲ Choose Process to define a color that will be printed as overlapping dots with percentages of cyan, magenta, yellow, and black inks or toner.

   ▲ Choose Don't Print to define a color that won't be printed.

4. Choose one of the following from the Model pop-up menu: CMYK, RGB, or HLS.

(continues on next page)

DEFINING AND CHANGING COLORS AND TINTS

5. Adjust the color components by dragging the sliders or typing percent values in the color text boxes (**Figure 7.42**).

As you drag a slider or change a value in a color text box, the current color definition appears in the New color box.

6. To make this color print on top of other colors when printing color separations, choose Overprint.

or

To make this color "knock out" any color that it overlaps, choose Knock Out (**Figure 7.43**).

Overprint is usually the best choice when you want to avoid gaps between colors. Knock Out is the better choice when you want to prevent colors from showing through.

7. Click Add and click Done.

The new color will appear on all Color menus no matter where they appear (**Figure 7.44**).

To change an existing custom color:

1. From the View menu, choose Color > Definitions.

2. In the Color Definitions dialog box, from the Name pop-up menu, choose the color you want to change.

You cannot change FrameMaker's preset standard colors.

3. Change settings in any part of the window.

The new color definition for the chosen color appears in the New color box.

4. Click Change.

The definition for the chosen color changes to the new settings.

To delete a custom color:

1. From the View menu, choose Color > Definitions.

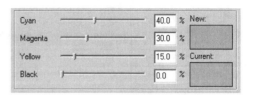

Figure 7.42 The New color box displays the current color values as you adjust the concentration of cyan, magenta, yellow, and black for the new color.

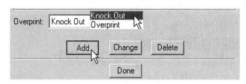

Figure 7.43 Choose Knock Out or Overprint. When you click Add, the Cancel button changes to Done.

Figure 7.44 This is how the new color in this example looks on the Color menu on the Tools palette.

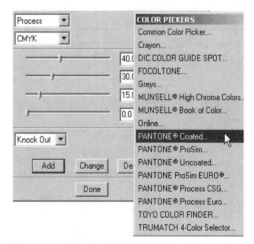

Figure 7.45 Choose a color library for a library of predefined colors.

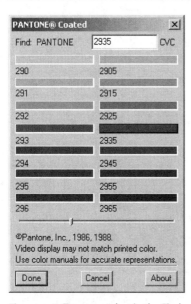

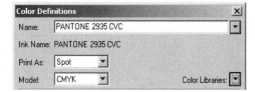

Figure 7.46 Type a number in the Find text box. For more information about the color library, click the About button at the bottom right.

Figure 7.47 A color from a color library.

Figure 7.48 The new color appears on Color menus.

2. In the Color Definitions dialog box, from the Color pop-up menu, choose the color you want to delete.

You cannot delete FrameMaker preset standard colors.

3. Click Delete.

To define a color from a color library:

1. From the View menu, choose Color > Definitions.

2. In the Color Definitions dialog box, from the Color Libraries pop-up menu, choose a library (**Figure 7.45**).

The first set of colors appears.

3. Type the name or number of the color in the Find text box (**Figure 7.46**).

In this example, PANTONE color number 2935 is used.

4. Click Done.

The color you chose appears in the Name text box (**Figure 7.47**) and on the Color menus (**Figure 7.48**).

✔ Tips

■ To ensure consistency throughout a document or book, use paragraph and character formats to assign color to text. For example, if you want to use a spot color for callouts, create and define it and then make it part of the paragraph or character format for callouts.

■ FrameMaker comes with these color libraries:

▲ **Crayon**, with common RGB colors using everyday names in alphabetical order. Do not use Crayon colors as spot colors.

▲ **Online**, with 216 colors that look the same on all platforms when viewed in a Web browser. The numbers and letters to the right are hexidecimal values that are exported to HTML.

Applying Drawing Properties

FrameMaker offers a number of features related to the application of drawing properties to objects created in FrameMaker that you should know about. You can:

- View and change an object's drawing properties in the Object Properties dialog box.

- Apply drawing properties to more than one object at the same time, grouped or ungrouped.

- Pick up object properties from one object and apply them to existing objects or new objects you draw.

To view and change object properties in the Object Properties dialog box:

1. Select an object.

2. From the Graphics menu, choose Object Properties.

    or

    Press Esc G O.

    The Object Properties dialog box appears.

3. To change the color or tint, choose a color or tint from the pop-up menus (**Figure 7.49**).

4. To change the border or line width, type a new value in the Border or Line Width text box.

5. Click Set.

    The new object properties are applied to the selected object.

✔ Tips

- If you select more than one object and try to display the Object Properties dialog box, an information message appears (**Figure 7.50**). Click OK and try again, but this time select only one object.

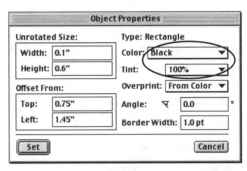

Figure 7.49 The Color and Tint pop-up menus in the Object Properties dialog box look identical to the same menus on the Tools palette and also behave the same way.

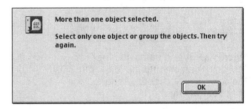

Figure 7.50 To display the Object Properties dialog box, select only one object.

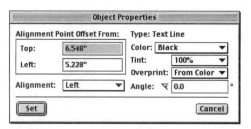

Figure 7.51 The Object Properties dialog box for a text line.

Figure 7.52 Fill and pen patterns, line properties, and color and tint properties are picked up.

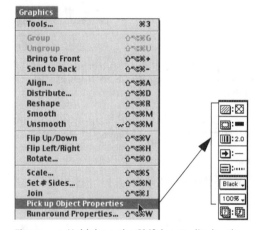

Figure 7.53 Hold down the Shift key to display the command to pick up object properties and make them the current properties on the Tools palette.

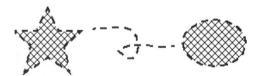

Figure 7.54 The properties you picked up are now the current drawing properties and you can apply them to one or more selected objects.

■ Settings in the Object Properties dialog box change depending on the selected object. **Figure 7.51** shows the dialog box displayed when you select a text line.

Throughout this chapter, you've seen how to apply properties to ungrouped objects either before you draw the objects or after you have created them. When you apply a property to a grouped object, the property is applied to each separate object in the group.

To apply object properties to a grouped object:

1. Choose a grouped object.

2. Apply properties by choosing them from the Tools palette.

or

Choose Graphics > Object Properties and change the color, tint, or line width in the Object Properties dialog box; then click Set.

The new properties are applied to the selected grouped object. If you used the Tools palette, the properties you chose are now the current properties.

To pick up object properties from one object and apply them to another:

1. Select the object that has the properties you want to pick up (**Figure 7.52**).

2. Hold down the Shift key and choose Graphics > Pick up Object Properties (**Figure 7.53**).

The selected object's drawing properties become the current properties on the Tools palette.

3. Select one or more objects.

4. On the Tools palette, click the drawing properties you want to apply.

The properties you picked up are now applied to the selected objects.

Any objects you draw will also have the same drawing properties (**Figure 7.54**).

Creating a Chart

People often create charts and diagrams in another application, save them to EPS format, for example, and then import them into FrameMaker. But they could just as easily have created the same chart or diagram in FrameMaker—and made it easier for someone who might work on the document later to modify or update it.

The best way to create multiple grouped objects, such as shadow boxes with text inside them, is to get one exactly the way you like it and then copy and paste or drag-copy several times. Then you just have to select and replace the text for the copies.

In the following tasks, you create a series of shadow boxes, such as you might use in a chart. Once you finish you'll have created what could be the first line of boxes in a corporate organizational chart.

To create a shadow box:

1. Draw a rectangle the size you need.

2. With the rectangle still selected, from the fill pop-up menu, choose white (the blank square in the middle).

3. Copy and paste the rectangle.

   The second rectangle appears on top of the first one, offset to the left and down (**Figure 7.55**). You can reposition the rectangle as you wish.

4. With the second rectangle still selected, from the Fill pop-up menu, choose a fill (**Figure 7.56**).

5. With the second rectangle still selected, send it to the back (**Figure 7.57**).

6. Shift-click the top rectangle to extend the selection and group (**Figure 7.58**).

   Now you have a basic shadow box. You can use the same steps to make shadow squares and shadow ovals.

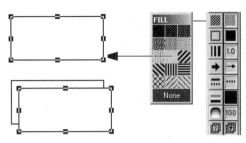

Figure 7.55 When you copy and paste a rectangle, you can reposition it if you wish.

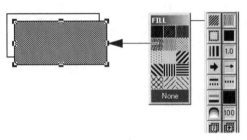

Figure 7.56 Pop-up menus for object properties, such as the Fill menu, are on the left side of the palette.

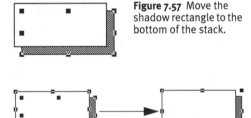

Figure 7.57 Move the shadow rectangle to the bottom of the stack.

Figure 7.58 Extend the selection (left) and group the rectangles (right).

Figure 7.59 Click where you want the text line to start (left), and then start typing (right).

Figure 7.60 Select and hold down the Ctrl (Windows) or Option (Mac OS) key as you drag. Hold down the Shift key to constrain movement to horizontal, vertical, or 45 degrees.

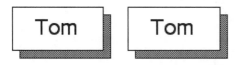

Figure 7.61 A copy appears where you dragged.

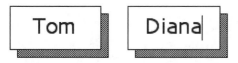

Figure 7.62 Select the text in the second box and change it.

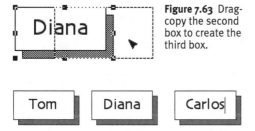

Figure 7.63 Drag-copy the second box to create the third box.

Figure 7.64 Type new text in the third box. Now all that's left is to distribute the boxes evenly on the line.

Figure 7.65 In addition to distributing these boxes, you could group and copy them, paste them somewhere else, and so on.

To add a text line to the shadow box:

1. On the Tools palette, click the Text Line tool to select it.

In the document window, the pointer becomes a crossed I-beam.

2. Click where you want the text line to start and then start typing (**Figure 7.59**).

3. With the text line still selected, apply a character format and microposition the text so that it's centered in the box.

4. Select the box, the shadow box, and the text line and group them.

This is the basic unit you'll copy and paste. If you don't group objects, when you paste them, individual objects will still be selected and will be more difficult to edit or reposition.

To drag-copy the shadow box:

1. Group the objects you want to drag-copy.

2. Hold down the Ctrl or Option key and drag the selected object (**Figure 7.60**).

In this example, also hold down the Shift key to constrain movement to horizontal and keep the boxes aligned (**Figure 7.61**).

Now you have a second box that's identical to the first (**Figure 7.62**). You can drag or double-click to select the text line as text and replace it with new text.

To complete the chart:

1. Drag-copy the second box to create a third box (**Figure 7.63**).

Be sure to hold down the Shift key as well to keep the boxes aligned.

2. Drag or select the text in the third box and type new text (**Figure 7.64**).

3. Select all three boxes and distribute them with either equidistant edges or centers (**Figure 7.65**). Since the boxes are the same size, both approaches yield the same results.

CREATING A CHART

GRAPHICS AND ANCHORED FRAMES

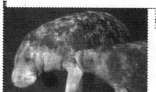

HELP RESEARCHER FIND MYRIAH THE MANATEE¶

Researchers are asking for the public's help in locating a rehabilitated. The manatee, named Myriah, recently lost her radio tag near Everglades City. Anyone who sees a manatee with a belt located at the base of the tail area is asked to call the Florida Fish and Wildlife Conservation Commission (FWC) dispatch.¶

Myriah when she was in the rehabilitation center.§

The video is a joint project between Save the Manatee Club (SMC) and International Video Projects of Florida and features beautiful underwater footage of manatees at Blue Spring State Park, Homosassa Springs Wildlife State Park, and other areas in

Anchored frame

Figure 8.1 A graphics file has been added to this newsletter inside an anchored frame located between paragraphs of text—and it includes callout text in a text frame.

Previous chapters have shown text frames, which contain flows of text in a document. When you want to add a graphic, you need to put it in a graphic frame. An anchored frame is a graphic frame that is anchored in the paragraph above or beside the frame; it stays in place relative to the text. even when text is added or deleted above the frame. You can draw an illustration in an anchored frame or you can copy or import graphics into the frame (**Figure 8.1**). You can add callouts in text lines or text frames.

You can even put a small graphic in an anchored frame in line with text or place an anchored frame in the top corner of a paragraph to add a drop capital letter.

An unanchored graphic frame isn't anchored to text and is used, for example, as a reference frame to hold graphics on reference pages (see page 260).

If you plan to create tagged PDF (see page 323) or XML documents from a FrameMaker document (see page 345), you can include object attribute information for an anchored frame, also known as "alternate text," or "altText." AltText is typically used for describing images so that screen readers can read descriptions aloud as an aid to people who are visually impaired.

Using Anchored Frames

All screen captures and illustrations in this book reside in anchored frames. Most of them are located inside a text column and span the width of the text column, but you can add anchored frames almost anywhere in a FrameMaker document.

Adding anchored frames automatically

An anchored frame is created automatically when you do either of the following:

- Paste an object into text at the insertion point.

- Import a graphic.

The pasted object or imported graphic appears in an anchored frame, centered below the current line (**Figure 8.2**). You can then change its properties in the Anchored Frame dialog box if you wish.

✔ Tips

- When an anchored frame is selected, any object or graphic you paste is pasted into the frame.

- When you select an object on a page and align it, the object is aligned relative to the page. When you select an object or graphic inside an anchored frame (**Figure 8.3**) and align it (**Figure 8.4**), the object or graphic is aligned relative to the anchored frame (**Figure 8.5**).

- When you copy, cut, and paste anchored frames, the contents come along too.

- To select an anchored frame, you can click it or you can select the anchor. When you select the anchor symbol, the frame is also selected.

attention as you would give to the thing you regard as most important, For it will be by those small things that you shall be judged.'

Figure 8.2 This graphic was imported into the document and appeared in its own anchored frame.

Figure 8.3 Select a graphic in an anchored frame.

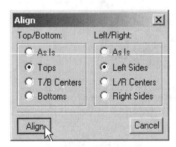

Figure 8.4 Select a graphic inside an anchored frame and choose Graphics > Align to display the Align dialog box.

Figure 8.5 Contents of anchored frames are aligned relative to the frame.

Figure 8.6 Choose Special > Anchored Frame.

Figure 8.7 Choose an anchoring position relative to the text or text column.

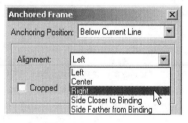

Figure 8.8 Choose an alignment for the anchored frame relative to the text column or the page.

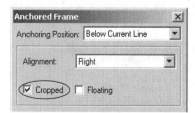

Figure 8.9 Select Cropped to ensure that the anchored frame crops its contents.

Placing anchored frames in text

You can place an anchored frame below a line of text, at the top or bottom of a text column, at the insertion point, outside a column or text frame, or run into a paragraph.

To add an anchored frame below a line of text:

1. Click at the end of a paragraph of text or in an empty paragraph.

2. From the Special menu, choose Anchored Frame (**Figure 8.6**).

   or

   Press Esc S A or Command-H.

   The Anchored Frame dialog box appears. It has the same settings as when you last displayed it or when you last added an anchored frame.

3. From the Anchoring Position pop-up menu, choose Below Current Line (**Figure 8.7**).

4. From the Alignment menu, choose one of the following options (**Figure 8.8**):

   ▲ Left side of text column

   ▲ Centered in text column

   ▲ Right side of text column

   ▲ Side of page closer to the binding in a double-sided document, which means the right side of a left page or the left side of a right page

   ▲ Side of page farther from the binding in a double-sided document, which means the left side of a left page or the right side of a right page.

5. If you want to prevent the contents of a frame from extending outside the frame, select Cropped (**Figure 8.9**).

   (continues on next page)

USING ANCHORED FRAMES

6. If you want the frame to "float" to the next column that can hold it but to leave the anchor in the same location, select Floating.

In this example, the anchor symbol stays in the first column, but the anchored frame appears at the top of the next column, and text backfills the space at the bottom of the first column (**Figure 8.10**).

7. In the Size area, change the values in the Width and Height text boxes if you wish.

8. Click New Frame.

An anchor symbol ($\perp$) appears at the insertion point, and the anchored frame appears below it (**Figure 8.11**).

By default, an anchored frame has no pen or fill pattern. It appears as an empty rectangle bordered by a dashed line, which is invisible unless borders are visible in the document.

To add an anchored frame at the top or bottom of a text column:

1. Click in the text column where you want to add the frame.

2. From the Special menu, choose Anchored Frame.

3. In the Anchored Frame dialog box, from the Anchoring Position pop-up menu, choose At Top of Column or At Bottom of Column (**Figure 8.12**).

4. Click New Frame.

An anchor symbol appears at the insertion point, and the anchored frame appears at the top or bottom of the text column (**Figure 8.13**). It will change position only when its anchor moves to another column.

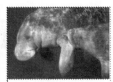

Figure 8.10 The anchor symbol stays in the first column and the anchored frame "floats" to the top of the next column.

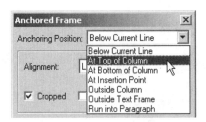

Figure 8.11 The anchored frame is aligned with the left side of the text column.

Anchored Frame

Anchoring Position: Below Current Line

- Below Current Line
- At Top of Column
- At Bottom of Column
- At Insertion Point
- Outside Column
- Outside Text Frame
- Run into Paragraph

Alignment:

☑ Cropped

Figure 8.12 From the Anchoring Position menu, choose At Top or At Bottom of Column.

Anchored frame
From a letter Gandhiji wrote at the request of an
American friend who visited him and conveyed an
invitation to visit the United States.
"It is a privilege for me to enjoy the friendship of so many
unknown American and European friends. It pleases me
to note that the circle is ever widening, perhaps more
Anchor

Figure 8.13 The anchor is in the column, in any location, and the frame is at the top or bottom.

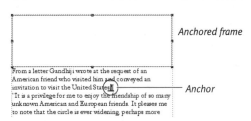

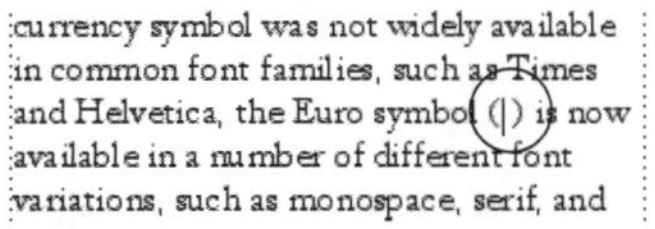

currency symbol was not widely available
in common font families, such as Times
and Helvetica, the Euro symbol (|) is now
available in a number of different font
variations, such as monospace, serif, and

Figure 8.14 Click in the text.

Anchored Frame
Anchoring Position: At Insertion Point
Distance above Baseline: 0.0 pt
Size:
Width: 0.25"
Height: 0.25"
New Frame
Cancel

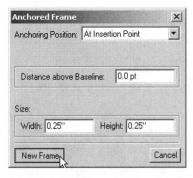

Figure 8.15 Make sure that the size of the anchored frame is relatively small.

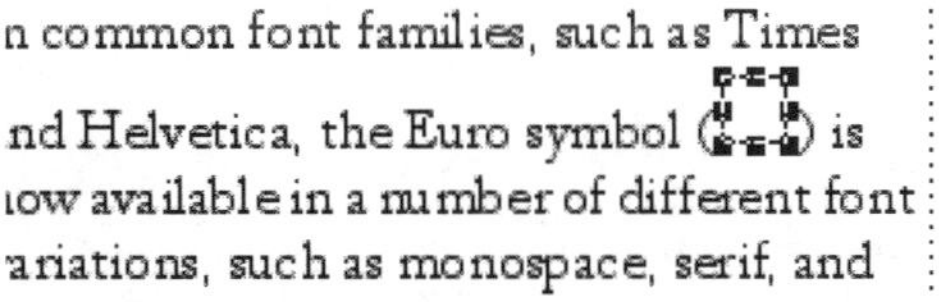

n common font families, such as Times
nd Helvetica, the Euro symbol ( ) is
ow available in a number of different font
ariations, such as monospace, serif, and

Figure 8.16 An anchored frame appears at the insertion point.

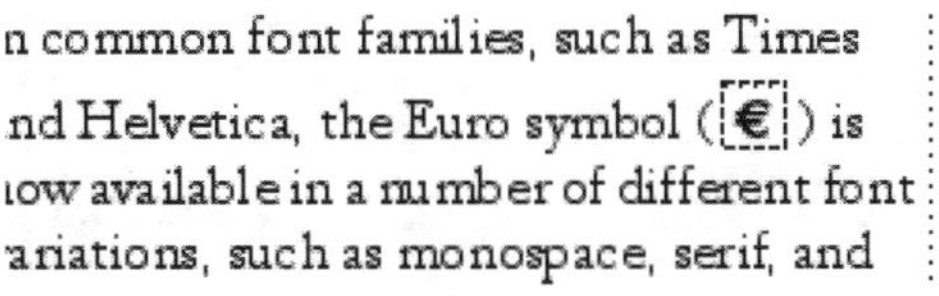

n common font families, such as Times
nd Helvetica, the Euro symbol (€) is
ow available in a number of different font
ariations, such as monospace, serif, and

Figure 8.17 Import a graphic into the frame.

An in-line anchored frame usually holds a small graphic, for example, the anchor symbol in step 8 on page 152.

To add an in-line anchored frame:

1. Click in a line of text where you want the anchored frame to appear (**Figure 8.14**).
2. From the Special menu, choose Anchored Frame.
3. In the Anchored Frame dialog box, from the Anchoring Position pop-up menu, choose At Insertion Point (**Figure 8.15**).
4. Change the value in the Distance above Baseline text box if you wish.

   A value of 0.0" in the Distance above Baseline text box aligns the bottom of the frame with the baseline of the text. A positive value moves the frame up; a negative value moves the frame down.
5. Click New Frame.

   An anchor symbol and an anchored frame appear at the insertion point (**Figure 8.16**). Usually you can't see the anchor symbol for an in-line anchored frame, because it's hidden behind the frame.

   With the frame selected, microposition it using the arrow keys if you wish.

   Now you are ready to add a graphic to the anchored frame (**Figure 8.17**).

✔ Tip

- If you are working in documents, as is the case of this book, that use the same type and size of anchored frame repeatedly, you can copy and paste an anchored frame when you need a new one. Then just delete its contents, add new contents, and resize (the height) if necessary.

To add an anchored frame outside a text column:

1. Click in the text near where you want to place the frame (**Figure 8.18**).

2. From the Special menu, choose Anchored Frame.

3. In the Anchored Frame dialog box, from the Anchoring Position pop-up menu, choose Outside Column.

4. From the Side pop-up menu, choose one of the following options (**Figure 8.19**):

   ▲ Left of the text column

   ▲ Right of the text column

   ▲ Side of page closer to the binding in a double-sided document, which means the right side of a left page or the left side of a right page

   ▲ Side of page farther from the binding in a double-sided document, which means the left side of a left page or the right side of a right page

   ▲ Side closer to the edge of the page in a two-column layout

   ▲ Side farther from the edge of the page in a two-column layout

5. Change the value in the Distance above Baseline text box if you wish.

6. Change the value in the Distance from Text Column text box to specify the space between the anchored frame and the text column.

   A value of 0.0" in the Distance from Text Column text box aligns the edge of the frame with the edge of the text column. A positive value moves the frame away from the column; a negative value moves the frame into the text column (**Figure 8.20**).

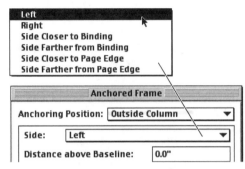

Figure 8.18 The insertion point is in the text column.

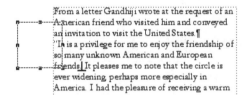

Figure 8.19 Choose where to position the frame relative to the text column.

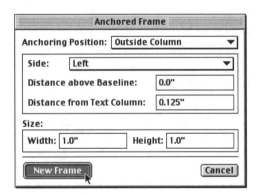

Figure 8.20 A negative value in the Distance from Text Column moves the frame into the column.

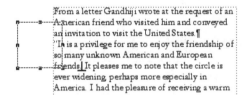

Figure 8.21 Click New Frame.

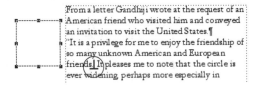

Figure 8.22 The anchored frame appears outside the text column as specified.

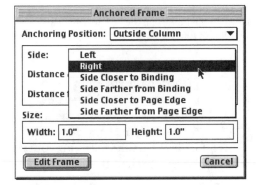

Figure 8.23 Select an anchored frame, with or without contents, to edit its properties.

Anchored Frame
Anchoring Position: Outside Column ▼
Side:	Left
	Right
Distance	Side Closer to Binding
	Side Farther from Binding
Distance	Side Closer to Page Edge
	Side Farther from Page Edge
Size:
Width: 1.0" Height: 1.0"
Edit Frame Cancel

Figure 8.24 Change anything about the frame, including its position or size.

Figure 8.25 In this example, the frame and its contents move to the Right side of the text column.

7. In the Size area, specify the width and height of the anchored frame.

Make sure that the width of the anchored frame fits in the margin.

8. Click New Frame (**Figure 8.21**).

An anchor symbol appears at the insertion point, and the anchored frame appears in the position you specified (**Figure 8.22**).

Now you are ready to copy or import a graphic into the anchored frame.

Once you've created an anchored frame, you can easily edit its properties in the Anchored Frame dialog box.

To edit an anchored frame:

1. Select the frame (**Figure 8.23**) and from the Special menu, choose Anchored Frame.

2. In the Anchored Frame dialog box, change the anchored frame type, position, or size (**Figure 8.24**).

3. Click Edit Frame.

The selected frame moves or changes size as you specified (**Figure 8.25**). The anchor, however, stays in the same place.

FrameMaker allows you to add an anchored frame so that the paragraph text runs around the frame. For example, you can use a run-in frame to add a drop cap at the top left of a paragraph.

To add an anchored frame run into paragraph text:

1. Click at the beginning of the paragraph or where you want the frame to appear.
2. If you are adding a drop cap, delete the first letter of the paragraph (**Figure 8.26**).
3. From the Special menu, choose Anchored Frame.
4. In the Anchored Frame dialog box, from the Anchoring Position pop-up menu, choose Run into Paragraph.
5. From the Alignment pop-up menu, choose an alignment option (**Figure 8.27**).
6. Change the value in the Gap text box is you wish.

   This specifies the gap between the anchored frame and the text around it.
7. In the Size area, specify the width and height of the anchored frame.
8. Click New Frame.

   An anchored frame appears at the insertion point, along with the anchor. The paragraph text now runs around the anchored frame at the specified distance from it (**Figure 8.28**).

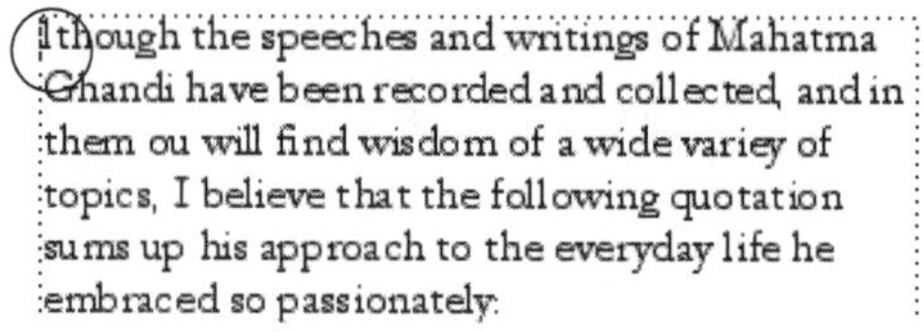

lthough the speeches and writings of Mahatma Ghandi have been recorded and collected, and in them ou will find wisdom of a wide variey of topics, I believe that the following quotation sums up his approach to the everyday life he embraced so passionately:

Figure 8.26 If you want to add a drop cap to the beginning of the paragraph, delete the first letter.

Anchored Frame
Anchoring Position:
Run into Paragraph
Alignment:
Left
Gap:
6.0 pt
Size:
Width:
0.75"
Height:
0.75"

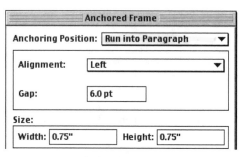

Figure 8.27 Specify the alignment, the gap between the frame and the text around it, and the size for the run-in frame.

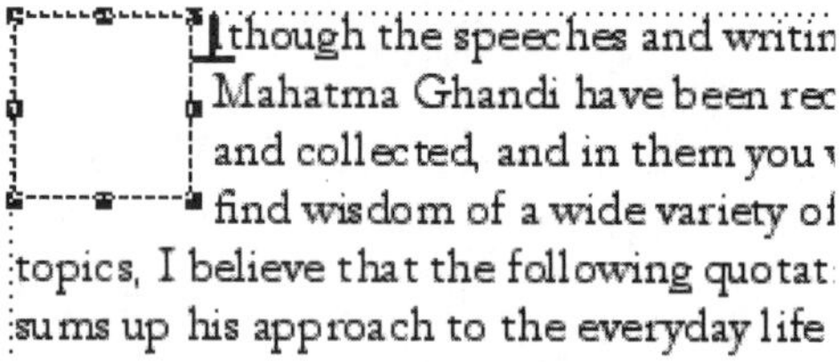

lthough the speeches and writin
Mahatma Ghandi have been rec
and collected, and in them you
find wisdom of a wide variety o
topics, I believe that the following quotat
sums up his approach to the everyday life

Figure 8.28 The text runs around the anchored frame.

lthough the speeches and writin
Mahatma Ghandi have been rec
and collected, and in them you
find wisdom of a wide variety of
topics, I believe that the following quotat
sums up his approach to the everyday life

Figure 8.29 Draw a text frame, the same size as the anchored frame, inside the frame.

Align
Top/Bottom:
As Is
Tops
T/B Centers
Bottoms
Left/Right:
As Is
Left Sides
L/R Centers
Right Sides
Align
Cancel

Figure 8.30 Align the text frame inside the anchored frame.

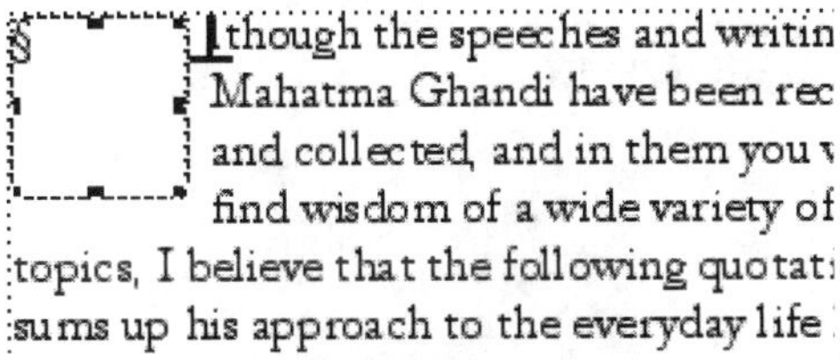

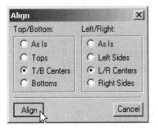

A
lthough the speeches and writin
Mahatma Ghandi have been rec
and collected, and in them you
find wisdom of a wide variety of
topics, I believe that the following quotat
sums up his approach to the everyday life

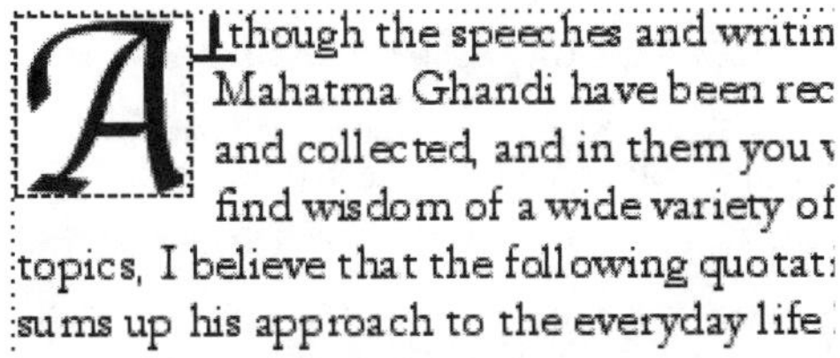

Figure 8.31 To create a drop cap, copy or import a graphic into the run-in anchored frame or type a letter and give it a distinctive format.

You can now add a drop capital letter by copying or importing the letter as a graphic. You can also use an actual letter typed into a text frame inside the anchored frame.

To add a drop cap:

1. Add an anchored frame as described in the previous task.
2. Inside the anchored frame, draw a text frame (see page 123) the same size as the anchored frame (**Figure 8.29**).
3. Select the text frame and align it centered left to right and top to bottom (**Figure 8.30**).
4. Click in the text frame and type the first letter of the paragraph.
5. Select the letter and use a character format to make the letter much larger, large enough to fill the text frame and, if you wish, apply a decorative font (**Figure 8.31**).

   Make the letter large enough to just fill the text frame (and the anchored frame).

Controlling placement of anchored frames

As you're adding anchored frames, you must make sure that space between the frame and its surrounding text is consistent throughout the document. If anchored frames are anchored below the current line at the end of a paragraph of text, as they often are, you can make the frame taller and wider than the graphic and then position the graphic in the frame (**Figure 8.32** and **Figure 8.33**). But this is an imprecise method of controlling the space above and below the graphic.

A better way to control the spacing is to anchor the frame in its own paragraph with a format that specifies the space above and below. (See *The Paragraph Designer* on page 63.) If you fit the graphic snugly inside the frame, the spacing you specified for the paragraph becomes the spacing above and below the graphic.

To create a new paragraph format for anchored frames:

1. From the Format menu, choose Paragraphs > Designer.

2. In the Paragraph Designer, from the Commands menu at the bottom left, choose New Format.

3. In the New Format dialog box, type a name for the format and click Create.

   In this example, the paragraph tag is Anchor (**Figure 8.34**).

4. In the Default Font properties, use the same font family as the body text, set the size to 2 points, and click Update All.

   The smallest font size you can specify in FrameMaker is 2 points.

5. In the Basic properties, specify values for Space Above and Space Below, and click Update All (**Figure 8.35**).

   You've created a format for anchored frames and stored it in the Catalog.

Then, perhaps, they will see the reality instead of

Figure 8.32 The frame (circled) is anchored in the paragraph above it and there is extra space at the top and bottom of the graphic …

Then, perhaps, they will see the reality instead of

Figure 8.33 … which looks fine in the final document but is difficult to keep consistent.

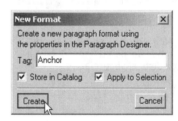

Figure 8.34 Click Create to create a new format.

Then, perhaps, they will see the reality instead of

Figure 8.35 The anchor for the frame (circled) is tiny because the font size of the Anchor paragraph format in this example is 2 points.

About Graphics File Formats

FrameMaker supports the import of the following formats, which are the formats most commonly used in educational, technical, and corporate documents:

◆ **BMP (Windows Bitmap).** Windows native graphics bitmap file format; usually has the file suffix `.bmp`. BMP files are not recommended for commercially printed documents but are acceptable for low-resolution or non-PostScript printers.

◆ **EPS (Encapsulated PostScript).** A graphics file format supported by many graphics applications, such as Adobe Illustrator. EPS files are often used for complex line art, such as you see in hardware, airplane, or automobile manuals. An EPS file contains PostScript code for printing and may also contain a preview image for viewing on the screen.

◆ **GIF (Graphics Interchange Format).** (Pronounced "jif") With JPEG, one of the two most common file formats for graphics images on the Web; usually has the file suffix `.gif`. It is commonly used for non-photographic images with no more than 256 colors. Most of the user interface elements in Web-based applications, such as buttons and icons, are GIF files.

◆ **JPEG (Joint Photographic Experts Group).** (Pronounced "JAY-peg") Commonly used to display photographs and other continuous-tone images on the Web; usually has the file suffix `.jpg`. When you create or convert to JPEG, you can make a trade-off between image quality and file size. Unlike GIF, JPEG retains all of the color information in an RGB image and uses compression that the reduces file size by discarding data not essential to the display of the image.

◆ **PNG (Portable Network Graphics).** A public-domain graphics file format that is best for images with no more than 256 colors. PNG format preserves all color information and uses lossless compression to reduce file size. PNG graphics files are best for Web-ready documents.

◆ **SVG (Scalable Vector Graphics).** A new graphics file format based on XML. When you import SVG graphics into a document, FrameMaker automatically rasterizes them, or converts them to bitmaps; when you create HTML, XML, and SGML files, you can choose to output the bitmap version or the original SVG code.

◆ **TIFF (Tagged-Image File Format).** A graphics file format used to exchange files between applications and computer platforms. The TIFF format supports LZW compression, a lossless compression method that does not discard details from the image. One of the most common graphic image formats, TIFF is commonly used in desktop publishing, commercial printing, faxing, 3-D applications, and medical imaging applications. The screen captures in this book are all TIFF files.

For a complete list of the graphics file formats FrameMaker supports for file import, go to the Adobe Web site: http://www.adobe.com/support/salesdocs/fbee.htm.

USING ANCHORED FRAMES

Adding Graphics Files to Documents

The past few chapters have covered how to create line (vector) art using FrameMaker's drawing tools and properties. If you work on technical manuals, you know that most of the graphics you use are screen captures (bitmaps) and other imported graphics. If you use FrameMaker to prepare presentations or other visually rich documents, you'll certainly need to add graphics scanned in or created in applications other than FrameMaker.

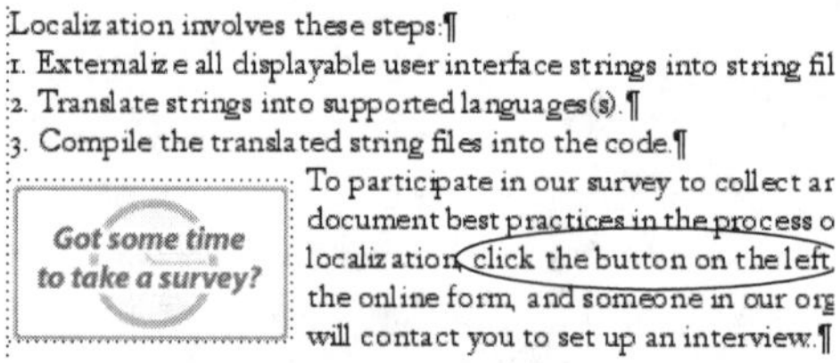

Although you can paste a graphic directly onto a page in a FrameMaker document (**Figure 8.36**), this is generally not the best approach. When text in the document is edited, the graphic will end up in the wrong place (**Figure 8.37**), so it's best to add an anchored frame and then import the graphic (**Figure 8.38**). Because the graphic is in an anchored frame, it stays with the paragraph it refers to.

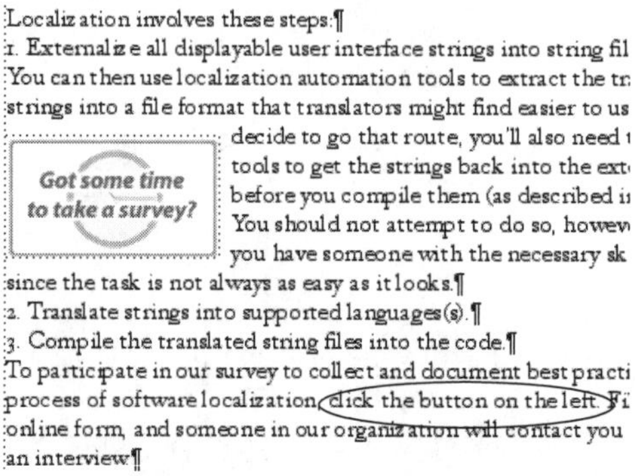

There are a number of ways to place a graphic into a frame:

- Drag a graphic from another location on the page into the frame.

- Paste a graphic into the frame.

- Import by reference or copy a graphic into an anchored frame.

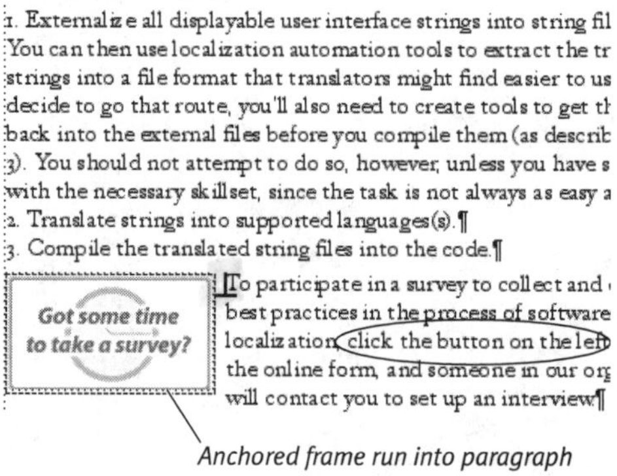

To paste a graphic into a graphic frame:

1. Select a graphic frame (either anchored or unanchored).

2. From the Edit menu, choose Paste.
   The graphic appears in the frame.

Figure 8.36 In this example, in which the graphic was pasted directly, the text to the right of the graphic instructs readers to "click the button on the left."

Figure 8.37 Text was added to the document and now the button is above the circled text, not to the left of it.

Anchored frame run into paragraph

Figure 8.38 Because the graphic is in an anchored frame, it stays with the right paragraph.

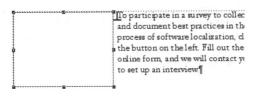

Figure 8.39 In this example, you'll import a PNG graphics file into an anchored frame.

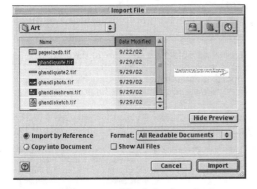

Figure 8.40 The Import File dialog box displays files in the folder you last used to import a file.

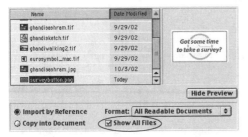

Figure 8.41 If you don't see the file you want to import and you know that FrameMaker supports its format, click Show All Files.

Importing graphics

You can import a graphic by reference or copy it into the document. When you import by reference, you create a link to an external graphics file. If the graphics file is updated and you're imported by reference, FrameMaker automatically updates the file in your document.

You can also import by reference using OLE (Windows) or Publish and Subscribe (Mac OS).

Importing graphics by copying them into a document dramatically increases the size of the document file. When you import by reference, only the *path* to the source file is stored in the document file, *not the graphic itself*, so the file size is much smaller.

To import a graphic by reference or copy it into a document:

1. Select a graphic frame (**Figure 8.39**).

   or

   Click outside all objects on the page to deselect everything.

2. From the File menu, choose Import > File.

   or

   Press Esc F I F or Ctrl-I or Command-I.

   The Import File dialog box appears (**Figure 8.40**). It displays files in the folder you last used to import a file.

3. Browse to select the graphics file you want to import.

   FrameMaker supports the import of most graphics file formats. For a complete list, go to the Adobe Web site referenced at the bottom of page 159.

   If you don't see the file you want to import, you may need to check the Show All Files check box (**Figure 8.41**).

4. Select Import by Reference or Copy into Document.

   (continues on next page)

5. Click Import.

If the graphic is a vector file, not a bitmap, it appears in the document.

If the imported file is a bitmap, the Imported Graphic Scaling dialog box appears.

6. In the Options area, select a resolution for the graphic (**Figure 8.42**).

or

Type a value in the Custom dpi text box.

The dimensions for the preset resolution values are displayed to the right of the value. The default is 72 dots per inch (dpi).

7. Click Set.

The graphic appears inside the graphic frame or on the page (**Figure 8.43**).

If you've imported or copied a graphic into a frame, you'll need to align the graphic in the frame, and you may want to resize the frame.

To fit an anchored frame to its graphic:

1. With the graphic still selected, align it in the frame.

In the example shown in **Figure 8.44**, the graphic is aligned with the top and left side of the anchored frame.

2. To resize the frame, drag the bottom-right corner of the frame (**Figure 8.44**) until the frame just fits around the graphic (**Figure 8.45**).

You can also open a graphic for viewing or editing from inside FrameMaker.

To open a graphic imported by reference:

◆ (Windows) Double-click the graphic.

or

(Mac OS) Double-click the graphic; then in the Object Properties dialog box, select the file format in the Facets list and click Open to open the graphic in an application window.

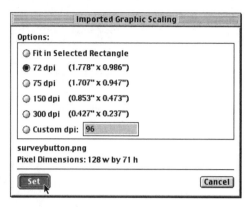

Figure 8.42 Select a resolution for the graphic you're importing. The name of the file you're importing appears below the Options area, along with the graphic's dimensions (in pixels).

Figure 8.43 The graphic is selected when it appears in the document.

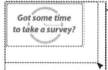

Figure 8.44 You can resize an anchored frame by selecting it and dragging a middle or a corner resize handle.

Figure 8.45 You should try to make the graphic fit snugly into the frame.

American friend who visited him and conveyed an invitation to visit the United States. ¶

"It is a privilege for me to enjoy the friendship of so many unknown American and European

Figure 8.46 If the anchored frame is smaller than the graphic ...

American friend who visited him and conveyed an invitation to visit the United States. ¶

"It is a privilege for me to enjoy the friendship of so many unknown American and European

Figure 8.47 ... and Crop is selected in the Anchored Frame dialog box, the frame hides part of the image.

American friend who visited him and conveyed an invitation to visit the United States. ¶

"It is a privilege for me to enjoy the friendship of so many unknown American and European

Figure 8.48 Drag the bottom-right corner handle until you can see the entire graphic.

✔ Tips

■ When you link graphics files instead of copying them into a document, you can create multiple links to the same graphics file and save storage space on your computer or server.

■ The higher the resolution (dpi value), the smaller the graphic will appear in the document.

■ If you intend to print a document, choose a dpi value that divides evenly into the resolution of your printer. For example, if you're printing to a 600-dpi laser printer, use 75 dpi, 100 dpi, 150 dpi, 200 dpi, or 300 dpi.

■ If a document will be viewed on a computer screen, choose a resolution that divides evenly into the screen resolution. Since you're not likely to know the screen resolution of your users' monitors, choose a standard resolution, such as 96 dpi (Windows) or 72 dpi (Mac OS).

■ If you import or copy a graphic into an anchored frame that's smaller than the graphic and Crop is selected in the Anchored Frame dialog box (**Figure 8.46** and **Figure 8.47**), you'll need to resize the anchored frame so as not to hide any part of the graphic (**Figure 8.48**)—unless you want to use the frame to crop the graphic.

■ If a graphic is too large for the space allocated for it, you can select the graphic and change its resolution to a higher value.

■ Be sure that Snap is off when you're fitting a frame to a graphic. You don't want the frame to snap to lines on the invisible grid, which will make it difficult to get an accurate fit.

ADDING GRAPHICS FILES TO DOCUMENTS

Resizing graphics

Once a graphic is imported into a document, you can resize it easily in the following ways:

◆ By dragging a resize handle

◆ By scaling it in the Scale dialog box

◆ By scaling it in the Object Properties dialog box

◆ By changing its resolution (dpi value) in the Imported Graphic Scaling dialog box

To resize a selected bitmap by dragging:

◆ Hold down the Shift key to constrain the proportions of the graphics to the original proportions and drag a corner resize handle.

To resize a selected bitmap by scaling:

◆ Choose Graphics > Scale and, in the Scale dialog box, type a new value in the Scale Factor text box (**Figure 8.49**).

To resize a bitmap in the Object Properties dialog box:

1. Select the graphic you want to resize.

2. From the Graphics menu, choose Object Properties.

   or

   (Mac OS only) Double-click the graphic.

3. In the Object Properties dialog box, do one of the following:

   ▲ To scale the graphic, change the value in the Scaling Percent text box (**Figure 8.50**).

   ▲ To change the graphic's resolution, click the Set dpi button and change the resolution in the Imported Graphic Scaling dialog box (**Figure 8.51**).

   ▲ To resize the graphic to 100 percent, in the Scaling Percent text box, type 100%.

4. Click Set.

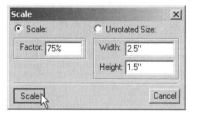

Figure 8.49 You can resize a bitmap in the Scale dialog box.

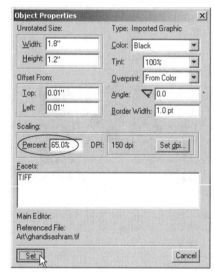

Figure 8.50 Change the value in the Scaling Percent text box.

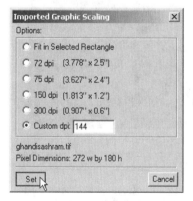

Figure 8.51 Change the resolution in the Imported Graphic Scaling dialog box.

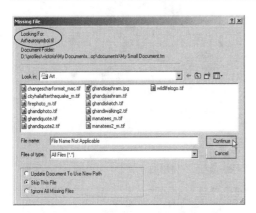

Figure 8.52 When the Missing File dialog box appears, Skip This File is selected by default.

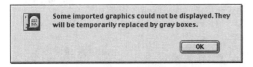

Figure 8.53 On Mac OS, this message appears if you tell FrameMaker to ignore one or more graphics files when it opens the document.

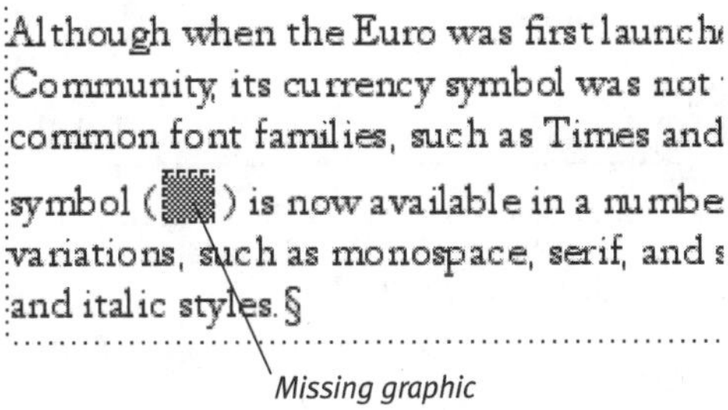

Although when the Euro was first launch Community, its currency symbol was not common font families, such as Times and symbol (　) is now available in a numbe variations, such as monospace, serif, and s and italic styles. §

Missing graphic

Figure 8.54 Any missing graphics in the document are replaced by gray boxes.

Handling missing graphics files

A graphics files imported by reference can be accidentally deleted, or a graphic may be renamed or moved. (This is more likely to happen when you're working on a server where number of colleagues may have write permission.) When FrameMaker can't find a linked graphics file, you have the option of opening the document anyway, respecifying the path to the file, or selecting another graphic to import.

To open a FrameMaker document with a missing graphics file:

1. Open a FrameMaker document.

   If FrameMaker can't find one of the imported graphics using its pathname, the Missing File dialog box appears (**Figure 8.52**).

   In this example, the missing file is eurosymbol.tif and FrameMaker is looking for it in the Art folder. On Windows, the name of the missing file is displayed at the top of the dialog box, and on Mac OS, it's displayed below the list of files.

2. Select Skip This File or Ignore All Missing Files.

3. Click Continue or Select.

   (Mac OS) A message appears (**Figure 8.53**) to let you know that at least one imported graphic will be replaced by a gray box. Click OK.

   The document opens, and missing graphics are replaced by gray boxes (**Figure 8.54**).

   The path for the original graphic is still stored in the document. If the graphics file is present in the correct location the next time you open the document, FrameMaker will find it.

To replace a missing graphics file imported by reference:

1. Open a FrameMaker document.

   If FrameMaker can't find one of the imported graphics using its path, the Missing File dialog box appears (**Figure 8.55**).

   In this example, the graphics file "ghandiwalking.tif" is no longer in the Art folder. There is a file named "ghandiwalking2.tif," however, and that's the one you want to import to replace the original file.

2. Select the new file in the scroll list.

   The Update Document to Use New Path radio button is now also selected (**Figure 8.56**).

3. Click Select.

   If there are no other missing files, the document opens.

   If you go to the page where the graphic is located, you'll see the new graphic has replaced the original graphic (**Figure 8.57**). Its position and resolution are the same as those of the original graphic.

✔ Tips

- Pay careful attention when you specify a graphics file replacement in the Missing File dialog box. Once you select a new file, you'll lose any record of the original file name and path. If you accidentally select the wrong file, you can't go back and try again, because this time you won't know the name of the missing file.

- FrameMaker stores *relative* pathnames. A relative pathname starts at the current folder or one folder up in the hierarchy and specifies its location from there. Even if the FrameMaker files are moved, as long as the graphics files stay in place relative to the FrameMaker document they are linked to, FrameMaker will find them.

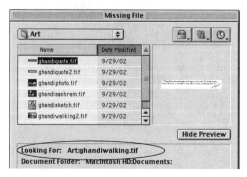

Figure 8.55 The name of the missing graphics file is displayed in the Looking For field.

Figure 8.56 Select the new file. If a Preview image is saved with the graphics file, it appears in the box to the right of the selected file.

Figure 8.57 The new graphic appears in the document.

approach to the everyday life he embraced so passionately.¶

Figure 8.58 A photographic image can be read aloud using an *alternate* text description.

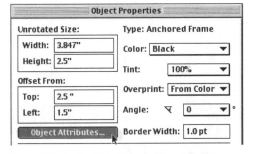

lthough the speeches and writings of Mahatma Ghandi have been recorded and collected, and in them you will find wisdom of a wide variety of

Figure 8.59 A drop cap in an anchored frame can be read aloud using *actual* text.

Object Properties

Unrotated Size:	Type: Anchored Frame
Width: 3.847"	Color: Black
Height: 2.5"	Tint: 100%
Offset From:	Overprint: From Color
Top: 2.5 "	Angle: 0 °
Left: 1.5"	
Object Attributes...	Border Width: 1.0 pt

Figure 8.60 In the Object Properties dialog box, click Object Attributes.

Text Attributes:

Alternate:	A photograph of the Satyagraha Ashram at Ah
Actual:	

Figure 8.61 The altText description of the photograph includes the word "photograph."

Text Attributes:

Alternate:	
Actual:	Although

Figure 8.62 The screen reader will say the word "Although" and then continue with the next complete word in the paragraph.

Using AltText for Accessibility

AltText is alternate text used in tagged PDF files that describes a graphic object for people who can't see it. When a screen reader encounters a graphic in an anchored frame with altText, it will read the alternate text aloud (**Figure 8.58**). Make sure you use text that makes sense when read out of context. For example, "An organization chart showing the following people in key positions in the organization ..." is better than just the callouts and captions, "CEO, Jack Thomas, CFO, Nance Thomas ...." You can also specify actual text, rather than altText, when you want the actual text read aloud, as in the case of a drop cap (**Figure 8.59**).

To add altText or actual text to an anchored frame:

1. Select an anchored frame, and from the Graphics menu, choose Object Properties.

2. In the Object Properties dialog box, click Object Attributes (**Figure 8.60**).

    The Object Attributes dialog box appears.

3. In the Text Attributes Alternate text box, type the text you want read aloud to describe the graphic in the anchored frame (**Figure 8.61**).

    The alternate text includes the word "photograph" to indicate that a photographic image is being described.

    or

    In the Text Attributes Actual text box, type the text you want read aloud for the drop cap (**Figure 8.62**). The screen reader will say the first word "Although" and then continue with the next complete word.

4. Click Set.

    The altText and actual text will be saved when you save the document as tagged PDF (see page 322) or export it to XML.

Using a Context Menu over Graphics

The context menu that is displayed when the pointer is over a graphic, includes commands from the Edit menu and the Graphics menu—commands you are likely to need when you're working with graphics.

To display a context menu:

◆ (Windows) Right-click (**Figure 8.63**).

or

(Mac OS) Control-click or right-click if you have a two-button mouse (**Figure 8.64**).

The context menu appears.

Undo Typing	Ctrl+Z
Cut	Ctrl+X
Copy	Ctrl+C
Paste	Ctrl+V
Bring to Front	
Send to Back	
Ungroup	
Align...	
Distribute...	
Flip Up/Down	
Flip Left/Right	
Rotate...	
Object Properties...	
Runaround Properties...	
Snap	

Figure 8.63 The context menu as it is displayed when the pointer is over a graphic (Windows).

Graphics
Undo
Cut
Copy
Paste
Bring to Front
Send to Back
Ungroup
Align...
Distribute...
Flip Up/Down
Flip Left/Right
Rotate...
Object Properties...
Runaround Properties...
Snap

Figure 8.64 The context menu as it is displayed when the pointer is over a graphic (Mac OS).

USING VARIABLES

A variable is text that is defined once but can be used several times. *User* variables, such as a company or product name, are defined by you, the user. *System* variables use information supplied by FrameMaker and your operating system, such as date and time, current page number, and total number of pages.

Variables are useful when you expect certain text to change often or when you know the same text will be used in several places. All variables are updated automatically when you change their definition (for user and system variables) or their value (for system variables) changes. You can define an unlimited number of *user* variables, such as a product name or book title. You can change the definition of most system variables.

On master pages, you can also define running header/footer variables by pulling in text from specified paragraphs on body pages, not unlike what you can do in cross-references. (See *Using Cross-References* on page 48.) For example, if you want to display the chapter number and chapter title at the top of left and right pages, a common feature of books or technical manuals, you can add a running header/footer system variable in a background text frame on the Left and Right master pages.

Using Variables

Most FrameMaker documents use system variables on master pages, and many include user variables on body pages. Standard FrameMaker templates do not include user variables, but if you're using templates designed for your workgroup, you will probably have a set of user variables already created for your site.

To insert a variable:

1. Click where you want the variable to appear (**Figure 9.1**).

2. From the Special menu choose Variable.

   or

   Press Command-B.

   The Variable dialog box appears.

3. In the Variables list, select a variable (**Figure 9.2**).

   The list includes both system and user variables. The system variables are listed first; the definition of the selected variable is displayed under the list box.

4. Click Insert.

   The variable you selected appears at the insertion point (**Figure 9.3**).

To insert a variable from the keyboard:

1. Click where you want the variable to appear, and press Ctrl-0 or Control-0 (zero).

   The Tag area reverses color, and you are prompted for a variable name.

2. Start typing the variable name until the variable you want to insert appears (**Figure 9.4**).

   In this example, once you're typed the first few letters, "Mod," the rest of the variable name appears. To display the next name in the list, click the down arrow; to display the previous name, click the up arrow.

3. Press Enter or Return to insert the variable.

Figure 9.1 Click where you want to insert the variable.

Figure 9.2 Select a variable from the list.

Figure 9.3 The variable you selected appears at the insertion point.

Figure 9.4 Insert a variable from the keyboard.

Join the Cruise of a Lifetime!

Your cruise on the Love Boat includes ship accommodations, meals, and most enterta aboard the vessel. Your cruise price does n

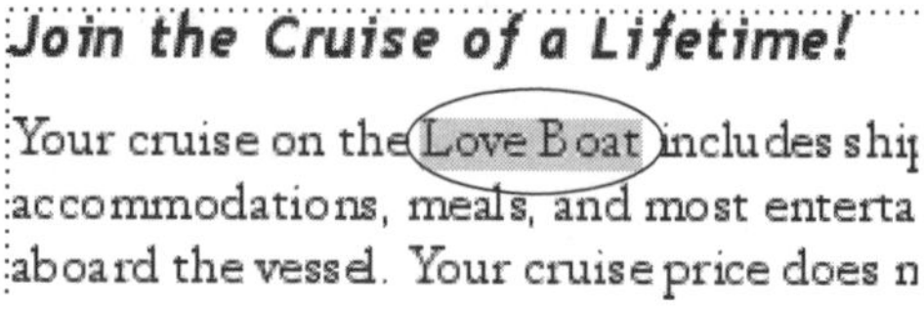

Figure 9.5 When you click a variable, the entire variable text is selected.

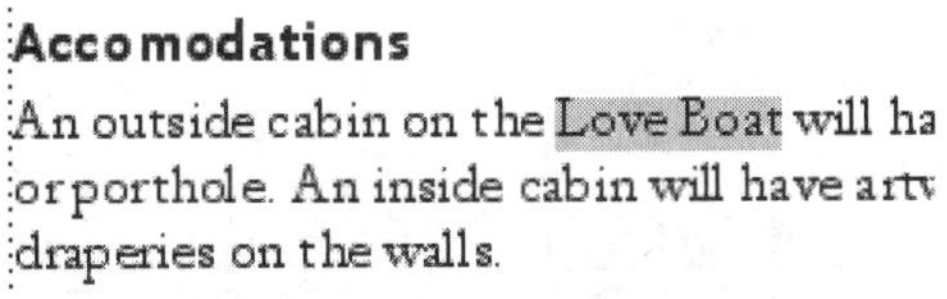

Accomodations

An outside cabin on the Love Boat will ha or porthole. An inside cabin will have arty draperies on the walls.

Figure 9.6 Paste a variable from the Clipboard, the same as you would do with ordinary text.

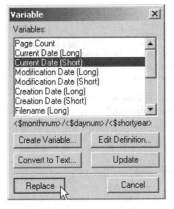

Figure 9.7 Double-click the variable.

Figure 9.8 Click a name in the Variables list and click Replace.

Figure 9.9 In this example, the long date format is replaced by the short date format.

Editing variables

You can copy, cut, delete, and paste variables the same way as you edit text. If you move text that contains a variable, the variable moves along with the text. To edit a variable in the document without changing all variables with the same name, you can convert the variable to text. Once you've done so, the text will no longer be treated as a variable.

To copy or move a variable:

1. Click the variable to select it.
   The entire variable text is selected (**Figure 9.5**).

2. Use the Edit > Copy or Edit > Cut command to copy the selected variable to the Clipboard.

3. Use the Edit > Paste command to paste the variable elsewhere in the document (**Figure 9.6**).

To replace a variable:

1. Double-click the variable you want to replace (**Figure 9.7**).

2. In the Variable dialog box, select the name of the new variable from the list (**Figure 9.8**).

3. Click Replace.
   The old variable is replaced by the new one (**Figure 9.9**).

To delete an occurrence of a variable in the document:

1. Click the variable to select it.

2. Press Back Space or Delete.
   The instance of the variable you selected is deleted, but the variable is still available for future use.

To convert a variable to editable text:

1. Double-click the variable to display the Variable dialog box.

   The variable name is selected in the list.

2. Click Convert to Text (**Figure 9.10**).

   The Convert Variables to Text dialog box appears.

3. Do one of the following:

   ▲ To convert only the variable you double-clicked, click the Selected Variable radio button (**Figure 9.11**).

   ▲ To convert all occurrences of the variable selected in the scroll list, click Variables Named.

   ▲ To convert all user and system variables in the document, click All Variables.

4. Click Convert.

   The Convert Variables to Text dialog box closes.

5. In the Variable dialog box, click Done (**Figure 9.12**).

   The selected variable is converted to editable text, but it will no longer be treated as a variable, that is, it is no longer defined globally in the document and will not change if you change its definition in the Edit User Variable dialog box.

6. Edit the variable you converted to text.

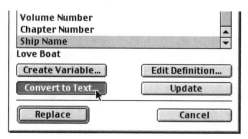

Figure 9.10 In the Variable dialog box, click Convert to Text.

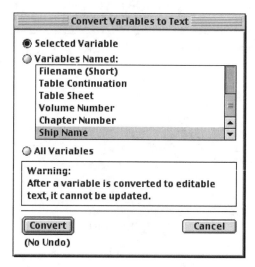

Figure 9.11 Select from the conversion options and click Convert.

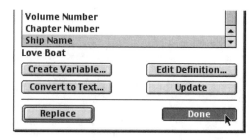

Figure 9.12 In the Variable dialog box, click Done.

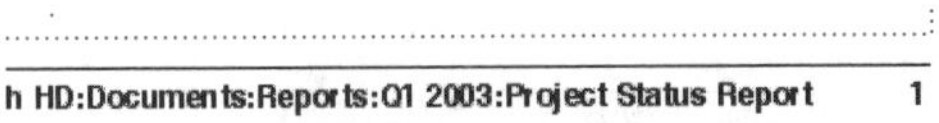

h HD:Documents:Reports:Q1 2003:Project Status Report   1

Figure 9.13 The footer includes a long pathname variable (left) along with a page number (right).

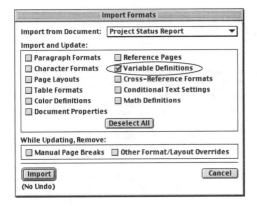

Figure 9.14 You can import variables from one FrameMaker file into another or into files in a book.

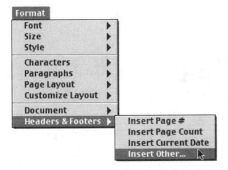

Figure 9.15 Choose Format > Headers and Footers > Insert Other.

✔ Tips

■ If you sometimes have trouble remembering the location of files on your system or server, include a Filename (Long) system variable in the header or footer on the master pages. When you look at the printed document (yours or someone else's), you'll see the pathname for the document (**Figure 9.13**).

■ You can import variable definitions from one document to another or from one document into all the files in a book (**Figure 9.14**). For details, see page 270.

■ When you copy and paste text that contains variables from one document to another, the variables are added to the list of variables in the document in which you copied the text. If you then delete the text that contained the variables, the variables remain in the document. If you don't want them there, you'll need to delete them (see page 177).

■ You can display the Variable dialog box by choosing Format > Headers and Footers > Insert Other (**Figure 9.15**), but only if you're on a master page.

Creating User Variables

User variable definitions consist of

◆ Text

◆ Optional character formatting

If you don't use character formats in the variable definition, the variable uses the format of the text at the insertion point.

To create a user variable:

1. Click in a text frame and choose Special > Variable.

2. In the Variable dialog box, click Create Variable (**Figure 9.16**).

   The Edit User Variable dialog box appears.

3. In the Name text box, type a name for the new variable.

   Make the name as descriptive as you can; don't abbreviate and end up with a cryptic name that won't mean anything to someone else who might work with the document at a later date. If you like to apply variables from the keyboard, use a name that will be uniquely identified within the first few keystrokes.

4. In the Definition text box, type the text for the new variable (**Figure 9.17**).

5. If you want to add a character format, click in the Definition text box where you want the format to start and select it in the Character Formats scroll list.

6. When the definition looks right, click Add.

   The new variable appears in the User Variables list (**Figure 9.18**).

7. Click Done to close the Edit User Variable dialog box.

   In the Variable dialog box, the new name appears in the list (**Figure 9.19**).

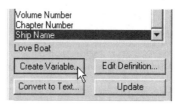

Figure 9.16 In the Variable dialog box, click Create Variable.

Figure 9.17 Type a name and a definition for the new variable in the Edit User Variable dialog box.

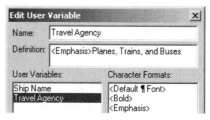

Figure 9.18 The new variable appears in the User Variables list.

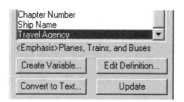

Figure 9.19 The new variable is added to the list in the Variable dialog box.

Join the Cruise of a Lifetime!

Your cruise on the (Love Boat) includes shi accommodations, meals, and most enterta

Figure 9.20 You can double-click a variable to display the Variable dialog box.

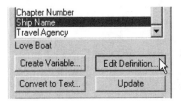

Figure 9.21 In the Variable dialog box, click Edit Definition.

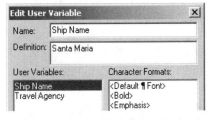

Figure 9.22 Replace the definition in the text box.

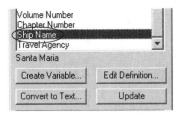

Figure 9.23 The new definition appears in the Variable dialog box.

Join the Cruise of a Lifetime!

Your cruise on the (Santa Maria) includes sl accommodations, meals, and most enterta

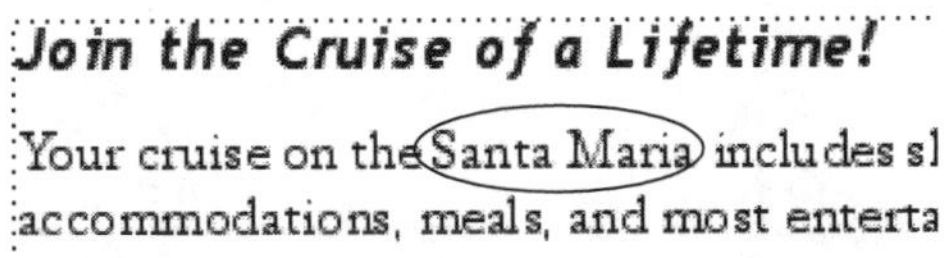

Figure 9.24 All occurrences of the Ship Name variable are changed to Santa Maria.

8. To insert the new variable immediately, click Insert.

or

To go back to the document without inserting the new variable, click Done.

The next time you insert a variable, you can use the new variable you created.

Editing user variables

You can add as many user variables as you wish in the Edit User Variable dialog box before you click Done and return to the Variable dialog box. You can also change the definition of an existing user variable.

To change the definition of a user variable:

1. Double-click the variable whose definition you want to change (**Figure 9.20**).

2. In the Variable dialog box, click Edit Definition (**Figure 9.21**).

3. In the Edit User Variable dialog box, replace the current definition in the Definition text box with the new definition (**Figure 9.22**) by typing and using building blocks.

4. To add a character format, click where you want the format to start and select a format in the list.

5. Click Change and click Done to close the Edit User Variable dialog box.

In the Variable dialog box, look for the new definition under the Variables list (**Figure 9.23**).

6. Click Done.

All occurrences of the Ship Name variable change from Love Boat to Santa Maria (**Figure 9.24**).

✔ Tips

■ If you are starting a technical manual early in the product's development cycle and the product name isn't final (yes, it's true; sometimes product names change right up to a few weeks before the product is released), create a user variable, Product Name, instead of using the current name. When you have a final product name, you then will need to change it in just one place and all occurrences of the product name will be updated.

■ You could use two variables for a long and a short version of a product name. The Product Name (Long) user variable could be defined as "Adobe FrameMaker 7.0," for example, and the Product Name (Short) could be just "FrameMaker" (**Figure 9.25** and **Figure 9.26**).

■ Defining user variables for a company name, product name, or book title ensures that everyone who works with the document uses the name in exactly the same way. For example, a company might be called "Acme" or "Acme, Inc." or "Acme, Incorporated." If the correct form is "Acme, Inc." with a comma separator and a period after the abbreviation "Inc.," use a variable and the name will always be correct (**Figure 9.27**).

■ Use a Book Title user variable if you need to refer to another publication that's still in development and doesn't have a final title. The editors of a secondary math series, for instance, might change the title of the series from "Essentials of Mathematics" to "General Mathematics" and back several times before the series is released. In this case, you should never let anyone know how easy it is to make the change!

■ To avoid errors, use a variable for a word or phrase that is long or difficult to type.

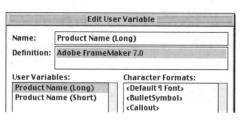

Figure 9.25 A long product name is often used in the introduction of a document ...

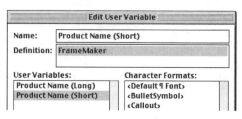

Figure 9.26 ... and a shorter version after that.

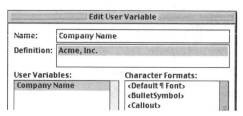

Figure 9.27 When you use a variable for content, such as a company name, it will always appear in the correct form with correct punctuation.

Chapter Number
Ship Name
Travel Agency
<Emphasis>Planes, Trains, and Buses
Create Variable...
Edit Definition...
Convert to Text...
Update
Insert
Cancel

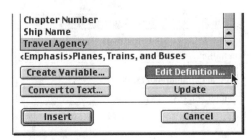

Figure 9.28 In the Variable dialog box, click Edit Definition.

Edit User Variable
Name:
Travel Agency
Definition:
<Emphasis>Planes, Trains, and Buses
User Variables:
Ship Name
Travel Agency
Character Formats:
<Default ¶ Font>
<Bold>
<Emphasis>
<EquationVariables>
<Note>
Add
Change
Delete
Done
Cancel

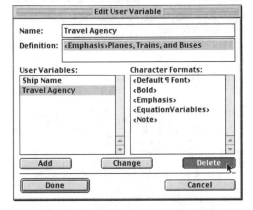

Figure 9.29 The variable you selected in the Variable dialog box is selected in the User Variables list. To Delete it, click Delete.

OK to convert references to variable Travel Agency to editable text? (Not undoable.)
Cancel
OK

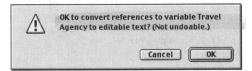

Figure 9.30 This alert box prompts you to think about what you're about to do. Click OK if you want to go ahead; click Cancel if you want to reconsider.

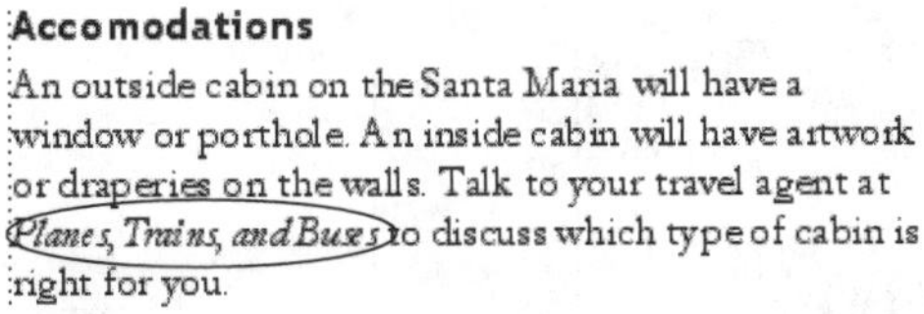

Accomodations
An outside cabin on the Santa Maria will have a window or porthole. An inside cabin will have artwork or draperies on the walls. Talk to your travel agent at Planes, Trains, and Buses to discuss which type of cabin is right for you.

Figure 9.31 The variable text looks the same, but you can no longer edit its definition as you would a variable.

Deleting user variables

You've seen how to delete one occurrence of a variable. You can also delete the variable itself to clean up a document or template and eliminate variables that are no longer current and shouldn't be used.

To delete a user variable from the Variables list:

1. From the Special menu, choose Variable to display the Variable dialog box.
2. Select the variable in the list and click Edit Definition (**Figure 9.28**).
3. In the Edit User Variable dialog box, click Delete (**Figure 9.29**).
4. Click Done.

   If you've used this variable anywhere in the document, an alert appears to let you know that all occurrences of the variable you just deleted will be converted to editable text and that you won't be able to undo this action (**Figure 9.30**).
5. Click OK.
6. In the Variable dialog box, click Done.

   The variable and its definition are deleted, and any occurrences of the variable are converted to editable text (**Figure 9.31**).

Using System Variables

System variables are more complicated than user variables, but also more powerful. Every FrameMaker template comes with a set of system variables. You can't add or delete system variables or change their names. You can, however, change the definition of a system variable.

A system variable definition can include any or all of the following:

◆ Building blocks for system information

◆ Optional character formatting

◆ Optional text

For example, the default definition of Modification Date (Long) (**Figure 9.32**) contains six building blocks and intervening spaces and punctuation as shown in **Table 9.1**.

Although the example shown in **Figure 9.33** places a system variable on a body page, system variables are more often used on master pages (see page 182). They are used in running headers and footers (**Figure 9.34**) in background text frames. A background text frame on a master page doesn't have a text flow. Its content appears on body pages, but you can't edit it on a body page.

The values of system variables on master pages are updated automatically. System variables on body pages, however, are updated automatically only when you open or print a file. You can manually update system variables on body pages when the file is open (see page 181).

✔ Tip

■ The Current Page # and Running H/F variables can be used *only in a background text frame on a master page.* If you display the Variable dialog box when you're on a body page, you won't see them in the list.

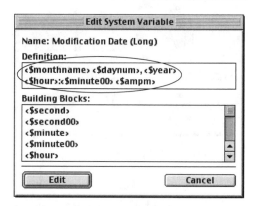

Figure 9.32 The default definition for Modification Date (Long) contains six building blocks.

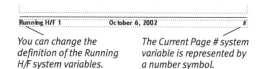

Figure 9.33 This system variable is placed on a body page. The displayed value for the variable comes from your computer's operating system.

Figure 9.34 Examples of system variables in a footer text frame on a master page.

You can change the definition of the Running H/F system variables.

The Current Page # system variable is represented by a number symbol.

Table 9.1

Default Definition for Mod. Date (Long)		
Building block	**Value**	**Followed by**
<$monthname>	October	Space
<$daynum>	3	Comma and space
<$year>	2002	Space
<$hour>	5	Colon
<$minute00>	31	Space
<$ampm>	pm	n/a

Figure 9.35 Click in a background text frame on a master page and add the word "Page."

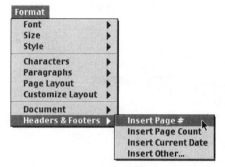

Figure 9.36 Choose Format > Headers and Footers > Insert Page #.

Figure 9.37 The number symbol represents the Page # system variable.

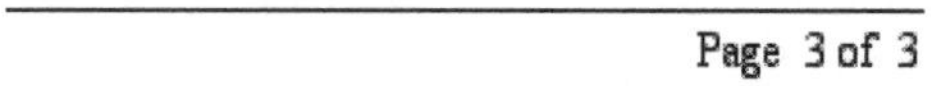

Page 3 of 3

Figure 9.38 The footer is displayed on a body page.

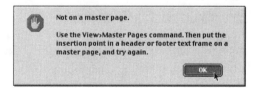

Figure 9.39 If you try to insert a system variable on a body page, this alert appears.

You insert and edit system variables in the same way as you work with user variables. You can also insert a system variable on a master page from the Format menu. In this example, you'll see how to insert two system variables—Page # and Page Count—and make them more descriptive by adding text. The Page # variable inserts the current page number and the Page Count variable inserts the total number of pages in the document or book.

To insert a system variable from the Format menu:

1. On a master page in a background text frame, click where you want the variable to appear.

2. Type Page and a space (**Figure 9.35**).

3. From the Format menu, choose Headers and Footers > Insert Page # (**Figure 9.36**). A number symbol appears in the footer text frame (**Figure 9.37**).

4. Since you're going to add the total page count, type of and a space.

5. From the Format menu, choose Headers and Footers > Insert Page Count.

   The actual page count appears in the footer.

   When you look on a corresponding body page, you'll see the footer with the system variables and any text you added on the master page (**Figure 9.38**).

✔ Tip

■ If you try to insert a system variable or display the Variable dialog box from the Format menu when you're on a body page, an alert appears (**Figure 9.39**). Click OK and go to a master page to insert the variable.

Editing system variables

Although you can't change the name of a system variable, you can change its definition.

To change the definition of a system variable:

1. From the Special menu, choose Variable.

   If you've used the system variable in the document (**Figure 9.40**), you can double-click it to display the Variable dialog box.

2. In the Variable dialog box, select the system variable you want to redefine.

3. Click Edit Definition (**Figure 9.41**).

4. In the Edit System Variable dialog box, change the definition in the Definition text box (**Figure 9.42**).

   You can use the system-supplied information building blocks or the character format building blocks from the Building Blocks list (scroll down to see the character format building blocks).

   In this example, the <$monthname> building block is moved in front of the <$daynum> building block and the comma is deleted.

5. Click Edit to close the Edit System Variable dialog box.

6. In the Variable dialog box, click Done.

   All occurrences of the Creation Date (Long) variable are updated to the new definition (**Figure 9.43**).

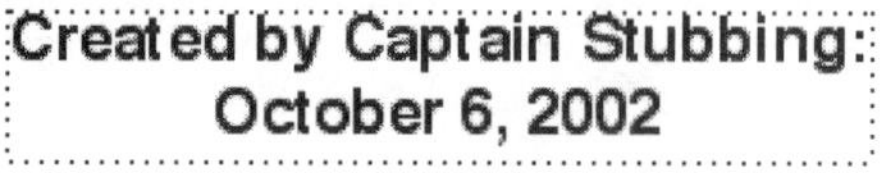

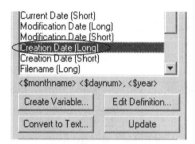

Figure 9.40 In this example, the Creation Date (Long) system variable looks like this. You've already used it in the document, so you can double-click it to open the Variable dialog box.

Figure 9.41 This is the default definition for the Creation Date (Long) system variable. Click Edit Definition to modify it.

Figure 9.42 Edit the definition using a combination of building blocks and text.

Created by Captain Stubbing:
6 October 2002

Figure 9.43 All occurrences of the system variable now use the new definition.

Figure 9.44 In the Variable dialog box, click Update.

Figure 9.45 When FrameMaker prompts you to confirm that you want to update all system variables, click OK.

✔ Tips

■ To see updated system variables on the screen, you may need to redraw the document by pressing Ctrl-L or Control-L.

■ If the Variable command is dimmed on the Special menu, your insertion point is not in a text column. Click in a text column and try again.

■ You can copy and paste building blocks in the definition text box.

Updating system variables

If the value of a system variable changes after you open or print the document, you can update variables manually.

To update system variables manually:

1. From the Special menu, choose Variable.

2. In the Variable dialog box, click Update (**Figure 9.44**).

   An alert appears to double-check that you want to update all system variables (**Figure 9.45**).

3. Click OK.

   All system variables in the document are updated.

USING SYSTEM VARIABLES

Using Running H/F System Variables

A running head or running foot is a header or footer in a background text frame on a master page, the text of which depends on the contents of a corresponding body page. For example, in this book the running head on the Left master page is Running H/F 1 (**Figure 9.46**). Its definition (**Figure 9.47**) means, "Display the word *Chapter*, then a space, and then the *autonumber only* of the Chapter Number paragraph format. If there's no Chapter Number paragraph on the page, search backward until one is found, and display its autonumber."

The running head on the Right master page uses a Running H/F 2 system variable, and its definition is <$paratext[Chapter Title, Appendix Title, Glossary, Index]>. This means, "Display the text in the first Chapter Title, Appendix Title, Glossary, or Index paragraph on the page. If this page doesn't contain one, search backward until you find one of these paragraph formats is found and then display its text."

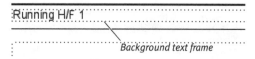

Background text frame

Figure 9.46 The portion of the Left master page for this book, showing a running header/footer system variable ...

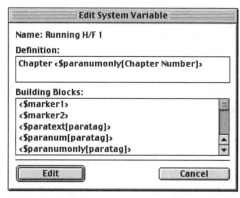

Figure 9.47 ... and the definition for that variable in the Edit System Variable dialog box.

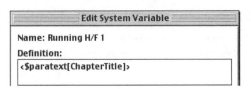

Figure 9.48 This is the default definition for the Running H/F 1 system variable.

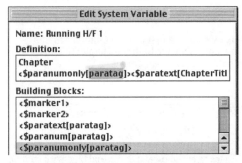

Figure 9.49 Select the building block and then the word "paratag." You will then type the paragraph tag of the paragraph whose autonumber you want to display.

Edit System Variable

Name: Running H/F 1

Definition:

Chapter <$paranumonly[ChapterNumber]>: <$paratext[ChapterTitle]>

Figure 9.50 The final variable definition in this example.

Table 9.2

Default Definitions for Running H/F Variables	
Variable name	**Default definition**
Running H/F 1	<$paratext[ChapterTitle]>
Running H/F 2	<$paratext[Heading1]>
Running H/F 3	<$marker1>
Running H/F 4	<$marker2>
Running H/F 5–12	<$paratext[paratag]>

Changing definitions of running header/footer system variables

Running header/footer variables can refer to a paragraph with a particular tag or to marker text. You can use the default definitions for the running header/footers as shown in **Table 9.2**, or you can change them. The paragraph tags between the square brackets ([ ]) are the actual tags of paragraph formats stored in the Paragraph Catalog.

To change the definition of a running header/footer system variable:

1. Double-click the running header/footer variable to display the Variable dialog box.

2. Click Edit Definition.

    The Edit System Variable dialog box appears (**Figure 9.48**).

    In this example, you're going to add the chapter title to the running head.

3. Use building blocks and text to change the definition of the running header/footer variable.

    You'll change the definition to a more complex one that will appear as "Chapter 1: The Inner Life of Dogs" in headers on body pages in the first chapter in this example.

4. Click at the beginning of the Definition text box and type Chapter and a space.

5. From the Building Blocks scroll list, select <$paranumonly[paratag]>.

6. In the Definition text box, select the word "paratag" (**Figure 9.49**) and type ChapterNumber.

7. After the angle bracket, type a colon and a space to complete the definition (**Figure 9.50**).

    You can include multiple paragraph tags in the square brackets; separate them with commas. When you use multiple tags, FrameMaker uses the first one it finds.

(continues on next page)

8. Click Edit to close the Edit System Variable dialog box.

9. In the Variable dialog box, click Done.

A Running H/F 1 system variable in a background text frame on a master page, displays the chapter number and title on body pages (**Figure 9.51**).

In this example, the autonumber and chapter title were picked up from the chapter opener (**Figure 9.52**).

✔ Tip

■ When you replace the word "paratag," you must type the paragraph tag exactly as it appears in the Catalog, including spaces and upper- and lowercase letters.

Using markers in running header/footer system variables

If the text you want to display in a running header/footer variable doesn't appear in a paragraph of its own, you can pull in text from a marker. You might also want to use a marker if the text of the paragraph is too long. First insert the marker and then include the marker building block in the variable definition.

To insert a marker:

1. Click in a body page where you want the marker to be located (**Figure 9.53**).

In this example, you want the marker in the heading that it will represent.

2. From the Special menu, choose Marker.

3. In the Marker dialog box, from the Marker Type pop-up menu, choose Header/Footer $1 or Header/Footer $2 (**Figure 9.54**).

4. In the Marker Text box, type the text you want to display.

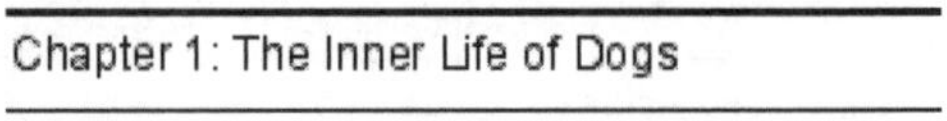

Figure 9.51 The running header for all left pages in Chapter 1.

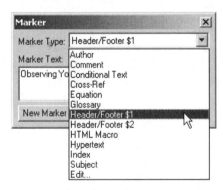

Figure 9.52 The first page of Chapter 1 in this example, showing both the ChapterTitle and ChapterNumber paragraphs.

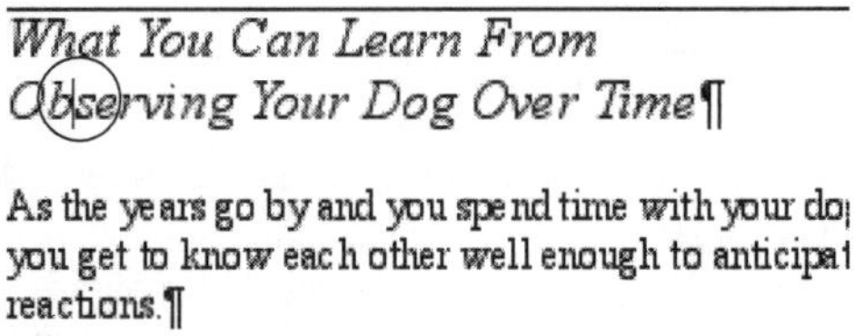

Figure 9.53 Click in the text where you want to insert the marker.

Figure 9.54 From the Marker Type menu, choose Header/Footer $1 or Header/Footer $2.

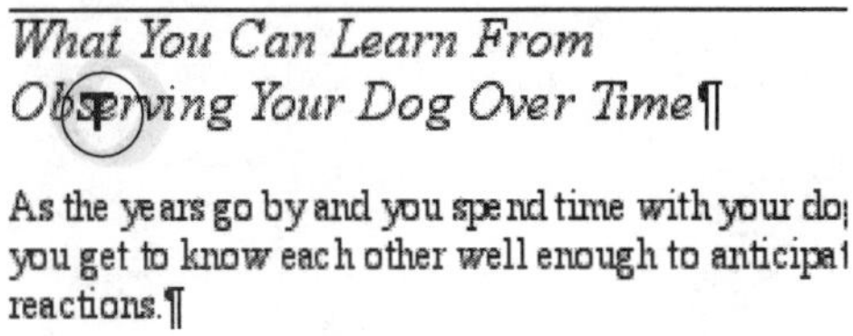
What You Can Learn From
Observing Your Dog Over Time¶
As the years go by and you spend time with your do
you get to know each other well enough to anticipa
reactions.¶

Figure 9.55 A marker text symbol appears at the insertion point.

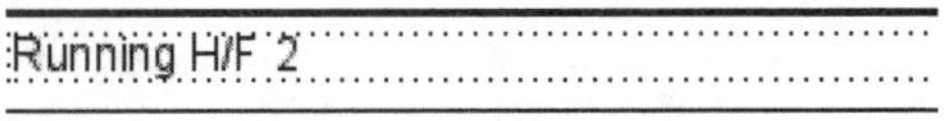
Running H/F 2

Figure 9.56 The running header/footer variable on a master page.

Edit System Variable
Name: Running H/F 2
Definition:
<$marker1>
Building Blocks:
<$marker1>
<$marker2>
<$paratext[paratag]>
<$paranum[paratag]>
<$paranumonly[paratag]>
Edit
Cancel

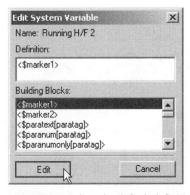

Figure 9.57 Replace the default definition with <$marker1>. Then click Edit.

Observing Your Dog

Figure 9.58 The text displayed on body pages is the marker text.

5. Click New Marker.

   A marker text symbol appears at the insertion point (**Figure 9.55**).

You've inserted a marker with the text you want to display in a running header/footer variable. Now you need to define the variable to pull in that text.

To display text from a marker:

1. On a master page in a background text column, insert a running header/footer system variable.

   In this example, the variable is Running H/F 2 (**Figure 9.56**).

2. From the Special menu, choose Variable to display the Variable dialog box.

3. With Running H/F 2 selected in the list, click Edit Definition.

4. In the Edit System Variable dialog box, select <$marker1> in the Building Blocks list.

5. Click Edit to close the Edit System Variable dialog box (**Figure 9.57**).

6. In the Variable dialog box, click Done.

   Now when you look at the display of the running header/footer variable on the body pages, you see the text you typed in the Marker Text box (**Figure 9.58**).

✔ Tips

■ FrameMaker uses the language of the paragraph in which a system variable is located to determine the language used in date and time variables. The language is specified in the Default Font paragraph properties.

For example, if a system variable displays the month in a paragraph whose language is US English (**Figure 9.59**), the month is displayed as "October"; but if the variable occurs in a paragraph whose language is French, the month appears as "octobre" (**Figure 9.60**).

The same does not apply, however, to user variables. FrameMaker is smart—but not smart enough to translate your user variable definitions!

■ If you change the language of a paragraph that contains a system variable, the language used to display the system variable is updated. For example, if you change the language of a paragraph from US English to French, the day of the week returned by a system variable changes from "Thursday" to "jeudi."

■ Even when you're on a master page, you can't insert a system variable in a template (tagged) text column, which is for text on body pages. If you try to do so, an alert appears (**Figure 9.61**) asking if you want to switch t to a background (untagged) text frame. Click OK (this just means that you've read the message; it doesn't change anything in the text frame) and then click in a background text frame.

You can tell whether a text frame is tagged or untagged by looking in the Tag area in the status bar at the bottom left of the document window. If the text frame is untagged, it doesn't have a flow tag (**Figure 9.62**). If the text frame is tagged, it has a flow tag; in **Figure 9.63**, the flow tag is A.

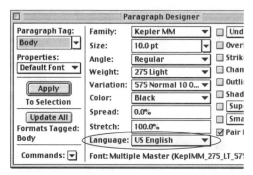

Figure 9.59 The paragraph's language is part of its Default Font properties.

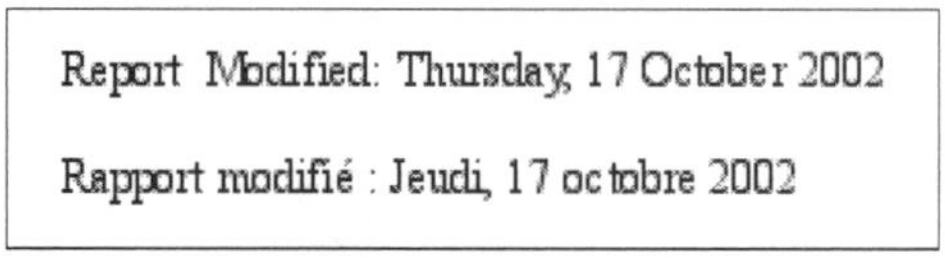

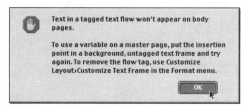

Figure 9.60 The Modification Date (Long) system variable in a US English paragraph (top) and in a French paragraph (bottom).

Figure 9.61 To dismiss this warning message, click OK and then click in a background text frame.

Figure 9.62 Click in a text frame on a master page and look in the Tag area at the bottom left to see if the flow is tagged or untagged. This text frame is untagged.

Figure 9.63 This text frame has a flow tag, Flow A, so you cannot insert a system variable.

10

CONDITIONAL TEXT

A FrameMaker document can contain content for multiple versions of the document. Typically, a conditional document contains mostly *unconditional* text, that is, text that appears in all versions, plus *conditional* text, which appears in only one or more versions. If you use conditional text, you don't have to keep multiple versions of a document in sync when you make a change to one version that applies to all versions. When you're ready to export or print a conditional document, you specify which text to include (show) and which text to exclude (hide) from that version.

Use conditional text in documents with a lot of content in common, but with minor differences. For example, if you're creating data sheets for several models of a product, where the only differences are the size, the speed, and the price, you can conditionalize this data and use the same document to create versions for all product models.

FrameMaker's conditional text feature allows you and/or someone else to add comments and then hide them before exporting or printing the document.

Working with Conditional Text

FrameMaker's conditional text feature allows you to create content for multiple versions of a document in the same document. Text is unconditional, unless you make it conditional by applying a condition. Like paragraph and character tags, a condition tag is just the name of the condition. Condition indicators make conditional text easy to identify by adding color or style changes.

Adding comments

In its simplest form, conditional text can be used to add notes to yourself within a document, and then hide them before you export or print the document. Every FrameMaker template (even the blank ones) comes with a Comment condition; any other conditions are created by users. Comments appear in red and are underlined by default as specified by their condition indicators.

To add conditional comments to a document:

1. Select the text that you want to become a comment (**Figure 10.1**).

2. From the Special menu, choose Conditional Text.

   or

   Press Command-5.

   The Conditional Text window appears.

3. Select the Comment tag in the Not In list (**Figure 10.2**) and click the left arrow button at the bottom of the list.

   The Comment condition tag moves into the In list and the Conditional radio button is selected at the top left (**Figure 10.3**).

   In the Conditional Text window:

   ▲ Condition tags in the In list will be applied to selected text and included in that version of the document.

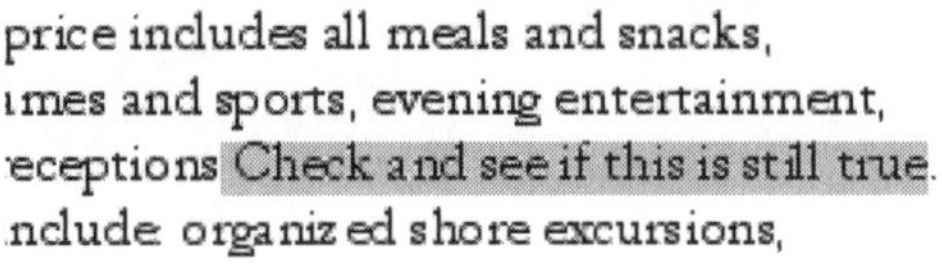

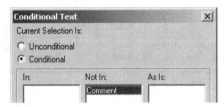

price includes all meals and snacks, imes and sports, evening entertainment, eceptions Check and see if this is still true. nclude organized shore excursions,

Figure 10.1 Select text to conditionalize.

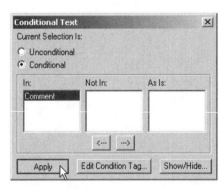

Figure 10.2 Select Comment in the Not In list.

Figure 10.3 Click the left arrow to move the selected condition into the In list; then click Apply.

Syncing Conditional Text

When you conditionalize text, check to make sure that you don't need to conditionalize something else to balance the text you've just changed.

For example, in a document that includes descriptions for two cruises, if you add the phrase "Wine included at no extra charge" for the luxury cruise, you might need to go back and conditionalize the existing phrase "Wine available for purchase" for the standard cruise, since it's no longer true for all cruises.

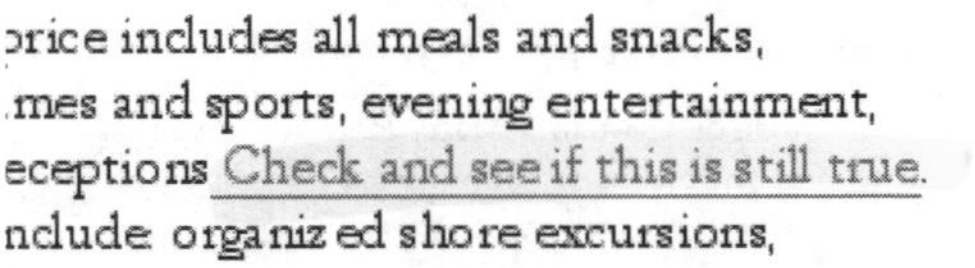

orice includes all meals and snacks,
.mes and sports, evening entertainment,
eceptions Check and see if this is still true.
nclude organized shore excursions,

Figure 10.4 The selected text now has the Comment condition tag.

Figure 10.5 In the Conditional Text window, click Show/Hide.

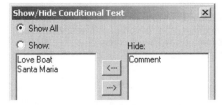

Figure 10.6 Select Show All to display all text, unconditional and conditional.

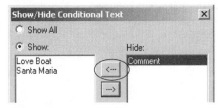

Figure 10.7 Move a condition tag to the Show list by selecting it in the Hide list and clicking the left arrow button.

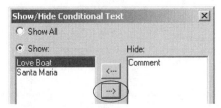

Figure 10.8 Move a condition tag to the Hide list by selecting it in the Show list and clicking the right arrow button.

▲ Condition tags in the Not In list will not be applied to selected text and will be excluded from that version of the document.

▲ Condition tags in the As Is list will be neither applied nor removed.

4. Click Apply.

The Comment condition is applied to the selected text—the text is now red and underlined (**Figure 10.4**).

Changing the view of a conditional document

Conditional text is distinguished from its surrounding text by condition indicators, which are associated with condition tags. When you want to view the conditional text for one version of a document and hide the text for another version of the same document, you can turn off the display of the version you don't want to view. You can also turn condition indicators on or off.

To show or hide conditional text:

1. From the Special menu, choose Conditional Text.

2. In the Conditional Text window, click Show/Hide (**Figure 10.5**).

   The Show/Hide Conditional Text dialog box appears.

3. Do one of the following:

   ▲ To show all text, including all conditional text, select Show All (**Figure 10.6**).

   ▲ To show text with certain tags, move those tags to the Show list by selecting them and clicking the left arrow button (**Figure 10.7**).

   ▲ To hide text with certain tags, move those tags to the Hide list by selecting them and clicking the right arrow button (**Figure 10.8**).

(continues on next page)

4. Click Set.

Depending on which action you performed in step 3:

▲ All text in the document is visible.

▲ Text with the condition tags you specified is now visible (**Figure 10.9**).

▲ Text with the conditional tags you specified is now hidden, and conditional text markers appear in its place (**Figure 10.10**).

To turn on or off condition indicators:

1. In the Conditional Text window, click Show/Hide.

2. In the Show/Hide Conditional Text dialog box, select the Show Condition Indicators check box (**Figure 10.11**).

3. Click Set.

If you turned on condition indicators, all conditional text appears with its condition indicators (color and/or style).

If you turned off condition indicators, they disappear, and all the text, unconditional and conditional, looks the same.

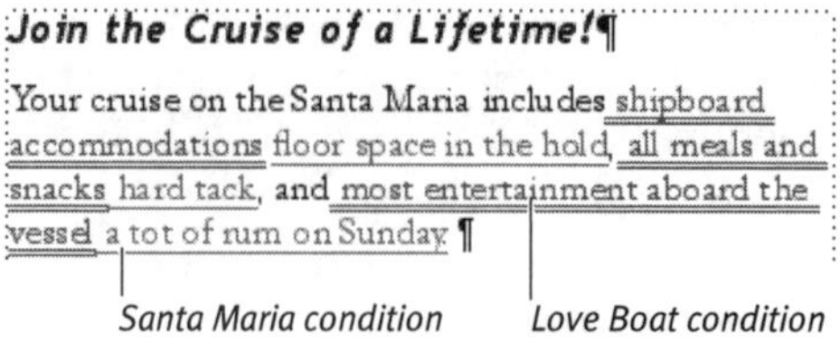

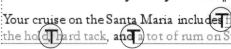

Santa Maria condition   Love Boat condition

Figure 10.9 In this example, the heading and introduction are unconditional, and the rest of the paragraph is mostly conditional—two condition tags are represented.

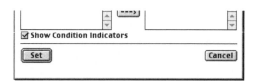

Figure 10.10 Conditional text markers appear where the conditional text would be if it were visible. in this example, the Love Boat condition is hidden.

☑ Show Condition Indicators

Set   Cancel

Figure 10.11 Select Show Condition Indicators to display conditional text with the color and/or style indicators.

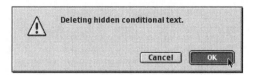

Figure 10.12 An alert appears if you delete text that contains hidden conditional text.

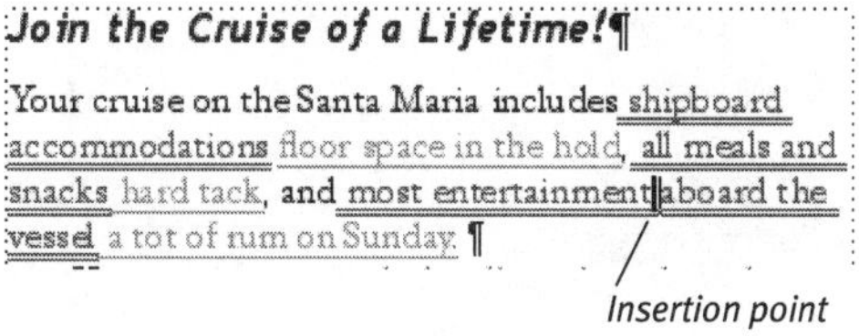

Figure 10.13 Click in the conditional text you want to select ...

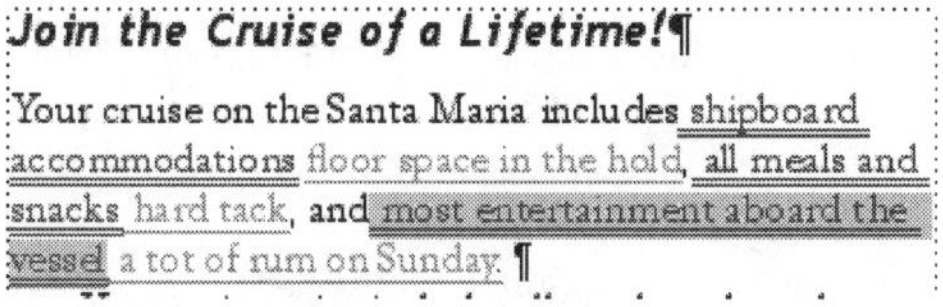

Insertion point

Figure 10.14 ... and then press Esc H Shift-C to select all the text around it with the same condition settings.

Variable or Conditional Text?

Sometimes either a variable or conditional text could potentially be used for the same purpose. For example, in a conditional document with information about several different cruises, you could conditionalize the names of the cruise ships whenever they occur, or you could create user variables for each of the cruise ships.

In this example, a variable is the better choice because variables are easier to work with. Words and phrases that occur frequently in a document are good candidates for variables.

✔ Tips

■ When you work in a conditional document, you should always do the following:

▲ Show all conditional text.

▲ Turn on condition indicators.

▲ Turn on text symbols (see page 12).

If you work with text symbols off, you risk deleting or moving conditional text unintentionally. If you delete text with hidden conditional text, an alert appears (**Figure 10.12**). To cancel the deletion, click Cancel; to delete the hidden conditional text, click OK.

■ FrameMaker searches for and spell checks *only the text that's showing*. If you want to search or spell check the entire document, including all conditional text, you must first show all text.

■ If you want to print a version of the document with your comments included, print the document on a color printer with the Comment condition showing and condition indicators on. If you create a PDF document the same way, you could send it to someone who could then view your comments along with the document.

■ To select all contiguous conditional text with the same conditional text settings, click in the text (**Figure 10.13**) and press Esc H Shift-C. All surrounding text with the same conditional text settings is selected (**Figure 10.14**).

■ If you apply a condition that's currently hidden to selected text, the text disappears immediately and a conditional text marker appears.

WORKING WITH CONDITIONAL TEXT

Applying and Removing Condition Tags

You can apply condition tags to selected text

- In the Conditional Text window
- From the keyboard
- By copying and pasting condition settings

You can apply more than one condition to the same text—and you can remove one or all conditions.

To apply a condition tag in the Conditional Text window:

1. Select the text you want to conditionalize (**Figure 10.15**).
2. From the Special menu, choose Conditional Text.
3. In the Conditional Text window, select the condition tag you want to apply and use the arrow button to move it to the In list (**Figure 10.16**).

   You can move as many tags as you want to the In list.
4. Click Apply.

   The condition is applied to the selected text (**Figure 10.17**), and it will appear in that version of the document.

✔ Tips

- When you select text or when the insertion point is in text with one or more conditions, the condition tag appears in parentheses in the Tag area at the bottom left of the document window (**Figure 10.18**). If the text has more than one condition, both tags appear (**Figure 10.19**).
- When text has more than one tag with different colors as condition indicators, the condition indicator is always magenta.

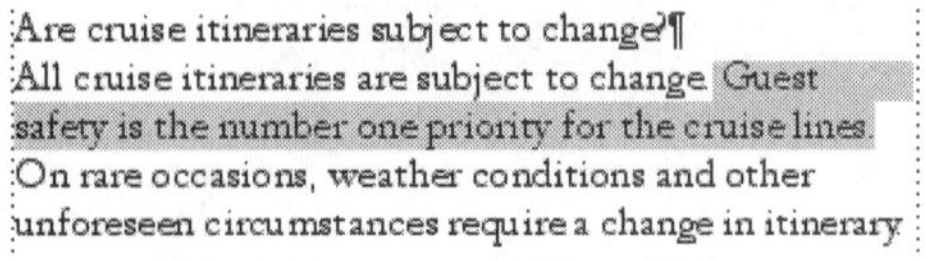

Are cruise itineraries subject to change?¶
All cruise itineraries are subject to change. Guest safety is the number one priority for the cruise lines.
On rare occasions, weather conditions and other unforeseen circumstances require a change in itinerary.

Figure 10.15 Select text to conditionalize.

Conditional Text
Current Selection Is:
Unconditional
Conditional
In:
Love Boat
Not In:
Comment
Santa Maria
As Is:
<---
--->
Apply
Edit Condition Tag...
Show/Hide...

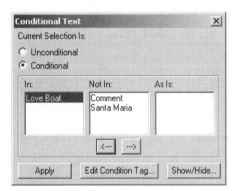

Figure 10.16 Move the condition tag(s) from the Not In list to the In list.

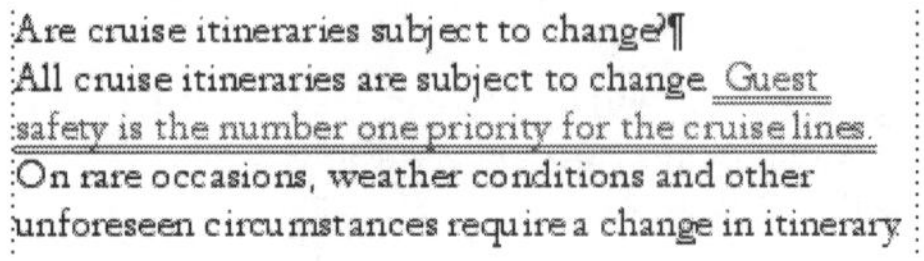

Are cruise itineraries subject to change?¶
All cruise itineraries are subject to change. Guest safety is the number one priority for the cruise lines.
On rare occasions, weather conditions and other unforeseen circumstances require a change in itinerary.

Figure 10.17 The selected text now has the condition(s) you specified.

(Love Boat) Flow: A ¶: Body

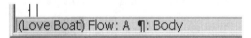

Figure 10.18 The condition tag appears in parentheses in the Tag area.

(Love Boat+Santa Maria) Flow: A ¶: Bo

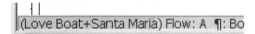

Figure 10.19 If you apply more than one condition to the same text, both tags appear in the Tag area.

Figure 10.20 On Windows, the first condition tag in the list appears with the prompt.

Figure 10.21 Start typing the condition tag until the one you want to apply appears.

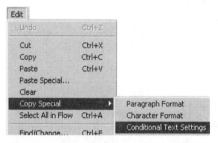

Figure 10.22 Select the text whose conditional text settings you want to copy.

Edit	
Undo	Ctrl+Z
Cut	Ctrl+X
Copy	Ctrl+C
Paste	Ctrl+V
Paste Special...	
Clear	
Copy Special ▶	Paragraph Format
Select All in Flow Ctrl+A	Character Format
Find/Change... Ctrl+F	Conditional Text Settings

Figure 10.23 Choose Edit > Copy Special > Conditional Text Settings.

photographs, gratuities, spa and beauty treatments, medical services, casino expenditures or other miscellaneous items you may purchase on board ¶ Before dawn, you start your physical conditioning program and it continues until the sun goes down.¶

Figure 10.24 Select the text you want to conditionalize.

photographs, gratuities, spa and beauty treatments, medical services, casino expenditures or other miscellaneous items you may purchase on board ¶ Before dawn, you start your physical conditioning program and it continues until the sun goes down.¶

Figure 10.25 The conditional text settings you copied to the Clipboard are applied.

To apply a condition tag from the keyboard:

1. Select the text you want to conditionalize.

2. Press Ctrl-4 or Control-4.

   The Tag area reverses color and prompts you for a condition tag. On Windows, the first condition in the list appears (**Figure 10.20**); on Mac OS, the Tag area displays only the prompt.

3. Start typing the condition tag until the tag you want to apply appears (**Figure 10.21**).

   In this example, you need to type only the first letter, "L." You can also press the down arrow key to display the next name in the list and the up arrow key to display the previous name.

4. Press Enter or Return to apply the condition tag.

To copy and paste condition tag settings:

1. Select text whose condition tags you want to copy to the Clipboard (**Figure 10.22**).

2. From the Edit menu, choose Copy Special > Conditional Text Settings (**Figure 10.23**).

   or

   (Mac OS only) Press Command-Option-C.

   The conditional text settings of the selected text are copied to the Clipboard.

3. Select the text to which you want to apply the conditional text settings (**Figure 10.24**).

4. From the Edit menu, choose Paste.

   The conditional text settings from the Clipboard are applied to the selected text (**Figure 10.25**).

To remove a condition tag from text:

1. Select the text from which you want to remove the condition tag (**Figure 10.26**).

2. From the Special menu, choose Conditional Text.

3. In the Conditional Text window, do one of the following:
   ▲ To make the text unconditional, select Unconditional (**Figure 10.27**).
   ▲ To remove a condition tag, select it in the In list and move it to the Not In list (**Figure 10.28**).

4. Click Apply.

   The selected text is now unconditional (**Figure 10.29**) or the specified condition tags are removed from the selected text (**Figure 10.30**).

✔ Tips

■ To make selected text unconditional using keyboard commands, select the text from which you want to remove the condition tags, and press Ctrl-6 or Control-6.

■ A quick way to remove all condition tags from conditional text is to select any unconditional text and choose Edit > Copy Special > Conditional Text Settings. Then select the text you want to make unconditional and choose Edit > Paste.

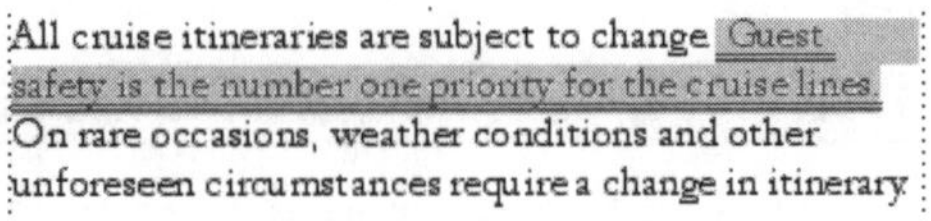

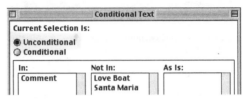

Figure 10.26 Select text that has one or more condition tags.

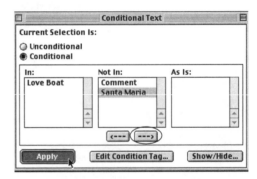

Figure 10.27 In the Conditional Text window, select Unconditional.

Figure 10.28 Move tags to the Not In list.

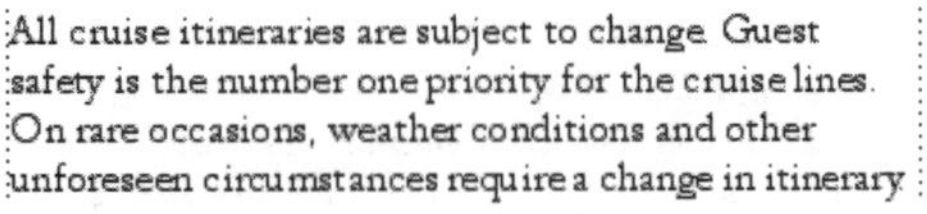

All cruise itineraries are subject to change. Guest safety is the number one priority for the cruise lines. On rare occasions, weather conditions and other unforeseen circumstances require a change in itinerary.

Figure 10.29 The text is now unconditional.

On rare occasions, weather conditions and other unforeseen circumstances require a change in itinerary. In these situations, the cruise line staff will do everything in their power to visit an alternate port of call.¶

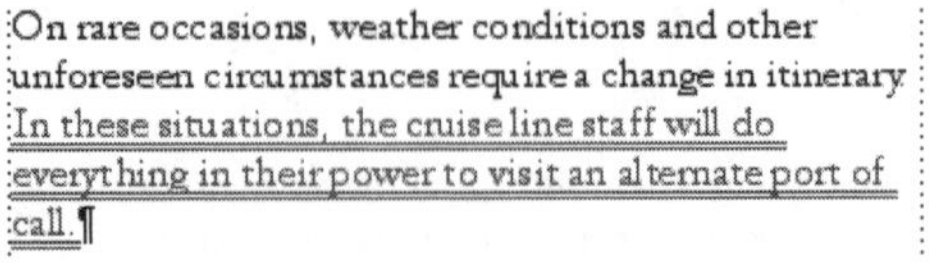

Figure 10.30 In this example, the Love Boat condition was removed, but the selected text still has the Santa Maria condition.

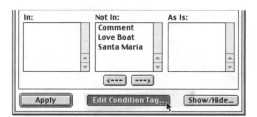

Figure 10.31 In the Conditional Text window, click Edit Condition Tag.

Figure 10.32 In the Tag text box, type a name for the new condition.

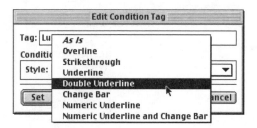

Figure 10.33 Choose a style for the condition indicators.

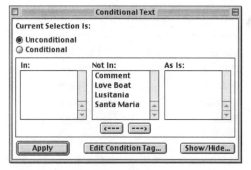

Figure 10.34 The new condition tag appears in the Not In list.

Creating, Changing, Deleting Condition Tags

If you are part or a workgroup or are using corporate templates, condition tags will most likely be set up in the templates and documents you work in. But you can also create your own condition tags.

To create a new condition tag:

1. From the Special menu, choose Conditional Text.

2. In the Conditional Text window, click Edit Condition Tag (**Figure 10.31**).

   The Edit Condition Tag dialog box appears.

3. Type a name for the new condition in the Tag text box (**Figure 10.32**).

4. From the Style pop-up menu, choose a style for the condition indicators (**Figure 10.33**).

5. From the Color pop-up menu, choose a color for the condition indicators.

   Be sure to use a color that you can read on the screen. The menu includes the FrameMaker standard colors along with custom colors that have been created.

6. Click Set.

   The new condition tag appears in the Conditional Text window (**Figure 10.34**).

✔ Tips

■ As with paragraph and character tags, when you create a condition tag, make its name meaningful so you'll remember what it stands for and so will others.

■ Even though you can't see the colors when you print the document on a black-and-white printer, if you use underline, strikethrough, and double-underline, you'll be able to see conditional text.

You can change the condition indicators for an existing condition, but you can't change the tag (condition name). If you try to do so, FrameMaker adds a new condition with the new condition tag.

To change condition indicators for an existing tag:

1. From the Special menu, choose Conditional Text.

2. In the Conditional Text window, select the tag you want to change and click Edit Condition Tag (**Figure 10.35**).

3. In the Edit Condition Tag dialog box, choose a new style and color for the tag in the Condition Indicators area (**Figure 10.36**).

4. Click Set.

   The condition now has new condition indicators. Any text in the document with that condition changes to match the new condition indicators.

✔ Tips

- Do not use magenta as a condition indicator, because FrameMaker reserves magenta for text with multiple conditions and different color condition indicators.

- Standard yellow or green FrameMaker colors are too hard to read on the screen. Create new colors that you can easily distinguish from black and from each other. (See *Defining and Changing Colors and Tints* on page 141.) **Table 10.1** shows some good color choices.

- Think carefully before you create a condition tag. Once you have named it, you can't change the name easily. The only way to do so is to create a new tag, find all text with the old tag in the Find/Change window, change it to the new tag, and finally delete the old tag.

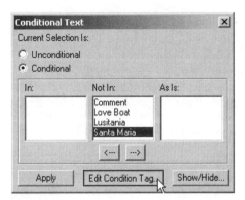

Figure 10.35 Select the tag you want to change and click Edit Condition Tag.

Figure 10.36 Choose a new color from the menu.

Table 10.1

Good Colors for Condition Indicators	
Name you can give the color	Online color library number
Medium Green	115-006633
Maroon	010-660033
Orange	189-FF6633
Navy Blue	071-000066
Purple	040-660099

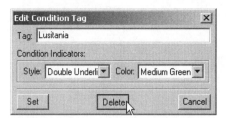

Figure 10.37 In the Edit Condition Tag dialog box, click Delete.

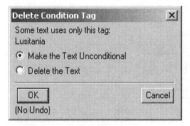

Figure 10.38 If text with the condition tag you deleted exists in the document, this dialog box appears.

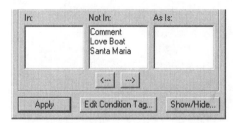

Figure 10.39 The deleted tag disappears from the list in the Conditional Text window.

To delete a condition tag:

1. From the Special menu, choose Conditional Text.

2. In the Conditional Text window, select the tag you want to remove and click Edit Condition Tag.

3. In the Edit Condition Tag dialog box, click Delete (**Figure 10.37**).

   If the condition tag you deleted is not used in the document, it is removed from the list in the Conditional Text window, and you're finished.

   If the condition tag you deleted is used in the document, the Delete Condition Tag dialog box appears (**Figure 10.38**).

4. If you want to make text with the deleted condition unconditional, select Make the Text Unconditional.

   or

   If you want to delete all text in the document with only the deleted condition, select Delete the Text.

5. Click OK.

   The tag disappears from the list in the Conditional Text window (**Figure 10.39**), and text with only the deleted condition is either made unconditional or deleted as you specified in step 4.

✔ Tip

- If you aren't sure whether a condition is used in a document, try to delete the condition tag. If the Delete Condition Tag dialog box appears, you'll know the condition is still used.

CREATING, CHANGING, DELETING CONDITION TAGS

Preparing the Final Document

Once you're ready to prepare files for final exporting or printing, you should follow these steps.

To prepare a final document:

1. Show the conditional text for only this version of the document (see page 189).

2. Check variable definitions for this version of the document. Choose Special > Variable to display the Variable dialog box. Scroll down to the user variables; then select each one and check its definition.

3. Turn off condition indicators (see page 190).

4. Spell check the document. Choose Edit > Spelling Checker to display the Spelling Checker window.

5. Update cross-references and resolve any unresolved cross-references (see page 51).

6. Turn off borders and text symbols (see page 12).

7. Make copies of the files and perform final production as follows:

   ▲ Page through the document, visually inspecting it and adjusting line and page breaks.

   ▲ If the document is part of a book, update generated files.

   ▲ Perform the checks you would for a book: check the TOC, index, and other generated files. (See *Troubleshooting generated files* on page 301.)

8. Export or print the document version. In other words, you branch the document, perform final production, and export or print the document.

To export or print another version of the same document, branch that version and perform final production on those files.

Other Items You Can Make Conditional in a Document

In this chapter you've seen how to work with text, but condition tags can also be applied to the following items in a document:

◆ An anchored frame (which includes its contents)—Select the frame and apply one or more condition tags.

◆ An entire table—Select the table anchor symbol or the table itself and apply one or more condition tags.

◆ One or more table rows (but not columns)—Select table rows and apply one or more condition tags. For more information about condition tags and tables, see *Using Conditional Text in Tables* on page 236.

◆ A cross-reference or variable—Select the cross-reference or variable and apply one or more condition tags.

◆ A footnote—Select the footnote reference in the main text and apply one or more condition tags.

◆ A marker—Select the marker, being careful not to select any surrounding text or spaces, and apply one or more condition tags.

Best Practices for Conditional Documents

The procedures for working in conditional documents are not difficult to implement. The challenge lies in planning and using best practices while you work.

Planning for conditional documents

Here are some planning guidelines:

◆ Plan for the number of versions you need to create now and the additional versions you may need to create in future.

◆ If you are part of a workgroup, get input from as many people in the group as is practical; one person may think of something another person may have overlooked.

◆ Decide which text will work better as conditional text and where you should use variables. For example, in a product guide, use variables for the company name, product name, and product model—but use conditional text where product features differ or where you need to include or exclude information.

Working with conditional documents

◆ Document the condition tags and how they should be used. Then make sure that everyone who subsequently works on the document has access to that information before they start working.

◆ Encourage others in your workgroup not to create ad hoc conditions that are specific to their work. If the condition stays in the document, the next writer will wonder what it's for and what to do with it. It will leave others in your workgroup scratching their heads and trying to find out who created it and whether it's OK to delete it.

◆ Copying and pasting content from one document to another brings in the condition tags from the source document. This is a workflow issue you need to take into account.

◆ Always use the same order for parallel conditional text whenever the conditions occur together. For example, if you're creating a travel brochure with versions for Mediterranean, Caribbean, and Alaskan cruises, put the three in a meaningful order, and each time you have content that needs to be conditionalized, always use the same order.

For technical manuals, you usually order conditions in the sequence in which they were added to the manual.

◆ Decide how to treat punctuation and spaces. When you conditionalize a sentence, phrase, or word, include the space before it *or* the space after it— and always do it the same way. If conditional text begins or ends with punctuation, always include the punctuation.

◆ Conditionalize meaningful units in a document. For example, if you are conditionalizing prices, conditionalize the currency symbol along with the numerical value. The next person who works on the document (and this could be you) needs to be able to make sense of the document with all content, conditional and unconditional, displayed.

WORKING WITH TABLES

TABLE 5: SPORTS BY SEASONS			Title
Season§	**Indoor§**	**Outdoor§**	Heading row
Spring§	Basketball§	Soccer§	
Summer§	Racquetball§	Softball§	Body rows
Fall§	Weight-lifting§	Football§	
Winter§	Hockey§	Skiing§	
Individual and team sports are placed indoors and outdoors.§			Footing row

Figure 11.1 A FrameMaker table and its parts.

FrameMaker tables are some of the best in the business. To determine the features for FrameMaker tables, David Murray, one of the founders of Frame Technology and the architect of the tables feature, looked for every different type of table he could find, from train schedules to financial tables in annual reports to weather reports. He put them all in a big, black binder and by the time FrameMaker shipped with its tables feature, he had most of them covered.

FrameMaker tables are easy to add to layouts, easy to use, and extremely versatile. You can change their structure and the way they look by using table ruling and shading properties. Text inside table cells is formatted the same way as text in a text frame. You can even insert graphics in table cells.

A table can have any or all of the following (**Figure 11.1**):

◆ Title

◆ One or more heading rows

◆ One or more body rows

◆ One or more footing rows

At a minimum, a table must have one body cell.

Adding Tables

When you insert a table into a FrameMaker document, you have a choice of formats. As with paragraph and character formats, the look of a table is determined by its format. All FrameMaker documents come with a choice of two table formats, Format A and Format B. They can be used as is or modified.

To insert a table:

1. From the Table menu, choose Insert Table (**Figure 11.2**).

   The Insert Table dialog box appears.

2. In the Table Format list, select a format for the table you want to insert (**Figure 11.3**).

   Formats A and B appear in the list along with other user-created table formats.

3. If you wish, type new values in the Columns, Body Rows, Heading Rows and Footing Rows text boxes.

   You can also change the number of rows and columns in a table after you add the table to a document (see page 224).

4. Click Insert.

   An anchor appears at the insertion point and a table appears below it (**Figure 11.4**). This is what Format A looks like in many FrameMaker templates. If you had inserted a table with Format B, it might look like the table in **Figure 11.5**.

   Both tables have a title, one heading row, five body rows, and three columns. The table with Format A is left aligned and has a double line between the heading row and the body rows, and the empty paragraphs are left aligned in the table cells.

   The table with Format B is center aligned and has thicker lines at the top and between the heading and body rows, and the empty paragraphs are center aligned in the table cells.

Figure 11.2 Choose Table > Insert Table.

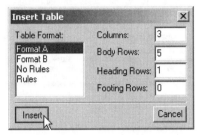

Figure 11.3 Specify a table format. If you wish, you can change the number of columns and rows for the table. Then click Insert

Insurance Rates¶

The following tables present typical rates for a 25-year-old male.

§	§	§
§	§	§
§	§	§
§	§	§
§	§	§
§	§	§

Figure 11.4 An anchor appears at the insertion point, and the table appears below it. This table uses Format A.

Insurance Rates¶

The following tables present typical rates for a 45-year-old male.

§	§	§
§	§	§
§	§	§
§	§	§
§	§	§
§	§	§

Figure 11.5 If you insert a table with Format B, it looks like this.

Table 1: Insurance Rates§		
§	§	§
§	§	§
§	§	§

Figure 11.6 The title frame appears above a table with a title in its format.

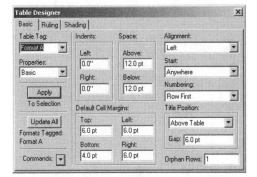

Figure 11.7 The Table Designer.

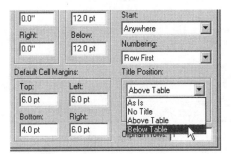

Figure 11.8 From the Title Position pop-up menu, choose Below Table.

§	§	§
§	§	§
§	§	§
Table 1: Insurance Rates §		

Figure 11.9 The table title moves below the table.

Modifying Table Titles

Technical documents usually include a title above or below a table. By default the title frame usually appears above the table (**Figure 11.6**), but you can move it below if you prefer.

To add a title to the table with a title in its format:

◆ Click in the table title frame and type a title.

To move the title below the table, you use the Table Designer. The Table Designer is similar to the Paragraph Designer and Character Designer, providing sets of properties that control the structure and look of the table.

Unlike the Paragraph Catalog and Character Catalog, the Table Catalog doesn't have its own window, but you can access the formats stored in the Table Catalog from the Insert Table dialog box and in the Table Designer.

To move a table title:

1. Click in the table title frame or the table itself.

2. From the Table menu, choose Table Designer.

   or

   Press Ctrl-Alt-T or Command-Option-T.

   The Table Designer appears (**Figure 11.7**).

3. From the Title Position pop-up menu at the bottom left, choose Below Table (**Figure 11.8**).

4. Click Apply.

   The table title moves from the top to the bottom of the table (**Figure 11.9**).

5. To update all tables with the same format, click Update All.

   The change is applied to all tables with the same format and is stored in the Table Catalog.

   (continues on next page)

✔ Tip

■ In the Table Designer, the value in the Gap text box specifies the space between the title text frame and the table (**Figure 11.10**). You can change the value and move the title closer or farther from the table.

To delete a table title:

1. Click in the table title frame or the table itself.

2. From the Table menu, choose Table Designer.

3. In the Table Designer, from the Title Position pop-up menu at the bottom left, choose No Title (**Figure 11.11**).

4. Click Apply.

   The title frame and the table title itself disappear (**Figure 11.12**).

5. To update all tables with the same format, click Update All.

   The change is applied to all tables in the document with the same format and stored in the Table Catalog. If you now insert a table with this format, there will be no table title.

Formatting table titles

A table title paragraph has a default paragraph format, TableTitle (**Figure 11.13**). The words and punctuation (Table 1:) are part of the autonumber properties for the TableTitle format (**Figure 11.14**). You can change the format of the table title in the Paragraph Designer.

To modify the format of a table title:

1. Click in the table title.

2. From the Format menu, choose Paragraphs > Designer.

   In the Paragraph Designer, modify any of the properties you wish. In this example, you'll remove the autonumber.

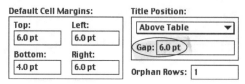

Figure 11.10 The Gap text box in the Table Designer.

Figure 11.11 From the Title Position pop-up menu, choose No Title.

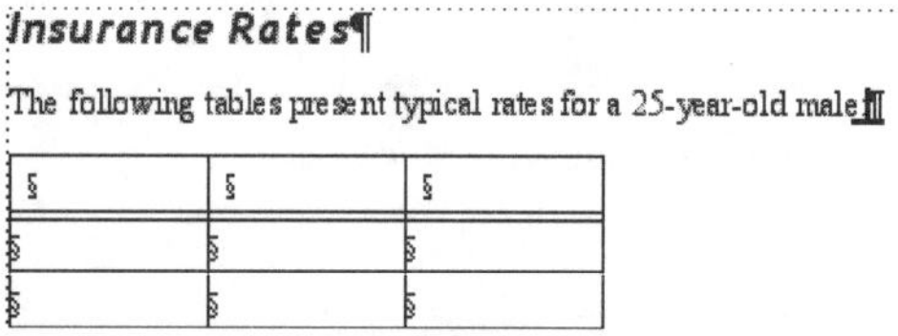

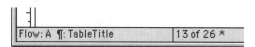

Figure 11.12 The title frame and the title itself are removed from the table.

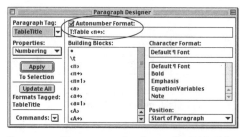

Figure 11.13 The default paragraph format of table titles is TableTitle.

Figure 11.14 The autonumber format for TableTitle paragraphs displayed in the Paragraph Designer.

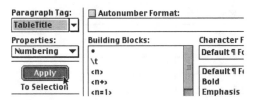

Figure 11.15 Click the Autonumber Format check box twice to remove the autonumber.

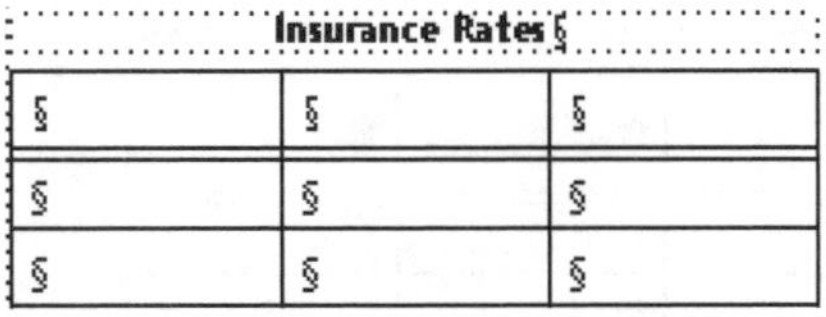

Insurance Rates §

§	§	§
§	§	§
§	§	§

Figure 11.16 In this example, the title now appears without an autonumber.

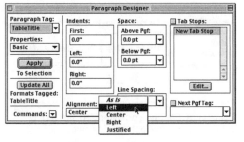

Figure 11.17 From the Alignment pop-up menu, choose a paragraph alignment, such as Left.

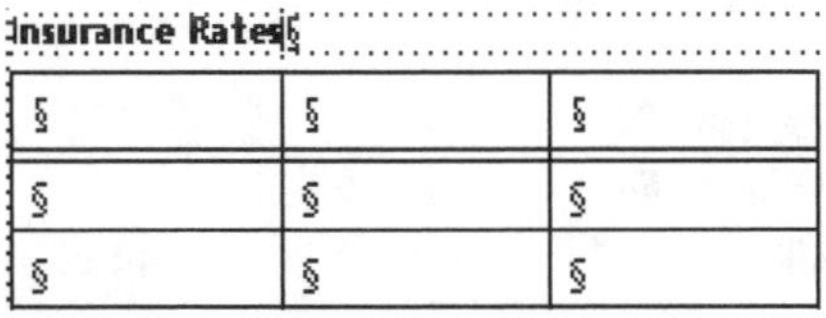

Insurance Rates§

§	§	§
§	§	§
§	§	§

Figure 11.18 In this example, the table title moves to the left side of the text frame.

3. From the Properties pop-up menu, choose Numbering.

4. Click the Autonumber Format check box twice, and click Apply (**Figure 11.15**).

The first click turns the check box to As Is, and the second click turns off autonumbering. When you click Apply, the change is applied to the current table (**Figure 11.16**).

5. To update all tables with the same format, click Update All.

The change is applied to all tables in the document with the same format and stored in the Table Catalog.

In the Basic properties of the Table Designer, you can change the alignment and margins of the title in its frame, as well as any other of the properties.

To change the alignment of a table title:

1. Click in the table title.

2. From the Format menu, choose Paragraphs > Designer.

3. In the Paragraph Designer, display the Basic properties.

4. From the Alignment pop-up menu, choose the paragraph alignment (**Figure 11.17**), and click Apply.

In this example, the title moves from the center to the left of the title text frame (**Figure 11.18**).

✔ Tip

- A table can continue on the next page, and if it does, the table title is repeated on the second page. In fact, the title appears on every page the table occupies, at the top or the bottom of the table, as specified.

Working in Tables

Once you've added a table to the document and modified the title, you'll want to populate the table cells.

To type in a table:

1. Click in the heading cell at the top left and type a column heading (**Figure 11.19**).

2. Press Tab.

   The empty paragraph in the next cell in the heading row is selected (**Figure 11.20**).

3. Type a heading for the second column and press Tab.

   The next cell in the row is selected.

4. Continue typing text and pressing the Tab key (**Figure 11.21**) until you've finished the heading row.

✔ Tips

- When you press Tab in a table cell, you move to the next cell. To enter a tab within a table cell, press Esc Tab.

- When you type in a cell, the text automatically breaks to the next line as if each cell were its own text frame. You can have more than one paragraph in a cell—just press Enter or Return or Shift-Enter or Shift-Return.

- As you type in a cell, its height increases to fit the text you type, as in the first heading cell shown earlier in **Figure 11.21**, but the width of the cell stays the same. To change the width of table cells, see page 228.

- To select the contents of a cell with more than one paragraph, press Esc T H A.

- You can use keyboard shortcuts to select the contents of cells (**Table 11.1**).

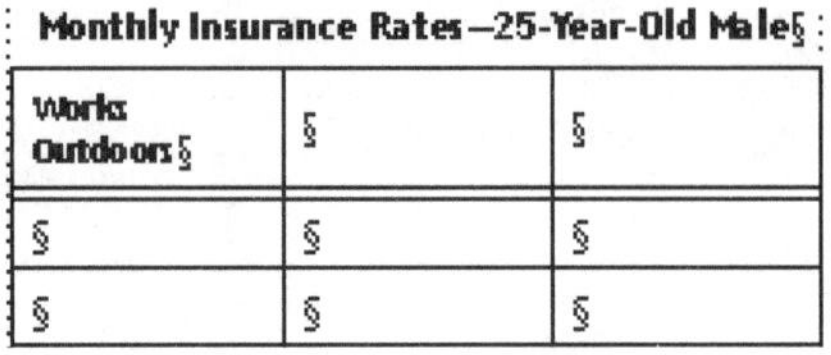

Figure 11.19 Click in the left heading cell and start typing.

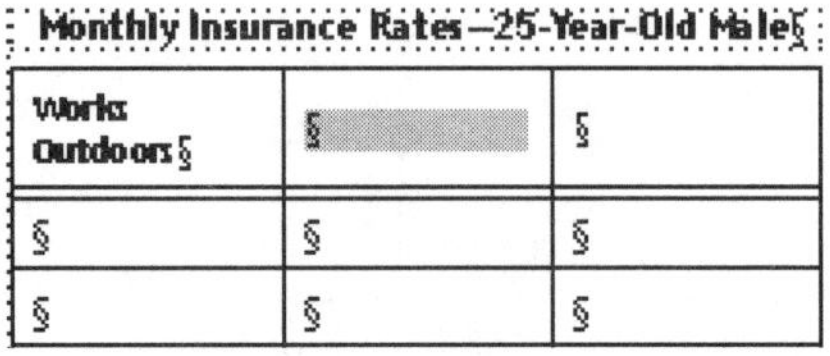

Figure 11.20 When you press Tab, the empty paragraph in the next cell is selected.

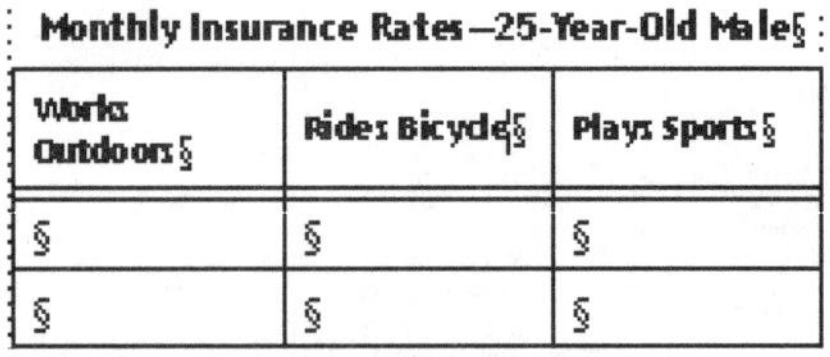

Figure 11.21 Continue pressing Tab and typing until you reach the last heading cell.

Table 11.1

Selecting Contents of Table Cells	
To select the contents of	Press
The next cell	Tab
The previous cell	Shift-Tab
The cell below	Ctrl-Alt-Tab or Control-Tab
The cell above	Ctrl-Alt-Shift-Tab or Control-Shift-Tab

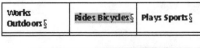

| Works Outdoors § | Rides Bicycles § | Plays Sports § |

| Works Outdoors § | Rides Bicycles § | Plays Sports § |

Figure 11.22 Cell contents selected (top) and cell selected (bottom).

Works Outdoors §	Rides Bicycles §	Plays Sports §
§	§	§
§	§	§
§	§	§

Figure 11.23 When you select a single cell or a block of cells, a selection handle appears on each of the rightmost cells.

Monthly Insurance Rates –25-Year-Old Male§		
Works Outdoors §	Rides Bicycles §	Plays Sports §
§	§	§
§	§	§
§	§	§

Figure 11.24 The entire table is selected, including the title frame.

✋	No table cells on the Clipboard.
	OK

Figure 11.25 This message appears when you paste text from the Clipboard.

Table 11.2

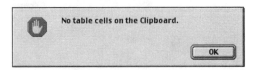

Shortcuts for Selecting in a Table	
To select	Click in a cell and press
An entire row	Esc T H R
An entire column	Esc T H C
The entire table	Esc T H T

Selecting table cells

Selecting table cells is different from selecting their contents (**Figure 11.22**).

To select a single table cell:

◆ Ctrl-click or Option-click the cell.

To select multiple cells:

◆ Drag across the cells you want to select.

or

Click in the first cell and then Shift-double-click or Shift-click in the last cell you want to include.

When you select a block of cells, a selection handle appears on each of the rightmost cells (**Figure 11.23**).

✔ Tips

■ If you select the anchor symbol, the table is selected for purposes of copying, cutting, or deleting, even though the table does not appear to be selected.

■ When the entire table is selected, the title frame is selected as well, and resize handles appear on each rightmost cell (**Figure 11.24**).

■ Use keyboard shortcuts to select a row, a column, or the entire table as shown in **Table 11.2**.

Copying and moving contents of table cells

You can copy, cut, and paste text in cells and from cell to cell in the same way as you do elsewhere in a document.

✔ Tip

■ If you try to paste text from the Clipboard when a cell is selected, an alert message appears (**Figure 11.25**). Click OK and select cell contents rather than the cell itself before pasting.

About the Table Designer and Table Formats

The Table Designer is very much like the Paragraph Designer and Character Designer. It includes the following groups of properties:

◆ **Basic.** Indents, Space Above and Below, Default Cell Margins, Alignment, Start, Numbering, Title Position, and Orphan Rows (**Figure 11.26**)

◆ **Ruling.** Column Ruling, Body Row Ruling, Heading and Footing Ruling, Outside Ruling

◆ **Shading.** Heading and Footing Shading, Body Shading

The left side of the Table Designer functions in the same way as the left side of the other Designers (**Figure 11.27**).

The Table Catalog doesn't have its own small palette like the other Catalogs (see page 28). To access table formats stored in the Table Catalog you use the Table Formats list in the Insert Table dialog box (**Figure 11.28**) or the Table Tag menu in the Table Designer (**Figure 11.29**).

Table formats can be applied to the current table or to all tables with the same table tag. When you apply table formats to an existing table, characteristics of the table, such as the number of rows and columns and column widths, remain unchanged.

The paragraph formats of table cell contents, such as the title, heading, and body cell paragraph formats, are stored with the table format. When you insert a new table, it includes the paragraph formats stored with the table format. When you apply a table format to an existing table, however, the paragraph formats remain unchanged.

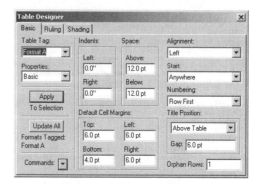

Figure 11.26 The Basic properties in the Table Designer.

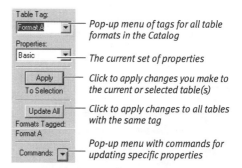

Figure 11.27 The left side of the Designer looks the same no matter which set of properties is displayed on the right.

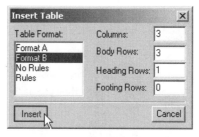

Figure 11.28 In the Insert Table dialog box, formats that have been created and saved appear in the Table Format list.

Figure 11.29 In the Table Catalog, formats appear on the Table Tag menu.

TABLE 1: SPORTS IN SEASON§		
Season§	Indoor§	Outdoor§
Spring§	Basketball§	Soccer§
Summer§	Racquetball§	Softball§
Fall§	Weight-lifting§	Football§
Winter§	Hockey§	Skiing§

] 12 pt

Of course, there are also other forms of exercise as running, aerobics exercise, hiking, and surfing.¶

Figure 11.30 In this example, the space between the bottom of the table and the top of the next line of text is 12 points. Click in the table to change the spacing.

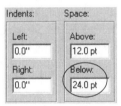

Figure 11.31 The Space Below setting is changed from 12 points to 24 points.

TABLE 1: SPORTS IN SEASON§		
Season§	Indoor§	Outdoor§
Spring§	Basketball§	Soccer§
Summer§	Racquetball§	Softball§
Fall§	Weight-lifting§	Football§
Winter§	Hockey§	Skiing§

] 24 pt

Of course, there are also other forms of exercise as running, aerobics exercise, hiking, and surfing.¶

Figure 11.32 The space below the table is now 24 points.

Using Basic Properties

The Basic properties in the Table Designer control the position of the table in its text column, the default cell margins, where the table starts, the number of rows that should be kept together, and the table's title properties (see page 203).

To control the space above and below a table:

1. Click in the table (**Figure 11.30**), and from the Table menu, choose Table Designer.

   The Table Designer appears.

2. In the Basic properties, type new value in the Space Above and/or Space Below text boxes (**Figure 11.31**).

   To determine the space between a table and the paragraph above or below, FrameMaker compares the space above or below the table with the space below or above the paragraph—and uses the larger value.

3. To apply the change to the current table, click Apply.

   or

   To apply the change to all tables with the same tag, click Update All.

   The space changes to the new value (**Figure 11.32**).

✔ Tip

■ The best way to control the space above and below anchored frames is to put anchored frames in their own paragraphs (see page 158). However, to control the space above and below *tables*, you should anchor them in the paragraph above. That way, the space above and below is specified in the table format, and all tables with the same format will have consistent spacing. In special cases, you can put tables into their own paragraphs, such as when tables follow each other with no intervening paragraphs.

Specifying the position of tables in text frames

The alignment of a table specifies how the table is positioned between its left and right indents. The left and right indents specify the indents for a left-aligned or right-aligned table.

To set table alignment:

1. Click in the table (**Figure 11.33**) and choose Table > Table Designer.

2. In the Basic properties of the Table Designer, choose from the Alignment pop-up menu (**Figure 11.34**) as follows:

   ▲ Choose Left, Center, or Right to left, center, or right align the table in its text column.

   ▲ Choose Side Closest to Binding to align the table with the side of the text column closest to the inside in a double-sided page layout.

   ▲ Choose Side Farthest from Binding to align the table with the side of the text column closest to the outside in a double-sided page layout.

3. To apply the change to the current table, click Apply.

   or

   To apply the change to all tables with the same tag, click Update All.

   The table's alignment changes (**Figure 11.35**).

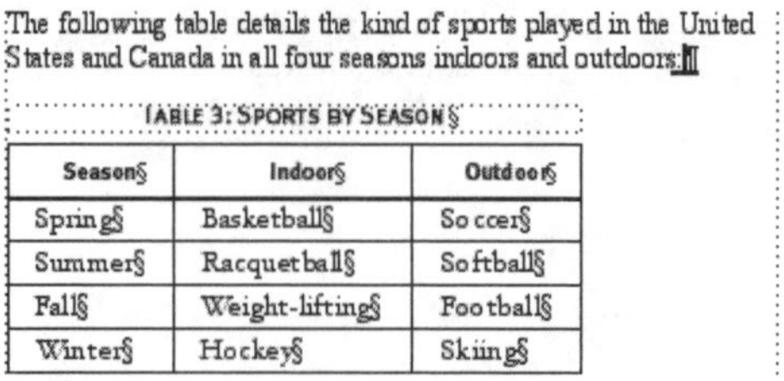

The following table details the kind of sports played in the United States and Canada in all four seasons indoors and outdoors.

Seasons	Indoors	Outdoors
Spring	Basketball	Soccer
Summer	Racquetball	Softball
Fall	Weight-lifting	Football
Winter	Hockey	Skiing

Figure 11.33 This table is left aligned in the text column.

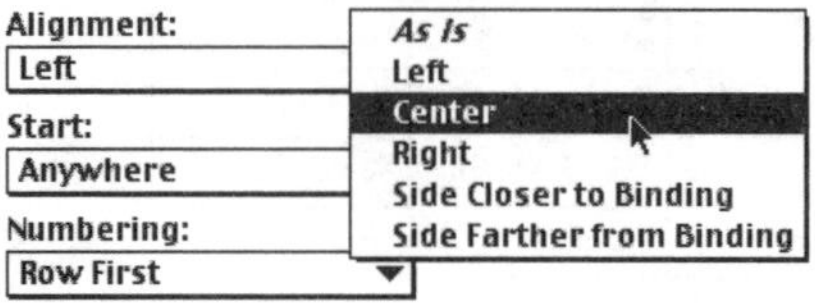

Alignment: Left — As Is / Left / Center / Right / Side Closer to Binding / Side Farther from Binding
Start: Anywhere
Numbering: Row First

Figure 11.34 The Alignment pop-up menu in the Basic properties of the Table Designer.

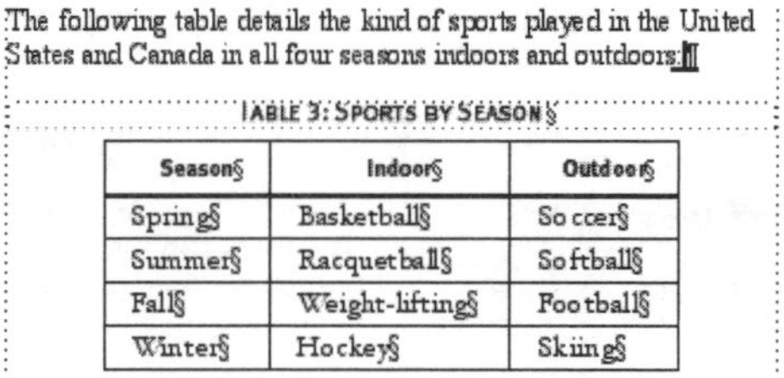

The following table details the kind of sports played in the United States and Canada in all four seasons indoors and outdoors.

Seasons	Indoors	Outdoors
Spring	Basketball	Soccer
Summer	Racquetball	Softball
Fall	Weight-lifting	Football
Winter	Hockey	Skiing

Figure 11.35 This table is now centered in the text column.

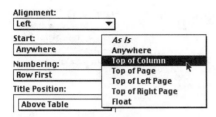

Figure 11.36 The Start pop-up menu in the Basic properties of the Table Designer.

Should I buy travel insurance?¶
We recommend the purchase of travel insurance. Trip insurance will cover you if you have to cancel due to injury, sickness, or death to you, a traveling companion, or family member. It does not cover unstable, pre-existing medical conditions. It will also cover you should something happen to you medically on your trip. Don't risk traveling without arranging for travel insurance in advance.¶
If you cancel your vacation for a covered reason, or incur medical expenses while on your trip, you would need to pay these fees in advance and then file a claim for reimbursement ¶
If you have specific questions about the insurance and its coverage, please contact a Cruise Customer

Trip§	Child§	Adult§
3 days§	$25§	$35§
5 days§	$35§	$45§
7 days§	$50§	$70§
10 days§	$75§	$100§
11+ days§	$100§	$150§

Travel Insurance Rates§

Service injury, sickness, or death to you, a traveling companion, or family member. It does not cover unstable, pre-existing medical conditions. It will also cover you should something happen to you medically on your trip. If you cancel your vacation for a covered reason, or incur medical expenses while on your trip, you would need

Figure 11.37 In this example of the Float setting, the table anchor is located in the first column, but the table starts at the top of the next column. Text backfills at the bottom of the first column.

To control where a table begins:

1. Click in the table and choose Table > Table Designer.

2. In the Basic properties of the Table Designer, choose from the Start pop-up menu (**Figure 11.36**) as follows.

   ▲ Choose Top of Column or Page to start the table at the top of the next column or page.

   ▲ Choose Top of Left or Right Page to start the table at the top of the next left or right page.

   ▲ Choose Float to keep the table anchor in the same position, but if there is not enough room in the text column with the table anchor, to float the table to the top of the first text column that can hold it. Text backfills the space below the line with the anchor (**Figure 11.37**).

3. To apply the change to the current table, click Apply.

   or

   To apply the change to all tables with the same tag, click Update All.

   The table changes position as specified.

USING BASIC PROPERTIES

To keep table rows together in the Table Designer:

1. Click in the table, and from the Table menu, choose Table Designer.

2. Go to the Basic properties in the Table Designer.

3. In the Orphan Rows text box at the bottom right, change the setting to a value larger than 1 (**Figure 11.38**).

4. To apply the change to the current table, click Apply.

   or

   To apply the change to all tables with the same tag, click Update All.

   FrameMaker will now try to keep at least three rows together when a table spans one or more pages.

To keep table rows together in the Row Format dialog box:

1. Click in the row you want to keep with the next or previous row, and from the Table menu, choose Row Format.

   The Row Format dialog box appears.

2. In the Keep With area, do one or both of the following (**Figure 11.39**):

   ▲ To keep the current row with the next row in the table, select Next Row.

   ▲ To keep the current row with the previous row in the table, select Previous Row.

3. Click Set.

   Now if the table spans one or more pages, these rows will stay together.

✔ Tip

■ You can also specify where a row starts in the Row Format dialog box. From the Start Row menu, choose where you want the current row to start (**Figure 11.40**).

Figure 11.38 To keep table rows together change the setting in the Orphan Rows text box to a value larger than 1.

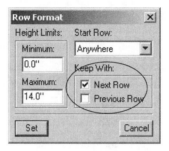

Figure 11.39 To keep table rows together, use the Keep With settings.

Figure 11.40 Choose where you want a row to start from the Start Row menu.

TABLE 1: SPORTS IN SEASON		
Season	**Indoor**	**Outdoor**
1. Spring	2. Basketball	3. Soccer
4. Summer	5. Racquetball	6. Softball
7. Fall	8. Weight-lifting	9. Football
10. Winter	11. Hockey	12. Skiing

Figure 11.41 Autonumbers for paragraphs in these table cells go across rows first.

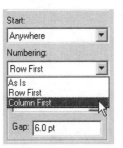

Figure 11.42 The Numbering pop-up menu in the Basic properties of the Table Designer.

TABLE 1: SPORTS IN SEASON		
Season	**Indoor**	**Outdoor**
1. Spring	5. Basketball	9. Soccer
2. Summer	6. Racquetball	10. Softball
3. Fall	7. Weight-lifting	11. Football
4. Winter	8. Hockey	12. Skiing

Figure 11.43 Autonumbers for paragraphs in these table cells now go down columns first.

Autonumbering in table cells

In a table where paragraphs in table cells have autonumbers, you need to tell FrameMaker whether to number them across rows (**Figure 11.41**) or down columns (**Figure 11.43**).

To specify the direction of autonumbering in a table:

1. Click in the table, and choose Table > Table Designer.

2. In the Basic properties of the Table Designer, choose an option from the Numbering pop-up menu (**Figure 11.42**).

3. To apply the change to the current table, click Apply.

   or

   To apply the change to all tables with the same tag, click Update All.

   The direction of autonumbering changes (**Figure 11.43**).

✔ Tip

■ Use autonumbering (rows first) in table cells to create a calendar (see **Figure 11.115** on page 231).

Specifying cell margins

You specify cell margins in two places:

◆ You set default cell margins in the Basic properties of the Table Designer (**Figure 11.44**).

◆ You make changes to the default cell margins in the Table Cell properties of the Paragraph Designer (**Figure 11.45**) for paragraphs in table cells.

FrameMaker uses the cell margins set in the Table Designer and then looks at the Paragraph Designer to see if any margins are customized.

To set default cell margins:

1. Click in the table (**Figure 11.46**) and choose Table > Table Designer.

2. In the Basic properties of the Table Designer, change any or all values in the Default Cell Margins area (**Figure 11.47**).

3. To apply the change to the current table, click Apply.

   or

   To apply the change to all tables with the same tag, click Update All.

   The new default cell margins are applied (**Figure 11.48**). The cell contents move within cells as specified, but column widths remain unchanged.

It's common in tables to position table heading paragraphs a little higher in the cell to make them appear visually centered top to bottom. You accomplish this by adding space to the bottom cell margin in the paragraph format used for heading cells, in this example, CellHeading paragraphs. In **Figure 11.45** shown earlier, the paragraph format is CellHeading.

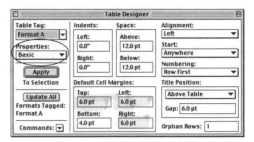

Figure 11.44 Default cell margins are set in the Basic properties of the Table Designer.

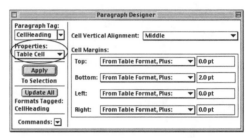

Figure 11.45 Customize cell margins for cells with particular paragraph formats in the Table Cell properties of the Paragraph Designer.

Season	Indoor	Outdoor
Spring	Basketball	Soccer
Summer	Racquetball	Softball
Fall	Weight-lifting	Football

Figure 11.46 In this example, the default left cell margin is 6 points.

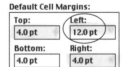

Figure 11.47 Change the value in the Left text box to 12 points.

Season	Indoor	Outdoor
Spring	Basketball	Soccer
Summer	Racquetball	Softball
Fall	Weight-lifting	Football

Figure 11.48 The default left cell margin is now 12 points.

Cell Margins:

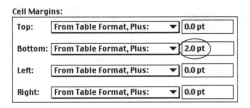

Figure 11.49 To change values in the text boxes, choose From Table Format, Plus from the pop-up menus. To increase the margin, type a positive value.

Cell Margins:

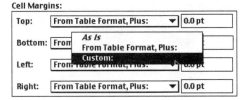

Figure 11.50 Choose Custom to *override* default cell margin values, rather than adding or subtracting space.

Cell Margins:

Top:	From Table Format, Plus: ▼	0.0 pt
Bottom:	Custom: ▼	0.0 pt
Left:	From Table Format, Plus: ▼	0.0 pt
Right:	From Table Format, Plus: ▼	0.0 pt

Figure 11.51 Choosing Custom from the pop-up menu resets the value in the text box to 0.

Cell Margins:

Top:	From Table Format, Plus: ▼	0.0 pt
Bottom:	Custom: ▼	8.0 pt
Left:	From Table Format, Plus: ▼	0.0 pt
Right:	From Table Format, Plus: ▼	0.0 pt

Figure 11.52 Type a value in the text box. The value you use will override the default cell margin.

To customize cell margins:

1. Click in the cell with the paragraph format you want to change, and from the Format menu, choose Paragraphs > Designer.

2. In the Paragraph Designer, display the Table Cell properties.

3. To add space to or subtract space from a default cell margin, choose From Table Format, Plus from the pop-up menu to the left of a text box, and then type a new value in the text box.

   ▲ To increase the margin, type a positive value (**Figure 11.49**). For example, if the default cell margin is 6 points and you add 2 points, the cell margin will be 8 points.

   ▲ To decrease the margin, type a negative value.

   or

   From the pop-up menu to the left of each text box, choose Custom (**Figure 11.50**). The value in the text box is reset to 0 (**Figure 11.51**). Type a value in the text box (**Figure 11.52**).

4. To apply the change to the current paragraph, click Apply.

   or

   To apply the change to all paragraphs with the same tag, click Update All.

   The cell margin is changed as specified.

✔ Tip

■ If you set a custom value and then decide to revert to the default cell margin value, you must go back to the Table Cell properties, choose From Table Format, Plus from the pop-up menu, and change the value in the text box to 0. If you change the value to 0 but still have Custom chosen from the pop-up menu, the default cell margin will be 0, which is probably not what you intend.

Setting Text Alignment in Table Cells

Both the vertical and horizontal alignment of text in table cells are specified in the Paragraph Designer as part of the paragraph's format. You set the horizontal alignment in the Basic properties and the vertical alignment in the Table Cell properties.

To set horizontal alignment of text in table cells:

1. Click in the paragraph you want to align (**Figure 11.53**), and from the Format menu, choose Paragraphs > Designer.

2. In the Paragraph Designer, display the Basic properties.

3. From the Alignment pop-up menu, choose a new alignment (**Figure 11.54**).

4. To apply the change to the current paragraph, click Apply.

   or

   To apply the change to all paragraphs with the same tag, click Update All.

   Paragraph horizontal alignment changes as specified (**Figure 11.55**).

✔ Tips

- If there is more than one paragraph in a table cell, they can have a different horizontal alignment.

- Horizontal and vertical alignment of cell contents apply within the cell area bounded by the cell margins, as shown in **Figure 11.56**, not the cell area bounded by the borders of the cell.

Season§	Indoor§	Outdoor§
Spring§	Basketball§	Soccer§
Summer§	Racquetball§	Softball§
Fall§	Weight-lifting§	Football§
Winter§	Hockey§	Skiing§

Figure 11.53 Body cell paragraphs in this table are left aligned.

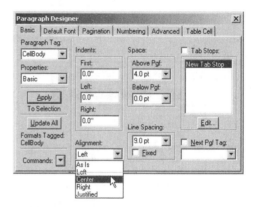

Figure 11.54 Choose from the Alignment pop-up menu in the Paragraph Designer.

Season§	Indoor§	Outdoor§
Spring§	Basketball§	Soccer§
Summer§	Racquetball§	Softball§
Fall§	Weight-lifting§	Football§
Winter§	Hockey§	Skiing§

Figure 11.55 The CellBody paragraphs in this example are now center aligned.

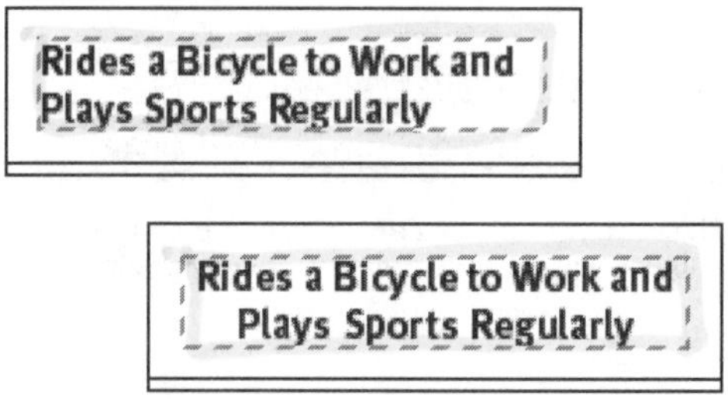

Rides a Bicycle to Work and Plays Sports Regularly

Rides a Bicycle to Work and Plays Sports Regularly

Figure 11.56 The same paragraph aligned left (top) and aligned center (bottom) within the cell margins, represented by the dashed lines.

Physical Condition	Rides a Bicycle to Work and Plays Sports Regularly	Works in the Garden
Unhealthy	$150.00	$100.00
Fair	$125.00	$100.00
Good	$100.00	$75.00
Very Good	$75.00	$75.00
Excellent	$50.00	$50.00

Figure 11.57 Heading cell paragraphs in this table are top aligned.

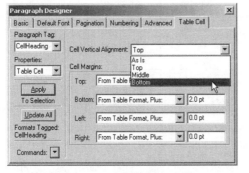

Figure 11.58 Choose from the Cell Vertical Alignment pop-up menu in the Table Cell properties.

Physical Condition	Rides a Bicycle to Work and Plays Sports Regularly	Works in the Garden
Unhealthy	$150.00	$100.00
Fair	$125.00	$100.00
Good	$100.00	$75.00
Very Good	$75.00	$75.00
Excellent	$50.00	$50.00

Figure 11.59 The CellHeading paragraphs in this example are now bottom aligned.

To set vertical alignment of text in table cells:

1. Click in the paragraph you want to align (**Figure 11.57**), and from the Format menu, choose Paragraphs > Designer.

2. In the Paragraph Designer, display the Table Cell properties.

3. From the Cell Vertical Alignment pop-up menu, choose a new alignment (**Figure 11.58**).

4. To apply the change to the current paragraph, click Apply.

   or

   To apply the change to all paragraphs with the same tag, click Update All.

   Paragraph vertical alignment changes as specified (**Figure 11.59**).

✔ Tips

■ Cell vertical alignment applies to *only the first paragraph in a cell*; the cell vertical alignment of subsequent paragraphs is ignored.

■ The paragraph formats of the first heading cell, first body cell, and first footing cell are stored as part of the table format in the Table Catalog. If you change the properties of any of these paragraphs and then store them with the table format by clicking Update All, tables you insert in the future with the same table format will use the custom settings.

Using Table Ruling Properties

Tables can look very different depending on the rules, or lines, they have around the outside and between rows and columns. Tables with no rules at all, for example, just look like lists. Ruling properties, shown in **Figure 11.60**, are saved with table formats and tables you insert will use these properties.

Setting ruling styles inside tables

In the Ruling properties of the Table Designer, you can set the ruling style for the following:

◆ Lines between columns, with a custom style for one designated column separator

◆ Lines between body rows, with a custom style every *n* rows, where *n* is a number you specify

◆ The line that separates heading or footing rows from body rows

To change column ruling:

1. Click in the table (**Figure 11.61**) and choose Table > Table Designer.

2. In the Table Designer, from the Properties menu, choose Ruling.

3. In the Column Ruling area, specify your choices. In this example, from the first pop-up menu, choose 1st, and from the second, choose Double (**Figure 11.62**).

   You're telling FrameMaker to use a Double line to the right of the first column and Thin lines to the right of all other columns.

4. To apply the change to the current paragraph, click Apply.

   In this example, a double line now appears to the right of the first column in the table (**Figure 11.63**).

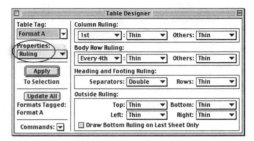

Figure 11.60 Choose Ruling from the Properties menu to display table ruling properties.

Physical Condition	Plays Sports	Works in the Garden
Unhealthy	$150.00	$100.00
Fair	$125.00	$100.00
Good	$100.00	$75.00
Very Good	$75.00	$75.00

Figure 11.61 In this example, all lines between columns are set to Thin.

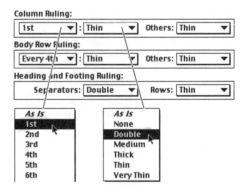

Figure 11.62 In this example, in the Column Ruling area, choose 1st from the first pop-up menu and then Double.

Physical Condition	Plays Sports	Works in the Garden
Unhealthy	$150.00	$100.00
Fair	$125.00	$100.00
Good	$100.00	$75.00
Very Good	$75.00	$75.00

Figure 11.63 The line after the first column is now set to Double.

USING TABLE RULING PROPERTIES

Season	Occupancy	Inside Cabin	Outside Cabin
Spring	Single/Double	$750/$1,000	$1,250/$1,500
Summer	Single/Double	$750/$1,000	$1,250/$1,500
Mid-Season	Single/Double	$1,000/$1,250	$1,500/$1,750
Fall	Single/Double	$1,250/$1,500	$1,750/$2,000
Winter	Single/Double	$1,500/$1,750	$2,000/$2,500

Figure 11.64 In this example, all lines between body rows are set to Thin.

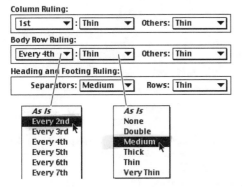

Figure 11.65 In the Body Row Ruling area, choose Every 2nd from the first pop-up menu and Medium from the second.

Season	Occupancy	Inside Cabin	Outside Cabin
Spring	Single/Double	$750/$1,000	$1,250/$1,500
Summer	Single/Double	$750/$1,000	$1,250/$1,500
Mid-Season	Single/Double	$1,000/$1,250	$1,500/$1,750
Fall	Single/Double	$1,250/$1,500	$1,750/$2,000
Winter	Single/Double	$1,500/$1,750	$2,000/$2,500

Figure 11.66 Every second line between body cells is now set to Medium.

Furnished Apartment For Rent!		
Room	**Floor Size**	**Area Rug**
Living Room	16' x 14'	10' x 12'
Dining Room	14' x 12'	8' x 10'
Kitchen	12' x 12'	n/a
Bathroom	10' x 8'	4' x 6'
Master Bedroom	14' x 10'	8' x 10'
Guest Bedroom	10' x 16'	5' x 9'

Figure 11.67 Example of a table with no rules.

To change body row ruling:

1. Click in the table (**Figure 11.64**) and choose Table > Table Designer.

2. In the Table Designer, from the Properties menu, choose Ruling.

3. In the Body Row Ruling area, specify your choices. In this example, from the first pop-up menu, choose Every 2nd, and from the second, choose Medium (**Figure 11.65**). You're telling FrameMaker to use a Medium line after every second body row and Thin for lines between all other rows.

4. To apply the change to the current table, click Apply.

   With these settings, medium lines now appear after the second and fourth body rows (**Figure 11.66**).

✔ Tips

- In the tasks on this and the previous page, you could have chosen a different ruling style from the Others menu (the rightmost pop-up menu) in addition to the styles shown in the examples.

- Try to make sure that the thickness of table ruling harmonizes with the weight of fonts in the document and other graphic elements.

- To create a list with multiple columns, use a table with no rules at all, such as the one shown in **Figure 11.67**. Choose None from all of the pop-up menus in the Ruling properties in the Table Designer.

To change separator ruling between heading and body rows:

1. Click in the table (**Figure 11.68**), and choose Table > Table Designer.

2. In the Table Designer, from the Properties menu, choose Ruling.

3. In the Heading and Footing Ruling area, from the Separators pop-up menu, choose an option, such as Medium (**Figure 11.69**).

4. To apply the change to the current table, click Apply.

   In this example, the ruling style of the line between the heading row and the first body row changes to Medium (**Figure 11.70**).

✔ Tips

- If there are multiple heading or footing rows, the separator ruling style is used between the row closest to the adjacent body row, as shown in **Figure 11.71**.

- Zoom in to a high magnification, say 200 percent, to see how different ruling styles look. You will find it easier to see the difference between Thin and Medium, or Medium and Thick lines.

- Ruling styles look different on the screen, printed on a laser printer, printed commercially, and in a PDF file. Before you finalize ruling styles for a table format, do some testing to see how things will look in their final form. If you'll be printing commercially, be sure you include a table in your printing test.

Season	Occupancy	Inside Cabin	Outside Cabin
Spring	Single/Double	$1,000/$1,250	$1,500/$1,750
Summer	Single/Double	$1,000/$1,250	$1,500/$1,750
Fall	Single/Double	$1,250/$1,500	$1,750/$2,000
Winter	Single/Double	$1,500/$1,750	$2,000/$2,500

Figure 11.68 In this example, the line between the heading and body rows is set to Double.

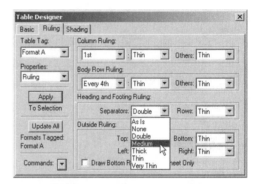

Figure 11.69 In this example, from the Separators menu, choose Medium.

Season	Occupancy	Inside Cabin	Outside Cabin
Spring	Single/Double	$1,000/$1,250	$1,500/$1,750
Summer	Single/Double	$1,000/$1,250	$1,500/$1,750
Fall	Single/Double	$1,250/$1,500	$1,750/$2,000
Winter	Single/Double	$1,500/$1,750	$2,000/$2,500

Figure 11.70 The lines separating the heading row from the first body row is now set to Medium.

Season	Inside Cabin Single/Double	Outside Cabin Single/Double
Spring	$1,000/$1,250	$1,500/$1,750
Summer	$1,000/$1,250	$1,500/$1,750
Fall	$1,250/$1,500	$1,750/$2,000
Winter	$1,500/$1,750	$2,000/$2,500

Figure 11.71 This table has two heading rows and uses a separator ruling style between the bottom heading row and the first body row.

Physical Conditions	Plays Sports §	Gardens§
Unhealthy§	$150.00	$100.00
Fair§	$125.00	$100.00
Good§	$100.00	$75.00
Very Good§	$75.00	$75.00
Excellent§	$50.00	$50.00

Figure 11.72 In this example, the top, bottom, left, and right outside rules are set to Thin.

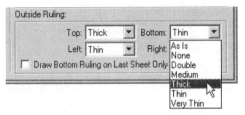

Figure 11.73 From the Top and Bottom pop-up menus, choose Thick.

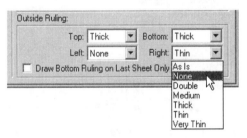

Figure 11.74 From the Left and Right pop-up menus, choose None.

Physical Conditions	Plays Sports §	Gardens§
Unhealthy§	$150.00	$100.00
Fair§	$125.00	$100.00
Good§	$100.00	$75.00
Very Good§	$75.00	$75.00
Excellent§	$50.00	$50.00

Figure 11.75 The table looks different with thick top and bottom outside lines and no left and right outside lines.

Setting table borders

You specify the outside borders separately, with one pop-up menu for each of the four borders: top, bottom, left, and right.

To change outside ruling style:

1. Click in the table (**Figure 11.72**) and choose Table > Table Designer.

2. In the Table Designer, from the Properties menu, choose Ruling.

3. In the Outside Ruling area, from the Top and Bottom pop-up menus, choose an option, such as Thick (**Figure 11.73**).

4. From the Left and Right pop-up menus, choose an option, such as None (**Figure 11.74**).

5. To apply the change to the current table, click Apply.

   The table in this example now has thick lines at the top and bottom and no lines on the sides, as you specified (**Figure 11.75**).

✔ Tip

■ When you remove rules from around the outside of a table, be careful that the table is still read as a table and doesn't float off the page. One way to do this is to ensure that text in table cells adjacent to an outside border is not too far from the outside border, to avoid unnecessary white space. You may need to experiment before you find exactly the right look.

Using Table Shading Properties

You can use table shading properties to create reverse text for a heading row or to shade alternate rows or columns. Shading properties are saved with table formats and tables you insert will use these properties.

To change heading and footing shading:

1. Click in the table (**Figure 11.76**) and choose Table > Table Designer.

2. In the Table Designer, from the Properties menu, choose Shading (**Figure 11.77**).

3. In the Heading and Footing Shading area, choose a percentage from the Fill pop-up menu (**Figure 11.78**).

   In this example, a 50 percent fill is selected for the heading row.

4. From the Color pop-up menu, choose a color if you wish.

   The Color pop-up menu contains FrameMaker standard colors plus all custom colors that have been created and saved.

5. To apply the change to the current table, click Apply.

   The table heading row in this example now has a 50 percent red fill (**Figure 11.79**).

✔ Tip

■ For black text to be readable on a fill, the fill must be a percentage less than 50 percent. To make the text more readable, you can also reverse the text to a light color.

Season	Occupancy	Inside Cabin	Outside Cabin
Spring	Single/Double	$750/$1,000	$1,250/$1,500
Summer	Single/Double	$750/$1,000	$1,250/$1,500
Mid-Season	Single/Double	$1,000/$1,250	$1,500/$1,750
Fall	Single/Double	$1,250/$1,500	$1,750/$2,000
Winter	Single/Double	$1,500/$1,750	$2,000/$2,500

Figure 11.76 The heading row in this table has no fill.

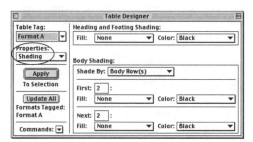

Figure 11.77 Choose Shading from the Properties menu to display table shading properties.

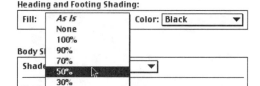

Figure 11.78 From the Fill menu, choose a percent shade, such as 50%.

Season	Occupancy	Inside Cabin	Outside Cabin
Spring	Single/Double	$750/$1,000	$1,250/$1,500
Summer	Single/Double	$750/$1,000	$1,250/$1,500
Mid-Season	Single/Double	$1,000/$1,250	$1,500/$1,750
Fall	Single/Double	$1,250/$1,500	$1,750/$2,000
Winter	Single/Double	$1,500/$1,750	$2,000/$2,500

Figure 11.79 The heading row now has a fill of 50% red.

Season	Occupancy	Inside Cabin	Outside Cabin
Spring	Single/Double	$750/$1,000	$1,250/$1,500
Summer	Single/Double	$750/$1,000	$1,250/$1,500
Mid-Season	Single/Double	$1,000/$1,250	$1,500/$1,750
Fall	Single/Double	$1,250/$1,500	$1,750/$2,000
Winter	Single/Double	$1,500/$1,750	$2,000/$2,500

Figure 11.80 Light text on a darker fill creates reverse type for cell headings.

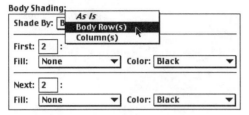

Figure 11.81 From the Shade By pop-up menu, choose Body Row(s).

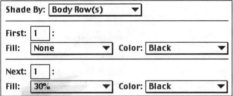

Figure 11.82 Type values in the First and/or Last text box and choose a percent shade from the Fill menu.

Season	Occupancy	Inside Cabin	Outside Cabin
Spring	Single/Double	$750/$1,000	$1,250/$1,500
Summer	Single/Double	$750/$1,000	$1,250/$1,500
Mid-Season	Single/Double	$1,000/$1,250	$1,500/$1,750
Fall	Single/Double	$1,250/$1,500	$1,750/$2,000
Winter	Single/Double	$1,500/$1,750	$2,000/$2,500

Figure 11.83 If you add more rows to the table, every second row will have a fill of 30%.

To reverse text color in table heading rows:

1. Click in the table cell with a fill, and from the Formats menu, choose Paragraphs > Designer.

2. In the Paragraph Designer, display the Default Font properties.

3. From the Color menu, choose a light color, for example, White.

4. Click Apply to check whether the text is readable (**Figure 11.80**).

You may need to go back and increase the fill percentage in the heading cells.

5. If the text looks right, you may want to create a new paragraph format and call it CellHeading Fill.

If you plan to use different formats for different effects, you might instead call the new heading format CellHeading 50%.

To shade alternate rows of a table:

1. Click in the table and choose Table > Table Designer.

2. In the Table Designer, from the Properties menu, choose Shading.

3. In the Body Shading area, from the Shade By pop-up menu, choose Body Row(s) or Column(s) (**Figure 11.81**).

4. In the First and/or Next text box, type a number of rows or columns.

In this example, you'll shade alternate rows by typing 1 in both text boxes.

5. From the Fill pop-up menu in the First and/or Next area, choose a percentage (**Figure 11.82**).

A 30-percent fill should not make the black text unreadable.

6. Click Apply.

Every second row now has a fill of 30 percent black (**Figure 11.83**).

USING TABLE SHADING PROPERTIES

Modifying Rows and Columns

You can add, delete, move, and resize rows and columns in FrameMaker tables.

Adding and deleting rows and columns

To add a row or column:

1. Click in a table (**Figure 11.84**).

2. From the Table menu, choose Add Rows or Columns (**Figure 11.85**).

   The Add Rows or Columns dialog box appears.

3. To add rows, type a number in the Add Row(s) text box and choose from the pop-up menu as follows:

   ▲ Choose Above or Below Selection to add one or more rows above or below the selected row or the row with the insertion point.

   ▲ Choose To Heading or To Footing to add one or more rows to the heading or footing rows below the current rows.

4. To add columns, type a number in the Add Column(s) text box and choose from the pop-up menu as follows (**Figure 11.86**):

   ▲ Choose Left of Selection to add one or more columns to the left of the selected column or the column with the insertion point.

   ▲ Choose Right of Selection to add one or more columns to the right of the selected column or the column with the insertion point.

5. Click Add.

   The new empty rows or columns appear in the specified location (**Figure 11.87**). Table cells in the new rows or columns have the same paragraph formats as the row or column with the insertion point.

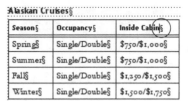

Figure 11.84 Click in the table to add a row or column. In this example, click the column to the left of where you want to add the new column.

Figure 11.85 Choose Table > Add Rows or Columns.

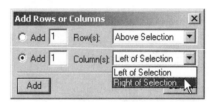

Figure 11.86 Type a number in the Add text box and choose an option from the pop-up menu.

Alaskan Cruises§

Season§	Occupancy§	Inside Cabin§	§
Spring§	Single/Double§	$750/$1,000§	§
Summer§	Single/Double§	$750/$1,000§	§
Fall§	Single/Double§	$1,250/$1,500§	§
Winter§	Single/Double§	$1,500/$1,750§	§

Figure 11.87 In this example, a new blank column appears to the right of the column with the insertion point.

Alaskan Cruises§

Season§	Occupancy§	Inside Cabin§	Outside Cabin§
Spring§	Single/Double§	$750/$1,000§	$1,250/$1,500§
Summer§	Single/Double§	$750/$1,000§	$1,250/$1,500§
Fall§	Single/Double§	$1,250/$1,500§	$1,750/$2,000§
Winter§	Single/Double§	$1,500/$1,750§	$2,000/$2,500§

Figure 11.88 Select rows or columns to delete.

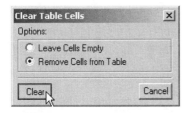

Figure 11.89 Select Remove Cells From Table to delete rows or columns. Then click Clear.

Alaskan Cruises§

Season§	Occupancy§	Inside Cabin§	Outside Cabin§
Spring§	Single/Double§	$750/$1,000§	$1,250/$1,500§
Fall§	Single/Double§	$1,250/$1,500§	$1,750/$2,000§
Winter§	Single/Double§	$1,500/$1,750§	$2,000/$2,500§

Figure 11.90 The selected row is deleted.

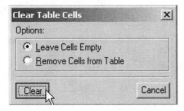

Figure 11.91 Select Leave Cells Empty to delete the text in selected table cells. Then click Clear.

To delete a row or column:

1. Select rows or columns you want to delete (**Figure 11.88**).

2. Press the Back Space or Delete key.

   The Clear Table Cells dialog box appears.

3. Select Remove Cells from Table and click Clear (**Figure 11.89**).

   The selected rows or columns are deleted (**Figure 11.90**).

To delete text in table cells:

1. Select the table cells whose contents you want to delete.

2. Press Back Space or Delete.

3. In the Clear Table Cells dialog box, select Leave Cells Empty and click Clear (**Figure 11.91**).

   The text in the selected table cells is deleted and the cells are now empty.

Copying and moving rows and columns

You can copy, cut, and move table rows and columns in much the same way as with text.

To copy or cut rows or columns:

1. Select the rows or columns you want to copy or cut.

2. To copy rows or columns, from the Edit menu, choose Copy.

   The selected rows or columns are copied to the Clipboard.

   or

   To cut rows or columns, from the Edit menu, choose Cut.

   The Cut Table Cells dialog box appears.

3. Select Remove Cells from Table and click Cut.

   The selected rows or columns are cut and copied to the Clipboard.

   (continues on next page)

✔ Tips

■ If you don't select entire rows or columns for deletion, the contents of table cells will be deleted without a prompt to delete the contents or the cells themselves. If this happens, choose Edit > Undo immediately and make sure that you select *all cells* in the rows or columns before deleting.

■ To select an entire row, Ctrl- or Option-double-click a column border in the row; to select an entire column, Ctrl- or Option-double-click a row border in the column (**Figure 11.92**).

To paste rows or columns:

1. Copy or cut rows or columns to the Clipboard.

2. Click in the row or column next to where you want to insert the rows or columns from the Clipboard.

3. From the Edit menu, choose Paste.

   ▲ If you copied rows to the Clipboard, the Paste Rows dialog box appears (**Figure 11.93**).

   ▲ If you copied columns to the Clipboard, the Paste Columns dialog box appears (**Figure 11.94**).

4. Select where you want the rows or columns from the Clipboard to be pasted.

   The rows or columns are pasted to the location as specified (**Figure 11.95**).

✔ Tips

■ To divide a table into two tables, cut rows or columns from the table and paste them where you want the new table.

■ To combine two tables, cut rows or columns from one table and paste them into another table.

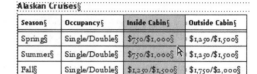

Figure 11.92 To select a column, Ctrl- or Option-double-click a row border in the column.

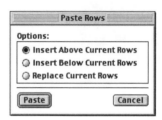

Figure 11.93 Select a location for the rows from the Clipboard.

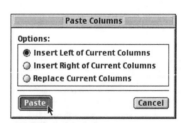

Figure 11.94 Select a location for the columns from the Clipboard.

Alaskan Cruises§			
Season§	Occupancy§	Inside Cabin§	Outside Cabin§
Spring§	Single/Double§	$750/$1,000§	$1,250/$1,500§
Summer§	Single/Double§	$750/$1,000§	$1,250/$1,500§
Fall§	Single/Double§	$1,250/$1,500§	$1,750/$2,000§
Winter§	Single/Double§	$1,500/$1,750§	$2,000/$2,500§

Figure 11.95 The rows or columns on the Clipboard are pasted into the table.

Alaskan Cruises§

Season§	Occupancy§	Inside Cabin§	Outside Cabin§
Spring§	1 Person/2 People§	$750/$1,000§	$1,250/$1,500§
Summer§	1 Person/2 People§	$750/$1,000§	$1,250/$1,500§
Fall§	1 Person/2 People§	$1,250/$1,500§	$1,750/$2,000§
Winter§	1 Person/2 People§	$1,500/$1,750§	$2,000/$2,500§

Figure 11.96 Select the rows or columns you want to substitute and copy them to the Clipboard.

Caribbean Cruises§

Season§	Occupancy§	Inside Cabin§	Outside Cabin§
Spring§	Single/Double§	$1,000/$1,250§	$1,500/$1,750§
Summer§	Single/Double§	$1,000/$1,250§	$1,500/$1,750§
Fall§	Single/Double§	$1,250/$1,500§	$1,750/$2,000§
Winter§	Single/Double§	$1,500/$1,750§	$2,000/$2,500§

Figure 11.97 Select the rows or columns you want to replace.

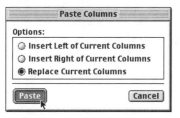

Figure 11.98 Click Replace Current Columns and click Paste.

Caribbean Cruises§

Season§	Occupancy§	Inside Cabin§	Outside Cabin§
Spring§	1 Person/2 People§	$1,000/$1,250§	$1,500/$1,750§
Summer§	1 Person/2 People§	$1,000/$1,250§	$1,500/$1,750§
Fall§	1 Person/2 People§	$1,250/$1,500§	$1,750/$2,000§
Winter§	1 Person/2 People§	$1,500/$1,750§	$2,000/$2,500§

Figure 11.99 The rows or columns on the Clipboard replace the selected rows or columns.

To replace selected rows or columns:

1. Select the rows or columns you want to use as replacements and copy or cut them to the Clipboard (**Figure 11.96**).

2. Select the rows or columns you want to replace (**Figure 11.97**).

3. From the Edit menu, choose Paste.

4. In the Paste Rows or Paste Columns dialog box, select Replace Current Rows or Replace Current Columns and click Paste (**Figure 11.98**).

   ▲ If the number of rows or columns on the Clipboard exactly matches the number of selected rows or columns, the rows or columns are replaced exactly.

   ▲ If the number of rows or columns on the Clipboard is greater than the number of selected rows or columns, FrameMaker pastes as many rows or columns as it can fit.

   ▲ If the number of rows or columns on the Clipboard is less than the number of selected rows or columns, FrameMaker pastes the rows or columns from the Clipboard once and then again, until the selected area is filled.

The rows or columns from the Clipboard replace the selected rows or columns (**Figure 11.99**).

MODIFYING ROWS AND COLUMNS

Resizing Rows and Columns

One of the most versatile features of FrameMaker tables is the ability to resize columns in a number of different ways:

◆ Drag a column boundary.

◆ Use options in the Resize Selected Columns dialog box for more precision.

◆ Copy the column width of one column and paste it to another column.

To resize a column by dragging:

1. Select a column or a cell in the column you want to resize.

   Handles appear on the right cell border (**Figure 11.100**).

2. To change the column width, making the entire table narrower or wider, drag the selection handle (**Figure 11.101**).

   or

   To change the border so that one column gets wider and the adjacent column gets narrower without changing the overall width of the table, Alt-drag or Shift-drag a selection handle

   The column width changes (**Figure 11.102**).

✔ Tips

■ You can select one or more columns to resize by dragging. If you select more than one column, the total width is changed, but each column maintains its width proportionally, as shown in **Figure 11.103**.

■ Although the examples here show resizing rightmost columns in a table, you can select and resize any column in a table, including inside columns.

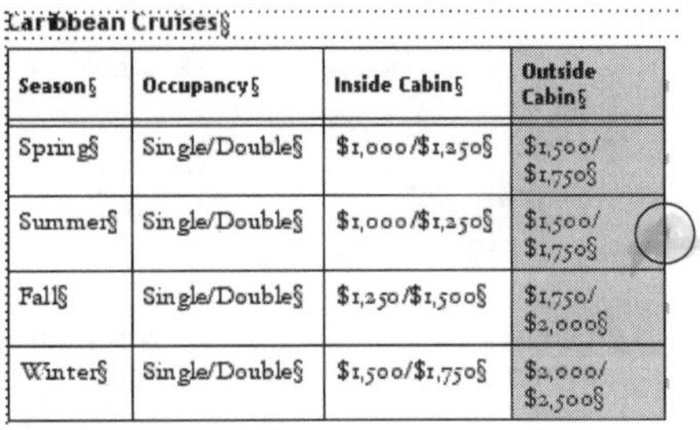

Figure 11.100 When you select a column, resize handles appear on the rightmost cells.

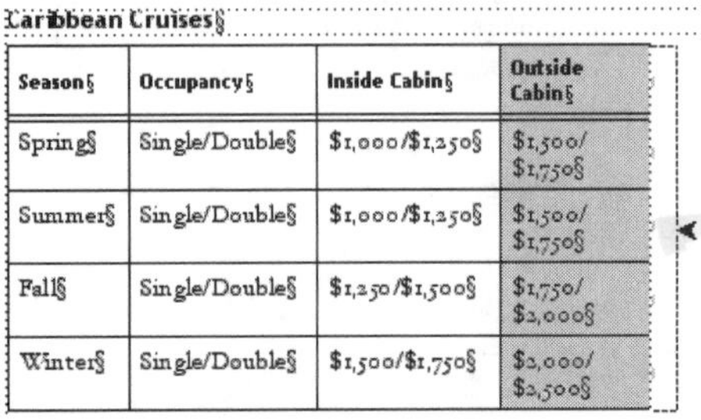

Figure 11.101 Dragging to make column wider.

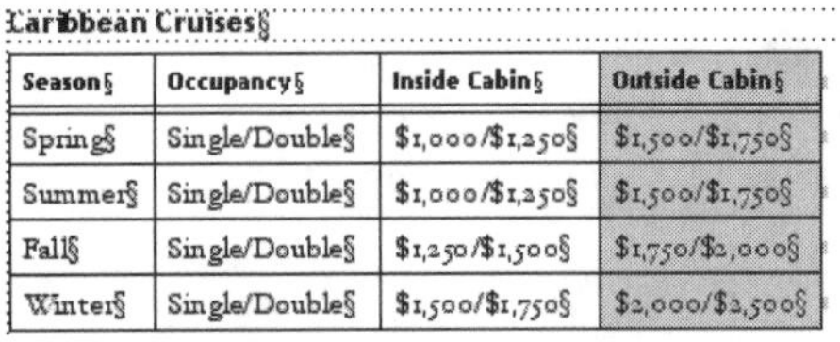

Figure 11.102 After dragging to make the column wider.

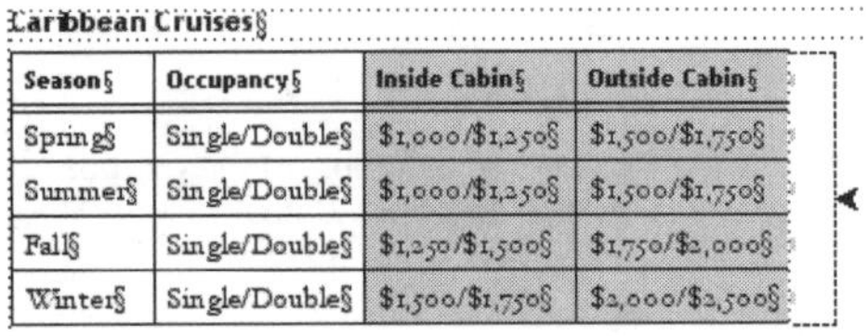

Figure 11.103 When you select and drag multiple columns to resize them, the columns' relative proportions stay the same.

Season§	Occupancy§	Inside Cabin§	Outside Cabin§
Spring§	Single/Double§	$1,000/$1,250§	$1,500/$1,750§
Summer§	Single/Double§	$1,000/$1,250§	$1,500/$1,750§
Fall§	Single/Double§	$1,250/$1,500§	$1,750/$2,000§
Winter§	Single/Double§	$1,500/$1,750§	$2,000/$2,500§

Width of text column = 5 "

Figure 11.104 Select one or more columns.

Figure 11.105 Choose Table > Resize Columns.

Table Window Help
Insert Table...

Table Designer...   Ctrl+T
Row Format...
Custom Ruling & Shading...
Add Rows or Columns...
Resize Columns...

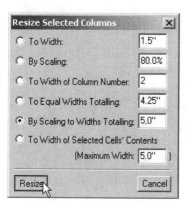

Resize Selected Columns

- To Width: `1.5"`
- By Scaling: `80.0%`
- To Width of Column Number: `2`
- To Equal Widths Totalling: `4.25"`
- By Scaling to Widths Totalling: `5.0"`
- To Width of Selected Cells' Contents
  (Maximum Width: `5.0"`)

Resize   Cancel

Figure 11.106 Use the Resize Selected Columns dialog box to resize columns precisely.

Season§	Occupancy§	Inside Cabin§	Outside Cabin§
Spring§	Single/Double§	$1,000/$1,250§	$1,500/$1,750§
Summer§	Single/Double§	$1,000/$1,250§	$1,500/$1,750§
Fall§	Single/Double§	$1,250/$1,500§	$1,750/$2,000§
Winter§	Single/Double§	$1,500/$1,750§	$2,000/$2,500§

Figure 11.107 After resizing by scaling to a width totalling the width of the text column.

■ Turn on Snap to align the column border to the invisible snap grid.

To resize columns in the Resize Selected Columns dialog box:

1. Select one or more columns or click in a column you want to resize (**Figure 11.104**).

2. From the Table menu, choose Resize Columns (**Figure 11.105**).

   The Resize Selected Columns dialog box appears (**Figure 11.106**).

3. Choose from the following resize options:

   ▲ To specify a width for the selected columns, type a value in the To Width text box.

   ▲ To scale the width of the selected columns, enter a percentage in the By Scaling text box.

   ▲ To make the width of the selected columns each equal to the width of another column in the same table, type a column number in the To Width of Column Number text box.

   ▲ To make the width of the selected columns equal and add up to a specific width, type a value in the To Equal Widths Totalling text box.

   ▲ To make the total width of the selected columns a specific width, while keeping their relative widths the same, type a value in the By Scaling to Widths Totalling text box.

   ▲ To set the width to match the widest paragraph or frame in the selected cells, select To Width of Selected Cells' Contents. To set a maximum width for the selected cells, type a value in the Maximum Width text box.

4. Click Resize.

   The selected column or columns are resized as specified (**Figure 11.107**).

   (continues on next page)

RESIZING ROWS AND COLUMNS

✔ Tip

- When you display the Resize Selected Columns dialog box, the values in the To Width and To Equal Widths Totalling text boxes represent the total width of the selected columns.

  The values in the By Scaling to Widths Totalling and To Width of Selected Cells' Contents text boxes represent the width of the text column that contains the table.

To copy and paste a column width:

1. Select or click in the column whose width you want to copy (**Figure 11.108**).

2. From the Edit menu, choose Copy Special > Table Column Width (**Figure 11.109**).

   The width of the column is pasted to the Clipboard.

3. Select or click in the column you want to resize (**Figure 11.110**).

4. From the Edit menu, choose Paste.

   The column width is pasted from the Clipboard and the column width changes (**Figure 11.111**). The total width of the table changes, but nothing else, including the column cell contents.

Alaskan Cruises§			
Season§	Occupancy§	Inside Cabin§	Outside Cabin§
Spring§	1 Person/2 People§	$750/$1,000§	$1,250/$1,500§
Summer§	1 Person/2 People§	$750/$1,000§	$1,250/$1,500§
Fall§	1 Person/2 People§	$1,250/$1,500§	$1,750/$2,000§

Figure 11.108 Select the column whose width you want to copy.

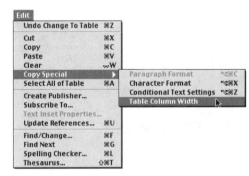

Figure 11.109 Choose Edit > Copy Special > Table Column Width.

Caribbean Cruises§			
Season§	Occupancy§	Inside Cabin§	Outside Cabin§
Spring§	Single/Double§	$1,000/$1,250§	$1,500/$1,750§
Summer§	Single/Double§	$1,000/$1,250§	$1,500/$1,750§
Fall§	Single/Double§	$1,250/$1,500§	$1,750/$2,000§
Winter§	Single/Double§	$1,500/$1,750§	$2,000/$2,500§

Figure 11.110 Select or click the column you want to resize.

Caribbean Cruises§			
Season§	Occupancy§	Inside Cabin§	Outside Cabin§
Spring§	Single/Double§	$1,000/$1,250§	$1,500/$1,750§
Summer§	Single/Double§	$1,000/$1,250§	$1,500/$1,750§
Fall§	Single/Double§	$1,250/$1,500§	$1,750/$2,000§
Winter§	Single/Double§	$1,500/$1,750§	$2,000/$2,500§

Figure 11.111 The column width is pasted from the Clipboard.

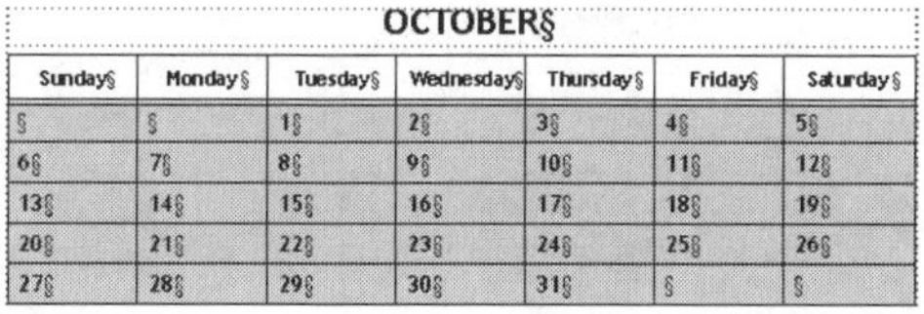

Figure 11.112 Select the rows whose height you want to set.

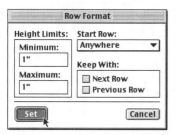

Figure 11.113 Choose Table > Row Format.

Figure 11.114 In the Row Format dialog box, specify minimum and maximum values for row height.

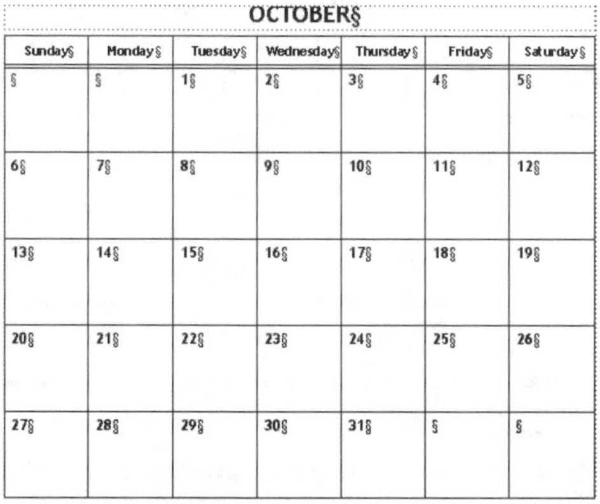

Setting the height of rows

As you type in a table cell, its height increases to accommodate the text. You can also specify the minimum and maximum height of rows to create, for example, a calendar with all table cells the same size.

To specify the height of a row:

1. Click in the row whose height you want to set or select rows (**Figure 11.112**).

2. From the Table menu, choose Row Format (**Figure 11.113**).

3. In the Row Format dialog box, type values in the Height Limits Minimum and Maximum text boxes (**Figure 11.114**).

4. Click Set.

   The selected rows are set to the specified minimum and maximum heights (**Figure 11.115**).

✔ Tip

■ In the Row Format dialog box, you can also set the start position for a specific row in a table by choosing an option from the Start Row pop-up menu as follows:

   ▲ Top of Column or Page

   ▲ Top of Left or Right Page

Figure 11.115 A calendar month with all date cells the same height.

Straddling and Rotating Table Cells

The ability to straddle and rotate table cells allows an almost dizzying array of design possibilities for FrameMaker tables. You can straddle, or merge, cells in rows, in columns, or across rows and columns. In a straddled cell, the group of cells acts as if it were one cell with no boundaries. If you later change your mind, you can unstraddle straddled cells.

For example, the score sheet in **Figure 11.116** uses straddled cells across rows at the top and a block of straddled cells toward the bottom to create a scoresheet for a custom version of a game called Yam.

When you want to group rows in a table, you can add a column to the left or right side of the table, straddle cells as needed, and then rotate the cells, as shown in **Figure 11.117**.

To straddle table cells:

1. Select the cells you want to straddle (**Figure 11.118**).

2. From the Table menu, choose Straddle.

   The selected cells are now merged and will behave as if they were a single cell (**Figure 11.119**).

   With borders on, you can see borders of the cells you straddled.

   In the straddle cell contents are positioned in their own paragraphs across rows first. In this example, there is only one paragraph, which was center aligned in the unstraddled cell. It is now center aligned in the new straddle cell.

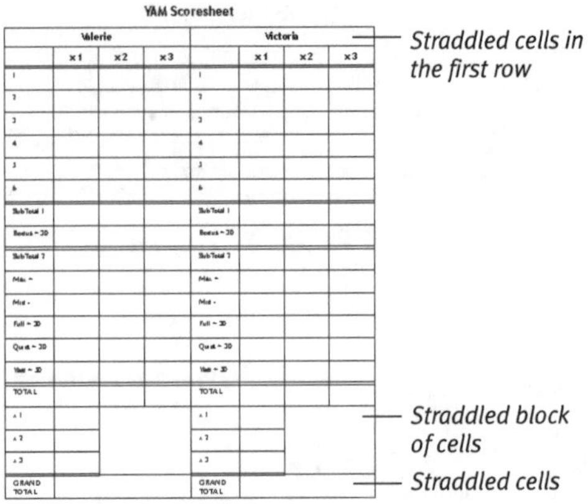

Figure 11.116 Example of straddled table cells.

Figure 11.117 Example of straddled and rotated cells in the leftmost column.

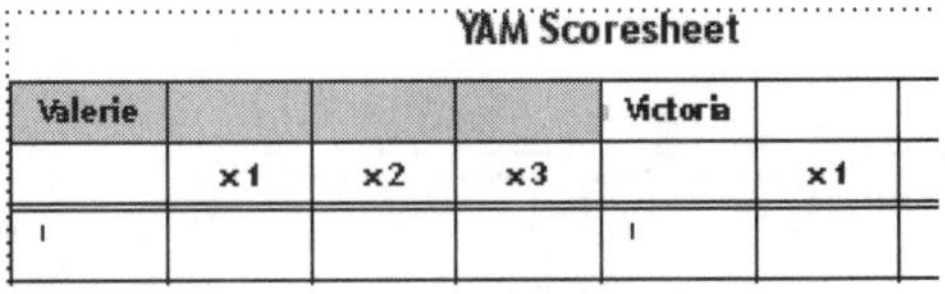

Figure 11.118 Select adjacent cells to straddle.

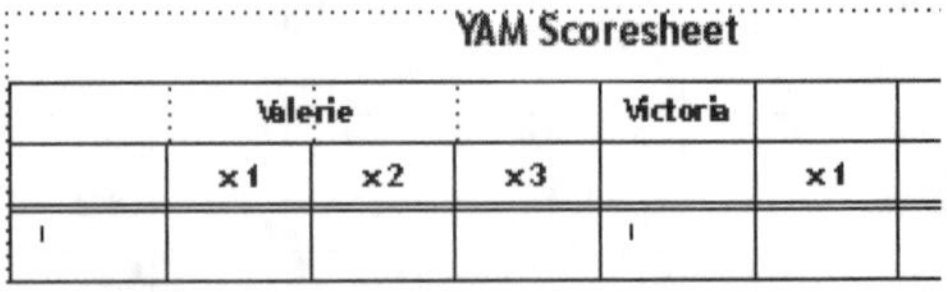

Figure 11.119 Straddled cells behave like a single cell. With borders turned on, you can see the borders of the cells you straddled.

	Inside Cabin§	Outside Cabin§
Season§	Single/Double§	Single/Double§
Spring§	$1,000/$1,250§	$1,500/$1,750§
Summer§	$1,000/$1,250§	$1,500/$1,750§
Fall§	$1,250/$1,500§	$1,750/$2,000§

Figure 11.120 Select the straddle cell.

Season§	Inside Cabin§	Outside Cabin§
§	Single/Double§	Single/Double§
Spring§	$1,000/$1,250§	$1,500/$1,750§
Summer§	$1,000/$1,250§	$1,500/$1,750§
Fall§	$1,250/$1,500§	$1,750/$2,000§

Figure 11.121 The cells are restored; the contents of the straddle cell appear in the top-left cell.

§	Living Room§	16' x 14'§	10' x 12' Carpet§
	Dining Room§	14' x 13'§	8' x 10' Carpet§
	Kitchen§	12' x 12'§	Tile§
	Bathroom§	10' x 8'§	Tile§
	Master Bedroom§	14' x 10'§	Wall to wall§
§	Guest Bedroom §§	10' x 16'§	5' x 9' Carpet§

Figure 11.122 Click or select the cell you want to rotate.

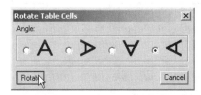

Figure 11.123 Click a radio button and click Rotate.

	Living Room§	16' x 14'§	10' x 12' Carpet§
§§	Dining Room§	14' x 13'§	8' x 10' Carpet§
Standard§	Kitchen§	12' x 12'§	Tile§
	Bathroom§	10' x 8'§	Tile§
	Master Bedroom§	14' x 10'§	Wall to wall§
§	Guest Bedroom §§	10' x 16'§	5' x 9' Carpet§

Figure 11.124 You can type in a rotated cell just as you do in any other cell. Click and start typing.

To unstraddle cells:

1. Select the straddle cell (**Figure 11.120**).

2. From the Table menu, choose Unstraddle.
   The command on the Table menu toggles between Straddle and Unstraddle depending the type of cells selected.
   The selected cells go back to being individual cells (**Figure 11.121**). The contents of the formerly straddled cell appear in the top-left cell, not back in their original, unstraddled cells.

✔ Tip

- You cannot straddle cells that are already straddled. You can, however, select more than one adjacent straddle cell to unstraddle at the same time.

To rotate a table cell:

1. Click in the cell or select the cell you want to rotate (**Figure 11.122**).

2. From the Graphics menu, choose Rotate.
   The Rotate Table Cells dialog box appears.

3. Select an option by comparing the rotation you want for the table cell with the rotation of an uppercase letter "A" (**Figure 11.123**).

4. Click Rotate.
   The cell rotates as specified. In this example, it rotates 90 degrees counterclockwise.
   Click in the cell to start typing (**Figure 11.124**).

Placing Graphics in Table Cells

To paste or import a graphic into a table cell, you need to place the graphic in an anchored frame. Before you insert the anchored frame, you should change the empty paragraph in the table cell so it is center aligned.

To change the alignment of the table cell paragraph:

1. Click in the paragraph whose alignment you want to change (**Figure 11.125**).

2. From the Format menu, choose Paragraphs > Designer.

3. In the Paragraph Designer, from the Alignment pop-up menu, choose Center (**Figure 11.126**).

4. Click Apply.

   The alignment of the paragraph changes to centered (**Figure 11.127**).

To insert an anchored frame in a table cell:

1. Click in the cell where you want to insert the anchored frame (**Figure 11.128**).

2. From the Special menu, choose Anchored Frame.

3. In the Anchored Frame dialog box, from the Anchoring Position pop-up menu, choose At Insertion Point (**Figure 11.129**).

4. Estimate the size of the anchored frame you'll need and specify the width and height by typing in the text boxes.

5. Click New Frame.

   The anchored frame appears in the table cell at the insertion point (**Figure 11.130**).

   If the anchored frame is wider than the table cell, you'll need to resize the column to accommodate the frame.

Icon§	Name§	Click to§
§	Help§	Display a Help window§

Figure 11.125 Click in the empty paragraph whose alignment you want to change.

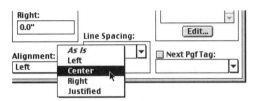

Figure 11.126 In the Paragraph Designer, from the Alignment menu, choose Center.

Icon§	Name§	Click to§
§	Help§	Display a Help window§

Figure 11.127 The paragraph is now centered.

Icon§	Name§	Click to§
§	Help§	Display a Help window§
§	Alert§	Display a warning§
§	Hint§	Display a tip or best practice§

Figure 11.128 In this example, the graphic will be placed in the top-left body cell.

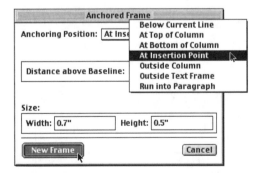

Figure 11.129 Specify an anchored frame at the insertion point.

Icon§	Name§	Click to§
	Help§	Display a Help window§
§	Alert§	Display a warning§
§	Hint§	Display a tip or best practice §

Figure 11.130 An anchored frame appears at the insertion point.

Icon§	Name§	Click to§
	Help§	Display a Help window§
§	Alert§	Display a warning§
§	Hint§	Display a tip or best practice §

Figure 11.131 The graphic is pasted into the anchored frame.

Unrotated Size:

Width: 0.594"

Height: 0.466"

Figure 11.132 Check the size of the graphic to estimate the size of the anchored frame you'll need.

Icon§	Name§	Click to§
	Help§	Display a Help window§
§	Alert§	Display a warning§

Figure 11.133 Click in the paragraph that contains the anchored frame ...

Icon§	Name§	Click to§
	Help§	Display a Help window§
§	Alert§	Display a warning§

Figure 11.134 ... and press Esc T W.

To copy a graphic into an anchored frame in a table cell:

1. Copy the graphic to the Clipboard.

2. Select the anchored frame and from the Edit menu, choose Paste (**Figure 11.131**).

✔ Tips

■ To estimate the size of the anchored frame you'll need, select the graphic, choosing Object Properties from the Graphics menu, and check the size of the graphic you want to use (**Figure 11.132**).

■ In this example, the column width was about right for the size of the graphic. If not, click in the paragraph that contains the anchored frame (**Figure 11.133**) and press Esc T W. The column is resized to comfortably fit the contents of the cell with the insertion point (**Figure 11.134**).

■ An anchored frame at the insertion point can be repositioned vertically but not horizontally. Select the frame and either microposition it (see page 116) or drag it up or down.

You can also select the anchored frame and in the Anchored Frame dialog box, type a value in the Distance Above Baseline text box. A positive value moves the frame up; a negative value moves it down.

PLACING GRAPHICS IN TABLE CELLS

Using Conditional Text in Tables

You can apply condition tags to an entire table or to selected rows in a table. You cannot, however, make a table column conditional.

To apply a condition to a row or to an entire table:

1. Select one or more rows to which you want to apply a condition tag (**Figure 11.135**) or select an entire table.
   You can also select just the table anchor.

2. From the Special menu, choose Conditional Text.

3. In the Conditional Text window, select the condition you want to apply and move it from the Not In list to the In list (**Figure 11.136**).

4. Click Apply.

5. One of the following will happen:
   - ▲ If the condition you applied is showing, the selected row or table now has the specified condition. If condition indicators are on, you will see the color override for the specified condition (**Figure 11.137**).
   - ▲ If the condition you applied is hidden (**Figure 11.138**), the selected row or table will disappear (**Figure 11.139**).

✔ Tips

- ■ The color condition indicator for table rows is crosshatched, not a solid color.

- ■ If you conditionalize a table but not the paragraph that contains it, when the condition is hidden, you will get an empty paragraph. As a general rule, you should conditionalize the paragraph that contains the table, not the table itself, to avoid an unnecessary empty paragraph.

3 days§	$25§	$35§	$40§
5 days§	$35§	$45§	$50§
7 days§	$50§	$70§	$75§
10 days§	$75§	$100§	$110§
11 + days§	$100§	$150§	$150§

Travel Insurance Rates§

Figure 11.135 Select table rows to conditionalize.

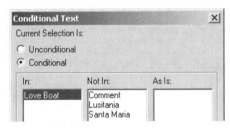

Figure 11.136 Move the condition to the In list.

3 days§	$25§	$35§	$40§
5 days§	$35§	$45§	$50§
7 days§	$50§	$70§	$75§
10 days§	$75§	$100§	$110§
11 + days§	$100§	$150§	$150§

Travel Insurance Rates§

Figure 11.137 The color condition indicator for conditional table rows is crosshatched.

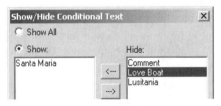

Figure 11.138 When the condition is hidden ...

3 days§	$25§	$35§	$40§
5 days§	$35§	$45§	$50§
7 days§	$50§	$70§	$75§

Travel Insurance Rates§

Figure 11.139 ... the selected rows disappear.

Figure 11.140 Select the text for the heading and body rows, but not the title.

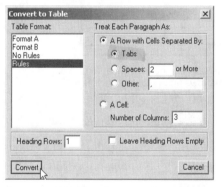

Figure 11.141 Choose Table > Convert to Table.

Figure 11.142 Select a format and other settings for the table.

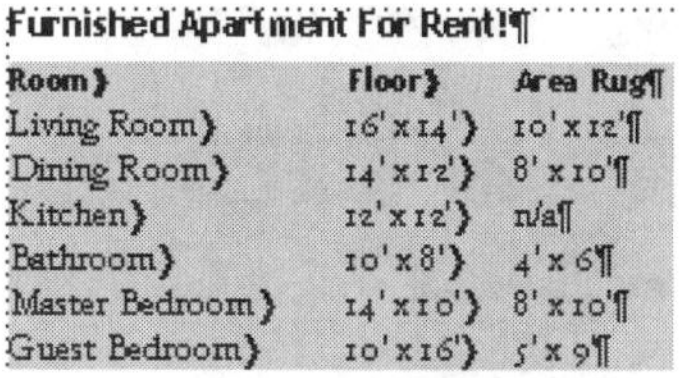

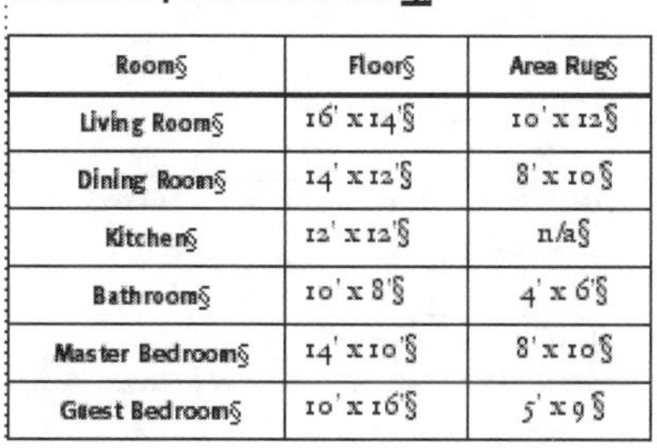

Furnished Apartment For Rent!¶

Room§	Floor§	Area Rug§
Living Room§	16' x 14'§	10' x 12§
Dining Room§	14' x 12'§	8' x 10§
Kitchen§	12' x 12'§	n/a§
Bathroom§	10' x 8'§	4' x 6'§
Master Bedroom§	14' x 10'§	8' x 10§
Guest Bedroom§	10' x 16'§	5' x 9§

Figure 11.143 The selected text is converted to a table anchored in the paragraph above.

Converting Between Text and Tables

If text in paragraphs is separated by tabs, for example, you can convert it to a table. For instance, if you save a spreadsheet as text with a tab or other separator character, you can convert it to a FrameMaker table. One advantage of having text in a table is that you can sort the table rows. You can also select a table and convert it to text.

To convert text to a table:

1. Select the text you want to convert (**Figure 11.140**).

   Select the heading and body row text, but not the title. You can add that to the table later if you wish.

2. From the Table menu, choose Convert to Table (**Figure 11.141**).

   The Convert to Table dialog box appears.

3. In the Table Format list, select a format (**Figure 11.142**).

4. In the Treat Each Paragraph As area, select options that describe how the text you selected is separated.

   In this example, the text is separated by tabs.

5. In the Number of Columns text box, change the value if you wish.

6. In the Heading Rows text box, type the number of heading rows for the table.

7. To add empty heading rows, not populated with the selected text, click the Leave Heading Rows Empty check box.

8. Click Convert.

   The selected text is converted to a table and it is anchored in the paragraph above (**Figure 11.143**).

To convert a table to text:

1. Select the table you want to convert (**Figure 11.144**).

   If you want to include the title, select the title using the keyboard shortcut Esc T H T instead of dragging to select.

2. From the Table menu, choose Convert to Paragraphs (**Figure 11.145**).

   The Convert to Paragraphs dialog box appears.

3. Select one of the following:

   ▲ To convert the table going across rows first, select Row by Row (**Figure 11.146**).

   ▲ To convert the table going down columns first, select Column by Column.

4. Click Convert.

   Paragraphs from each of the table cells now appear in their own paragraphs, ordered as specified (**Figure 11.147**).

To sort table columns or rows:

1. To sort all columns or rows, click anywhere in the table (**Figure 11.148**).

   or

   To sort only some of the rows, select the rows you want to sort.

   FrameMaker sorts only body rows, not heading or footing rows.

2. From the Table menu, choose Sort.

   The Sort Table dialog box appears (**Figure 11.149**).

3. Do one of the following:

   ▲ To sort the rows of the table, click Row Sort.

   ▲ To sort the columns of the table, click Column Sort.

TABLE 3: INDOOR AND OUTDOOR SPORTS BY SEASON§		
Season§	Indoor§	Outdoor§
Spring§	Basketball§	Soccer§
Summer§	Racquetball§	Softball§
Fall§	Weight-lifting§	Football§
Winter§	Hockey§	Skiing§

Figure 11.144 Select the entire table, including the title, using the keyboard shortcut.

Figure 11.145 Choose Table > Convert to Paragraphs.

Figure 11.146 Choose whether to convert across rows first or down columns first.

TABLE 2: INDOOR AND OUTDOOR SPORTS BY SEASON¶		
	Season¶	
	Indoor¶	
	Outdoor¶	
Spring¶		
Basketball¶		
Soccer¶		

Figure 11.147 In this example, FrameMaker goes across rows first (the figure shows paragraphs from the first body row, not the entire table).

Family Name§	Given Name§	City§	Country§
Garbo§	Greta§	Stockholm§	Sweden§
Cruz§	Penelope§	Madrid§	Spain§
Bragga§	Sonia§	Buenos Aires§	Brazil§
Fonda§	Jane§	Atlanta§	USA§
Dietrich§	Marlena§	Berlin-Schoneberg§	Germany§
Fonda§	Bridget§	Los Angeles§	USA§

Figure 11.148 Click in the table.

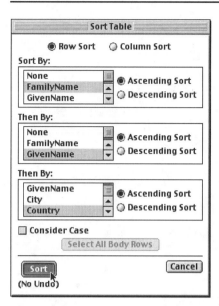

Figure 11.149 In the Sort Table dialog box, specify how you want to sort body rows in the table.

Family Name§	Given Name§	City§	Country§
Bragga§	Sonia§	Buenos Aires§	Brazil§
Cruz§	Penelope§	Madrid§	Spain§
Dietrich§	Marlena§	Berlin-Schoneberg§	Germany§
Fonda§	Bridget§	Los Angeles§	USA§
Fonda§	Jane§	Atlanta§	USA§
Garbo§	Greta§	Stockholm§	Sweden§

Figure 11.150 In this example, the body rows in the table are now sorted alphabetically in ascending order, first by family name and then by given name.

Figure 11.151 The settings for putting text in a list into a table to sort.

4. Choose a primary sort key by selecting from the Sort By text box, and then selecting Ascending Sort or Descending Sort.

You can also choose a second and third sort key in the Then By areas.

5. To sort uppercase letters apart from lowercase letters, select Consider Case.

6. Click Sort.

Body rows or columns are sorted as specified (**Figure 11.150**).

✔ Tips

- If there are conditional rows in the table and you want them to be included in the sort, make sure they are showing.

- Save the document before you start sorting. If the sort produces unexpected results, you can revert to the last saved version.

- When a sorted table includes numbers, text is sorted after numbers, but dollar signs and other symbols are ignored.

- You can sort dates or times as long as they are typed as text, use a consistent format, and include leading zeros. For example, for *dd/mm/yy* and *hh:mm:ss* formats, type 04/12/01 or 09:30:25.

- FrameMaker doesn't sort text in paragraphs, only text in tables. If you have a long list of information to sort, you might want to put it into a table to sort. You could use a table with no rules to make it look like a list, or if necessary, you could export it back out to text.

  In the Convert to Table dialog box (**Figure 11.151**), use the following settings:

  ▲ Any table format

  ▲ Treat Each Paragraph As: A Cell: Number of Columns: 1

  ▲ Heading Rows: 0

Using the Context Menu for Tables

The context menu that is displayed when one or more table cells are selected includes commands from the Edit menu and the Table menu—commands you are likely to need when you're working in tables.

To display a context menu:

◆ (Windows) Right-click (**Figure 11.152**).

or

(Mac OS) Control-click or right-click if you have a two-button mouse (**Figure 11.153**).

The context menu appears.

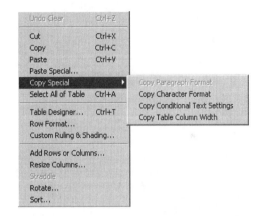

Figure 11.152 The context menu as it is displayed when one or more table cells are selected (Windows).

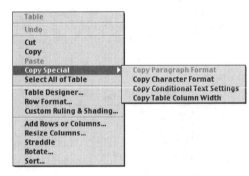

Figure 11.153 The context menu as it is displayed when one or more table cells are selected (Mac OS).

12

PAGE LAYOUT

Previous chapters have covered some of the concepts associated with page layout, such as master pages and flow tags. In Chapter 9, for instance, system variables were inserted on master pages. If you use FrameMaker templates, or if you work with documents that are already set up, you won't need to think too much about page layout, but you'll still find it helpful to know how page layout works.

Here are some of the components of page layout:

◆ Page size and margins

◆ Whether a document is single-sided or double-sided

◆ The number of columns on each page and their sizes and locations

◆ Background content on body pages: for example, headers or footers

In this chapter, you'll see how FrameMaker's page layout features function behind the scenes to make your work easier.

You'll also see how to open a FrameMaker template, customize it, and save it so it's available the next time you want a similar document.

About FrameMaker Pages

Every FrameMaker document comes with three types of pages:

◆ **Body pages**, where you add content to the document. Most of your work in a FrameMaker document is on body pages (**Figure 12.1**).

◆ **Master pages**, where you specify page layout and background text for body pages (**Figure 12.2**).

◆ **Reference pages**, where you find graphic elements used throughout the document (**Figure 12.3**).

Every body page in a FrameMaker document has a corresponding master page. A page layout override occurs when the layout on a body page is different from the layout of its corresponding master page. You can create layouts directly on body pages for one-time-only use, which then override the layout on the corresponding master page.

A single-sided document has at least one default master page, called Right; a double-sided document has default Right and Left master pages. You cannot delete these master page, but you can create additional custom master pages. The first page in a chapter file or a blank page for the last page are good examples.

To navigate from body to master pages and back, choose View > Body Pages or Master Pages. On master pages, the name of the current master page appears in the Page Status area at the bottom of the document window (**Figure 12.4**).

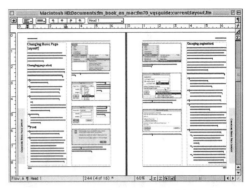

Figure 12.1 Facing body pages from this book ...

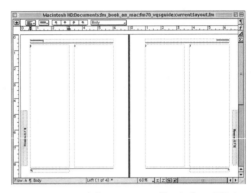

Figure 12.2 ... and the corresponding Left and Right master pages.

Figure 12.3 This book has only one reference page.

Figure **12.4** The name of the master page appears in the Page Status area of the status bar.

Figure **12.5** The end-of-flow symbol appears at the end of the text in a text flow when text symbols are on.

Flow: A ¶: Body   243

Figure **12.6** The flow tag of the text frame with the insertion point appears in the Tag area.

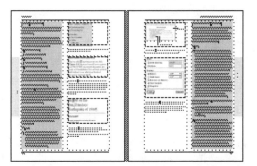

Figure **12.7** this book has two text flows, one for text (selected) and one for graphics.

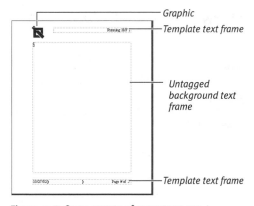

Figure **12.8** Components of a master page.

Text Flows, Flow Tags, and Text Frames

A text flow is a series of connected text frames in which the text flows in a document. When you add text and graphics on body pages, FrameMaker adds pages and automatically uses the page layout from the Left or Right master page. Most documents have a single text flow, from the first page to the last; and FrameMaker handles the text frame connections automatically.

The end-of-flow symbol (**Figure 12.5**) appears at the end of the text in a text flow. The flow tag of the current text frame appears in the Tag area of the status bar (**Figure 12.6**). A text flow with no flow tag is untagged.

This book has two text flows: one for the text columns and one for the graphics columns (**Figure 12.7**). When the flow reaches the end of a text column, FrameMaker moves to the text column on the next page that has the same flow tag. The same is true for the columns that contain the graphics, with flow tag B.

A master page can include any or all of the following (**Figure 12.8**):

◆ **Template text frames** with a tagged text flow, or a named text flow. These frames appear on corresponding body pages, which is where you add content (text and graphics).

◆ **Background text frames** with an untagged text flow. The contents of background text frames appear on corresponding body pages, but you can edit them *only on master pages*.

◆ **Graphics** imported or pasted directly on the page.

Changing Basic Page Layout

Basic components of page layout can be handled from the body page: for instance, changes to the page size, margins, pagination, or column layout.

Changing page size

You can change the page size to that of a standard page, or you can specify a custom page size.

To change a document's page size:

1. Click in the document whose page size you want to change.

2. From the Format menu, choose Page Layout > Page Size (**Figure 12.9**).
   The Page Size dialog box appears.

3. From the Page Size menu, choose a standard page size (**Figure 12.10**).

   or

   To change to a custom size, choose Custom and type the new dimensions in the Width and Height text boxes (**Figure 12.11**).

4. Click Set.
   The document is resized as specified. Margins are maintained, and text frames are resized.

✔ Tips

■ FrameMaker can accommodate a page size as large as 216 inches by 216 inches!

■ If the document whose page size you want to change includes custom master pages with text frames that won't fit in the new page size, FrameMaker displays a message shown in **Figure 12.12**. Click OK, go to the custom master pages that have been added to the document, and change the size of the text frames so they'll fit in the new page size—then try again.

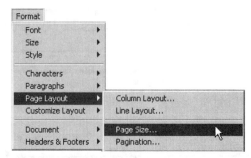

Figure 12.9 Choose Format > Page Layout > Page Size.

Figure 12.10 Choose a standard page size from the Page Size menu.

Figure 12.11 Type custom values in the Width and Height text boxes.

Figure 12.12 If the new page layout can't accommodate text frames on custom master pages, this message appears.

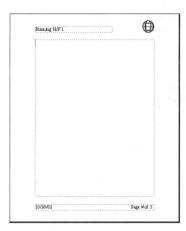

Figure 12.13 The Right master page in a single-sided document.

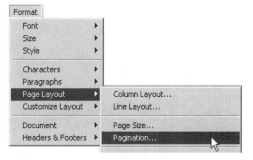

Figure 12.14 Choose Format > Page Layout > Pagination.

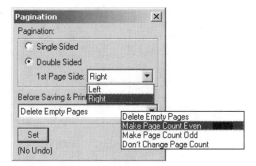

Figure 12.15 The Pagination dialog box with choices for a double-sided document.

Changing pagination

Many documents you create are single-sided: letters, presentation slides, reports, or online help. Others may require a double-sided layout: brochures or technical manuals that will be printed. If your document's page layout is symmetrical and it uses no master pages other than the standard Right and Left master pages, you can change the basic layout.

To change a document's pagination:

1. Click in the document whose pagination you want to change.

   In **Figure 12.13**, a single-sided document is changed to double-sided.

2. From the Format menu, choose Page Layout > Pagination (**Figure 12.14**).

   The Pagination dialog box appears.

3. In the Pagination area, select Single Sided or Double Sided.

   If you select Double Sided, then from the 1st Page Side pop-up menu, choose Left or Right (**Figure 12.15**).

   FrameMaker will assign that master page to the first page in the document.

   If the document is part of a book, a blank page may be added to the previous file in the book so that the document can start on the page you specified.

4. From the Before Saving & Printing pop-up menu, choose an option as follows:

   ▲ To have empty pages deleted, choose Delete Empty Pages.

   ▲ To make the page count even or odd, choose Make Page Count Even or Odd. FrameMaker will add an extra page to this file if necessary.

   ▲ To ensure that FrameMaker doesn't change the page count when you save or print the document, choose Don't Change Page Count.

   (continues on next page)

5. Click Set.

If the document contains page layout overrides on a body page, a warning dialog box appears (**Figure 12.16**).

6. Do one of the following:

▲ To retain the page layout overrides even with the new pagination, click Keep Overrides.

▲ To assign the default master page layouts (Left master page for left pages and Right master page for right pages), even for pages with overrides, click Remove Overrides.

7. Click Continue.

The dialog box disappears.

8. In the Pagination dialog box, click Set.

In this example, the document, which previously had only a Right master page (**Figure 12.13**), now has Left and Right master pages (**Figure 12.17**). The changes made to the master pages are applied to corresponding body pages (**Figure 12.18**).

✔ Tip

■ If you tell FrameMaker to delete empty pages when you save or print a document, FrameMaker deletes a blank page only under the following conditions:

▲ It uses a Left or Right master page.

▲ It doesn't contain the start of a text flow.

▲ It has no layout overrides.

▲ It contains an empty paragraph.

If, after printing, you find unwanted blank pages you thought would be deleted, check to make sure that these conditions are met.

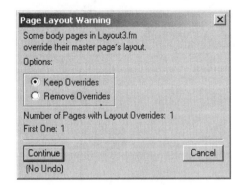

Figure 12.16 The Page Layout Warning dialog box.

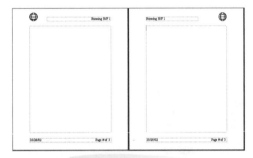

Figure 12.17 Left and Right master pages after changing from single-sided to double-sided pagination ...

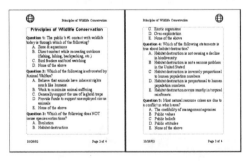

Figure 12.18 ... and the corresponding body pages.

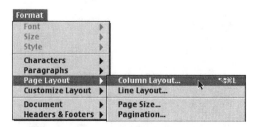

Figure 12.19 Choose Format > Page Layout > Column Layout.

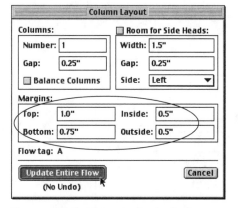

Figure 12.20 Change page margins in the Column Layout dialog box.

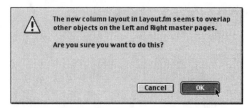

Figure 12.21 Click OK and then check the master pages and fix overlaps.

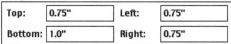

Figure 12.22 View a document's page margins in the Column Layout dialog box.

Changing page margins

When you open a new document in FrameMaker, you have the opportunity to specify its margins. You can also change the margins of an existing document.

To change a document's margins:

1. Click in the document whose page margins you want to change.

2. From the Format menu, choose Page Layout > Column Layout (**Figure 12.19**). The Column Layout dialog box appears.

3. Change any of the values in text boxes in the Margins area (**Figure 12.20**).

4. Click Update Entire Flow.
   If the new margins will overlap other text frames or graphics on the master pages, a warning appears (**Figure 12.21**).

5. Click OK and then go to the master pages, fix any overlaps, and try again.

✔ Tips

■ To view a document's page margins, choose Format > Page Layout > Column Layout and look at the values in the Margins area (margins for a single-sided document are shown in **Figure 12.22**).

■ To use the Column Layout dialog box to make room for side headings, see page 75.

Page layout on body pages

Although it's generally best practice to make layout changes on master pages so they are applied consistently throughout the document, there will be times when you want to create a one-time-only page layout on a body page. For example, the side bars on page 242 and page 243 are one-time-only page layouts on body pages (**Figure 12.23**) that override their corresponding Left and Right master pages (see **Figure 12.2** earlier in the chapter).

Another example of a body page layout override is a side bar across the bottom of the page; the side bar contains two text frames side by side and no graphics (**Figure 12.24**).

On those pages, the text frames are narrower and shorter and include a rectangle with a 1-point black pen pattern and a 10 percent fill.

You can also use one-time-only page layouts to do the following, for example:

◆ Place a graphic directly on the body page.

◆ Add an extra text frame on the body page.

◆ Stretch the bottom of a text frame to fit a little extra text if you don't want it to break over to the next page.

✔ Tips

■ If you have one-time-only layout overrides on body pages, when you go to master pages and then come back to body pages, a message appears (see **Figure 12.16** earlier in the chapter). Make sure that Keep Overrides is selected and click Continue.

■ Text typed into a background (untagged) text frame on a master page is displayed on corresponding body pages but you cannot edit it on the body pages. Text typed into a template text frame *on a master page* is not displayed on corresponding body pages; you add text on the body pages.

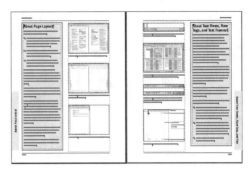

Figure 12.23 Both of these pages have page layouts that override the layout on their corresponding master pages.

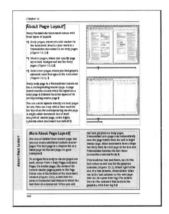

Figure 12.24 Another example of a one-time-only body page layout override.

CHANGING BASIC PAGE LAYOUT

Figure 12.25 The master page corresponding to the current body page appears.

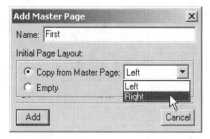

Figure 12.26 Give the new master page a name and initial page layout.

Figure 12.27 In this example, the First master page looks like the Right master page.

Creating Custom Master Pages

Single-sided documents have a default Right master page, and double-sided documents have Left and Right master pages. For many of the documents you create, that's enough. But if you want the opening page of a document to look different from the other pages, for example, you'll need to create a custom master page.

To create a custom master page:

1. To display master pages, from the View menu, choose Master Pages.

   The master page corresponding to the body page appears (**Figure 12.25**).

2. From the Special menu, choose Add Master Page.

   The Add Master Page dialog box appears.

3. Type a name for the new master page in the Name text box.

4. Choose an option from the Copy from Master Page pop-up menu as follows:

   ▲ To add a new master page based on the Left master page's layout, choose Left.

   ▲ To add a new master page based on the Right master page's layout, choose Right (**Figure 12.26**). All existing master pages, including custom pages, are included in the menu.

   or

   To add a new master page with nothing on it, select Empty.

5. Click Add.

   The new master page appears with the initial layout you specified (**Figure 12.27**). You can make modifications (see page 251) and then assign the master page to one or more body pages (see page 256).

To create a custom master page based on the layout of a body page:

1. Make the layout changes you want on a body page.

   or

   Display the body page you want to use for the custom master page.

2. From the Format menu, choose Page Layout > New Master Page (**Figure 12.28**). The New Master Page dialog box appears.

3. Type a name for the new master page in the Master Page Name text box (**Figure 12.29**).

4. Click Create.

   A message confirms that a page has been created (**Figure 12.30**).

5. Click OK.

   A new master page is created, but it will not be associated with any body pages until you assign it (see page 256).

✔ Tips

■ For a body page that is completely blank, that doesn't have even headers or footers, create a custom master page with nothing on it called Blank and assign it to the empty pages.

■ If you have two variations of a particular page, such as a chapter opener where the chapter title could be one line or two lines, create two master pages: one for the first page of chapters with one-line titles and one for chapter titles with two-line titles.

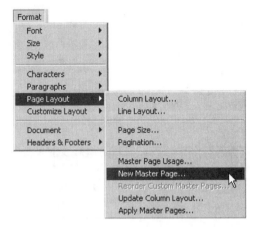

Figure 12.28 Choose Format > Page Layout > New Master Page.

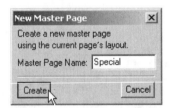

Figure 12.29 Type a name for the new master page.

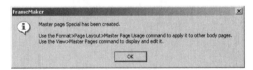

Figure 12.30 This message lets you know that the new master page has been created.

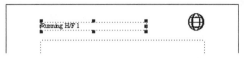

Figure 12.31 Select and delete the background header text frame.

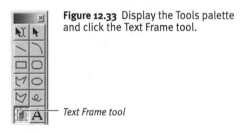

Figure 12.32 Select the main template text frame and resize it.

Figure 12.33 Display the Tools palette and click the Text Frame tool.

Text Frame tool

Figure 12.34 Draw a text frame at the top of the page.

Figure 12.35 Add a template text frame you can type into on a body page.

Modifying Page Layout on Master Pages

Once you've added a new master page, whether you've based it on the layout of an existing master page or body page, you can still modify the layout. For example, on the first page in a document or chapter, you can:

◆ Delete the header.

◆ Change the main text column so that it starts lower on the page.

◆ Add a background text frame for a large chapter number or graphic.

To make changes on a custom master page:

1. Create a custom master page (in the procedure on page 249, it was called First).

   In a double-sided document, a custom page for the first page is usually copied from the Right master page.

2. Select and delete the background header text frame (**Figure 12.31**).

3. Select the main template text frame, hold down the Shift key and drag the top-middle selection handle down to start the column lower on the page (**Figure 12.32**).

4. Display the Tools palette and click the Text Frame tool to select it (**Figure 12.33**).

5. Draw a text frame at the top of the page (**Figure 12.34**).

   The Add New Text Frame dialog box appears.

6. In the Text Frame Type area, select Template for Body Page Text Frame and click Add (**Figure 12.35**).

   The new text frame appears at the top of the page. Because you added a template text frame with flow tag A, a message appears to tell you that the new frame has been added to the end of flow A.

Controlling Text Flow

In the previous section you added a text frame with flow A at the top of a First master page, but it was added to *the end of the flow* on the page, and you really needed it connected to the beginning so that the text you type on a body page will flow from the smaller text frame at the top of the page to the main text frame,

In the following exercises, you will see how to disconnect a text frame from the previous or next text frame and then connect two text frames.

To disconnect text frames:

1. Select the text frame you want to disconnect from the previous or next text frame (**Figure 12.36**).

   You need to disconnect the text frame so you can reconnect it and have text flow from the top to the main text frames.

2. From the Format menu, choose from the Customize Layout submenu as follows:

   ▲ To disconnect the selected text frame from the one that comes before it in the flow, choose Disconnect Previous (**Figure 12.37**).

   ▲ To disconnect the selected text frame from the that comes after it in the text flow, choose Disconnect Next.

   ▲ To disconnect the selected text frame from both the one before it and the one after it, choose Disconnect Both.

   A warning message appears telling you that you now have two or three untagged text flows on the page and what you need to do to assign new flow tags (**Figure 12.38**).

3. Click OK.

   The warning message disappears, but the top text frame is now disconnected and untagged (**Figure 12.39**).

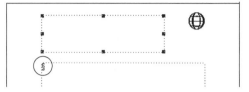

Figure 12.36 Select the frame you want to disconnect so you can connect it to the main text flow, the one with the end-of-flow symbol.

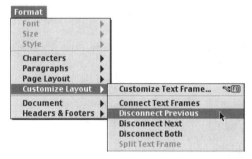

Figure 12.37 Choose Format > Customize Layout > Disconnect Previous.

Figure 12.38 A warning message telling you that the page now has two untagged text frames.

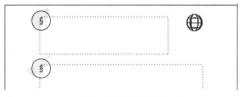

Figure 12.39 The top text frame is now disconnected and untagged—each of the text frames has its own end-of-flow symbol.

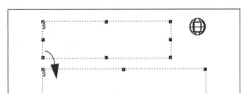

Figure 12.40 Select the two text frames in the order you want text to flow.

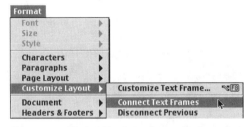

Figure 12.41 Choose Format > Customize Layout > Connect Text Frames.

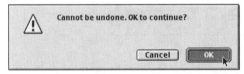

Figure 12.42 A warning message tells you that the connection cannot be undone.

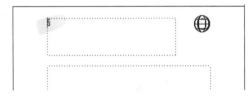

Figure 12.43 Now that the columns are connected, there is only one end-of-flow symbol.

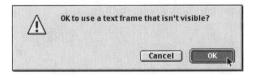

Figure 12.44 When one of the frames you want to connect is not visible on the screen, this warning message appears.

To connect two text frames:

1. Ctrl-click or Option-click to select the frame you want text to flow from.

2. Shift-Ctrl-click or Shift-Option-click to extend the selection to the frame you want text to flow to (**Figure 12.40**).

3. From the Format menu, choose Customize Layout > Connect Text Frames (**Figure 12.41**).

   An alert message appears (**Figure 12.42**).

4. Click OK.

   The columns are now connected and there is only one end-of-flow symbol in the top frame (**Figure 12.43**). On a body page, when you finish typing in the top text frame, text will flow into the main text frame on the page.

✔ Tips

- You can connect text frames on different pages, even nonadjacent pages. When you extend the selection to the second frame, the first frame appears to be deselected, but FrameMaker keeps track of the first selection, and the frames will be connected. A warning message asks you to confirm that you want to connect to that frame, as shown in **Figure 12.44**. Click OK.

- Text frames are containers for text. When you make changes to text frames on master pages or on body pages, you do not affect the text and graphics inside the text frames.

(continues on next page)

CONTROLLING TEXT FLOW

- If you try to connect text frames in a situation where the connection would create a circular text flow, an alert appears, (**Figure 12.45**). Click OK and think about what you're trying to do. You may need to disconnect one or more text frames before connecting them up to other text frames to achieve the connection you want.

Figure 12.45 An alert message tells you that the connection you want to make is not possible.

Adding new, disconnected pages

Most of the time, you'll want FrameMaker to add pages for you and give you the correct Left or Right master page automatically. For documents where each page stands on its own, such as a slide presentation, you can have FrameMaker add new pages for you and let text flow from page to page, or you can add a new, disconnected page.

When you add a disconnected page:

- ▲ Text from the page before flows around the page and into a new page added after the disconnected page.

- ▲ When you get to the end of the disconnected page, text doesn't flow to the next page.

To add new, disconnected pages:

1. While on a body page, from the Special menu, choose Add Disconnected Pages (**Figure 12.46**).

2. In the Add Disconnected Pages dialog box, from the Add pop-up menu, choose from the following (**Figure 12.47**):

   - ▲ To add a page before the page displayed in the text box, choose Before Page.

   - ▲ To add a page after the page displayed in the text box, choose After Page.

3. If you wish, change the page number in the text box.

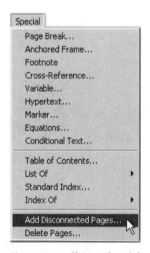

Figure 12.46 Choose Special > Add Disconnected Pages.

Figure 12.47 Specify where you want to add the new, disconnected page, how many to add, and which master page to use.

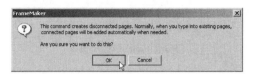

Figure 12.48 A warning message warns you that you're adding disconnected pages.

Figure 12.49 Choose Special > Delete Pages.

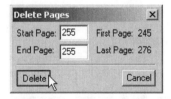

Figure 12.50 Type a page range into the text boxes and click Delete.

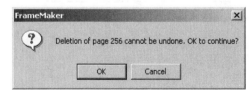

Figure 12.51 A warning message asks you to confirm the deletion.

4. In the Number of Pages text box, type the number of pages you want to add.

5. From the Use Master Page pop-up menu, choose a master page from the list of default and custom master pages.

All of the pages you add will be based on this master page.

6. Click Add.

A warning message (**Figure 12.48**) reminds you that you're creating disconnected pages, and that when you get to the end of the page, FrameMaker will not add pages automatically.

7. Click OK.

A new, disconnected page is added to the document.

To delete disconnected pages:

1. Click in a page you want to delete, and from the Special menu, choose Delete Pages (**Figure 12.49**).

The Delete Pages dialog box appears.

2. Type a range of pages in the Start Page and End Page text boxes and click Apply (**Figure 12.50**).

A warning message appears asking you to confirm the deletion (**Figure 12.51**).

3. Click OK.

The specified pages and their contents are deleted from the document.

✔ Tip

■ Deleting a disconnected page in a FrameMaker document cannot be undone. To be on the safe side, save your document before you delete disconnected pages. If you accidentally delete content you didn't want to delete, revert to the saved document and try again.

Assigning Master Pages to Body Pages

When you add a custom master page to a document, nothing happens on body pages until you assign them a master page. When you assign a master page to one or more body pages, FrameMaker:

◆ Displays graphics and text from the background (untagged) text frames, typically headers and footers.

◆ Uses the template text frames from the master page to hold text and graphics on the body page.

To assign a custom master page to a body page:

1. Display the body page whose master page you want to change (**Figure 12.52**).

2. From the Format menu, choose Page Layout > Master Page Usage (**Figure 12.53**).
   The Master Page Usage dialog box appears.

3. In the Use Master Page area, from the Custom menu, choose the master page you want to assign (**Figure 12.54**).
   Figure 12.55 shows the First master page in this example.

4. In the Apply To area, specify how to assign the custom master page as follows:
   ▲ To assign it to the current page only, click Current Page.
   ▲ To assign it to a range of pages, type the first and last page numbers in the range in the Pages text boxes.
   ▲ To assign it to only the even or odd pages in the range, click the Even or Odd check box.

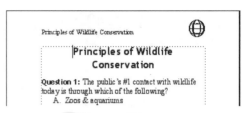

Figure 12.52 Top of the body page with the default Right master page.

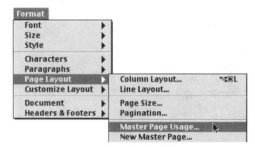

Figure 12.53 Choose Format > Page Layout > Master Page Usage.

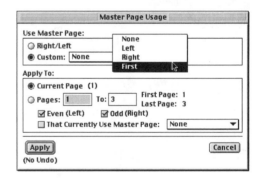

Figure 12.54 From the Custom menu, choose First.

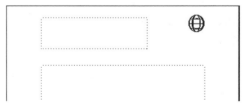

Figure 12.55 The top of the First master page in this example.

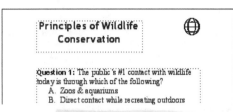

Figure 12.56 Top of the body page after the custom First master page is assigned.

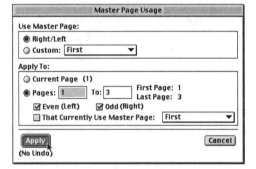

Figure 12.57 In the Use Master Page area, click Right/Left.

▲ To assign it to all of the body pages in the range that currently use a specific master page, choose a master page from the That Currently Use Master Page pop-up menu.

5. Click Apply.

The custom master page is assigned to the body page (**Figure 12.56**).

You may sometimes want to reassign a default master page to a body page to which a custom master page has been assigned.

To assign default master pages to body pages:

1. Display the body page whose master page you want to change.

2. From the Format menu, choose Page Layout > Master Page Usage.

In the Master Page Usage dialog box, in the Use Master Page area, click Right/Left (**Figure 12.57**).

3. In the Apply To area, specify how to assign the default Right and Left master pages.

4. Click Apply.

The Right and Left master pages are assigned as specified.

✔ Tip

■ If you're working with a large document *with no one-time-only page layouts on body pages* but lots of custom master pages, and you feel as if you can't figure out what's going on with page layout, here is a remedial strategy. Make a backup of the document before you start, just in case. Then apply default Left and Right master pages to all of the pages in the document and again start applying custom master pages as appropriate.

Managing Master Pages

If you're working in a document with multiple custom master pages, you'll eventually need to delete, rename, or reorder master pages.

To rename a master page:

1. Display the master page you want to rename.

2. Click the page name at the bottom of the document window (**Figure 12.58**).

   The Master Page Name dialog box appears.

3. Type a new name for the master page and click Set (**Figure 12.59**).

   The new name appears in the Page Status area (**Figure 12.60**).

To delete a master page:

1. Display the master page you want to delete.

2. From the Special menu, choose Delete Page (**Figure 12.61**).

   If any body pages use the master page you want to delete, an alert appears, as shown in **Figure 12.62**. It tells you which body pages are using the master page you want to delete.

3. Click OK, go to the affected body pages, and assign one of the other master pages to all of the affected body pages.

   Without any further messages, the master page is deleted.

Figure 12.58 Click the master page name in the Page Status area.

Figure 12.59 Type a new name for the master page and click Set.

Figure 12.60 The new name appears in the Page Status area.

Figure 12.61 Choose Special > Delete Page.

Figure 12.62 This alert lets you know that you cannot delete the master page.

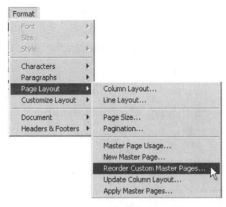

Figure 12.63 Choose Format > Page Layout > Reorder Custom Master Pages.

Figure 12.64 The Reorder Custom Master Pages dialog box.

Figure 12.65 Select a master page, click Move Up or Move Down to reorder the pages, and click Set.

When custom master pages were added to the document, they were added in the order they were created. You might want to reorder them so you can view them in an order that you prefer. You cannot, however, change the order of the standard master pages, Left and Right. They always come first and in that order.

To reorder custom master pages:

1. Display a master page.

2. From the Format menu, choose Page Layout > Reorder Custom Master Pages (**Figure 12.63**).

   The Reorder Custom Master Pages dialog box appears (**Figure 12.64**).

3. Reorder the master page names in the list as follows:

   ▲ To move a name up, select it and click Move Up

   ▲ To move a name down, select it and click Move Down.

4. When the master pages are in the order you want them, click Set (**Figure 12.65**).

   The custom master pages in the document are reordered as specified.

✔ Tip

■ As for all named items in a FrameMaker document (paragraph and character tags, variable names, table tags, and so on), you should try to use meaningful names.

   For example, the names Special and Extra Special don't really tell another person who might work with the document what to do with this master page. But the name First 2 Line Title, if there's a custom master page called First, gives another person a clue that this is a variation of the First master page to use for chapters with two-line titles.

Using Reference Pages

On reference pages, you can store graphics, such as icons or logos, you might want to use throughout a document. Graphics are stored in named reference frames, which are unanchored graphic frames on a reference page. A FrameMaker document normally has at least one reference page; a template usually includes four graphics in reference frames (**Figure 12.66**).

Specialized reference pages can contain hypertext commands, formatting information for generated files such as TOCs and indexes and mappings for conversion to XML and HTML.

Linking graphics to paragraph formats

You link graphics in reference frames on a reference page to paragraph formats by using the Advanced properties in the Paragraph Designer.

You can add an icon, for example, on a reference page (**Figure 12.67**), and then use it above a paragraph on a body page (**Figure 12.68**). If you put the graphic on a reference page and add it to the paragraph format the graphic appears automatically each time you use the paragraph—and it's sized and positioned consistently throughout the document.

You can include a line or other graphic that appears above or below a paragraph in the paragraph format. A heading paragraph format, for example, could include a single line that appears below the text of the paragraph.

To add a graphic to a paragraph format:

1. Click in the paragraph whose format you want to change (**Figure 12.69**).

2. From the View menu, choose Paragraphs > Designer to display the Paragraph Designer.

Graphic in reference frame

Reference frame

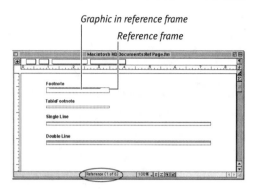

Figure 12.66 Graphics on reference pages are placed in reference frames.

Figure 12.67 A tip icon has been added to a reference frame on a reference page.

TIP: Evolutionary Units are segments of biological diversity that contain the potential for a unique evolutionary future.

Figure 12.68 An example of a graphic added above a paragraph on a body page.

An understanding of wildlife populations is fundar cessful management and conservation. Populatio the study of changes in the number and composit uals in a population, and the factors that influen changes. Population dynamics involves five basic of interest to which all changes in populations ca birth, death, sex ratio, age structure, and disper

The following glossary should be used in conjunc course material you'll be using from week to wee

Glossary for Week 1

Density is a measure of animal abundance in which the number of animals is given per unit area (i.e., 100 elk/km2).

Figure 12.69 The text before adding a line to the heading paragraph format; click in the paragraph whose format you want to change.

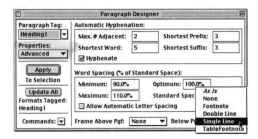

Figure 12.70 Choose a reference frame.

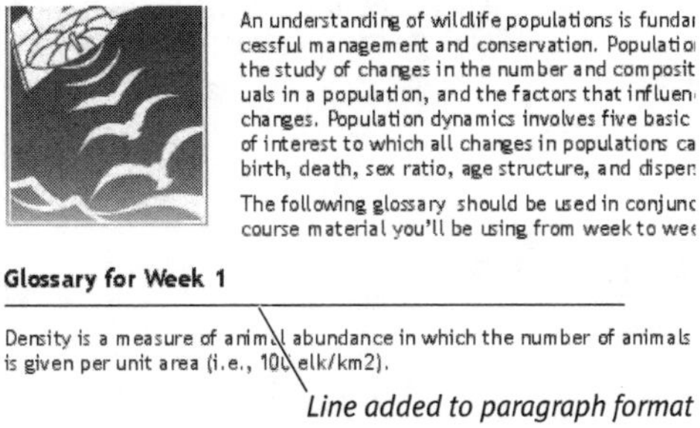

An understanding of wildlife populations is funda
cessful management and conservation. Populatio
the study of changes in the number and composit
uals in a population, and the factors that influen
changes. Population dynamics involves five basic
of interest to which all changes in populations ca
birth, death, sex ratio, age structure, and disper

The following glossary should be used in conjunc
course material you'll be using from week to wee

Glossary for Week 1

Density is a measure of animal abundance in which the number of animals
is given per unit area (i.e., 100 elk/km2).

Line added to paragraph format

Figure 12.71 A single line appears below the heading paragraph ...

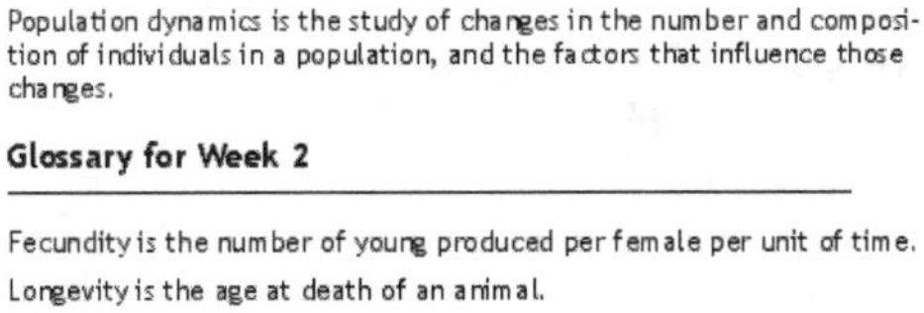

Population dynamics is the study of changes in the number and composi-
tion of individuals in a population, and the factors that influence those
changes.

Glossary for Week 2

Fecundity is the number of young produced per female per unit of time.
Longevity is the age at death of an animal.

Figure 12.72 ... every time it's used.

3. From the Properties pop-up menu, choose Advanced.

4. At the bottom of the window, choose as follows:

▲ To add a graphic above the paragraph, choose the name of the reference frame from the Frame Above Paragraph pop-up menu.

▲ To add a graphic below the paragraph, choose the name of the reference frame from the Frame Below Paragraph pop-up menu (**Figure 12.70**).

In this example, a single line is added below the paragraph (**Figure 12.71**).

Names of all of the reference frames stored on reference pages appear on both menus.

5. Click Update All to apply the change to all paragraphs with the same tag and to add the change to the Paragraph Catalog for future use.

The graphic is added to the current paragraph and to all paragraphs with the same format (**Figure 12.72**).

✔ Tip

■ In the Advanced properties of the Paragraph Designer, you can place graphics only above or below a paragraph, not to the right or left, so you can't use these settings to put boxes around text.

To place a box around text, use a single-cell table with outside ruling. (See page 218 for tasks associated with table ruling properties.)

USING REFERENCE PAGES

Adding reference frames and graphics on reference pages

You can add a graphic to an existing reference page if there's room, or you can add a new reference page (see page 263).

To create a reference frame on a reference page:

1. From the View menu, choose Reference Pages to display the reference pages.

2. On the Tools palette, click the Graphic Frame tool to select it (**Figure 12.73**).

3. Draw a frame a little larger than the graphic it will contain (**Figure 12.74**).
   The Frame Name dialog box appears.

4. Type a name for the new frame in the text box and click Set (**Figure 12.75**).

   The name you type is the name that FrameMaker displays on the Frame Above and Below Paragraph pop-up menus in the Paragraph Designer.

5. Click above the reference frame and add a text line with the name of the frame (**Figure 12.76**).

   The name you add should correspond exactly to the name you used in step 4.

6. Select the frame you just created and copy or import a graphic into the frame (**Figure 12.77**).

✔ Tips

- The height of the reference frame and the position of the graphic inside it affects the space between the graphic and the text above and below it on a body page (**Figure 12.78**). To add more space above or below the graphic when it's used on a body page, resize the reference frame to increase its height and microposition the graphic inside the frame if you wish.

Figure 12.73 Display the Tools palette and click the Graphic Frame tool.

Graphic Frame tool

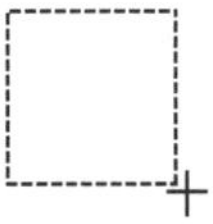

Figure 12.74 Drag to draw a graphic frame on the reference page.

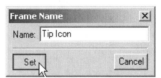

Figure 12.75 Type a name for the new reference frame.

Figure 12.76 Add a text line above the reference frame.

Figure 12.77 Import or copy a graphic into the reference frame.

- To make the reference frame title text line the same font as the other titles on the page, before you click to add the name, click one of the other names on the page.

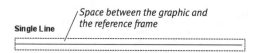

Single Line

Space between the graphic and the reference frame

Figure 12.78 The height of the reference frame and the position of the graphic inside the frame determine the space above and below the graphic on a body page.

Figure 12.79 Choose View > Reference Pages.

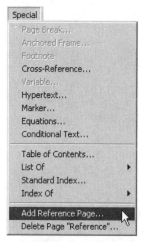

Figure 12.80 Choose Special > Add Reference Page.

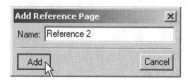

Figure 12.81 Type a name for the reference page.

Managing reference pages and reference frames

When you choose View > Reference Pages, if the document doesn't have a reference page, the Add Reference Page dialog box appears. You can either create a reference page or click Cancel. You navigate through reference pages that same way you navigate through body or master pages.

To display reference pages:

◆ From the View menu, choose Reference Pages (**Figure 12.79**).

The fist reference page appears. A FrameMaker document normally has at least one reference page, named Reference, and may have others.

To add a reference page:

1. Display the reference pages, and from the Special menu, choose Add Reference Page (**Figure 12.80**).

2. In the Add Reference Page dialog box, type a name for the reference page in the text box and click Add (**Figure 12.81**).

A new reference page is added.

To delete a reference page:

1. Display the reference pages, and from the Special menu, choose Delete Page.

2. When a warning message appears, click OK (**Figure 12.82**).

   The current reference page and its contents are deleted. If any of the graphics in deleted reference frames were linked to any paragraph formats, the link is undone, and any graphics that appeared on body pages disappear.

To rename a reference frame:

1. Select a frame and click its name in the Page Status area at the bottom of the document window (**Figure 12.83**).

2. In the Frame Name dialog box, type a new name in the text box and click Set (**Figure 12.84**).

   The name of the reference frame is changed. You should now change the name displayed in the text line to match.

   If the renamed reference frame was linked to any paragraph formats, the link is undone, and any graphics that appeared on body pages disappear.

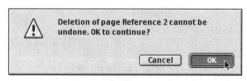

Figure 12.82 A warning message tells you that the deletion cannot be undone.

Figure 12.83 Click the name of the reference frame you want to change.

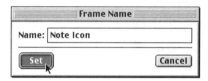

Figure 12.84 Type a new name for the reference frame.

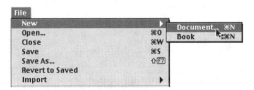

Figure 12.85 Choose File > New > Document.

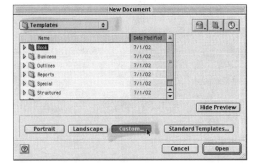

Figure 12.86 Click Custom to customize the page layout of a new, blank document.

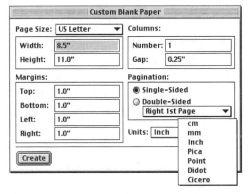

Figure 12.87 In the Custom Blank Paper dialog box, you can customize the page layout of a new blank document.

Introduction to FrameMaker Templates

If you work in a corporate environment, most of the time you'll work with documents that have been created for you. But you can also start with a new, blank document or a FrameMaker template.

Opening a new, blank document

Even a "blank" document includes a few basic formats. You can use them as is, change them, or create new formats.

To open a new blank document:

1. From the File menu, choose New > Document (**Figure 12.85**).

2. In the New Document dialog box (**Figure 12.86**), click one of the following buttons:
   ▲ To open a blank, 8-1/2 x 11-inch document, click Portrait.
   ▲ To open a blank, 11 x 8-1/2-inch document, click Landscape.
   ▲ To open a blank document and customize layout options, such as page size and margins, click Custom.
   The Custom Blank Paper dialog box appears.

3. To set units of measurement for the document, choose from the Units pop-up menu at the bottom right (**Figure 12.87**).

4. Change any of the following: page size, margins, number of columns and gap between them, pagination, and first page choice.

5. Click Create.
   A new, blank document appears with the page layout you specified.

✔ Tip

■ New, blank documents have only one text flow, and its flow tag is A.

Using standard templates

You can find out a little about FrameMaker's standard templates before you open one.

To explore standard FrameMaker templates:

1. From the File menu, choose New > Document.

2. In the New Document dialog box, click (Explore) Standard Templates (**Figure 12.88**).

   The Standard Templates window appears (**Figure 12.89**).

3. Select the template you want to explore in the list on the left side of the window (**Figure 12.90**).

   Details about the selected template appear in the middle of the window, and the page layout appears on the right.

4. To display more of the list of templates, click the Up or Down button at the bottom left (**Figure 12.91**).

   More of the list of available templates appears.

5. At this point, you can proceed as follows:

   ▲ To open a blank template, that is, a template with the page layout and formats, but no content, click Create.

   ▲ To view a template with sample text and graphics (most of it in Latin), click Show Sample.

   ▲ To close the window, click Done.

   The Standard Templates window disappears.

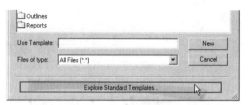

Figure 12.88 In the New Document dialog box, click Explore Standard Templates.

List of available templates

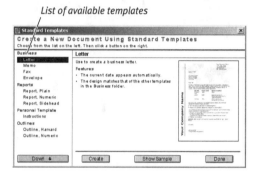

Figure 12.89 The Standard Templates window lists available templates on the left side ...

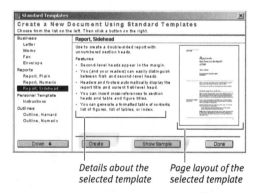

*Details about the   Page layout of the
selected template   selected template*

Figure 12.90 ... and gives details about the template and shows you the page layout on the right side.

Figure 12.91 Click Up or Down to see the templates not currently visible in the list.

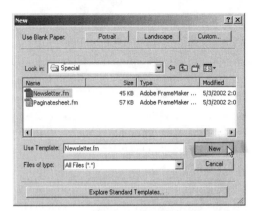

Figure 12.92 Browse in the scroll list to find the template you want to open or click the (Explore) Standard Templates button.

Figure 12.93 A new, untitled document appears.

Figure 12.94 Save and name the new document.

Once you become familiar with FrameMaker's standard templates, you can open a template from the New Document dialog box.

To open and save a FrameMaker template:

1. From the File menu, choose New > Document.

2. In the New Document dialog box, navigate to the document you want to use as a template (**Figure 12.92**).

   You can use any FrameMaker document as a template, or you can navigate to the FrameMaker Templates folder.

3. Select the document and click New.

   A new, untitled document appears (**Figure 12.93**). It contains the formats and content from the template.

4. To save and name the document, from the Edit menu, choose Save.

5. In the Save Document dialog box, navigate to where you want to save the document, type a name for the new document in the text box, and click Save (**Figure 12.94**).

   The new document is saved in the location you specified.

   Once you've saved the template, you can add and edit text on body pages. You will want to go to the master pages and replace some of the placeholder text, for example, in the newsletter template, selecting and replacing the placeholder text for the company name and the name of the newsletter.

INTRODUCTION TO FRAMEMAKER TEMPLATES

Customizing Templates

If you want to use FrameMaker to create more personal documents, you'll want to customize the templates you use, whether they're standard FrameMaker ones or from other sources. Once you have a certain type of document looking exactly as you like it, you can save it in the Templates folder for future use.

Figure 12.95 This is FrameMaker's envelope template.

For example, you might create a customized envelope template. Anything you want to appear on all body pages, such as your return address, should be added to the master page as background text. Similarly, any graphic placed on a master page will appear on corresponding body pages. The text you add to a background text frame on a master page cannot be edited from a body page.

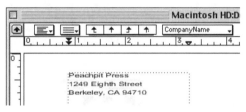

Figure 12.96 Change the return address on a master page.

To add a background text frame on a master page:

1. Open the template or document that you want to customize.

   This example uses FrameMaker's envelope template (**Figure 12.95**).

2. From the View menu, choose Master Pages to display the master pages.

3. Change any of the text in the existing background text frames.

   In this example, you'll customize the return address (**Figure 12.96**).

4. Display the Tools palette, click the Text Frame tool, and draw a text frame where you want the text to appear on the body page.

   The Add New Text Frame dialog box appears.

5. In the Text Frame Type area, select Background Text and click Add (**Figure 12.97**).

   The background text column appears.

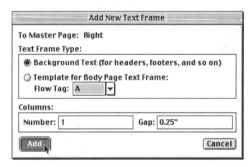

Figure 12.97 When you draw a text frame, the Add New Text Frame dialog box appears.

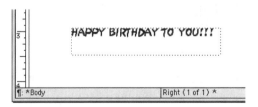

Figure 12.98 Text in a background text frame on a master page appears on a body page.

Figure 12.99 In this example, add destination addresses on body pages.

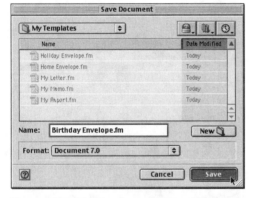

Figure 12.100 Save the document you want to use as a template in the Templates folder.

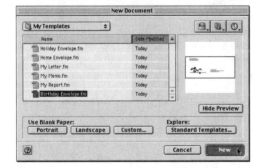

Figure 12.101 In the New Document dialog box, the template you customized appears with its new name.

6. Type the text you want to appear on the body page and format it (**Figure 12.98**).

7. If you wish, import or copy a graphic to the master page.

This graphic is from FrameMaker's clip art (page 3 of the Balloons.fm file).

8. Go back to the body pages, and continue working (**Figure 12.99**).

In this envelope example, type a destination address in the template text frame on the body page. Add disconnected body pages for each envelope you want to address (see page 254).

To use your own document as a template:

1. Create a new folder in the FrameMaker Templates folder.

In this example, it's called My Templates.

2. Once a document looks just the way you want it to, save it in the folder you created (**Figure 12.100**).

The next time you use the File > New > Document command to open a new document, the document you saved will be available as a template.

3. In the New Document dialog box, select the document you saved and click New (**Figure 12.101**).

The template opens as a new, untitled document, ready to be saved and used.

✔ Tip

■ Think about all of the documents that you create in different applications, and see if you can re-create them in FrameMaker. The more you practice the better you'll get. Don't be afraid to work on master and reference pages. If you always save your document before you start experimenting, you'll always be able to revert to the saved document.

CUSTOMIZING TEMPLATES

Importing Formats

One of FrameMaker's most astonishing features is the ability to import formats, layout, definitions, and other settings from one document into another. Although the following procedure refers to the document you import formats from as a template, it can be any FrameMaker document.

To import formats from a template into another document:

1. Open the document that contains the formats you want to use.

   The document can be a template or any FrameMaker file.

2. Make the document you want to format active, and from the File menu, choose Import > Formats (**Figure 12.102**).

   or

   Press Esc F I O or Command-Option-O.

   The Import Formats dialog box appears.

3. From the Import From Document pop-up menu at the top of the dialog box, choose the document to import formats from (**Figure 12.103**).

4. In the Import and Update area, click Deselect All, and then select the items you want to import.

   See page 272 for more information about the effect of importing the items shown in **Figure 12.103**.

5. To remove page break overrides in paragraphs that have them and other formatting overrides, select options in the While Updating Remove area.

   If the document you're importing formats into is currently unformatted, you don't need to select anything.

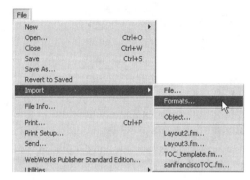

Figure 12.102 Choose File > Import > Formats.

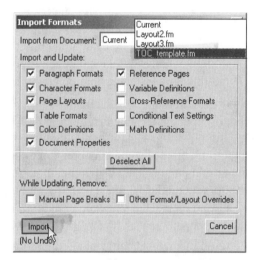

Figure 12.103 Specify the document to use formats from and what items you want to import and update.

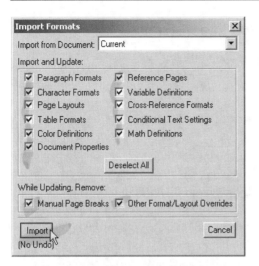

Figure 12.104 Import formats into the current document to remove format overrides.

6. Click Import.

FrameMaker merges the information into the document. When you import paragraph and character formats, FrameMaker adds them to the Catalogs. If any formats have the same name, FrameMaker overwrites the original format with settings from the template. Formats that are not overwritten remain in the document with the same settings.

If there are a lot of formatting overrides in a document, you can remove them all at once by reimporting a document's own formats.

To revert to a document's default formatting:

1. Choose File > Import > Formats.

2. In the Import from Document pop-up menu, choose Current, and select the items you want to revert to the document's defaults.

3. In the While Updating Remove area, select both options (**Figure 12.104**).

FrameMaker removes format overrides and restores default settings from the Paragraph, Character, and Table Catalogs.

FrameMaker reapplies default formats from the Catalog to, for example, paragraphs and characters that contain formatting overrides.

✔ Tips

■ Importing formats is a *very powerful* feature. Save the document or make a backup before you import formats into it. Check that you've chosen the right document to import formats from, and that you've selected the right items to import.

■ Format names are case-sensitive; for example, body is not the same as Body. So if you import a paragraph format named Body, it won't override a paragraph format named body.

What Changes When You Import Formats

The document you import formats from is referred to as the "template" in this section, but it could be any FrameMaker document.

♦ **Paragraph Formats.** The template's Paragraph Catalog is merged into the document and all formats in the Catalog are reapplied in the document.

♦ **Character Formats.** The template's Character Catalog is merged into the document and all formats in the Catalog are reapplied in the document.

♦ **Page Layouts.** All the template's master pages are merged into the document and body pages are updated with the master page changes. If the template and the document have a master page with the same name, the template's master page replaces the document's master page.

♦ **Table Formats.** The template's Table Catalog and ruling styles are merged into the document and all formats in the Catalog are reapplied in the document.

♦ **Color Definitions.** The template's color definitions and views are merged into the document.

♦ **Document Properties.** The template's custom marker types, footnote properties, numbering, and settings in the Text Options dialog box are merged into the document.

♦ **Reference Pages.** All the template's reference pages are merged into the document. If the template and the document have a reference page with the same name, the template's reference page replaces the document's reference page.

♦ **Variable Definitions.** The template's variables and their definitions are merged into the document.

♦ **Cross-Reference Formats.** The template's cross-reference formats are merged into the document, and the internal cross-references are updated.

♦ **Conditional Text Settings.** The template's condition tags and Show/Hide settings are merged into the document and applied to conditional text.

BOOKS AND GENERATED FILES

The ability to group files into a book is one of FrameMaker's most powerful features. This book, for example, has a file for each chapter and appendix, in addition to files for the preface, TOC, glossary, and index. If I were part of a workgroup, different writers could be working on different files in the book.

When files are part of a book, you can add generated files such as a table of contents (TOC) or an index. A generated file is a file FrameMaker populates by extracting paragraph text or marker text from one or more source documents. A TOC is a list of chapter title and heading paragraphs; an index is an alphabetized list of text stored in index markers. When you update the book, you can regenerate the TOC and index as well.

You can use book files for more than books in the traditional sense; you could add files to a book file for easy access. For example, a program coordinator could create a book that contains all of the most common type of documents that need to be printed or faxed. It could contain an introduction to the program, schedules, program descriptions, a registration form, an information sheet, a confirmation form, directions to the facilities, and an invoice form.

About Book Files and the Book Window

A book file is a special FrameMaker file that allows you to group a number of files together, so you can work with them as a unit. When files are part of a book, pages can be numbered consecutively from one file to another. You can perform operations, such as spell checking or updating of cross-references, across all the files in the book at the same time.

Files in the book appear in a book window. They can be added and rearranged in a logical order from front to back (**Figure 13.1**). You can also access book commands from the icon bar at the bottom of the window (**Figure 13.2**).

To build a book, you assemble its components, which can be:

◆ Files such as the forward, introduction, chapters, appendixes, and glossary.

◆ Generated files that are added to the book and generated as part of the book building process, such as the TOC and index.

When the book is updated, FrameMaker updates generated files and numbering throughout the book (**Figure 13.3**).

Each file can have its own numbering system and style. You can start numbering the front matter in a book using lowercase roman numerals (i, ii, iii, and so on), for example, and then switch to arabic numbers (1, 2, 3, and so on) for the rest of the book.

Paragraph numbering, such as the autonumbering used for figure captions or table numbering, can be started or reset in the book file. Settings in the book file override settings in individual files.

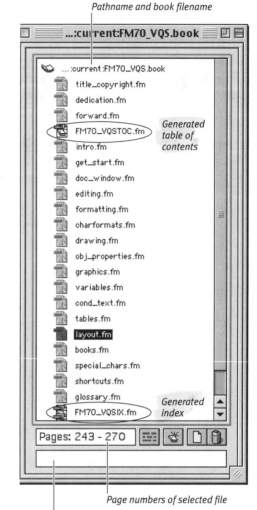

Figure 13.1 A book window with component files, including a generated TOC and index.

Figure 13.2 You can access book commands by clicking buttons on the bar at the bottom of the book window.

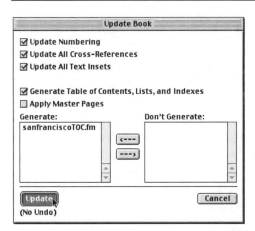

Figure 13.3 The Update Book dialog box displays items that can be updated across the book.

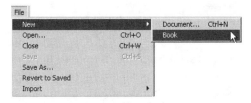

Figure 13.4 Choose File > New > Book.

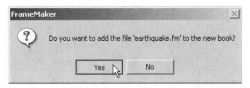

Figure 13.5 You can include the document you started from in the book, or you can start a new book without including an open document.

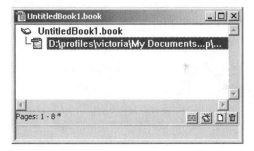

Figure 13.6 An untitled book window appears.

Building a Book

Here is an overview of the tasks involved in building a book file:

◆ Create the book file.

◆ Add all of the other files that you want to be part of the book.

◆ Add filenames for generated files.

◆ Set up numbering for the book.

◆ Update the book to add content to, or generate, the generated files.

◆ Generate and update on an ongoing basis as you add files to the book or change the content of existing files.

Creating a book and adding files

You can create a book file from any document or from a document that will be part of the book.

To create a book file:

1. Open a document that you want to be part of the book, and from the File menu, choose New > Book (**Figure 13.4**).

    (Mac OS only,) You can press Esc F Shift-N to create a new book without opening a document first.

    A warning message appears (**Figure 13.5**).

2. To open a new book file without including the document, click No.

    or

    To open a new book file that includes the document you started from, click Yes.

    A new, untitled book window appears with the document from which you created the book if you included it (**Figure 13.6**).

    (continues on next page)

3. From the File menu, choose Save Book As (**Figure 13.7**).

The Save Book dialog box appears.

4. Navigate to where you want to save the book and type a name for the book in the text box (**Figure 13.8**).

5. Click Save.

The book file is saved and the name appears in the title bar of the book window (**Figure 13.9**).

You can now add more files to the book.

✔ Tips

■ Keep all the documents that are part of a book, including the book file itself, in the same folder.

■ Don't include any numbering in filenames for files in a book, such as chapter_1 or Appendix A. If you reorder the files, the filenames will be misleading.

■ Always open files in a book from the book window. That way you know you're working in the most current and correct version, and that you haven't accidentally opened a .backup or a .auto file.

■ When you're working with documents that are part of a book, pay attention to whether you're choosing commands from the document menus (**Figure 13.10**) or the book menus (**Figure 13.11**). When a document is active, the document menus are displayed; when a book is active, the book menus are displayed. The book menus are a subset of the document menus, with one additional menu, the Add menu.

To add documents to a book:

1. In the book window, from the Add menu, choose Files (**Figure 13.12**).

or

Click the Add File icon (see **Figure 13.2**).

Figure 13.7 Choose File > Save Book As.

Figure 13.8 Save the book file in the same folder as the files that will be included in the book.

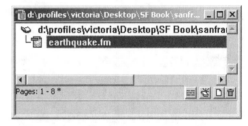

Figure 13.9 The book file is now saved and named.

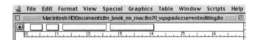

Figure 13.10 The document menus.

Figure 13.11 The book menus.

BUILDING A BOOK

Figure 13.12 Choose Add > Files.

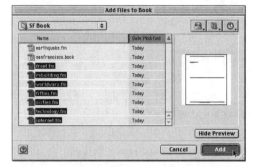

Figure 13.13 Select files from the list to add to the book file.

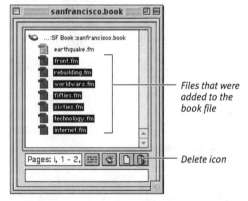

Files that were added to the book file

Delete icon

Figure 13.14 The files you added appear in the book window.

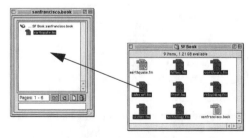

Figure 13.15 Select and drag files into the book window to add them to the book.

The Add Files to Book dialog box appears, displaying all the files in the current folder. You can navigate to any folder, but you can add only FrameMaker files.

2. Select one or more files in the list to add to the book (**Figure 13.13**).

   (Windows) Shift-click to select contiguous files; Ctrl-click to select noncontiguous files.

   (Mac OS) Command-Shift-click to select a range of files; Shift-click to select noncontiguous files.

3. Click Add.

   The files are added to the book file and appear in the book window (**Figure 13.14**).

It may be more convenient for you to drag and drop files from another book window or from a window on the desktop.

To drag and drop files:

◆ Drag files from another book window or a file manager window into the book window (**Figure 13.15**).

Once you have some of the component files in the book, you can rearrange them.

To rearrange files in the book window:

◆ In the book window, select one or more files and drag them to the correct position in the book window.

If you accidentally add a file you didn't intend to add or later want to remove a file, you can delete files from the book.

To delete files from the book:

1. In the book window, select the files you want to delete.

2. From the Edit menu, choose Delete File from Book.

   or

   Click the Delete icon.

   The selected files are deleted from the book and disappear from the window.

BUILDING A BOOK

Adding Generated Files to the Book File

When you add a TOC or an index to the book, you add a placeholder filename, which contains some information about the file itself. But these generated files are not populated until you update the book.

To add a TOC to a book and set it up:

1. In the book window, select a file next to where you want to add the TOC (**Figure 13.16**).

2. Choose Add > Table of Contents.

   The Set Up Table of Contents dialog box appears.

3. To add the TOC before the selected file in the book window, from the Add File pop-up menu, choose Before (**Figure 13.17**).

   or

   To add the TOC after the selected file in the book window, from the Add File pop-up menu, choose After.

4. To include the text from a type of paragraph in the TOC, select the paragraph tag in the Don't Include list and click the left arrow button.

   The selected paragraph tag moves to the Include Paragraphs Tagged list.

   or

   To remove a paragraph from the TOC, select the paragraph tag in the Include list and click the right arrow button.

5. To add hypertext links from the TOC entry to the source of the paragraph in the book, select Create Hypertext Links.

   Adding hypertext links in a generated file means that you can use a keyboard shortcut to click an entry and will FrameMaker take you to the source (see page 301). If you create a PDF file of the book, users will be able to click any entry and go to the source.

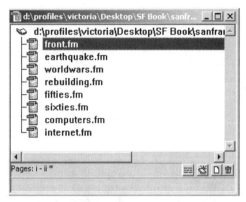

Figure 13.16 Select a file in the book next to where you want to add the TOC.

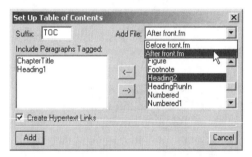

Figure 13.17 Specify where to add the file, what paragraphs to include, and whether to add hypertext links to the TOC entries.

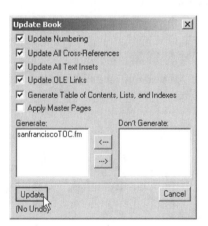

Figure 13.18 The Update Book dialog box with the default options selected. At this point you can choose to populate the TOC or to wait until later.

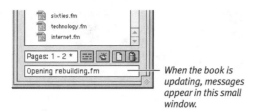

When the book is updating, messages appear in this small window.

Figure 13.19 When a book is updating, FrameMaker opens, closes, and saves the files in the book.

Figure 13.20 The generated TOC appears in the book window.

Figure 13.21 This message appears if you try to open a generated file that hasn't been updated for the first time from the book window.

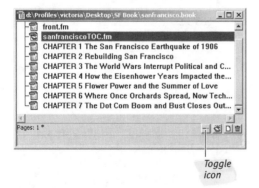

Toggle icon

Figure 13.22 Click the Toggle icon to switch between the filename and the text of the first paragraph.

6. Click Add.

The Update Book dialog box appears (**Figure 13.18**). By default, all options are selected except Apply Master Pages, and generally these are the ones you should use.

7. To generate the TOC, that is, to populate it with text from the included paragraphs, click Update.

As files in the book are opened and closed, status messages appear in the small white area at the bottom of the book window (**Figure 13.19**). When the new, generated file opens on the screen, save and close it.

or

To add the TOC filename without generating the book and populating the file, click Cancel.

The TOC is added to the book and appears in the book window (**Figure 13.20**).

✔ Tips

■ If you try to open a generated file from a book window and the file has not been updated at least once, a message appears (**Figure 13.21**). Click OK and update the book (see page 287).

■ To toggle display of files in the book window between the filename and the text of the first paragraph of the main text flow, click the Toggle icon (**Figure 13.22**). Toggling to text from the files in a book window is a good way to remind yourself of the chapter numbers, if chapter numbers are the first paragraph in each chapter.

ADDING GENERATED FILES TO THE BOOK FILE

To add a standard index to the book and set it up:

1. In the book window, select a file next to where you want to add the index, and from the Add menu, choose Standard Index (**Figure 13.23**).

2. In the Set Up Standard Index dialog box, from the Add File pop-up menu, specify whether to add the index file before or after the selected file (**Figure 13.24**).

    For a standard index, Index will appear in the Include Markers of Type list. You don't need to do anything further.

3. To add hypertext links from the index entry to the source of the entry in the book, select Create Hypertext Links.

4. Click Add.

    The Update Book dialog box appears.

5. To generate the index, that is, to populate it with index marker text, click Update.

    When the new, generated file opens on the screen, save and close it.

    or

    To add the index filename without generating the book and populating the file, click Cancel.

    The index is added to the book and appears in the book window (**Figure 13.25**).

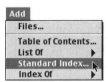

Figure 13.23 Choose Add > Standard Index.

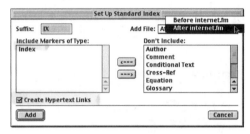

Figure 13.24 Specify where to add the file, what marker text to include, and whether to add hypertext links to the index entries.

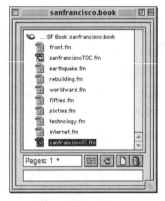

Figure 13.25 The generated index appears in the book window.

About Indexes

Standard indexes are generated using the text from index markers, which is then sorted alphabetically. You insert index markers manually in source documents and add text in the Marker window as shown in **Figure 13.28**. Entries with the same text are merged into a single entry, with multiple page references.

You can specify multiple levels for entries; even though for most books you'll use only first- and second-level index entries. You can add special building blocks to marker text to format index entries. Using building blocks, you can specify page ranges, suppress display of page numbers for cross-reference entries, or apply character formats.

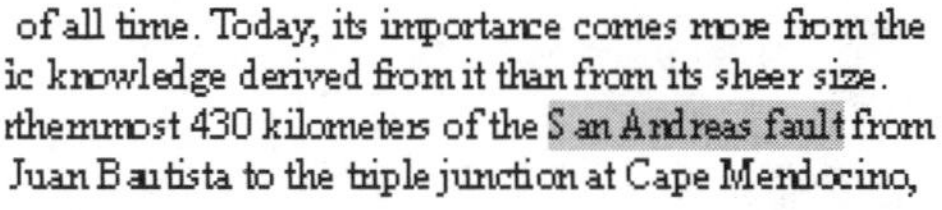

of all time. Today, its importance comes more from the
ic knowledge derived from it than from its sheer size.
rthernmost 430 kilometers of the San Andreas fault from
Juan Bautista to the triple junction at Cape Mendocino,

Figure 13.26 Select text you want to appear in the Marker Text box.

Special
Page Break...
Anchored Frame... ⌘H
Footnote ⌘E
Cross-Reference... ⌘K
Variable... ⌘B
Hypertext... ⌥⌘J
Marker... ⌘J
Equations... ⌘4
Conditional Text... ⌘5

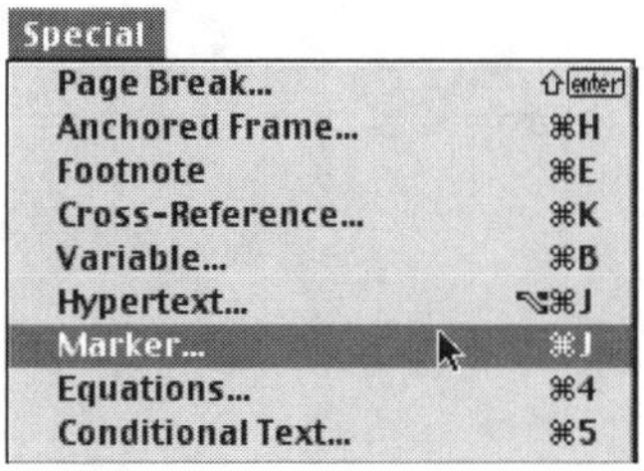

Figure 13.27 Choose Special > Marker.

Marker Type: Index
Marker Text:
San Andreas fault
New Marker
Author
Comment
Conditional Text
Cross-Ref
Equation
Glossary
Header/Footer $1
Header/Footer $2
HTML Macro
Hypertext
Index
Subject
Type 21
Edit...

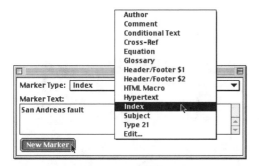

Figure 13.28 Edit the text in the Marker Text box and click new Marker.

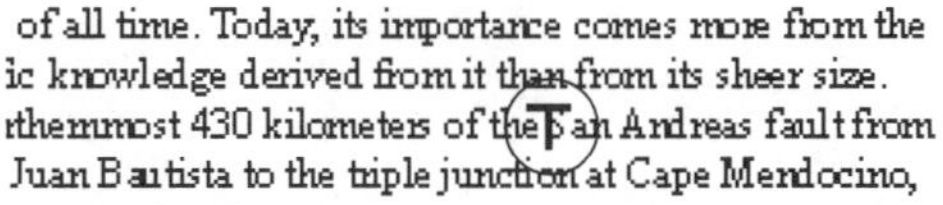

of all time. Today, its importance comes more from the
ic knowledge derived from it than from its sheer size.
rthernmost 430 kilometers of the San Andreas fault from
Juan Bautista to the triple junction at Cape Mendocino,

Figure 13.29 A marker symbol appears in the document when text symbols are on.

Using Index Markers

Whereas TOC entries are generated from the text of paragraphs in documents in the book, index entries are generated from text you add in the Marker window, similar to the way you added cross-reference marker text (see page 49). Before generating an index, you insert markers in the document. You can add different types of markers in the Marker window, such as a cross-reference marker (see page 49) or an index marker.

Adding index markers

Inserting an index marker in a FrameMaker document can be as simple as selecting text and using that text as the index entry.

To insert an index marker:

1. Click where you want to insert the marker.

   or

   In the document, select the text that you want to appear in the Marker Text box (**Figure 13.26**).

   As long as the selected text does not itself contain a marker, it automatically appears in the Marker Text box.

2. From the Special menu, choose Marker (**Figure 13.27**).

   or

   (Mac OS only) Press Command-J.

3. In the Marker window, from the Marker Type menu, choose Index (**Figure 13.28**).

4. In the Marker Text box, edit or add the text for the index entry.

   You can enter up to 255 characters.

5. Click New Marker.

   A marker symbol appears in the document (**Figure 13.29**).

To index a word automatically:

1. Click at the beginning of the word, and from the Special menu, choose Marker.

   You don't need to type anything in the Marker Text box.

2. In the Marker window, click New Marker.

   When the index is generated, the text to the right of the marker, up to the first space, becomes the entry.

Creating special marker text

When you add index markers, you use a special syntax to structure the entry as it will appear in the index.

To include several entries in one marker:

- In the Marker Text box, add the entries separated by semicolons (;) (**Figure 13.30**).

  Each of the entries between semicolons will become its own index entry. In this example, there will be one entry for "duration of earthquake" and another entry for "earthquake duration" (**Figure 13.31**).

To use subentries in an index:

- In the Marker Text box, add a subentry separated from the higher-level entry by a colon (:) (**Figure 13.32**).

  In this example, the first-level entry will be "reports" and under it, the second-level entry will be "Lawson's report (1908)" (**Figure 13.33**). If any other reports are indexed similarly, they will also appear as second-level entries under "reports."

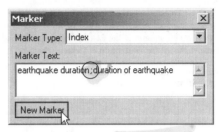

Figure 13.30 Separate multiple entries in one marker with semicolons ...

D
damage from the 1908 earthquake 2–4
duration of earthquake 2

E
earthquake damage 3
earthquake duration 2

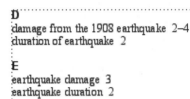

Figure 13.31 ... for separate index entries.

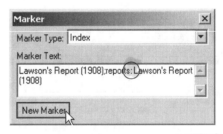

Figure 13.32 Use colons to create subentries ...

L
Lawson's report (1908) 2

R
reports
  Lawson's report (1908) 2

Figure 13.33 ... such as this second-level entry under "reports."

Table 13.1

Building Blocks for Index Entries	
Building block	**Meaning**
<$startrange>	Beginning of a range
<$endrange>	End of a range
<$nopage>	Suppresses the page number in the entry
<$singlepage>	Restores the page number for an entry that had been suppressed
Character tag between angle brackets, for example, <Emphasis>	Changes the character format of an entry
<Default Paragraph Font>	Restores the paragraph's default font

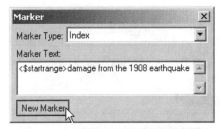

Figure 13.34 A marker for the beginning of a range of page numbers in an index entry.

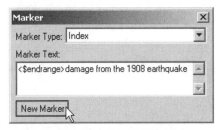

Figure 13.35 A marker for the end of a range of page numbers in an index entry.

D
damage from the 1908 earthquake 13–17
density of soil 15
duration of earthquake 8

Figure 13.36 A page range entry in an index.

You can use building blocks in marker text. **Table 13.1** lists some of the building blocks for index marker text. You can use building blocks for the following:

◆ For a page range, for example, 34–37

◆ To suppress the display of a page number for entries that cross-reference another entry, for example, See also Hayward fault.

◆ To use character formats stored in the Character Catalog, in the same way that you used character format building blocks for cross-references (see page 99) and variables.

To specify a page range in index entries:

1. Click in the document where you want the page range to begin.

2. In the Marker Text box, type <$startrange> and the entry (**Figure 13.34**).

3. Click New Marker.

   A marker is inserted at the beginning of the range.

4. Click in the document where you want the page range to end.

5. In the Marker Text box, type <$endrange> and the entry (**Figure 13.35**).

6. Click New Marker.

   A marker is inserted at the end of the range. If the <$startrange> marker is on page 13 and the <$endrange> marker is on page 17, the index entry would appear as "damage from the 1908 earthquake, 13–17" (**Figure 13.36**).

To suppress page number display:

◆ In the Marker Text box, type `<$nopage>` at the beginning of the text (**Figure 13.37**).

   In this example, the index entry would display the marker text, but not the page number, "San Andreas fault. See also Hayward fault" (**Figure 13.38**).

✔ Tips

■ If the same marker text occurs on consecutive pages, FrameMaker automatically creates page ranges in the index entry.

■ To be certain that identical text is used for the start and end markers, insert the start marker, copy the start marker symbol, and paste the symbol where you want to insert the end marker. Select the end marker symbol, and in the Marker Text box, change <$startrange> to <$endrange> and click Edit Marker (**Figure 13.39**).

■ After you add index markers, be sure to spell check the document. You may have accidentally copied and pasted letters or spaces if you copied and pasted index markers—or deleted letters or spaces.

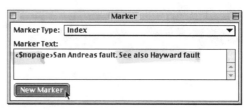

Figure 13.37 Cross-reference marker text with display of the page number suppressed.

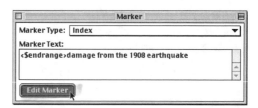

Figure 13.38 When you suppress display of the page number, the entry displays the marker text.

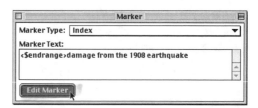

Figure 13.39 Edit the building block in the marker text and click Edit Marker.

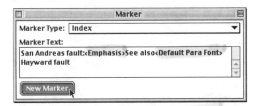

Figure 13.40 Use any character tag in the Character Catalog in angle brackets to format text in an index entry.

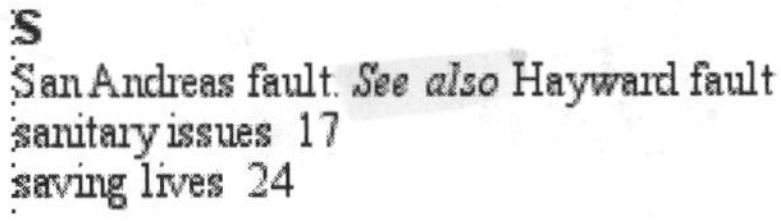

S

San Andreas fault. *See also* Hayward fault
sanitary issues 17
saving lives 24

Figure 13.41 In this example, Emphasis character format produces an italic font.

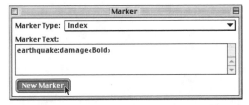

Figure 13.42 Adding the character format at the end of the marker text formats the page number.

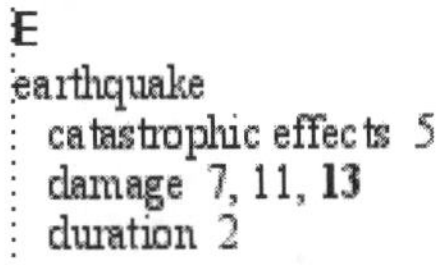

E

earthquake
  catastrophic effects 5
  damage 7, 11, **13**
  duration 2

Figure 13.43 Bold format for the page number indicates the most significant page reference.

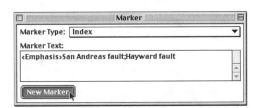

Figure 13.44 Character formatting affects only the entry it precedes.

Formatting Index Entries

You can add character formatting to parts of an index entry, including the page number. Often words in a cross-reference, such as "See also," are in italic text. And you might want to use bold text for a page number to indicate that this is where the most significant information is located.

To use a character format in an index entry:

◆ In the Marker Text box, type the character tag between angle brackets (< and >) at the beginning of the text you want to format. When you want to end the character format, type `<Default Para Font>` (**Figure 13.40**).

In this example, the index entry would appear as "San Andreas fault. *See also* Hayward fault" (**Figure 13.41**).

To format only a page number in an index entry:

◆ Type the character tag between angle brackets (< and >) at the end of the marker text.

Bold character formatting is often used to indicate the most significant page number from among several. If the entry "earthquake:damage<Bold>" (**Figure 13.42**) were inserted on page 13 among other entries on nonconsecutive pages in the same chapter, the entry would appear as "earthquake damage, 7, 11, **13**" (**Figure 13.43**).

✔ Tip

■ Character formatting affects only the entry it precedes. For example, "<Emphasis>San Andreas fault;Hayward fault" (**Figure 13.44**) generates two entries, but only the first entry would have the Emphasis character format.

Formatting Generated Files

As a general rule, you'll want generated files, such as a TOC and index, to look different from the rest of the book files. The first time you update a book after you add generated files, the generated file uses the page layout of the first nongenerated file in the book.

You can format a generated file:

◆ By working in the file itself, creating page layouts and paragraph and character formats for the generated file.

◆ By using a template or an existing generated file with page layouts and formatting already set up. You can use the template in one of the following ways:

▲ Put the template or existing file in the folder that contains the book files (**Figure 13.46**).

▲ Import formats from the template or existing file into the generated file.

Once you've formatted a generated file, the formatting stays in place, even when you regenerate the file.

To format a generated file by copying a template into the book folder:

1. Add the generated filename to the book file, *but don't generate the file.*

2. Copy the template into the folder that contains the book files and rename it to match the generated filename that appears in the book window.

   Now you need to update the book to pick up the formatting.

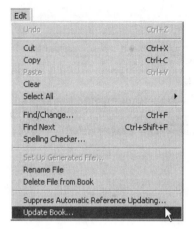

Figure 13.45 Choose Edit > Update Book.

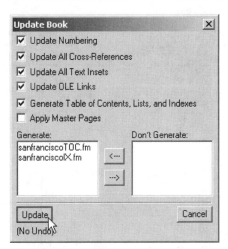

Figure 13.46 When you update the book, generated files pick up page layout and formatting if a a template with the same name as the generated files is present in the same folder.

To update a book:

1. In the book window, from the Edit menu, choose, Update Book (**Figure 13.45**).

or

Press Esc F G or Command-U.

or

Click the Update Book icon (see page 274).

The Update Book dialog box appears (**Figure 13.46**).

2. Make sure that the Generate Tables of Contents, Lists, and Indexes check box is selected and that the files you want to format are in the Generate list.

To move a file from one list to the other, select the file and click the left or right arrow, or double-click the filename.

To move all files from one list to the other, Shift-click an arrow.

3. Click Update.

The files in the Generate List are updated, and when you open them, you'll see the page layout and formatting from the template.

✔ Tip

■ Be sure that you update a book after you make any of the following changes:

▲ Perform editing that affects pagination

▲ Change a chapter or index title

▲ Add or delete files

▲ Change the order of files in the book.

▲ Add a new color

▲ Change conditional text settings

FORMATTING GENERATED FILES

Working in Book Files

Many tasks you perform in a file, such as searching and spell checking, are the same even when you perform them across all files in a book. Other tasks, such as renaming files in a book or the book file itself, work a little differently.

Renaming book files

Even after you've built a book, you may want to rename a file in the book.

To change the filename of a document in a book:

1. In the book window, select the file you want to rename (**Figure 13.47**).

2. From the Edit menu, choose Rename File. A box appears around the filename.

3. Type a new name for the file and press Enter or Return (**Figure 13.48**). The first of two warning messages appears.

4. Read the warning message and click OK (**Figure 13.49**). A second warning message appears.

5. Read the second warning message and click OK (**Figure 13.50**). The corresponding file is renamed and cross-references, hypertext links, and text inset links are updated in the other files in the book (**Figure 13.51**).

Figure 13.47 Select the file you want to rename.

Figure 13.48 Type a new name for the file and press Enter or Return.

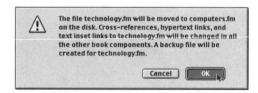

Figure 13.49 Read the first warning message ...

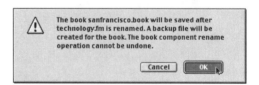

Figure 13.50 ... and the second warning message.

Figure 13.51 The file is renamed, and the new name appears in the book window.

Figure 13.52 Choose File > Save Book As.

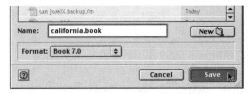

Figure 13.53 Type a new name for the book.

Figure 13.54 The book is renamed and so are generated files.

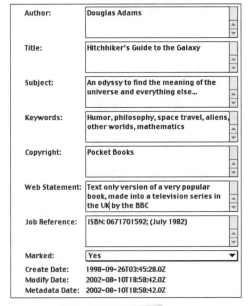

Figure 13.55 The metadata form.

To change the name of a book:

1. In the book window, choose File > Save Book As (**Figure 13.52**).

2. In the Save Book dialog box, type a new name for the book in the Name text box and click Save (**Figure 13.53**).

   The book is saved with the new name and any generated files are renamed to match the new book filename (**Figure 13.54**).

✔ Tips

- When you add a generated file to a book, it is assigned a filename based on the book's filename. If you rename a book, FrameMaker renames the generated files to match the new filename for the book. If you rename a *generated* file so it no longer has this default filename, renaming the book won't rename the generated file.

- If you are saving the book to a new location, you will need to open and save each file in the book individually to the new location.

Adding metadata to a book

FrameMaker includes built-in Extensible Metadata Platform (XMP) support. Metadata is descriptive information about the file and its contents that can be searched and processed by a computer, for example, as part of a content management system.

To add metadata to a book file:

1. In the book window, from the File menu, choose File Info.

   The File Info for Selected Files dialog box appears.

2. Add descriptive information in the form fields (**Figure 13.55**) and click Set.

   If the book becomes part of a knowledge database, for example, the metadata you added will be used to track, manage, and retrieve this document.

Opening, closing, and saving files from a book window

You can use a book window to open, save, print, and close individual files in the book. You can also open, save, and close all of the files in the book at once, and you can print and update the format of several files or all files at once.

To open files from a book window:

◆ To open one file in a book, select the file and double-click it.

◆ (Windows) To open several files, select the files you want to open and press Enter.

or

(Mac OS) To open several files, select the files you want to open and double-click one of the files.

◆ To open all the files in the book, hold down the Shift key and from the book's File menu, choose Open All Files in Book (**Figure 13.56**).

The documents in the book open one at a time until all the files are open.

When FrameMaker opens all files in a book, updating the files can take time. You can avoid this processing by suppressing automatic updating.

To suppress automatic updating:

1. From the book's Edit menu, choose Suppress Automatic Reference Updating (**Figure 13.57**).

2. In the Suppress Automatic Reference Updating dialog box, click the check box and click Set (**Figure 13.58**).

Now when you open all the files in a book, cross-references and text insets will not be updated, and files will open more quickly.

Remember to turn automatic updating back on when you no longer need to open all of the files at once. Do the same as before, but *turn off* Suppress Automatic Updating.

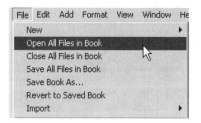

Figure 13.56 Choose File > Open All Files in Book.

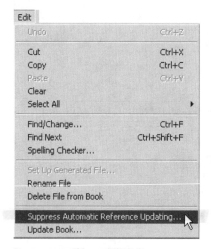

Figure 13.57 Choose Edit > Suppress Automatic Reference Updating.

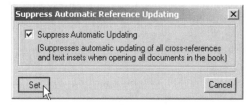

Figure 13.58 Click the Suppress Automatic Updating check box and click Set.

WORKING IN BOOK FILES

Books and Generated Files

Figure 13.59 Choose File > Save All Files in Book.

Figure 13.60 Choose File > Close All Files in Book.

Figure 13.61 Choose File > Revert to Saved Book.

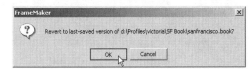

Figure 13.62 Click OK when prompted to confirm revert to saved.

To save all files in a book:

◆ Hold down the Shift key, and from the book's File menu, choose Save All Files in Book (**Figure 13.59**).

All files in the book are saved, including the book itself.

To close all files in a book:

◆ Hold down the Shift key, and from the book's File menu, choose Close All Files in Book (**Figure 13.60**).

All files in the book are closed, but the book window stays open.

Reverting to the last saved book

Settings for a book and for individual files in a book are saved with the book file. To change the contents of an individual file, you work in the file itself. Contents of individual files are not affected by reversion to the last saved book.

To revert to the last saved book:

1. From the book's File menu, choose Revert to Saved Book (**Figure 13.61**).

2. When the alert message appears, click OK (**Figure 13.62**).

Files that have been added are deleted; files that have been deleted are added back. Settings, such as numbering, pagination, or file setup for generated files, revert to the last saved version.

✔ Tip

■ The File > Revert to Saved Book command affects files that have been added or deleted as well as setting that have been applied to documents in the book, but the contents of the documents are not affected.

Setting up Numbering in a Book

Autonumbering of chapters, pages, paragraphs, and footnotes are all updated at the book level. By default, FrameMaker uses an arabic numbering style (1, 2, and so on) starting with page 1 for page numbering. You can change both the starting number and the numbering style by choosing an option from the Numbering Style and Format menus, which appear in multiple dialog boxes (**Figure 13.63**).

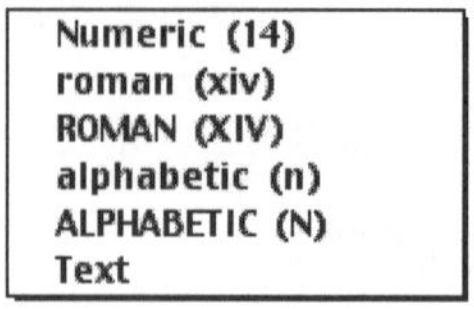

Specifying chapter numbering

All body pages in the same document use the same numbering style, but you can change the numbering style from document to document. For example, in this book, all documents up to Chapter 1 are numbered consecutively using lowercase roman numerals. After that, all the rest of the pages to the end of the book are numbered consecutively using arabic numbers.

To specify chapter numbering:

1. In the book window, select a document and from the Format menu, choose Document > Numbering (**Figure 13.64**). The Numbering Properties dialog box appears.

2. From the pop-up menu at the top of the dialog box, choose Chapter (**Figure 13.65**) or (Windows only) click the Chapter tab (**Figure 13.66**).

3. Do one of the following:
   - ▲ To specify a chapter number, type a number in the text box, and from the Format pop-up menu, choose a numbering style.
   - ▲ To increment the chapter number in the previous document in the book and use the same numbering style, select Continue Numbering From Previous File in Book (**Figure 13.67**).

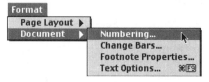

Figure 13.63 The numbering styles available for page numbering.

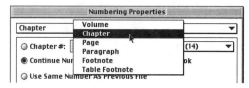

Figure 13.64 Select the file in the book window and choose Format > Document > Numbering.

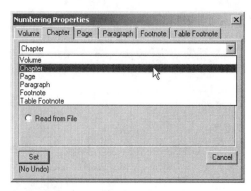

Figure 13.65 Choose an option from the pop-up menu at the top of the dialog box.

Figure 13.66 Choose from the menu or click a tab to display other numbering properties.

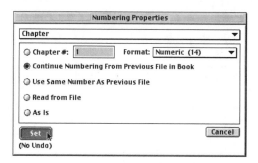

Figure 13.67 Select an option for chapter numbering.

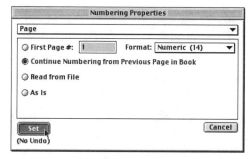

Figure 13.68 Set page numbering properties.

Volume and Chapter Numbering Building Blocks

Volume and chapter numbering variables are available only in FrameMaker 6.0 and above. If you are upgrading to FrameMaker 7.0 from a version earlier than version 6.0, you may want to replace building blocks such as <$paranum> and <$paranumonly> with <$volume> and <$chapnum> building blocks to take advantage of this feature.

You'll find <$volume> and <$chapnum> building blocks in the Numbering properties of the Paragraph Designer (see page 77), Edit Cross-Reference Format dialog box (see page 99), Edit System Variable dialog box (see page 180), and Edit User Variable dialog box (see page 174).

▲ To use the same chapter number as for the previous file, select Use Same Number As Previous File.

▲ To use chapter numbering from a selected document, select Read From File.

▲ If you selected more than one file in the book window, select As Is to use the numbering values specified in the selected documents.

4. Click Set.

✔ Tips

■ The Use Same Number As Previous File setting is the right choice if you have a very long chapter broken into two or more files.

■ You can select several files in the book and set chapter numbering as long as all of the settings are identical, for example, for all the chapters after the first.

Specifying page and paragraph numbering

Page numbering affects the page number system variables on master pages; paragraph numbering affects paragraph autonumbering and cross-reference formats.

To specify page numbering:

1. In the book window, select a document and from the Format menu, choose Document > Numbering.

2. In the Numbering Properties dialog box, from the pop-up menu at the top of the dialog box, choose Page (**Figure 13.68**) or (Windows only) click the Page tab.

3. Do one of the following:

▲ To specify the starting page number, type a number in the text box, and from the Format pop-up menu, choose a numbering style.

(continues on next page)

▲ To continue numbering from the last page of the previous file in the book, select Continue Numbering From Previous Page in Book.

▲ To use page numbering from a selected document, select Read From File.

▲ If you selected more than one file in the book window, select As Is to use the numbering values specified in the selected documents.

4. Click Set.

To specify paragraph numbering:

1. In the book window, select a document and from the Format menu, choose Document > Numbering.

2. In the Numbering Properties dialog box, from the pop-up menu at the top of the dialog box, choose Paragraph (**Figure 13.69**) or (Windows only) click the Paragraph tab (**Figure 13.70**).

3. Do one of the following:

▲ To reset paragraph autonumbering, select Restart Paragraph Numbering.

▲ To continue paragraph numbering from the previous file in the book, select Continue Numbering From Previous Page in Book.

▲ To use paragraph numbering from the selected document, select Read From File.

4. Click Set.

✔ Tips

■ Instead of setting numbering properties in the file, select the file in the book window and use the book's numbering properties. The book's numbering properties override the numbering properties set in individual files in the book.

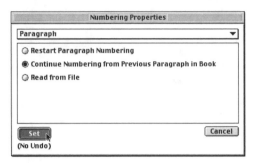

Figure 13.69 Set paragraph numbering properties.

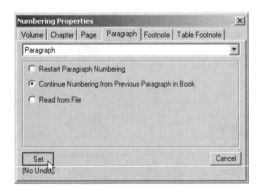

Figure 13.70 Choose from the menu or click a tab to display the paragraph numbering properties.

■ When you use the Chapter Number and Current Page # variables in page headers and footers on master pages of individual files—and building blocks such as <$chapnum> and <$pagenum> in cross-reference formats and paragraph autonumbering—their values are kept current when the book is updated.

Figure 13.71 Compound numbering style in footer.

Click here

Figure 13.72 Click in front of the Current Page # variable.

Figure 13.73 Add a Chapter Number variable in the page number of a master page.

Figure 13.74 A compound number in the footer on a master page.

Setting up compound numbering

To set up compound page numbering, such as you might find in technical manuals, you edit the definition of the Current Page # system variable. For example, you might want to use page 3-12 for page 12 of Chapter 3 (**Figure 13.71**). You will need to do this on all master pages that include page numbers in all of the individual files that you want to display compound numbering.

To set up compound page numbering in a document:

1. Go to the master pages and click in front of the Current Page # variable in a footer text frame (**Figure 13.72**).

2. From the Special menu, choose Variable to display the Variable dialog box.

3. In the Variables list, select Chapter Number and click Insert (**Figure 13.73**). The actual chapter number appears.

4. Type a separator character, such as a hyphen (**Figure 13.74**).

   Page numbers of body pages now display compound numbering.

✔ Tip

■ Set up compound page numbering in one file in the book and then import formats for Page Layout and Variables to specific files in the book that will use the same numbering (see page 365).

Troubleshooting Books

When you work with books, you may encounter problems or errors you need to correct so that the book will be generated and updated properly.

◆ If the generated file is empty, make sure that the name of the generated file in the book window has this icon (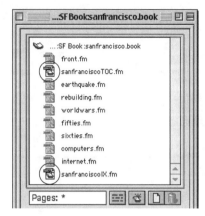) (**Figure 13.75**). If it does not, the file was added to the book as a document file rather than generated. Select the file in the book window and choose Edit > Delete File from Book. Make sure that the file has the correct default name, add a generated filename to the book, and then update the book. The update should generate a new file and pick up formatting from the nongenerated (bad) file.

◆ If one or more chapters start on the wrong side, select the document in a book window, choose Format > Page Layout > Pagination, and correct the pagination.

The Book Error Log reports all errors that occur when you perform book tasks (**Figure 13.76**). Click a link in the Book Error Log to display the problem document.

Understanding book error messages

Here are some of the messages you might see in the Book Error Log and explanations. The following errors will not stop a book from generating.

◆ Unresolved cross-references—Search for unresolved cross-references in the problem document and resolve them.

◆ Conditional text settings—The file has conditional text settings that differ from those of the previous file in the book. To make settings consistent, make the settings in one file correct, and then import them into the book.

Figure 13.75 The book has two generated files.

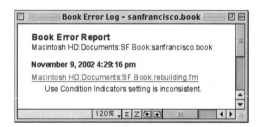

Figure 13.76 In the Book Error Log, you can click a link to display the problem document.

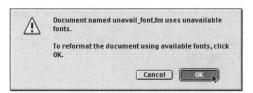

Figure 13.77 This warning about unavailable fonts is common, especially if you're moving files across platforms.

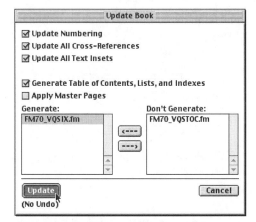

Figure 13.78 You can generate the index without generating the TOC.

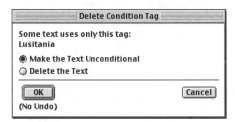

Figure 13.79 If this dialog box appears when you try to delete a condition, you know that the condition is used somewhere in the document.

◆ **Inconsistent color settings**—The file has color definitions or color separation settings that differ from those in the previous file in the book. To make settings consistent, make the settings in one file correct and then import them into the book. At the same time, you may have to delete unused color definitions.

The following error *will stop a book from generating* and can be one of the most frustrating messages to receive. If you can't open even one file in a book, you can't print the book and you can't create a PDF file.

◆ **Couldn't open file**

Open the individual file with the error— the alert message that appears tells you why the file can't be opened (**Figure 13.77**). The most common cause of this issue is unavailable fonts, especially if you're moving files across platforms (see page 359).

✔ Tips

■ When you are doing final production on a book, you may want to be more selective about what you update. For example, if you've done some touch-up on the TOC, you may want to exclude it from being generated when you perform a final update of the index (**Figure 13.78**).

■ To find out what conditions are being used in a document, try to delete them one at a time. Choose Special > Conditional Text, and in the Conditional Text window, select a condition and click Edit Condition Tag. In the Edit Condition Tag dialog box, click Delete. If the Delete Condition Tag dialog box (**Figure 13.79**) appears, you know the condition is used somewhere in the document. Click Cancel to abort the deletion.

Generated Files for Single Documents

The content for generated files is extracted from one or more source documents. You can generate TOCs and other generated lists for a book, but you can also generate a standalone file for a single document as the source.

Generating lists for a single document

You can generate files, such as a TOC or index, for single documents. You can also generate files for information purposes, for example, to see a list of condition tags used in the document.

To generate a TOC for a single document:

1. From the Special menu of the document for which you want to generate a TOC, choose Table of Contents (**Figure 13.80**).

   A prompt appears to confirm that you want to create a standalone TOC.

2. Click Yes (**Figure 13.81**).

   The Set Up Table of Contents dialog box appears. Note that the Add File pop-up menu is inactive.

3. Move the paragraph tags you want to include in the TOC to the Include Paragraphs Tagged list (**Figure 13.82**).

4. To add hypertext links from the TOC entry to the source of the paragraph in the document, select Create Hypertext Links.

5. Click Set.

   FrameMaker generates the TOC, with the same page layout as the original file but with no paragraph formatting, and displays it (**Figure 13.83**).

6. Save the generated TOC in the same folder or use the Save As command to save it in a different location.

GENERATED FILES FOR SINGLE DOCUMENTS

Figure 13.80 In the document, choose Special > Table of Contents.

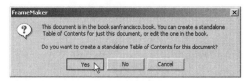

Figure 13.81 When prompted to confirm that you want to create a standalone TOC, click Yes.

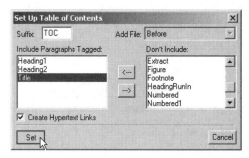

Figure 13.82 Move paragraphs to the Include list. When you're finished, click Set.

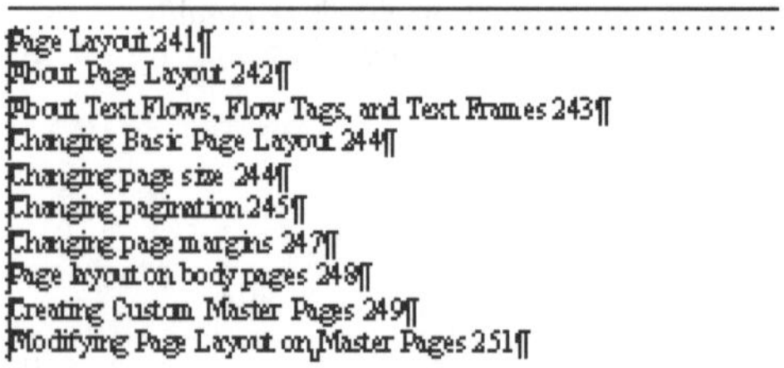

Page Layout 241¶
About Page Layout 242¶
About Text Flows, Flow Tags, and Text Frames 243¶
Changing Basic Page Layout 244¶
Changing page size 244¶
Changing pagination 245¶
Changing page margins 247¶
Page layout on body pages 248¶
Creating Custom Master Pages 249¶
Modifying Page Layout on Master Pages 251¶

Figure 13.83 The TOC has the same page layout as the original file and the paragraphs aren't formatted.

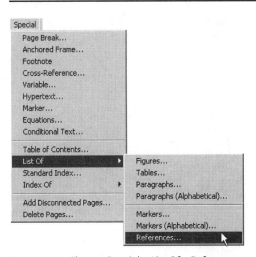

Figure 13.84 Choose Special > List Of > References.

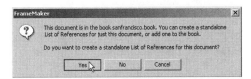

Figure 13.85 When prompted, click Yes.

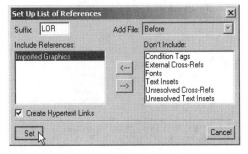

Figure 13.86 In this example, move Imported Graphics to the Include list and click Set.

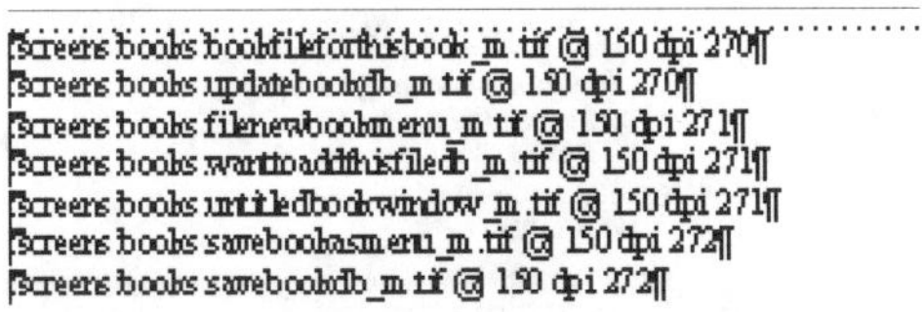

```
[Screens\books\bookfileforthisbook_m.tif @ 150 dpi 270¶]
[Screens\books\updatebookdb_m.tif @ 150 dpi 270¶]
[Screens\books\filenewbookmenu_m.tif @ 150 dpi 271¶]
[Screens\books\wanttoaddthisfiledb_m.tif @ 150 dpi 271¶]
[Screens\books\untitledbookwindow_m.tif @ 150 dpi 271¶]
[Screens\books\savebookasmenu_m.tif @ 150 dpi 272¶]
[Screens\books\savebookdb_m.tif @ 150 dpi 272¶]
```

Figure 13.87 The list of references has the same page layout as the original file and the paragraphs aren't formatted.

✔ Tips

■ You can generate a standard index from a single document in much the same way as a TOC. Choose Special > Standard Index.

■ If you close a TOC or list that you generate from a single document without saving it the first time, the document disappears. You must save it the first time you generate it.

In addition to a TOC and a standard index, you can generate several types of lists. For example, you can generate a list of figure titles or table titles. One of the most widely used lists is a list of imported graphics.

To generate a list for a single document:

1. From the Special menu of the document for which you want to generate a list, choose List Of > References (**Figure 13.84**).

   A prompt appears to confirm that you want to create a standalone list of references.

2. Click Yes (**Figure 13.85**).

   The Set Up List of References dialog box appears. Note that the Add File pop-up menu is inactive.

3. Move the items you want to include in the list to the Include References list (**Figure 13.86**).

4. To add hypertext links from the list entry to the source of the paragraph in the document, select Create Hypertext Links.

5. Click Set.

   FrameMaker generates the list, with the same page layout as the original file but with no paragraph formatting, and displays it (**Figure 13.87**).

6. Save the generated list in the same folder, or use the Save As command to save it in a different location.

✔ Tips

■ Lists present entries in the order in which paragraphs occur in the source document; indexes, such as an index of references (**Figure 13.88**), present entry paragraphs in alphabetical order.

■ Lists and indexes of references help you track special categories of information, such as a fonts used in the document (**Figure 13.89**). You can generate lists of all the items shown in **Figure 13.90**, including condition tags, external cross-references, publishers, text insets, unresolved cross-references, and unresolved text insets.

To add a title to a generated file:

1. Type the title before the first entry on the first body page after you generate the file for the first time.

2. Create a new paragraph format for the title, such as TOC Title or Index Title.

   Do not use a standard suffix, such as TOC, IX, or LOR, for this paragraph tag.

   When the file is regenerated, the title will remain in place as long as you haven't used a standard FrameMaker suffix (**Figure 13.91**).

Updating standalone generated files and changing file setup

When a generated file is part of a book, it can be regenerated when you update the book. You can also update standalone generated lists.

To change the setup of or update a standalone TOC or list:

1. Make changes in the document that is the source for the generated file.

2. In the source document, from the Special menu, choose the same command you used to generate the file originally.

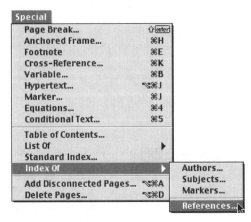

Figure 13.88 Choose Special > Index Of > References.

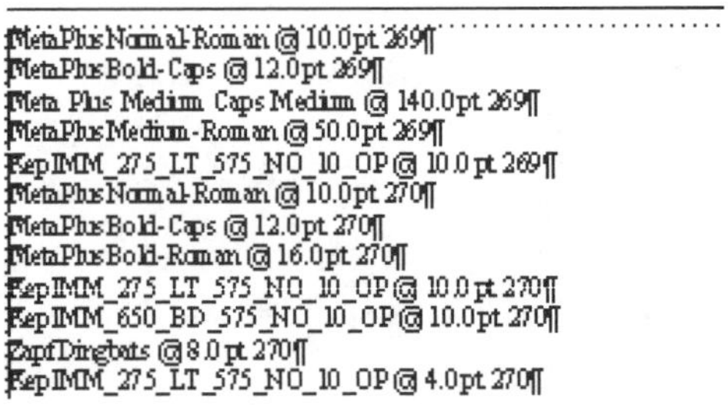

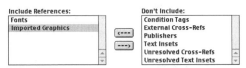

Figure 13.89 A list of references with fonts used in the document.

Figure 13.90 All of the special information about a document you can include in lists.

Contents

Figure 13.91 The next time the TOC in this example is regenerated, the title, "Contents," will remain in place.

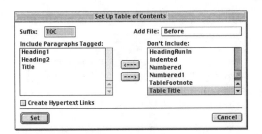

Figure 13.92 To change the setup, move items between lists.

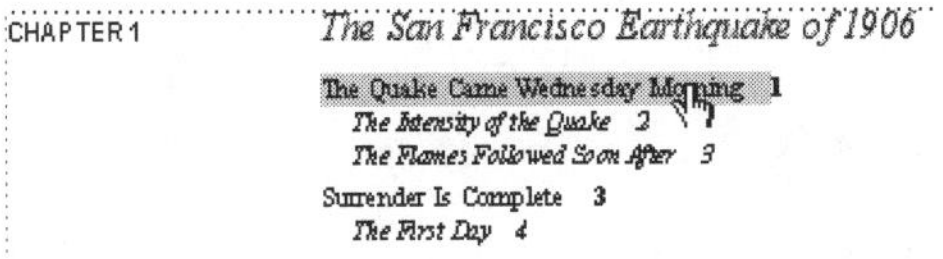

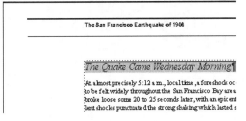

Figure 13.93 Alt-Ctrl-click or Control-Option-click an entry ...

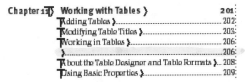

Figure 13.94 ... to go to the source.

Chapter 13 Working with Tables 201
  Adding Tables 202
  Modifying Table Titles 203
  Working in Tables 206
  206
  About the Table Designer and Table Formats ... 208
  Using Basic Properties 209

Figure 13.95 Example of an empty TOC entry.

3. When prompted to create a standalone document, click Yes.

4. To change the setup, in the dialog box that appears, move items between lists (**Figure 13.92**).

5. Click Set.

Entries in the generated file are updated and reflect the new setup. Any formatting you've made in the file is retained.

Finding the source of an entry

When you spell check an index or other generated file, you might find a spelling error and if so, you'll need to correct the marker text for that entry. Or you might see some first-level entries that you should change to second-level entries. You could go to the page in the entry and select marker symbols to find the right one. But if you selected Create Hypertext Links when you generated the file, you can easily find the source of an entry.

To find the source of a list entry by using a link:

◆ In the generated list, Alt-Ctrl-click or Control-Option-click the page number in an entry (**Figure 13.93**).

FrameMaker opens the source document, displays the page with the source paragraph or marker, and selects the source paragraph or marker (**Figure 13.94**).

Troubleshooting generated files

◆ If you find a spelling or other error, go back to the source document, fix the error, and regenerate the file.

◆ An empty entry in a TOC (**Figure 13.95**) means that you may have an empty paragraph in the source document tagged with an included tag. Delete the empty paragraph in the source document and regenerate the TOC.

(continues on next page)

GENERATED FILES FOR SINGLE DOCUMENTS

- Because FrameMaker allows you to index a word automatically by inserting an index marker with no marker text (see page 282), if you insert an "empty" index marker, the index entry displays the next word from the source document (**Figure 13.96**). If you see a word that clearly doesn't belong in the index, this could be the problem. Go to its source and delete the index marker.

- If a list contains an entry that doesn't appear to belong there, go to the source paragraph and check the entry's tag—you may need to apply a different tag so that the paragraph will not be included.

- If an index is missing an entry, its marker may be a marker type other than Index. Go to the source and display the Marker window (choose Special > Marker). From the Marker Type pop-up menu, choose Index and click Edit Marker.

- Double question marks in an index (**Figure 13.97**) mean that FrameMaker can find only one of the start or end markers or that the marker text doesn't match exactly (see page 283). Search for double question marks, and if you find them, check that you have both start and end range markers and that marker text is identical, including spelling, punctuation, and capitalization.

- You can make changes in entries in generated lists, but the next time the list is updated, the change will be overwritten. If you find an error or something you want to change in a generated list, change the paragraph or marker text at its source and then regenerate the file.

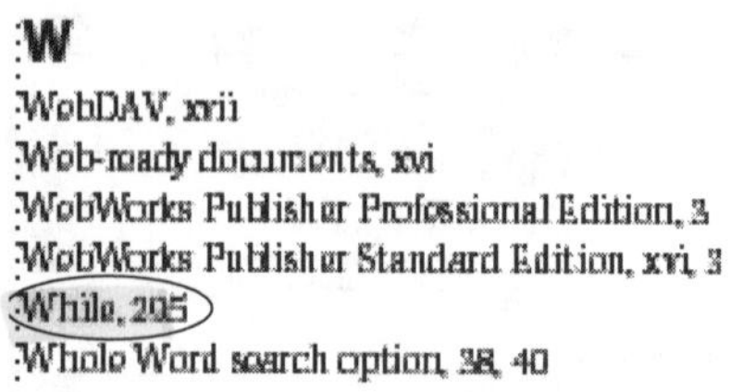

W

WebDAV, xvii
Web-ready documents, xvi
WebWorks Publisher Professional Edition, 3
WebWorks Publisher Standard Edition, xvi, 3
While, 295
Whole Word search option, 38, 40

Figure 13.96 An example of a bogus index entry caused by an index marker with no marker text. An empty index marker has been accidentally inserted before the word "While" in the source document.

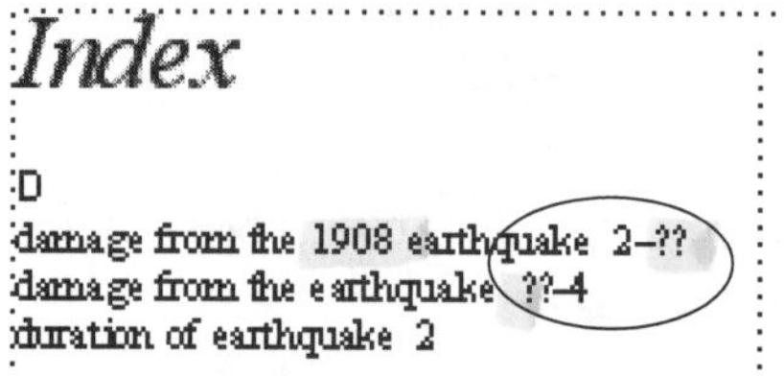

Index

D

damage from the 1908 earthquake 2–??
damage from the earthquake ??–4
duration of earthquake 2

Figure 13.97 In this example, because the marker text doesn't match, FrameMaker thinks it's two different ranges with missing markers in each.

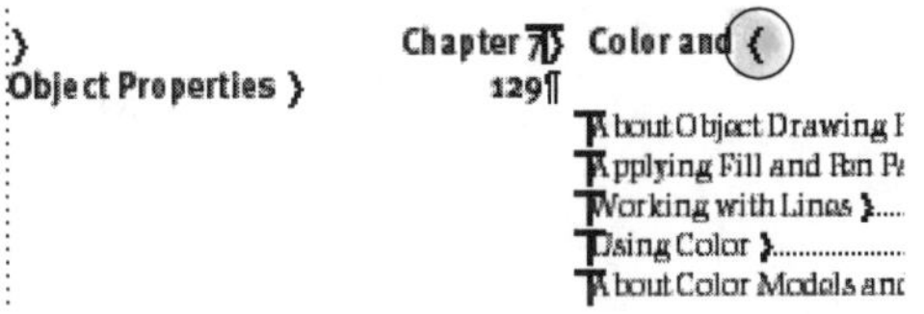

Figure 13.98 Example of a forced return in a TOC chapter title entry.

Figure 13.99 After deleting the forced return.

Touching up generated files

While you are getting your files ready for print or PDF, you need to do a few thing in the TOC and the index after the content in source files is frozen.

◆ Fix bad line breaks. In a TOC, if a paragraph in the source document contains a forced return, it will appear as an unneeded forced return (**Figure 13.98**). Delete the forced return symbol in the TOC (**Figure 13.99**).

◆ Insert page breaks.

◆ Visually inspect the file and apply any custom master pages, such as a Blank page for a last page with no entries.

✔ Tips

■ Touch-up formatting is overwritten when you regenerate the file, so plan to perform touch-up work only at the end of the production process, when you won't be regenerating the file. Of course, if you need to create a draft document, you may want to touch up generated files, even though you know you'll have to repeat the process again (probably several more times) later.

■ Although many writers do this, it is not necessary to re-import formats from templates during final production. In fact, it's better practice not to do so. When you import formats from a template, you may accidentally impact parts of the document you don't intend to change.

GENERATED FILES FOR SINGLE DOCUMENTS

PRINTING AND CREATING PDF FILES

Printing a document or a book in FrameMaker works much the same way as printing from other applications. And as with other applications, the available options vary slightly depending on the platform and printer you're using. With the exception of nonprinting text symbols and borders, what you see in the document window is what is printed.

Generating PDF files from a FrameMaker document or book is a completely automated task. When you save a FrameMaker file as PDF file, FrameMaker creates an interim PostScript file, which is then distilled using Acrobat Distiller. The result is a PDF file, which can be opened in Acrobat or Acrobat Reader on any platform.

Before starting the process, you can specify options that determine the attributes that your PDF file will contain. Possible attributes include bookmarks, the addition of tags for structured PDF, and automatically generated hyperlinks.

Setting Up For Printing

When you print a document, you can specify a number of options. Some of these options are specific to FrameMaker, such as whether or not to print crop marks. Others depend on the printer driver and printer description you're using.

Your computer's printer driver allows a desktop application to communicate with a printer. A printer description, such as a PostScript printer description (PPD) file, is specific to a printer model and describes the fonts, paper sizes, resolution capabilities, and other standard features for a PostScript printer.

Before you print, you should check settings in the Print Setup (Windows) or Page Setup (Mac OS) dialog box. You probably won't need to change these settings if you print on 8-1/2 x 11-inch paper (Letter) in portrait orientation.

To set up for printing on Windows:

1. From the File menu, choose Print Setup (**Figure 14.1**).

    The Print Setup dialog box appears (**Figure 14.2**). The current printer appears in the Name menu at the top.

2. To use a different printer, choose a printer from the Name menu.

3. To view the printing features supported by your current printer, click Properties.

    The Document Properties dialog box appears (**Figure 14.3**). The tabs and settings in each of the tabs are determined by the current printer.

4. Click OK to return to the Print Setup dialog box.

5. In the Print Setup dialog box, specify settings such as page size, paper source, and orientation and click OK.

    You're now ready to print using these settings.

Figure 14.1 Choose File > Print Setup.

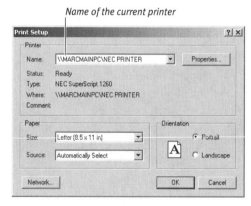

Figure 14.2 In the Print Setup dialog box, check settings such as page size and orientation.

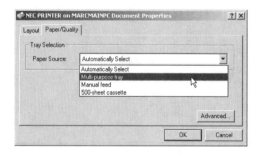

Figure 14.3 In this example, the printer does not have a large number of features, so the Document Properties dialog box is mostly empty.

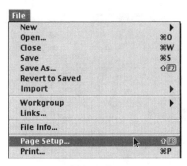

Figure 14.4 Choose File > Page Setup.

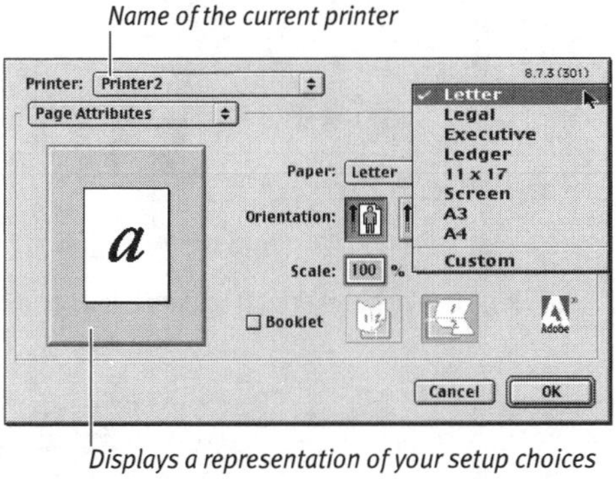

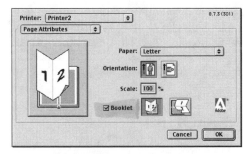

Name of the current printer

Displays a representation of your setup choices

Figure 14.5 The Page Attributes settings in the Page Setup dialog box.

Figure 14.6 Booklet settings allow you to specify double-sided printing across the short or long (shown) side of the page.

When you set up for printing on Mac OS, the Page Attribute settings in the Page Setup dialog box are determined by the current printer driver.

To set up for printing on Mac OS:

1. From the File menu, choose Page Setup (**Figure 14.4**).

   In the Page Setup dialog box, the first set of properties are Page Attributes.

2. Specify settings such as page size, orientation, and scale (printing at a greater or smaller percentage than the original).

   A representation of your choice appears in a display area on the left side of the dialog box each time you make a selection (**Figure 14.5**).

3. To specify how double-sided documents are printed, select Booklet and click one of the icons.

   The icon you selected appears in the display area (**Figure 14.6**).

   Settings elsewhere in the Page Setup dialog box are used for preparing files for offset printing and for creating PDF files. In general, you won't need to change any of these default settings.

4. Click OK.

   You're now ready to print using these settings.

✔ Tips

■ Your printer comes with documentation that tells you about its features and how to access them from your desktop. If you work in a corporate environment, make sure that you keep track of the documentation when a new printer is installed. If you keep it in a safe place, it will be available for everyone.

■ See the Adobe Web site for information on the latest PostScript drivers for both Windows and Mac OS: www.adobe.com/products/printerdrivers/main.html.

SETTING UP FOR PRINTING

Printing Documents

You can print documents to a networked printer or you can create PostScript files to provide to a commercial printer.

To print a document to a printer on Windows:

1. From the File menu, choose Print.

   or

   Press Esc F P or Ctrl-P.

   The Print Document dialog box appears. The name of the current printer is displayed at the bottom of the dialog box.

2. If you want to go back and change Print Setup settings at this point, click Setup (**Figure 14.7**).

   The Print Setup dialog box appears. Change any settings you wish and click OK to return to the Print Document dialog box.

3. Fill in print settings.

   See *Setting Print Options* on page 310 for details.

4. When you're ready, click Print.

   The print job is sent to the current printer.

To print a document to a printer on Mac OS:

1. From the File menu, choose Print.

   or

   Press Esc F P or Command-P.

   The Print dialog box appears. The name of the current printer is displayed at the top left of the dialog box.

2. From the Destination pop-up menu at the top right, choose Printer (**Figure 14.8**).

3. Fill in the print settings.

   See *Setting Print Options* on page 310 for details.

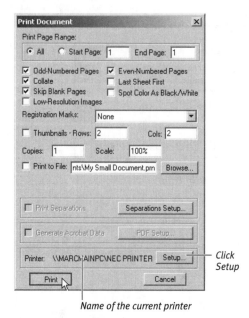

Click Setup

Name of the current printer

Figure 14.7 The Windows Print Document dialog box.

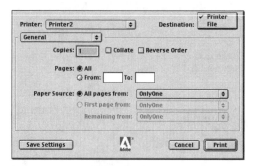

Figure 14.8 The General print settings.

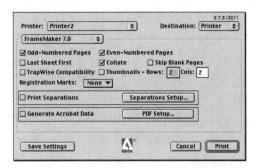

Figure 14.9 The FrameMaker 7.0 print settings.

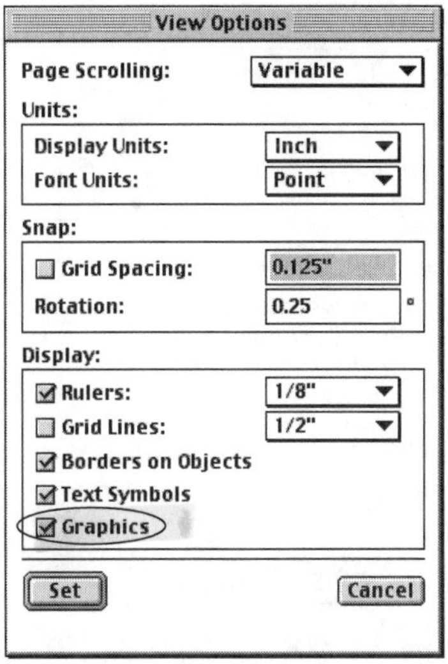

View Options

Page Scrolling: Variable ▼

Units:

Display Units: Inch ▼
Font Units: Point ▼

Snap:

☐ Grid Spacing: 0.125"
Rotation: 0.25 °

Display:

☑ Rulers: 1/8" ▼
☐ Grid Lines: 1/2" ▼
☑ Borders on Objects
☑ Text Symbols
☑ Graphics

Set   Cancel

Figure 14.10 Make sure Graphics is selected.

4. To access additional settings, choose from the pop-up menu under the Printer menu.

You'll most often need the General and FrameMaker 7.0 (**Figure 14.9**) settings.

5. To save a particular group of settings displayed in the dialog box, click Save Settings at the bottom left.

The settings will apply to any jobs you send to the printer until you change them.

6. When you're ready, click Print.

The document is sent to the printer.

✔ Tips

■ If you have graphics display turned off, graphics will not print. To turn on graphics display, choose View > Options, and in the View Options dialog box, in the Display area, select Graphics (**Figure 14.10**) and click Set.

■ For PostScript printing, FrameMaker recommends a PostScript Level 2 or higher output device.

■ (Windows only) FrameMaker has no control over the abilities or limitations of any printer driver; it can support only printer drivers that have been approved for use in the version of Windows on which FrameMaker is running.

If you're using an outdated printer driver, you may experience problems, such as lost graphics and characters and the inability to open documents.

PRINTING DOCUMENTS

Setting Print Options

The options described in this section are available for all printers from the Print dialog box. You may have additional print options available depending on the printer you're using. For more information, see the documentation for your printer.

On Windows, print options are displayed all together in the Print Document dialog box (**Figure 14.11**). On Mac OS, they are divided up into groups of options; choose from the pop-up menu below the Printer menu to display a group of properties (**Figure 14.12**).

◆ In the Print Page Range or Pages area, select All or enter a start page and an end page.

(Mac OS only) Enter only the starting page number to print from that page to the end; enter only the ending page number to print from the start to that page.

◆ Select Odd-Numbered Pages or Even-Numbered Pages.

FrameMaker will print only the odd-numbered pages (1, 3, 5, and so on) or only the even-numbered pages (2, 4, 6, and so on). If you want to print all of the pages in the file or book, be sure to keep both options selected.

◆ If you're printing multiple copies, to print one complete copy before printing the next copy, select Collate (**Figure 14.13**).

Printing may be slower when Collate is selected.

◆ To print a document starting with the last page, select Last Sheet First.

◆ To suppress printing of blank pages, select Skip Blank Pages.

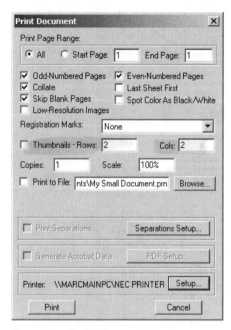

Figure 14.11 On Windows, print options are displayed in the Print Document dialog box.

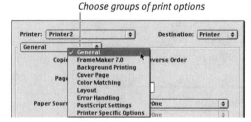

Figure 14.12 On Mac OS, choose from the pop-up menu below the Printer pop-up menu to display groups of print options.

SETTING PRINT OPTIONS

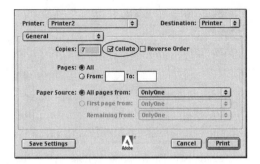

Figure 14.13 Select Collate in the General print options on Mac OS.

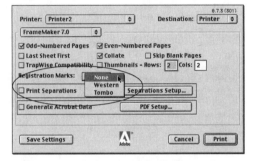

Figure 14.14 Turn crop and registration marks on or off in the FrameMaker 7.0 print options on Mac OS.

◆ (Windows) Select Spot Color As Black/White.

or

(Mac OS) With the AdobePS Printer Driver 8, in the Color Matching properties, choose Black and White from the Print Color pop-up menu, and click OK.

Colored items (FrameMaker-drawn images and text) are printed in black and white rather than in shades of gray.

◆ (Windows only) To print a document more quickly, select Low-Resolution Images. Imported images are printed as gray boxes.

◆ From the Registration Marks pop-up menu, choose None, Western, or Tombo (**Figure 14.14**).

FrameMaker will add crop and registration marks to the printed document. You may need to scale down the printed page image so that crop marks and registration marks will fit on the page size you can print.

◆ Thumbnails are small images of several pages on one page. FrameMaker sizes the thumbnail pages to fit on the paper size specified. The larger the values in the text boxes, the smaller the thumbnails will be.

In the Thumbnails Rows text box, type the number of thumbnails you want to print down the page; in the Columns text box, type the number of thumbnails you want to print across the page.

◆ Type the number of copies to print in the Copies text box.

◆ (Windows) Enter a percentage in the Scale text box.

or

(Mac OS) From the File menu, choose Page Setup, and enter a percentage in the Reduce or Enlarge text box.

SETTING PRINT OPTIONS

Printer driver version

If you need to troubleshoot printing problems, whether you use Adobe support or search the Adobe knowledgebase (see page 366), you'll need to know what version of printer driver is installed on your computer.

To find out what version of Mac OS PS printer driver is installed:

1. On Mac OS v9.2, from the Apple menu, choose Apple System Profiler.

2. In the System Profile tab, scroll down to the Printer overview (**Figure 14.15**).

   You may need to click the right arrow to display the overview (**Figure 14.16**).

   The overview includes every printer instance that appears on the desktop (**Figure 14.17**).

Figure 14.15 Scroll down in the System Profile tab to the Printer overview. You may need to click the right arrow (circled) to display the overview.

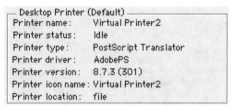

Figure 14.16 This is the overview for the Virtual Printer 2 printer instance.

Figure 14.17 (Mac OS) Three printer instance icons on the desktop.

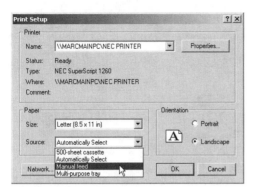

Figure 14.18 From the Source menu, choose Manual Feed.

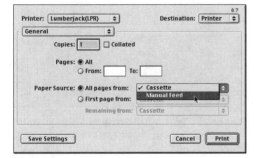

Figure 14.19 From the Paper Source menu, choose Manual Feed.

Manual printing

Even if your printer does not have a duplex (double-sided printing) option, you can print double-sided manually.

To print double-sided manually:

1. Print the odd-numbered pages.

2. Turn the paper over in the printer.

3. Print the even-numbered pages.

   Depending on how your printer produces pages, you may need to select Last Sheet First, because turning the paper over in the printer may reverse the page order.

To feed paper manually:

To print the document on paper that is not in your printer's paper cassette:

◆ (Windows) From the File menu, choose Print Setup; from the Source menu, choose Manual Feed (**Figure 14.18**) and then click OK.

   or

   (Mac OS) From the pop-up menu in the Paper Source area, choose Manual Feed (**Figure 14.19**).

✔ Tip

■ (Windows only) The Print Document dialog box in FrameMaker contains some options that may also appear in the Windows printer Properties dialog box, such as the number of copies. *FrameMaker printer settings override Windows printer settings.*

SETTING PRINT OPTIONS

Creating PostScript Files

Instead of printing a document to a local printer, you can create a PostScript (PS) file, which can then be converted to PDF via Adobe Distiller, downloaded to a PostScript printer using a download utility, or given to a commercial printer.

To create a PS file for a single document:

1. From the File menu, choose Print.

2. (Windows) Select Print to File and check the path and the filename in the text box. Click Browse to specify a different folder and filename (**Figure 14.20**).

   or

   (Mac OS) From the Destination pop-up menu, choose File.

3. Specify a .ps extension for the file (**Figure 14.21**).

4. Click Print or Save.

   The PS file for the document is saved into the location you specified.

To create a single PS file for a book:

1. In the book window, from the File menu, choose Print Book.

   or

   In the book window, select the documents you want to print, and from the File menu, choose Print Book.

2. (Windows) Select Print to File and check the path and the filename in the text box. Click Browse to specify a different folder and filename. From the Save As pop-up menu, choose Single File.

   or

   (Mac OS) From the Destination pop-up menu, choose File.

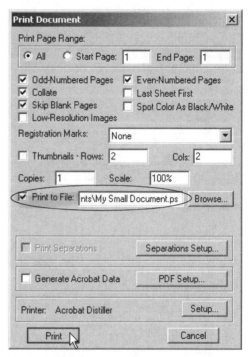

Figure 14.20 Specify a folder and a filename. Note that in this example, the current printer is Acrobat Distiller.

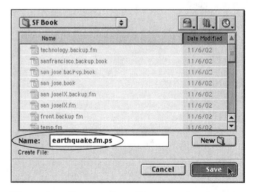

Figure 14.21 Type a name with a .ps extension.

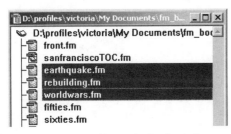

Figure 14.22 Select files in the book window.

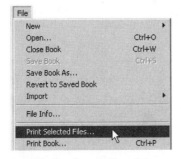

Figure 14.23 Choose File > Print Selected Files.

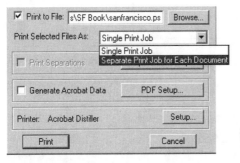

Figure 14.24 From the Print Selected Files As menu, choose Separate Print Job for Each Document.

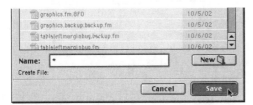

Figure 14.25 To save selected files or each file in a book separately, type an asterisk (*) in the Name text box.

3. Specify a `.ps` extension for the file, and click Print or Save.

The PS file for the book is saved in the location you specified.

To create separate PS files for files in a book:

1. In the book window, from the File menu, choose Print Book.

or

In the book window, select the documents you want to print (**Figure 14.22**), and from the File menu, choose Print Selected Files (**Figure 14.23**).

2. (Windows) Select Print to File and check the path and the filename in the text box. Click Browse to specify a different folder and filename. From the Print Selected Files As menu, choose Separate Print Job for Each Document (**Figure 14.24**).

or

(Mac OS) From the Destination pop-up menu, choose File and then click Save. Type an asterisk (*) in the Name text box (**Figure 14.25**).

3. Click Print or Save.

Separate PS files are saved in the location you specified.

Preparing files for offset printing

If you need to prepare files for commercial (offset) printing, ask your print vendor for the specifications for the imagesetter that will be used for your files. The printer may be able to provide you with detailed instructions for creating a PostScript file from FrameMaker. Some of the settings you should ask for are:

◆ Line screen specifications

◆ Specification of positive or negative film up

◆ Halftone screen specifications

CREATING POSTSCRIPT FILES

Creating PDF Files

If you want to get started creating PDF files from FrameMaker, you can use default settings. When you're more comfortable with PDF features and how to use them, you can configure settings to meet you particular needs.

Generating PDF files with default settings

Although FrameMaker and Distiller provide a variety of settings for your PDF files, use the following tasks to create PDFs with default settings.

The FrameMakerPDFWriter Printer Instance

On a Mac OS desktop, you'll see icons that represent printer instances. A printer instance is a connection to your printer set up by a system-level driver. Each printer instance is customized for a particular output device's print features.

To create the FrameMakerPDFWriter printer instance on Mac OS:

1. Confirm that Acrobat Distiller 5.05 is installed on your computer.

2. From the Apple menu, select Chooser and click the AdobePS printer driver icon (**Figure 14.26**).

3. With the Chooser open, launch FrameMaker.

4. From FrameMaker's File menu, choose Print.

   A new printer is available on the Printer menu (**Figure 14.27**) and a new printer instance called FrameMakerPDFWriter is created on the desktop.

5. In the Print dialog box, click Cancel to return to FrameMaker, and close the Chooser.

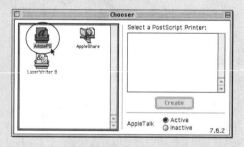

Figure 14.26 Click the AdobePS printer icon.

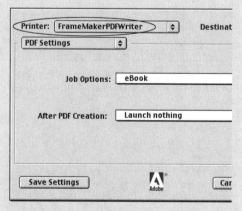

Figure 14.27 The new FrameMakerPDFWriter printer choice.

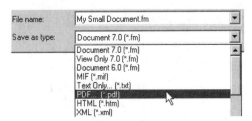

Figure 14.28 Choose PDF from the Format menu.

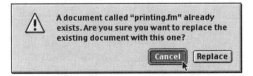

Figure 14.29 FrameMaker warns you if you continue with the .fm file extension, you will overwrite the FrameMaker file with the PDF file.

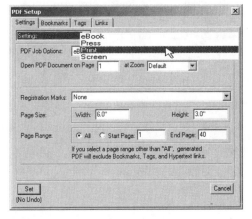

Figure 14.30 Choose a PDF Job Options setting.

To save a document or book as PDF using default settings:

1. From the File menu of a document or book window, choose Save As.

   To save an entire book as PDF, in the book window, from the File menu, choose Save Book As.

2. In the Save Document dialog box, navigate to a location on your computer to save the PDF file.

3. In the File name text box, change the file extension from the default (.fm) to .pdf.

4. From Save as type or Format pop-up menu, choose PDF (**Figure 14.28**).

5. Click Save.

   (Windows) If you didn't give the filename a .pdf extension, FrameMaker prompts you to do so. Click Yes.

   (Mac OS) If you didn't give the filename a .pdf extension, FrameMaker warns you that if you continue with the .fm file extension, you will overwrite the FrameMaker file with the PDF file (**Figure 14.29**). Click Cancel and in the Save Document dialog box, add a .pdf file extension.

   The PDF Setup dialog box appears.

6. From the PDF Job Options pop-up menu, choose from the following (**Figure 14.30**):

   ▲ To optimize the PDF file for both viewing on the screen and printing to desktop printers, choose eBook.

   ▲ To generate a PDF file optimized for output through commercial print service providers, choose Press.

   ▲ To optimize the PDF file for output on desktop printers, choose Print.

   ▲ To generate a PDF file optimized *for screen viewing only*, choose Screen.

   (continues on next page)

CREATING PDF FILES

7. Click Set.

A PostScript file is generated and distilled by Acrobat Distiller to create a PDF file. The PDF file appears in the location you specified when you started the job.

✔ Tips

■ The eBook and Screen PDF job options produce the most compact PDF files.

■ If the original document contains many high resolution images, the quality of those images will be better preserved with the Print option than with the eBook option.

■ The quality of high resolution images will be preserved best with the Press option, but the file size will be much larger than with the other options.

■ With the Screen option, all grayscale and color images with a resolution greater than 108 dpi will be downsampled to 72 dpi. If the PDF file is then printed, the images will have jagged details.

Reducing the Size of a PDF File

Here are a couple of ways you can reduce the size of a PDF file:

◆ Embedding fonts, especially Asian fonts, increases the size of a PDF file. To control font embedding, create or modify a job options file using Acrobat Distiller and then choose the file you created or modified from the PDF Job Options menu in the Settings options in the PDF Setup dialog box.

◆ If you don't intend to repurpose the PDF file, do not use the Generate Tagged PDF option in the Tags settings in the PDF Setup dialog box. Although when you click Set to start creating the PDF file, you may see an error message (see page 324), it doesn't mean the links in your FrameMaker document won't be present in the PDF file you create.

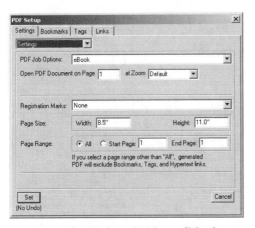

Figure 14.31 The Windows PDF Setup dialog box.

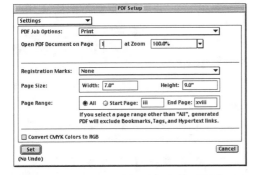

Figure 14.32 The general Settings in the PDF Setup dialog box.

Figure 14.33 Type a page number and choose a zoom value.

Figure 14.34 Choose an option from the Registration Marks menu.

Configuring PDF Setup

FrameMaker provides options for adding bookmarks and hypertext links to a PDF file in the PDF Setup dialog box. For a more detailed information about PDF setup, see *PDF with Acrobat 5: Visual QuickStart Guide* by Jennifer Alspach (Peachpit Press).

To configure general settings in PDF Setup:

1. To display the PDF Setup dialog box, follow steps 1 through 5 starting on page 317.

   The Settings options appear in the PDF Setup dialog box (**Figure 14.31** and **Figure 14.32**).

2. From the PDF Job Options menu, choose an option for the PDF file.

   For information on the job options, see step 6 on page 317.

3. Type the page number to which the PDF file will open in Acrobat or Acrobat Reader (**Figure 14.33**).

4. Choose the zoom percentage at which the PDF file will open.

5. To add crop and registration marks to the PDF file, from the Registration Marks menu, choose Roman or Tombo (Japanese) (**Figure 14.34**).

   Although the menu is labeled Registration Marks, it specifies both crop and registration marks.

6. To change the size of the page, enter measurements in the Width and Height text boxes.

   (continues on next page)

CONFIGURING PDF SETUP

7. In the Page Range area, select All or enter start and end page numbers in the text boxes (**Figure 14.35**).

8. (Mac OS only) Leave the Convert CMYK Color to RGB option turned off (**Figure 14.36**).

You may want to turn on this option when your document includes a large number of CMYK images and art that you want to convert to RGB so that display of the PDF file will be faster.

9. If you don't need to configure settings elsewhere in the dialog box, click Set.

Otherwise, click another tab or from the menu at the top left, choose another set of options.

✔ Tip

■ While you're configuring your PDF file in the PDF Setup dialog box, refrain from clicking Set until you're ready to start the process of creating a PDF file. You might be tempted to click Set after working on one group of settings instead of waiting until you've completed the setup.

Configuring bookmarks

Bookmarks settings enable you to generate bookmarks in a PDF file based on paragraphs with specific formats in your FrameMaker document. You can also expand bookmarks to different levels as shown in **Figure 14.37**.

To configure bookmarks in PDF setup:

1. (Windows only) With the PDF Setup dialog box still displayed, click the Bookmarks tab.

or

From the pop-up menu at the top left of the dialog box, choose Bookmarks.

The Bookmarks options appears in the PDF Setup dialog box.

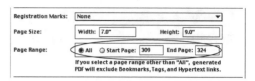

Figure 14.35 Select All to include all document pages in the PDF, or enter start and end pages.

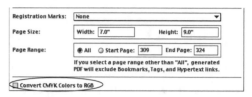

Figure 14.36 Leave the Convert CMYK Color to RGB option off (Mac OS).

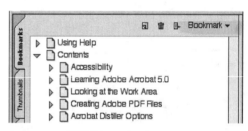

Figure 14.37 In this example, the Contents bookmark is expanded one level in the Bookmarks palette on the left side of the PDF window.

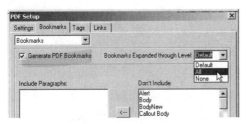

Figure 14.38 Choose the number of levels to expand the bookmarks in the PDF file.

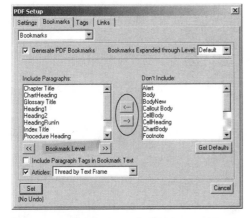

Figure 14.39 Move paragraphs that you want to include in bookmarks to the Include Paragraphs list.

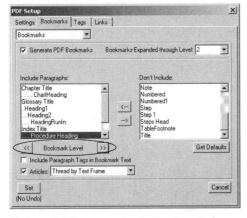

Figure 14.40 Change the level of bookmarks for a paragraph in the Include Paragraphs list.

2. To include bookmarks in the PDF file, select the Generate PDF Bookmarks option.

3. From the Bookmarks Expanded through Level menu at the top right, choose All or None (**Figure 14.38**).

   or

   Type the number of levels for bookmarks to be expanded in the text box.

4. To specify which paragraphs to include as bookmarks in the PDF file, move paragraphs from the Don't Include list to the Include Paragraphs list.

   Initially you may need to click in the Include Paragraphs list and, holding down the Shift key, click the right arrow to move all items to the Don't Include list.

   To move a paragraph to the Include Paragraphs list, select it and click the left arrow. You can also double-click a paragraph to move it to the other list (**Figure 14.39**).

   When you move a paragraph into the left list, it appears at the far left, that is, at the first level.

5. To change the levels of bookmarks for a paragraph in the left list, select the paragraph and click one of the Bookmark Level arrows at the bottom of the list once to move one level (**Figure 14.40**).

6. To include the actual paragraph tag with the text of each bookmark in the PDF document, select Include Paragraph Tags in Bookmark Text.

7. Leave the Articles option set to its default setting, Thread by Text Frame.

8. If you don't need to configure settings elsewhere in the dialog box, click Set.

   Otherwise, click another tab or from the menu at the top left, choose another set of options.

✔ Tips

- In the Include Paragraphs list, to move all paragraphs to the far left (top level), select one paragraph, hold down the Shift key, and keep clicking the left Bookmark Level arrow until all the paragraphs are positioned at the far left.

- Use the Include Paragraph Tags in Bookmark Text option (**Figure 14.41**) only for checking the assigned levels of bookmarks in a draft PDF document. Turn off this option when you generate the final PDF file.

Figure 14.41 Use the Include Paragraph Tags as Bookmark Text option during development and turn it off for the final PDF.

About tagged PDF

Using tagged PDF, you can create Adobe PDF files from FrameMaker with a logical document structure and extensive metadata for repurposing content. Logical structure refers to the organization of the document, such as the title page, chapters, sections, and subsections. With each of the structural components in a document tagged, the resulting PDF and its content is more easily repurposed.

For example, tagging a PDF file's components promotes the reflow of its content on devices with less screen real estate, such as an eBook reading device. On page 167, you saw how to add alternative text descriptions for graphics in anchored frames for tagged PDF files to be read by screen readers.

Tagged Adobe PDF files include the author's contents, but don't include information not considered useful when repurposing the document contents, such as headers, footers, graphical design elements, and typographic information.

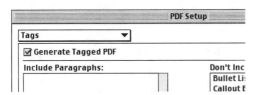

Figure 14.42 To include structural tags in the PDF file, select the Generate Tagged PDF option.

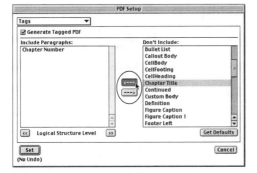

Figure 14.43 Select a paragraph and click the left arrow to move it to the Include Paragraphs list.

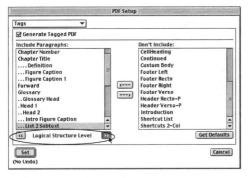

Figure 14.44 Select a paragraph in the Include Paragraphs list and click a Logical Structure Level arrow to move it up or down in the hierarchy.

Configuring tags

The tags you configure in PDF setup are displayed in the logical structure tree of a tagged PDF document.

To configure tags in PDF setup:

1. (Windows only) With the PDF Setup dialog box still displayed, click the Tags tab.

   or

   From the pop-up menu at the top left, choose Tags.

   The Tags properties appear in the PDF Setup dialog box.

2. To include tags in the PDF file, select Generate Tagged PDF (**Figure 14.42**).

   Adding tags to a PDF includes additional information in the form of metadata that further defines the logical structure of your document.

3. To specify which paragraphs to include in the logical structure of the PDF file, move paragraphs from the Don't Include list to the Include Paragraphs list.

   To move a paragraph to the Include Paragraphs list, select it and click the left arrow (**Figure 14.43**). You can also double-click a paragraph to move it to the other list.

4. To change the level of a paragraph in the hierarchy of the document's logical structure, select it in the Include Paragraphs list, and click a Logical Structure Level arrow at the bottom of the list once for each level change (**Figure 14.44**).

5. If you don't need to configure settings elsewhere in the dialog box, click Set.

   Otherwise, click another tab or from the menu at the top left, choose another set of options.

Adding links

A FrameMaker document generated from a single file or from a book file may include hypertext links in cross-references or links generated automatically in TOCs and indexes. But it does not contain links to other documents. You can add those links after the PDF file is created.

If you intend to add links to the document from other documents after you create the PDF file, you can use named destinations to identify paragraphs that are referenced by cross-references and hypertext links. If the Create Named Destinations for All Paragraphs option is *not* on and you add a link or cross-reference from one FrameMaker document to another, you'll need to resave both documents as PDF.

To configure links in PDF setup:

1. (Windows only) With the PDF Setup dialog box still displayed, click the Links tab.

   or

   From the pop-up menu at the top left, choose Links.

   The Create Named Destinations for All Paragraphs is on by default (**Figure 14.45**).

2. To turn the option off, click the check box (**Figure 14.46**).

3. Click Set.

   FrameMaker starts to create the PDF file. If an error log window appears, you can ignore it and close the window (**Figure 14.47**).

✔ Tip

- Selecting this option significantly increases the size of the PDF file, so use the Create Named Destinations for All Paragraphs option only if you do not regenerate PDF files after adding links.

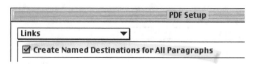

Figure 14.45 The Create Named Destinations for All Paragraphs option is selected by default.

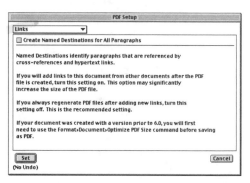

Figure 14.46 On the Links page, leave the default settings as is and click Set.

Figure 14.47 The error log message doesn't mean that the links inside your FrameMaker document won't be present in the PDF file you create.

15

XML PUBLISHING

Traditional FrameMaker contains no structure ...

... and XML contains no formatting information.

The two come together in Structured Framemaker.

Figure 15.1 Structured FrameMaker brings together formatting and structure.

The Structured FrameMaker interface allows you to work with documents that have an explicitly defined organization. Instead of following the free-flowing approach covered in the rest of the book, where you can place any type of paragraph anywhere in a document, structured documents require that certain elements, or units of information, be placed in a certain order (**Figure 15.1**).

For example, a chapter must contain a chapter title element, followed by one or more first-level heading elements. Each first-level heading, in turn, must contain one or more paragraphs of text. Elements can also be markers, graphics, and cross-references.

In this chapter, you'll learn about XML (Extensible Markup Language), how it differs from HTML (Hypertext Markup Language), how to work in structured documents, and how to use FrameMaker to publish structured documents in XML. You'll create a new structured document and add content to it. You'll find out how to bring XML documents into Structured FrameMaker and export them back out to XML. You'll also add structure to an unstructured document.

This chapter uses both the terms "FrameMaker" and "Structured FrameMaker" to refer to Structured FrameMaker.

About XML and Structured FrameMaker

Using FrameMaker, you can import existing XML documents, edit them, and save them again as XML. This is called "round-tripping" (see page 342). You can also apply structure to unstructured documents or create new structured documents based on an EDD (Element Definition Document), which describes a structured document in much the same way as a FrameMaker template describes an unstructured one (**Figure 15.2**).

HTML versus XML

HTML became a popular format for displaying Web pages because it's easy to use and has a relatively small set of tags that a user needs to master. Anyone with a text editor and a bit of time can create Web pages using HTML—and WYSIWYG HTML editors make it even easier. That small set of tags, however, limits what you can do with HTML. Various companies have tried to extend HTML, but these extensions are usually designed for one type or version of browser and can be problematic when used with other browsers.

XML takes the opposite approach, trading a simple method for a robust and flexible one. Like HTML, XML provides a way of formatting data for display on Web pages. It can also be used for creating other types of output, such as printable pages. Unlike HTML, XML is designed to manage the information it displays by assigning it labels (tags). Tags show the relationships between elements, attributes that can provide information about an element, and attribute values that describe specific instances of an element. The information in an XML file is identified in a way that makes it available for use elsewhere, for instance, in a content management system.

However, the rules for using XML are stricter than those for HTML. An XML document must be both well formed and valid. A *well-formed* XML document adheres to XML coding standards. For example, every element must have both opening and closing tags, and the elements must be properly nested.

To be considered *valid*, an XML document must also adhere to a set of structural rules called a DTD (Document Type Definition), which spells out which elements and attributes are allowed in a document. When you work with an XML document in FrameMaker, you will probably use a predefined DTD, either an industry standard, such as `DocBook.dtd` or one that's been specially defined or adapted for your company. DocBook is a DTD maintained by a standards committee and is particularly well suited to content about computer hardware and software.

Structured FrameMaker

Unstructured, FrameMaker enables you to format a document but does not describe the document's structure, whereas XML describes the contents of a document but not how the contents are to be formatted. Structured FrameMaker brings the two together, allowing you to edit structured files and using the structure to determine how the text should be formatted (**Figure 15.1**).

The FrameMaker EDD provides the connection between format and structure. Like a DTD file in XML, an EDD describes a document's structure; it also associates FrameMaker styles with each element. Usually, you start with an EDD that was created for you. However, you can also create your own EDD.

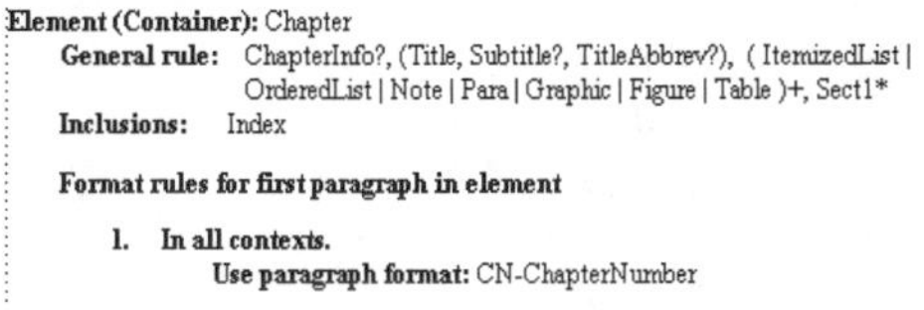

Element (Container): Chapter
  General rule: ChapterInfo?, (Title, Subtitle?, TitleAbbrev?), (ItemizedList |
        OrderedList | Note | Para | Graphic | Figure | Table)+, Sect1*
  Inclusions: Index

  Format rules for first paragraph in element

    1. **In all contexts.**
        Use paragraph format: CN-ChapterNumber

Figure 15.2 This snippet of an EDD shows the definition for a chapter. The general rule describes the structure of the elements in the chapter; the format rules describe the FrameMaker formatting used to display the chapter.

Figure 15.3 Choose File > Preferences > General to display the Preferences dialog box.

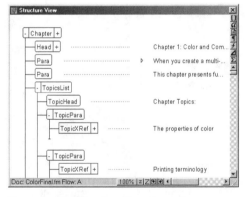

Figure 15.4 The Structure View shows the relationships of parent, child, and sibling elements.

Figure 15.5 Element boundaries enclose the element content.

TopicsList › *TopicHead* › **Chapter Topics:** ‹*TopicHead*

Figure 15.6 Element boundaries as tags appear as tag names at the beginning and end of the element content.

Working in Structured FrameMaker

FrameMaker 7.0 provides two interfaces: one for working with unstructured documents, and another for working with structured documents.

To display Structured FrameMaker:

1. From the File menu, choose Preferences > General to display the Preferences dialog box.

2. From the Product Interface menu, choose Structured FrameMaker (**Figure 15.3**).

3. Click Set and restart FrameMaker to make the interface change take effect.

From FrameMaker's point of view, a structured document consists of the document's content, which appears in the document window, and its structure, which appears in the Structure View (**Figure 15.4**). In the document window you can turn element boundaries on or off or display them as tags (they look like HTML tags).

To display element boundaries:

◆ From the View menu, choose Element Boundaries.

    The element boundaries appear as matching opening and closing square brackets around the element content (**Figure 15.5**).

To display element boundaries as tags:

◆ From the View menu, choose Element Boundaries (as Tags).

    Element boundaries as tags appear as tag names at the beginning and end of the element content (**Figure 15.6**).

The Structured FrameMaker window

The Structured FrameMaker window has an additional item on the main menu, the Element menu, plus three extra buttons at the top right of the window (**Figure 15.7**), which display the following items:

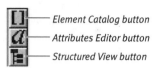

Figure 15.7 Buttons to display tools for working with structured documents.

◆ Element Catalog (**Figure 15.8**)—Displays a list of available elements. Every element can contain additional elements; unlike the Paragraph and Character Catalogs, the list changes depending on the current element.

Figure 15.8 The Element Catalog shows the elements that are currently available.

◆ Attributes dialog box (**Figure 15.9**)— Displays the information associated with an element. For each attribute you can add, edit, or remove a value. For example, attributes for a chapter might be the author's name and the version number.

◆ Structure View—Shows how the elements in a document relate to each other. The highest-level element in a document is called a parent. All subsequent levels are called child elements. Elements at the same level are called siblings.

In the Structure View shown previously in **Figure 15.4**, Chapter is the parent element and Head is a child element. Because both Para and TopicsList can appear at the same level of the structure, they are siblings.

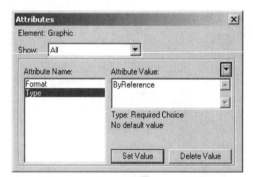

Figure 15.9 The Attributes dialog box displays the information associated with a selected attribute.

✔ Tip

■ A structured FrameMaker document is not an XML document; it's a FrameMaker document that contains additional structural information. However, the fact that it's structured allows you to easily save the document as an XML document. Likewise, FrameMaker's ability to handle structure allows you to easily convert an XML document to Structured FrameMaker.

About the Element Catalog

The information in the Element Catalog comes from content rules in the definition for the current element. The *current element* is the element that contains the insertion point or that is selected. The *current location* is the position of the insertion point or selection within that element.

The Element Catalog will be empty if you click or select in an unstructured flow, if the document does not have any element definitions, or if no more elements are required at the current location and no optional elements are available.

The Element Catalog (**Figure 15.10**) uses the following symbols to identify whether an element is valid:

- Bold check mark (✓)—The element is valid at the current location. If you insert the element, the current (parent) element will be correct and complete up to this location.

- Question mark (?)—The element is a possible replacement for the element right after the insertion point or for the selected elements. It is valid at the current location, but will make child elements below it invalid.

- Light check mark (✓) —The element is valid later in the current element. If you insert one of these elements, the current (parent) element will be correct but incomplete up to this location.

- No symbol—If an element in the catalog has no symbol, it is not valid at the current location or later in the current element.

The Element Catalog may also include the following information about the current location:

- <TEXT>—You can type text at this point.

- <UNDEFINED>—The current element does not have a definition in the document.

- <INVALID>—The contents of the current element are invalid.

You can use the buttons at the bottom of the Element Catalog to do the following (the last two commands are beyond the scope of this book):

- Insert an empty element (see page 333).

- Wrap an element around contents— You can add structure to contents already in a document by wrapping a new element around the contents (see page 337).

- Change the type of an existing element— You can change an existing element to another element of the same type.

- Display the Set Available Elements dialog box, where you can select from among options for what is displayed in the Element Catalog.

Figure 15.10 The Element Catalog displays all elements that are valid for the current location.

Getting Started

Typically, you begin working with structured documents by creating a new document (usually from a template) or by opening an existing document in Structured FrameMaker. When you select a structured template, it contains element definitions and attributes, as well as the usual paragraph tags, characters tags, table definitions, and so on.

Creating a new structured document

You can create a new structured document based on a structured template or without a template.

To create a new structured document based on a structured template:

1. From the File menu, choose New > Document.

2. In the New (Document) dialog box, navigate to the template that you want to use and select it (**Figure 15.11**).

3. Click New.

   The new document appears on the desktop (**Figure 15.12**).

4. Click the Element Catalog button to display the Element Catalog.

   When you open a document and display the Element Catalog, it will be empty (**Figure 15.13**).

When you don't have a template to work from, you can create a new structured document from scratch by importing elements from another structured document or from an EDD file.

To create a new structured document without a template:

1. From the File menu, choose New > Document.

Figure 15.11 Select a template in the New (Document) dialog box.

Figure 15.12 When you open a document in Structured FrameMaker ...

Figure 15.13 ... there are no items in the Element Catalog.

```
EDD Version is 7.0

Structured Application: XDocBook

Element (Container): Title
   Valid as the highest-level element.
   General rule:   (<TEXT> | FootnoteRef | XRef | Abbrev | Acronym | Citation | CiteRefEntry
                   | CiteTitle | Emphasis | FirstTerm | ForeignPhrase | GlossTerm | footnote |
                   Phrase | Quote | Trademark | WordAsWord | Link | OLink | ulink | Action |
                   Application | Classname | MethodName | InterfaceName | ExceptionName |
                   OoClass | OoInterface | OoException | Command | ComputerOutput |
                   Database | Email | EnVar | ErrorCode | ErrorName | ErrorType | Filename |
                   Function | GUIButton | GUIIcon | GUILabel | GUIMenu | GUIMenuItem |
                   GUISubmenu | Hardware | Interface | KeyCap | KeyCode | KeyCombo |
                   KeySym | Literal | Constant | Markup | MediaLabel | MenuChoice |
                   MouseButton | Option | Optional | Parameter | Prompt | Property |
                   Replaceable | ReturnValue | SGMLTag | StructField | StructName | Symbol |
                   SystemItem | Token | Type | UserInput | VarName | Anchor | Author |
                   AuthorInitials | CorpAuthor | ModeSpec | OtherCredit | ProductName |
                   ProductNumber | RevHistory | remark | Subscript | Superscript |
                   InlineGraphic | InlineMediaObject | InlineEquation | IndexTerm)*
   Inclusions:    Index
                  Cross-Ref
```

Figure 15.14 The Element Document Definition (EDD) is itself a structured FrameMaker document.

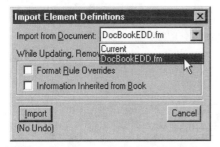

Figure 15.15 Choose the EDD from the Import from Document menu and click Import.

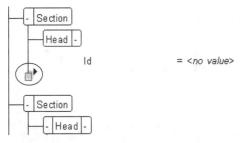

Figure 15.16 In this example, a red square indicates an element that is missing according to the DTD.

2. In the New (Document) dialog box, select Portrait or Landscape and click New.

A new, blank, structured document appears.

Importing elements into a structured document

Importing elements from another document is an easy way to create a structured document from an unstructured one.

To import elements into a structured document:

1. Open the structured document or the EDD file that contains the element definitions you want to use (**Figure 15.14**).

2. From the File menu of the document that you want to import elements into, choose Import > Element Definitions.

The Import Element Definitions dialog box appears.

3. Select a structured document or EDD from the Import from Document menu (**Figure 15.15**).

The menu lists all open, saved documents.

4. If you've made text or paragraph formatting changes to elements and want to return to the formatting described in the element definitions, select While Updating, Remove Format Rule Overrides.

5. If the document used to be included in a book but is now a standalone document, select While Updating, Remove Information Inherited from Book.

6. Click Import.

FrameMaker adds the definitions to the document's Element Catalog, replacing any definitions that are already there. Then it validates the document, identifies errors it finds in the Structure View (**Figure 15.16**), and reapplies format rules from the definitions.

Working in a Structured Document

All of the content in a structured document must eventually be located inside an element. As you work, you can add text to existing elements, add empty elements and then insert text, or add text and wrap an element around the text.

As you work, you should have the Element Catalog and the Structure View open and element boundaries displayed (**Figure 15.17**).

FrameMaker provides visual cues to show you where the insertion point is in an element in the Structure View (**Figure 15.18**). With element boundaries displayed, you can easily place the insertion point inside an element in the document window (**Figure 15.19**).

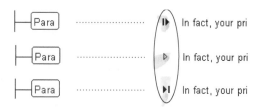

Figure 15.18 The small arrowheads in the Structure View indicate whether the insertion point is at the beginning (top), in the middle (center), or at the end (bottom) of the element.

Figure 15.19 With element boundaries (left) or element boundaries with tags (right) on, you can easily place the insertion point inside an element.

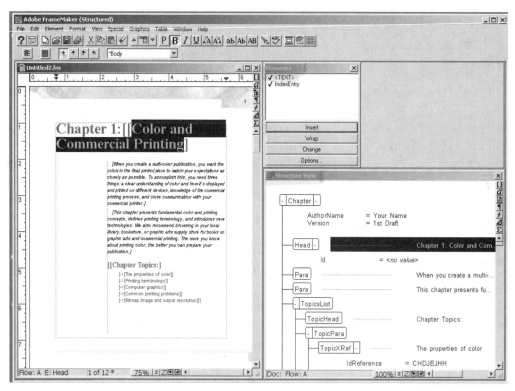

Figure 15.17 Desktop for working in Structured FrameMaker.

Figure 15.20 The current element tag is displayed in the Tag area.

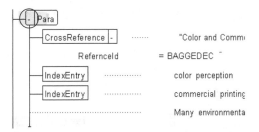

Figure 15.21 Click the small minus sign (-) on the left side of the element bubble ...

Figure 15.22 ... to collapse the contents of the element.

Figure 15.23 Select an element in the Catalog and click Insert.

Figure 15.24 An empty element appears in the document with the insertion point between the element boundaries ready for you to add content.

The current element tag is displayed in the Tag area of the status bar at the bottom left of the structured document window (**Figure 15.20**).

✔ Tips

■ The Structure View is similar to other FrameMaker windows in some ways but not in others. You can use zoom and page commands in the status bar at the bottom of the window. The active document and flow tag are displayed in the Tag area at the bottom left. However, you cannot print the contents of the Structure View.

■ Just a single element, for example, a paragraph element, can contain multiple index entries and cross-references. To make the Structure View more compact for editing, click the small minus sign on the left side of the parent element (**Figure 15.21**) to collapse the child elements (**Figure 15.22**). The minus sign changes to a plus sign (+), and the elements in the element bubble now appear to be stacked on each other.

To expand the element, click the small plus sign.

You can add an empty element and then add text inside the element.

To add an empty element:

1. Click where you want to insert the element.

   The Element Catalog displays the elements that are valid for you to insert.

2. Select a a valid element in the Element Catalog and click Insert (**Figure 15.23**).

   An empty element is added to the document, and the insertion point appears between the element boundaries (**Figure 15.24**). You can now type content into the element.

To add text to an element:

◆ Click between the boundaries of an element and start typing text.

The text you type is contained within the element boundaries (**Figure 15.25**).

Selecting text and elements

You can select entire elements and any part of a document's contents in a document window. When you select an entire element, the contents are selected as well. If an element has contents, you can select all or part of the content without selecting the element itself. When an element consists of a single object, such as an index entry or cross-reference, you must select the entire element.

To select text but not the element:

◆ In the document window, drag to select a range of text, but do not include an element boundary.

To select an element:

◆ In the document window, drag from anywhere inside the element to outside one of its element boundaries.

or

In the Structure View, click in the middle of the element bubble to select it.

The element, along with its contents, is selected in the document window and the Structure View (**Figure 15.26**).

Assigning attribute values to an element

An attribute is a piece of information associated with an element. For example, a Graphic element may have attributes to describe its format and whether it was imported by reference or copied into the document (**Figure 15.27**). Attributes can be required or optional, depending on how they are defined in the EDD. When you insert an element with attributes, FrameMaker

printing process, and close communication with your commercial printer.]

[In fact, your printer is your partner in the printing process and will want to assist you in any way possible. Remember that the results of your print job will reflect on the quality processes at the printer as much as anything else.]

[This chapter presents fundamental color and printing concepts, defines printing terminology, and introduces new

Figure 15.25 The text you add is contained within the element boundaries.

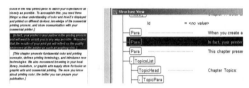

Figure 15.26 A paragraph selected in the document window (left) and in the Structure View (right).

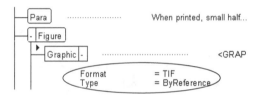

Figure 15.27 In this example, the Graphic element shown in the Structure View has two attributes (circled).

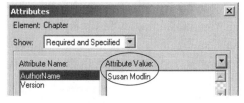

Figure 15.28 The TopicXRef element in this example has an ID attribute.

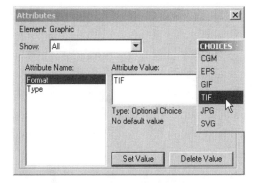

Figure 15.29 You can type a value in the Attribute Value text box.

Figure 15.30 You can select an attribute in the Attribute Name list and, if you have a choice, choose an attribute value from the Choices menu.

prompts you to enter values by displaying the Attributes for New Element dialog box (see **Figure 15.35** in a later section).

FrameMaker uses ID attributes in cross-reference and source elements to maintain the connection between these two elements. You can see these attributes in the Structure View (**Figure 15.28**), but you usually don't need to do anything with them.

To assign or edit attribute values:

1. Select an element that has attributes.

2. From the Element menu, choose Edit Attributes.

   or

   Click the Attributes button on the right side of the document window.

   or

   Double-click an attribute name or value in the Structure View.

   The Attributes dialog box appears.

3. For each attribute value that you want to enter or edit, select the attribute in the Attribute Name list, enter the value in the Attribute Value text box (**Figure 15.29**), and click Set Value.

4. If an attribute has a set of predefined values, choose from the Attribute Value menu rather than entering a value (**Figure 15.30**).

5. If you displayed the Attributes dialog box by double-clicking in the Structure View, click Done.

If you have multiple instances of an element that should have the same attribute values (for example, several section headings), you can copy the values from one element to the Clipboard and paste them to one or more elements. If you paste values to an element that does not have corresponding attributes defined, the attributes will be invalid.

To copy and paste attribute values:

1. Select the element with the attribute values that you want to copy.

2. From the Edit menu, choose Copy Special > Attribute Values (**Figure 15.31**).

   The attribute values associated with the selected element are copied to the Clipboard.

3. Select the element to which you want to apply the attribute values, and from the Edit menu, choose Paste.

   The attribute values are pasted to the selected element. To preserve element-based cross-references, an ID attribute value is not pasted.

If an attribute has an invalid value or is not defined for the document, in the Structure View, a red X appears to the left of the attribute name and its value is red. If an attribute does not have a value, <no value> appears to the right of the attribute name. If the attribute requires a value, <no value> is red, and a red square appears to the left of the attribute name (**Figure 15.32**).

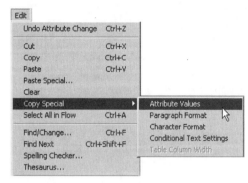

Figure 15.31 Choose Edit > Copy Special > Attribute Values.

Figure 15.32 If an attribute is missing, a red square appears in the Structure View window.

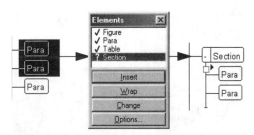

Figure 15.33 Select elements to wrap; then, in the Element Catalog, select a wrapper element and click Wrap.

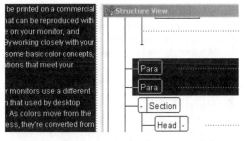

Figure 15.34 Select text in the document window (left) or elements in the Structure View (right).

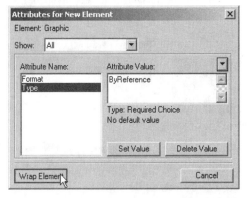

Figure 15.35 Enter attribute values for the element and click Wrap Element.

Editing Elements

You can easily edit elements in FrameMaker's Structure View. You can add a new parent element and wrap elements in it, remove a parent element and unwrap its elements, and merge and split elements. You can select elements and drag them to a new location.

Wrapping elements

After you've added text to a document you can add structure by wrapping a new element around existing text or other elements. When you wrap an element around other elements, the existing elements become children of the new element (**Figure 15.33**). You can select text or an element in the document view or one or more elements in the Structured View.

To wrap an element around content:

1. In the Structure View, select the text or other elements you want to include in the new element (**Figure 15.34**).

2. In the Element Catalog, select a wrapper element and click Wrap.

   If the element has attributes, the Attributes for New Element dialog box appears (**Figure 15.35**).

(continues on next page)

3. Enter attribute values for the element and click Wrap Element.

A new bubble appears in the Structure View (**Figure 15.36**), and a pair of element boundaries appears around the wrapped elements in the document window (**Figure 15.37**).

You can also remove a parent element from around its child elements by unwrapping the elements. Unwrapping deletes an element but leaves its contents in the same place in the document. For example, if you plan to remove a parent Section element, the Para elements it contains stay in place.

To unwrap elements:

1. In the Structure View, select the parent-level element you want to remove (**Figure 15.38**).

In this example, it's a Section element.

2. From the Element menu, choose Unwrap (**Figure 15.39**).

The parent Section element disappears from the Structure View (**Figure 15.40**), and the Para elements lose their boundaries in the document window.

Merging and splitting elements

If you're not satisfied with the way that the content in your document is organized, you can merge two or more elements into one. The elements to be merged must be adjacent to each other. Merging retains the attributes of the first element only but not of any of the others.

To merge elements:

1. In the Structure View, select the elements that you want to merge.

2. From the Element menu, choose Merge.

The contents of the second element (including any child elements) are merged at the end of the first element (**Figure 15.41**).

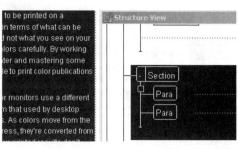

Figure 15.36 After you wrap elements, a new set of boundaries appears in the document window, and a new bubble appears in the Structure View.

[[In fact, your printer is your partner in the printing process and will want to assist you in any way possible. Remember that the results of your print job will reflect on the quality processes at the printer as much as anything else.]

[This chapter presents fundamental color and printing concepts, defines printing terminology, and introduces new technologies. We also recommend browsing in your local library, bookstore, or graphic arts supply store for books on graphic arts and commercial printing. The more you know about printing color, the better you can prepare your publication.]]

Figure 15.37 A pair of element boundaries appear around the Para elements that were wrapped.

Figure 15.38 Select the parent level element you want to unwrap.

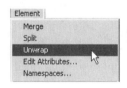

Figure 15.39 Choose Element > Unwrap.

Figure 15.40 The parent element disappears from the Structure View.

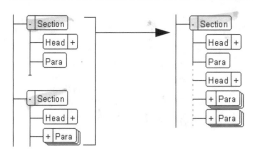

Figure 15.41 In this example, in the Structure View, two sections (left) were merged into one (right).

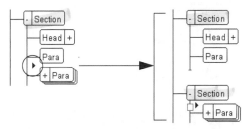

Figure 15.42 In the Structure View, click where you want to split the element (left); the element is split into two identical elements (right).

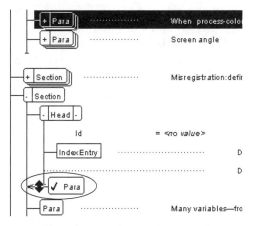

Figure 15.43 When you drag an element in the Structure View, the pointer changes to a solid up-and-down arrowhead, and an arrow on the left indicates where the bubble will go.

You can split a single element into two elements at the same level and with the same tag. The new element will have the same parent element as the original one.

To split elements:

1. In the Structure View, click where you want to split the element (**Figure 15.42**).

2. From the Element menu, choose Split.

   The element is split into two elements that have the same tag and are at the same level.

   You may need to edit the document after splitting an element. In this example, after splitting the Section element into two Section elements, you would add a Head for the new second Section.

You can cut and paste elements within a document or between documents. You can also move an element to another location in a document by dragging its bubble in the Structure View.

To move an element by dragging:

◆ In the Structure View, drag the element's bubble to the location you want.

   As you drag, the pointer changes to a solid up-and-down arrowhead, and an arrow moves to indicate where the bubble will go if you release the mouse button (**Figure 15.43**).

   When you move an element, its contents all move along with it.

✔ Tip

■ If the element you want to move has many child elements, collapse it before you drag it (see page 333).

Finding and Correcting Structural Errors

When you work in a structured document, elements must be in the correct sequence, with none missing and with attributes assigned to each element. If elements are out of sequence, they are invalid. If you pasted an element from another document, it may be invalid if it wasn't defined for this document. FrameMaker displays missing and invalid elements in red in the Structure View (**Figure 15.44**) as follows:

◆ A red square indicates that an element is missing.

◆ A red dotted line indicates an element is in an invalid location.

◆ A red element bubble indicates that the element is not valid in this document.

Validating documents

As you work, you can test the validity of a document to help you to spot structural errors or missing elements. You can validate an element, a flow, a single document, or an entire book.

To validate a document:

1. Click in an element that you want to validate, and from the Element menu, choose Validate (**Figure 15.45**).

   The Element Validation window appears (**Figure 15.46**).

2. In the Scope area, specify validation of one of the following:

   ▲ The entire document

   ▲ The current flow (in a document with multiple flows)

   ▲ The current element

3. If you want FrameMaker to skip over missing elements or attribute values, select Ignore Missing Elements and/or Ignore Missing Attribute Values.

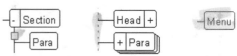

Figure 15.44 Missing and invalid elements are flagged in red in the Structure View in three ways: as a **red square** (left), as a **red dotted line** (center), and as a **red element bubble** (right).

Figure 15.45 Choose Element > Validate.

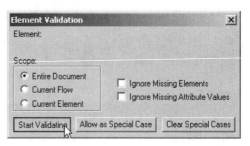

Figure 15.46 Specify the scope of the validation in the Element Validation window.

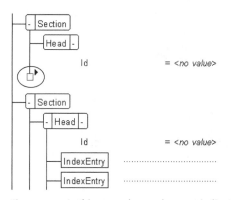

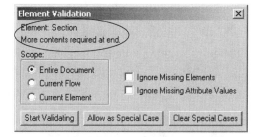

Figure 15.47 In this example, a red square indicates a missing element.

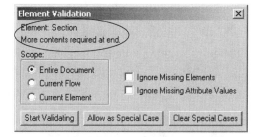

Figure 15.48 Validation errors are flagged at the top of the Element Validation window.

4. Click Start Validating.

If FrameMaker finds an error, the error is flagged in the Structure View (**Figure 15.47**), and a message appears at the top of the Element Validation window (**Figure 15.48**).

5. Do one of the following:

▲ To ignore the error and go back to validating, click Start Validating.

▲ To mark the error as an exception to the rule so that FrameMaker will skip it the next time FrameMaker encounters it during validation, click Allow as Special Case.

6. Click Start Validating and repeat step 5 until all errors have been flagged.

FrameMaker displays a message to tell you that all errors have been flagged at the top of the Element Validation window.

If you assume ownership of a structured document, you may want to see what errors the previous owner skipped. You can clear all special cases and validate to find the errors and then decide how to handle them as you validate.

To clear all special cases:

1. From the Element menu, choose Validate.

2. In the Element Validation window, select a scope for the action and click Clear Special Cases.

FrameMaker clears all of the special cases that have been marked in the document, flow, or current element.

✔ Tip

■ Missing elements and missing attribute values are the most common errors that occur in a work in progress. You may want to ignore them early in a project.

Taking Documents on Round Trips

Because Structured FrameMaker can import and export XML documents, you can use it to take a document on a round trip from FrameMaker to XML and back to FrameMaker (**Figure 15.49**), or from XML to FrameMaker and back to XML (**Figure 15.50**).

Although this chapter focuses on XML, Structured FrameMaker can import and export any type of structured document, such as SGML and HTML.

Read/Write rules

Some elements are represented differently in Structured FrameMaker than in XML (or other structured languages), including tables, markers, graphics, and variables. When files, are imported or exported, these differences are handled by a set of read/write rules. The lines from a rules file shown in **Figure 15.51** map XML attribute values to FrameMaker graphics alignment properties.

Structured application

Although it's a difficult concept to grasp, FrameMaker defines a structured application as a collection of files that describe how to process a structured file in FrameMaker. A structured application usually includes a DTD, which defines the elements and attributes, and other items, such as read/write rules and an import template. You can think of a structured application as a specification for a FrameMaker structured document, with information about what files to use and where to find them. Structured applications are defined in a special FrameMaker file named structapps.fm (**Figure 15.52**).

To work with a structured file, an application needs to be associated with the file. Typically, this application is set up for you and you then

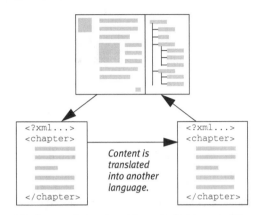

Figure 15.49 A structured FrameMaker document is exported to XML. The file is translated into another language for localization purposes, and the translated document is imported into FrameMaker.

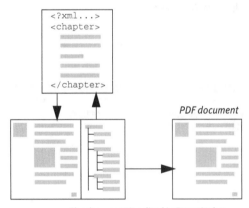

The document is edited in FrameMaker and used to generate a PDF document.

Figure 15.50 An XML file is imported to Structured FrameMaker. The FrameMaker document is edited and used to generate a PDF document, and the file is exported back to XML.

```
attribute "align"
  {
    is fm property alignment;
    value "left" is fm property value align
left;
    value "middle" is fm property value
align center;
    value "right" is fm property value
align right;
```

Figure 15.51 Lines from the rules file.

associate it with the appropriate files. You can also select the application yourself as you open or save the file, or you can change the application while the file is open.

An SGML or XML file does not include any specifications on how its contents are to be formatted, but your structured application may have a template that formats the file in FrameMaker. If you use a structured application that does not have a template, the file opens using basic default formatting.

Structured FrameMaker provides predefined structured applications, including:

◆ XHTML (**Figure 15.53**), an extension to HTML based on XML, which can be viewed, edited, and validated like standard XML. XHTML is convenient for migration from HTML to XML.

(continues on next page)

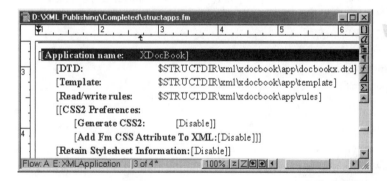

Figure 15.52
The structapps.fm file.

```
Application name:        XHTML
    DOCTYPE:             html
    File Extension Override: htm
    DTD:                 $STRUCTDIR\xml\xhtml\app\dtd
    Template:            $STRUCTDIR\xml\xhtml\app\template
    Read/write rules:    $STRUCTDIR\xml\xhtml\app\rules
    CSS2 Preferences:
        Generate CSS2:       Disable
        Add Fm CSS Attribute To XML:  Disable
    Retain Stylesheet Information: Disable
    XML Stylesheet
        Type:                css
        URI:                 /$STRUCTDIR/xml/xhtml/app/xhtml.css
```

Figure 15.53 The XHTML structured application is described in this section of the structapps.fm file.

◆ XDocBook, an XML implementation of the DocBook DTD, which is commonly used in the publishing industry. It was originally developed for use with SGML, but has now been adapted to XML.

When you open an XML document, you will choose a structured application to associate with the document.

To open an XML document:

1. From the File menu, choose Open.

2. In the Open dialog box, select the XML file you want to open.

3. Select XML as the file type and click Open.

4. If the Unknown File Type dialog box appears, select XML in the Convert From list and click Convert (**Figure 15.54**).

   The User Structured Application dialog box appears. All of the structured applications in the `structapps.fm` file are available for you to choose.

5. From the Use Structured Application menu, choose a structured application and click Continue (**Figure 15.55**).

   The XML document opens in Structured FrameMaker.

✔ Tips

■ Although you can open an XML document as a text file in FrameMaker and edit the XML code, a better approach to editing XML code is to use a text editor.

■ In a corporate environment, the structured application and all supporting files will have already been set up for you, and hopefully someone will provide you with the information you need to get started. As a technical writer, you will not be expected to create EDDs or DTDs or any of the other of the supporting documents.

Figure 15.54 Select XML and click Convert.

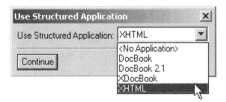

Figure 15.55 Choose a structured application and click Continue.

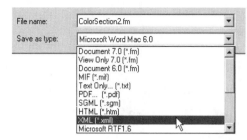

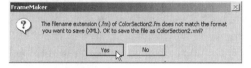

Figure 15.56 From the Save as type menu, choose XML.

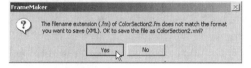

Figure 15.57 To add the .xml extension to the filename, click Yes.

To save a document as XML:

1. In an open document, from the File menu, choose Save As.

2. In the Save As dialog box, from the Save as Type menu, choose XML (**Figure 15.56**).

   (Windows) If you didn't give the filename a .xml extension, FrameMaker prompts you to do so. Click Yes(**Figure 15.57**).

   (Mac OS) If you didn't give the filename a .xml extension, FrameMaker warns you that if you continue using the .fm file extension, you will overwrite the FrameMaker file with the XML file. Click Cancel, and in the Save Document dialog box, add a .xml file extension.

3. Click Save.

   FrameMaker uses the application associated with the file to specify its structure.

TAKING DOCUMENTS ON ROUND TRIPS

Converting Unstructured Documents

If you already have a set of unstructured FrameMaker documents, you need to add structure to them before you can use the structural features of Structured FrameMaker.

In Chapters 4 and 5, you saw that formatting in traditional FrameMaker documents is best applied using paragraph and character tags. To convert a document to Structured FrameMaker, you create a conversion table that describes how paragraphs tags, character tags, tables, variables, markers, cross references, and graphics should be replaced with XML elements.

The success of the conversion depends on how well you have organized the unstructured documents. If a document is well organized and has a predictable structure, it will probably convert with little intervention.

To create a new conversion table:

1. From the File menu, choose Structure Tools > Generate Conversion Table (**Figure 15.58**).

   The Generate Conversion Table dialog box appears.

2. Select Generate New Conversion Table and click Generate (**Figure 15.59**).

   An untitled document window appears displaying a generation table that is partially filled in (**Figure 15.60**).

3. Save the conversion table document as a FrameMaker document, giving it any name you wish.

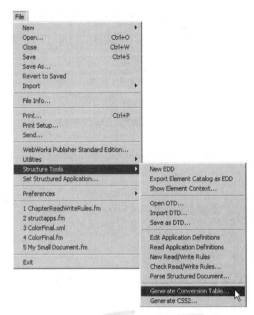

Figure 15.58 Choose File > Structure Tools > Generate Conversion Table.

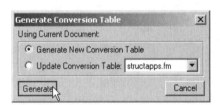

Figure 15.59 Select Generate New Conversion Table and click Generate.

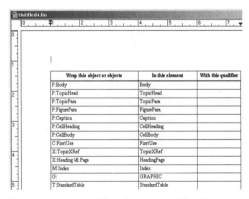

Wrap this object or objects	In this element	With this qualifier
P:Body	Body	
P:TopicHead	TopicHead	
P:TopicPara	TopicPara	
P:FigurePara	FigurePara	
P:Caption	Caption	
P:CellHeading	CellHeading	
P:CellBody	CellBody	
C:FirstUse	FirstUse	
X:TopicXRef	TopicXRef	
X:Heading \& Page	HeadingPage	
M:Index	Index	
G:	GRAPHIC	
T:StandardTable	StandardTable	

Figure 15.60 An untitled document with a three-column table appears.

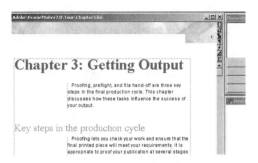

Figure 15.61 Even though the unstructured document can be opened in Structured FrameMaker, it has no structure.

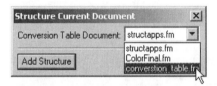

Figure 15.62 In this example, from the Conversion Table Document menu, choose conversion_table.fm.

Figure 15.63 FrameMaker lets you know that the unstructured document has been converted.

Exploring the conversion table

When FrameMaker adds structure to a document using the conversion table, it applies the rules in the table in order, beginning with the first row and working down:

◆ The left column describes the objects to be converted. A letter before each of the objects identifies the object's type (XML elements do not require a letter). The object specified in the first column can be as simple as a character tag, or it can be a complex statement that describes a number of different tags and elements found in a particular order.

◆ The middle column lists the element with which to wrap the object in the first column. You can also specify attributes that are to be assigned to the element.

◆ The right column, which is empty when the document first opens, allows you to give a special qualifier to the wrapped object. Content in this column is optional.

To use a conversion table:

1. With the conversion table open, click in the file that you want to convert (**Figure 15.61**).

2. From the File menu, choose Utilities > Structure Current Document.

3. In the Structure Current Document dialog box, from the Conversion Table Document menu, choose the conversion table that you want to use (**Figure 15.62**).

   All open FrameMaker documents are displayed in the menu.

4. Click Add Structure.

   Although you can't observe the conversion directly, a message appears telling you that the operation was completed normally (**Figure 15.63**).

(continues on next page)

5. Click OK.

The structured document opens in its own window on top of the unstructured document; it is untitled (**Figure 15.64**).

6. Save the new structured document.

Even though FrameMaker was able to add structure to the document, you should always expect to do some manual touch-up.

Developing a conversion table

Usually it takes a number of tries to develop a fully functioning conversion table. You start with the basic table generated by FrameMaker and replace the placeholder names in the middle column with actual elements and attributes.

Once you can convert paragraph and character tags to elements, you can start developing more complex rules to describe how to convert nested structures, such as lists and heading levels.

Finally, when the fundamental structure is in place, you can describe the conversion of tables, variables, markers, cross-references, and graphics.

Additional references

♦ For information about EDDs and other general information, see the *Structure Application Developer's Guide*, which is included in FrameMaker's online manuals. For more information on how to construct conversion tables, see Appendix A.

♦ For information on the DocBook DTD, see *Using the DocBook Starter Kit*, which comes with FrameMaker 7.0.

♦ For a good tutorial, see the *XML Cookbook*, also provided with FrameMaker 7.0 (**Figure 15.65**).

♦ For information about XML, see *XML for the World Wide Web: Visual QuickStart Guide*, by Elizabeth Castro (Peachpit Press).

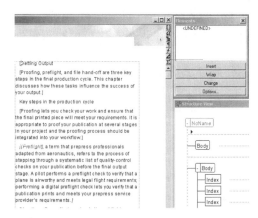

Figure 15.64 The document opens in a structured window, and now the Structure View displays the document's structure.

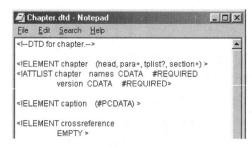

Figure 15.65 This DTD file is included in the FrameMaker *XML Cookbook*.

TIPS AND BEST PRACTICES

Most of the FrameMaker users I know and those I meet love it. To elicit tips for this chapter, I contacted people who love FrameMaker and sent out messages to several groups of people I thought might be FrameMaker lovers.

I've acknowledged each tip or best practice by listing the contributor, but I also want to thank anyone who sent me a tip—but was not first person—and everyone who responded to my call for tips with encouraging messages.

The tips are good ones, and you should peruse them and try them out. If you're a beginner, you may find that you don't need all of them right away. When you have more experience, you could come back to this chapter and see if there are tips you can make part of your work habits.

Tips

The tips in this section are grouped around interface areas where possible, and include a few tips for Microsoft Word users.

Indexes and markers

Lisa Kelly, Writers Plus, Cupertino, CA: "You can use FrameMaker's hypertext links to quickly change index entries."

To edit index marker text from the index:

1. When you generate an index, make sure Create Hypertext Links is selected (**Figure 16.1**).

2. Choose Special > Marker and leave the Marker window open on your desktop (**Figure 16.2**).

3. Open the index and locate an entry that needs to be updated, for example, an incorrect spelling.

4. Alt-Ctrl-click or Control-Option-click the entry.

   FrameMaker automatically opens the document that contains the Index marker, selects the marker, and displays the marker text in the Marker window.

5. Change the marker text and click Edit Marker.

Editing marker text

Bob Silva, Consultant, Stockton, CA: "When you're editing index markers, it's best to use the Find/Change window to select the marker. You should never select markers with the mouse, since markers can sometimes be stacked on top of each other."

To find and edit marker text:

1. Choose Special > Marker to open the Marker window and move it so it doesn't interfere with the document window.

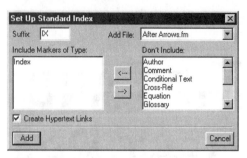

Figure 16.1 When you set up an index, make sure Create Hypertext Links is selected.

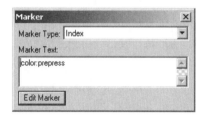

Figure 16.2 Leave the Marker window open on your desktop.

TIPS

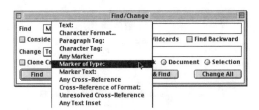

Figure 16.3 Choose Any Marker or Marker of Type and enter the marker type in the text box.

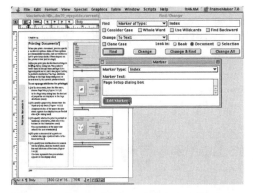

Figure 16.4 Use the Marker window to edit marker text.

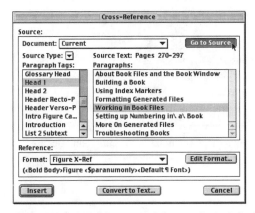

Figure 16.5 Select the paragraph formats in the left list, find the paragraph text in the right list, and click Go to Source.

2. Choose Edit > Find/Change to open the Find/Change window.

3. From the Find pop-up menu, choose Any Marker.

or

From the Find pop-up menu, choose Marker of Type and type a marker type, such as Index, in the text box (**Figure 16.3**).

4. Click Find.

5. Edit the marker text in the Marker window, and when you're finished, click Edit Marker (**Figure 16.4**).

6. In the Find/Change window, click Find to display the next marker text.

Cross-Reference dialog box

Bob Silva, Consultant, Stockton, CA: "One undocumented navigation technique that I find saves time is using the Cross-Reference dialog box to go to specific sections in a long document."

To navigate using the Cross-Reference dialog box:

1. Choose Special > Cross-Reference.
The Cross-Reference dialog box appears.

2. From the Source Type pop-up menu, choose Paragraphs.

3. In the Paragraph Tags list on the left, select the paragraph tag of the paragraph you want to locate.

4. In the Paragraphs list on the right, select the text of the paragraph.

5. Click Go to Source (**Figure 16.5**).
FrameMaker takes you to the page that contains the start of the paragraph.

Here is another task you can do in the Cross-Reference dialog box. When I accidentally type in an Anchor paragraph, which shouldn't contain any text, I usually don't

TIPS

notice it (a tiny gray box may appear just above the anchored frame on my printed copy). Since the default font is so small, this text is difficult to see on the screen.

To check for stray text in Anchor paragraphs:

1. Choose Special > Cross-Reference to display the Cross-Reference dialog box.

2. From the Source Type pop-up menu, choose Paragraphs.

3. In the Paragraph Tags list on the list, select the Anchor paragraph tag (or the tag of the format you're using for anchored frames) (**Figure 16.6**).

   In this example, the word "text" has been typed in an Anchor paragraph.

4. If any text is displayed in the Paragraphs list, select it and click Go to Source.

   FrameMaker takes you to the paragraph, so that you can delete the stray text. You may need to zoom in to 200% or higher to actually see the text.

Templates

Lisa Kelly, Writers Plus, Cupertino, CA: "If you design FrameMaker templates, it can be difficult to remember all the possible items to include, for example, variable definitions and cross-reference formats. You can use the Import Formats dialog box as a checklist."

To use the Import Formats dialog box as a checklist for templates:

1. Choose File > Import > Formats to display the Import Formats dialog box (**Figure 16.7**).

2. Check that you've included all the items in the Import and Update area.

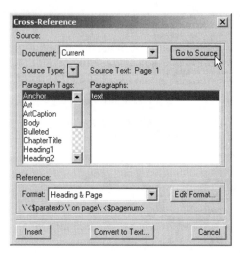

Figure 16.6 Use the Cross-Reference dialog box to find stray text in Anchor paragraphs.

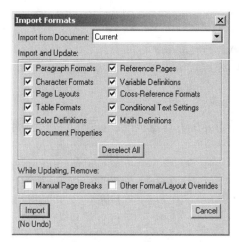

Figure 16.7 The items in the Import and Update area serve as a checklist for templates.

TIPS

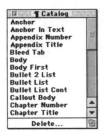 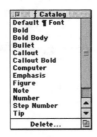

Figure 16.8 The paragraph and character formats, stored in Catalogs in FrameMaker correspond to Word styles.

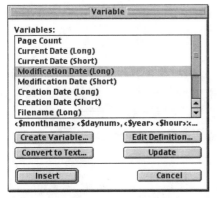

Figure 16.9 Choose Special > Variable to display the Variable dialog box.

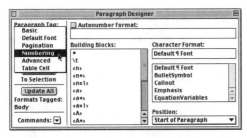

Figure 16.10 FrameMaker's Numbering properties in the Paragraph Designer correspond to Word Bullets and Numbering/Numbered/Restart Numbering.

For former Microsoft Word users

Dobbie Roisen, A Stable Link, Sunnyvale, CA: "The Paragraph and Character Designers fulfill the same function as the Styles menu option in Word (**Figure 16.8**)."

See Chapter 4, "Formatting Paragraphs," and Chapter 5, "Character Formatting."

Ron Rothbart, Financial Engineering Associates, Berkeley, CA: "AutoText in Word translates into FrameMaker variables (**Figure 16.9**)."

See Chapter 9, "Using Variables."

"In Word, if you use Restart Numbering in the Bullets and Numbering dialog box, in FrameMaker, use autonumbers in the Numbering properties in the Paragraph Designer (**Figure 16.10**)."

See *Autonumbering paragraphs* on page 77.

Chris Klemmer, The Graphic Word, San Jose, CA: "To add graphics to a Word document, you first open the graphic, copy it, and paste it. In FrameMaker you copy graphics or import them directly using the Import File dialog box. Using anchored frames gives you much more control over placement of graphics."

See Chapter 8, "Graphics and Anchored Frames."

"In Word, you open header and footer dialog boxes to add header and footer content. In FrameMaker, you go to master pages to add header and footer content, including system variables, including special Running H/F variables."

See *Using markers in running header/footer system variables* on page 184.

TIPS

Converting Microsoft Word documents to FrameMaker

Jennifer Foster, Blue Coat Systems, Sunnyvale, CA:

"If you try to paste text from Word documents into FrameMaker, the text will come in as a graphic in an anchored frame, not as editable text. Although you can always save the Word document to a text file, and then copy and paste the text into FrameMaker, this is incredibly boring, and no formats come through at all.

"I once converted a 500-page Word document to FrameMaker without knowing about this. I discovered the feature when I was on about page 450!"

To convert a Word file to FrameMaker (Windows only):

1. In the Word file, select and copy all the text you want to bring into FrameMaker (**Figure 16.11**).

   The text is copied to the Clipboard.

2. In FrameMaker, choose Edit > Paste Special to display the Paste Special dialog box.

3. In the As list, select Rich Text Format and click OK (**Figure 16.12**).

   After several seconds, the text appears in the FrameMaker document as editable text (**Figure 16.13**).

   You'll still have to update most of the formats, but at least they're closer than they would otherwise be, and you can update formatting globally instead of having to format each paragraph individually. In some cases the paragraph style (tag) is already there.

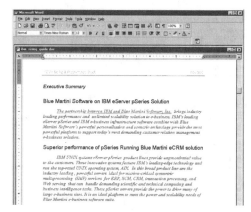

Figure 16.11 Here is what the text looks like in the Word document.

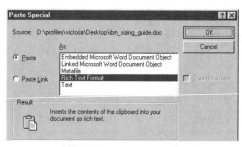

Figure 16.12 Select Rich Text Format in the As list in the Paste Special dialog box in FrameMaker.

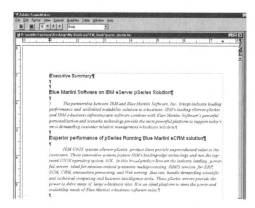

Figure 16.13 Here is what the text looks like when you use the Paste Special command to paste it into FrameMaker.

TIPS

ever widening, perhaps more especially in America.
I had the pleasure of receiving a warm invitation

Figure 16.14 Graphic pasted into a document; FrameMaker places it in an anchored frame.

ever widening, perhaps more especially in America.
I had the pleasure of receiving a warm invitation

Figure 16.15 Select anchored frame or graphic and shrink wrap the graphic inside the frame.

Paragraph Designer
Paragraph Tag:
Body
Properties:
Default Font
Apply
To Selection
Update All
Formats Tagged:
Body
Commands:
Family:
Hoefler Text
Size:
14.0 pt
Angle:
Regular
Weight:
Regular
Variation:
Regular
Color:
Black
Spread:
-1.0%
Stretch:
100.0%
Language:
US English
Underline
Overline
Strikethrough
Change Bar
Outline
Shadow
Superscript
Small Caps
Pair Kern
Font: TrueType on Screen (PS Font: HoeflerText-Regular)

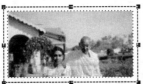

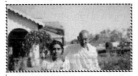

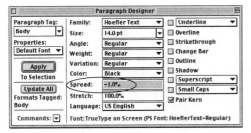

Figure 16.16 Use a small, negative value in the Spread text box.

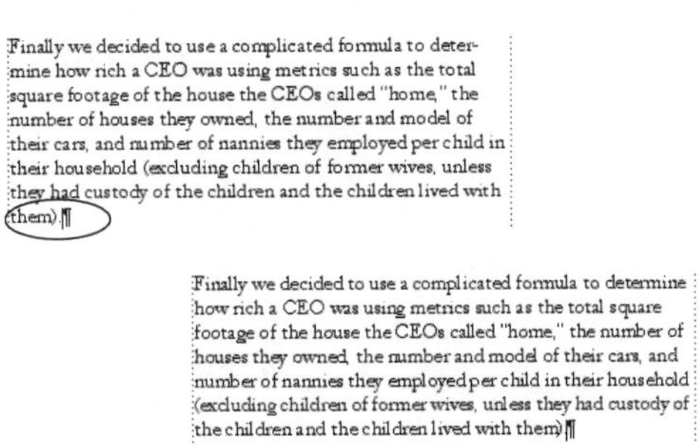

Finally we decided to use a complicated formula to determine how rich a CEO was using metrics such as the total square footage of the house the CEOs called "home," the number of houses they owned, the number and model of their cars, and number of nannies they employed per child in their household (excluding children of former wives, unless they had custody of the children and the children lived with them).
Finally we decided to use a complicated formula to determine how rich a CEO was using metrics such as the total square footage of the house the CEOs called "home," the number of houses they owned, the number and model of their cars, and number of nannies they employed per child in their household (excluding children of former wives, unless they had custody of the children and the children lived with them).

Figure 16.17 Before (left) and after (right) applying 1.0% spread to eliminate the orphan word.

Shrink wrapping graphics in anchored frames

Cindy Bloch, Sun Microsystems, San Jose, CA: "For more painless image handling. instead of manually adjusting an anchored frame around an image, shrink wrap the anchored frame around the image and any callouts. When I learned this, it was a happy, happy day. It seemed like magic!"

To shrink wrap a graphic in an anchored frame:

- Select a graphic or an anchored frame (**Figure 16.14**) and press Esc M P to shrink wrap the anchored frame around the image (**Figure 16.15**).

  If you change the image or its callouts, using Esc M P also correctly adjusts the anchored frame.

Note that shrink wrapping a graphic in an anchored frame changes the anchoring position to At Insertion Point.

Using the Spread font property

Ron Rothbart, Financial Engineering Associates, Berkeley, CA:
"My company uses a very heavy font (Imago ExtraBold) and all uppercase for some headings, so some letters fuse together when I save as PDF. To prevent this, I use a relatively small Spread value, such as 0.1 percent."

Becky Morgan, Peachpit Press, Berkeley, CA: "Use a small, negative spread value to avoid having an orphan word stranded on the last line of a paragraph or to create a more even right rag."

Start with 1% (**Figure 16.16**) and if that works (**Figure 16.17**), decrease the value until you're using the lowest value that still works. You may need to increase the value, but don't go higher than 2%. You can also use this technique to achieve a more even right edge for left-aligned paragraphs with ragged right edges.

Tips

Hyperlink cross-references

Ron Rothbart, Financial Engineering Associates, Berkeley, CA:
"How do you get hyperlink cross-references to automatically appear blue (in FrameMaker and/or PDF), so that users know they are links?"

To format cross-references as links:

1. Create a character format with As Is settings, except for Color, which you could specify as Blue (**Figure 16.18**).

2. For any cross-reference formats that you want to display in a different color, use a character format with the format you created (**Figure 16.19**).

Managing cross-references

Carol J. Elkins, A Written Word, Pueblo, CO:
"Cross-references are active in FrameMaker documents. In Windows, you can jump to the source of the cross-reference by Ctrl-Alt-clicking the cross-reference. Once there, however, it's often cumbersome to work your way back to the cross-reference. There is no convenient Back button in FrameMaker."

(Windows only) The solution is to use Ctrl-Tab to switch between open documents. This is extremely handy when checking index markers. You can quickly click a term in the index to go to its source and then click Ctrl-Tab to go back to the index and resume where you left off.

Numbering PDF pages to match FrameMaker page numbering

John Wolley, Santa Rosa, CA:
"This is one of the tips I've compiled over the years for quick reference."

This procedure is useful when you create PDF files for books where the front matter is numbered with lowercase roman numerals and the main part of the book uses arabic numbers, like this one.

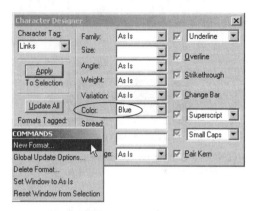

Figure 16.18 Create a character format for hypertext links.

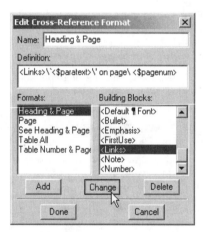

Figure 16.19 Add the character format to the cross-reference definition wherever you want cross-references to appear in a different color.

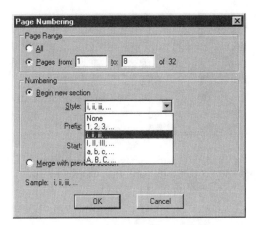

Figure 16.20 Specify a page range and a numbering style for the front pages ...

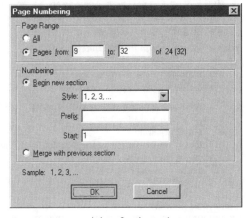

Figure 16.21 ... and then for the main text pages.

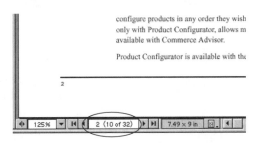

Figure 16.22 The FrameMaker page number in the footer matches the Acrobat page number (circled).

To number PDF pages to match FrameMaker footers:

1. Open the PDF file in Adobe Acrobat.

2. Choose Document > Number Pages.

3. In the Page Numbering dialog box, specify the front pages in the Page Range text boxes.

4. In the Numbering area, from the Style menu, choose a numbering style and click OK (**Figure 16.20**).

   The Acrobat front page numbers now match the FrameMaker footers.

5. Choose Document > Number Pages again.

6. Repeat steps 3 and 4 for the main text pages (**Figure 16.21**).

   The Acrobat main page numbers now match the FrameMaker footers (**Figure 16.22**).

7. Save changes and close the file.

   Although it's not absolutely necessary, having the FrameMaker page number in the footer match the Acrobat page number provides a professional finishing touch.

Better spell checking

Nandini Y. Garud, San Jose, CA:
"If you're not happy with FrameMaker's spell checking dictionaries (and there are a number of people who don't like them), when bringing a document into FrameMaker from Word, for example, use the Word spell checker before bringing the document into FrameMaker."

TIPS

Bob Silva, Consultant, Stockton, CA:
"Remember that the spell checker doesn't check index marker text or text on master pages unless they are showing. You should spell check the generated index to find any typos in index markers. Display master pages to spell check text on these pages."

"To facilitate spell checking, consider setting Language to None when you create paragraph and character fonts for code samples and computer terms (**Figure 16.23**). This can save time, as FrameMaker skips over text that the spelling checker would otherwise flag."

Keeping indents consistent

Shelley Hoy, San Jose, CA:
"Make sure that indents for all related tags are the same, so that when they appear on the same page, they create a clean left indent margin. For example, make sure that bullet indents match numbered list indents, and so on (**Figure 16.24**)."

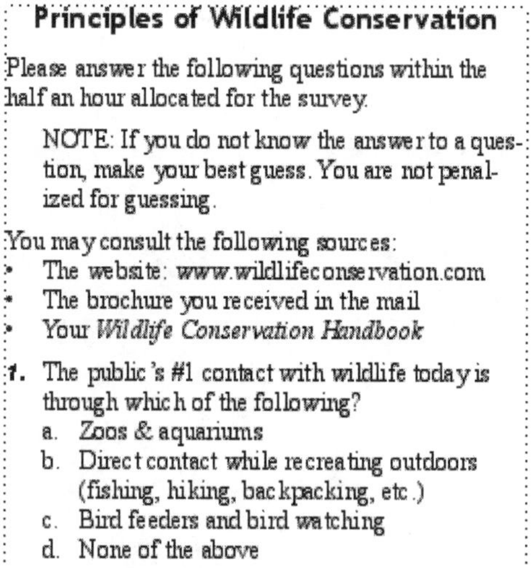

Finding a better and faster way

Debbie Wible, Cisco Systems, CA:
"Any time you find yourself doing something repetitive in FrameMaker, there is always a better and faster way to do it. Stop what you're doing and read the manual, use online help, ask a colleague, or check online (see page 366)."

"Experiment with the powerful Find/Change capabilities of FrameMaker (that is, when you're not on a deadline). Have fun becoming a power user. If you're a manager, make sure that your writers are all power users, so that the content developers' energy and creativity are not expended on tedious formatting issues, but on content development."

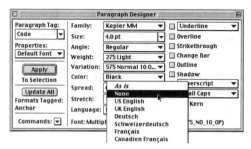

Figure 16.23 Create a paragraph or character format for computer terms or code samples and set Language to None.

Principles of Wildlife Conservation

Please answer the following questions within the half an hour allocated for the survey.

NOTE: If you do not know the answer to a question, make your best guess. You are not penalized for guessing.

You may consult the following sources:
- The website: www.wildlifeconservation.com
- The brochure you received in the mail
- Your *Wildlife Conservation Handbook*

1. The public's #1 contact with wildlife today is through which of the following?
   a. Zoos & aquariums
   b. Direct contact while recreating outdoors (fishing, hiking, backpacking, etc.)
   c. Bird feeders and bird watching
   d. None of the above

Figure 16.24 In this example, left indents are aligned for indented body paragraphs and for bulleted and numbered paragraphs.

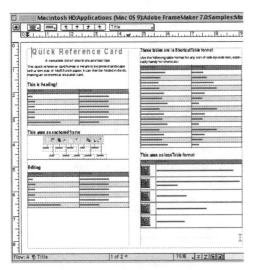

Figure 16.25 Sample quick reference card.

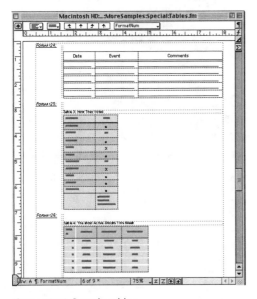

Figure 16.26 Sample tables.

Using FrameMaker sample files

In addition to templates and clip art, FrameMaker includes a set of documents showing you how to use FrameMaker to create a dizzying array of documents. Here is a partial list of the sample files included in the Samples\MoreSamples or Samples: MoreSamples folder within the folder in which FrameMaker is installed:

◆ Report templates

◆ Quick reference card (**Figure 16.25**)

◆ Data sheet

◆ Article for a scholarly journal or template for a thesis

◆ Technical specifications

◆ Buying guide (and many other books)

◆ Encyclopedia or glossary document

◆ Tables, tables, and more tables—in fact, 33 different tables (**Figure 16.26**)

Troubleshooting font errors

When you try to open a document, especially one that someone else has been working on, you may see an unavailable fonts message. The document may have been edited on a different system that uses fonts not installed on your system, a font may have been removed or become damaged, or the default printer for your system may have been changed.

If the Remember Missing Font Names option in the Preferences dialog box is selected (**Figure 16.27**), you can go ahead and open the document. Because FrameMaker preserves the names of unavailable fonts, the original fonts will reappear when you open the document on a computer that has the fonts installed. But if the file is part of a book, you won't be able to update or print the book with substitute fonts.

TIPS

Here are some of the remedies you might consider:

◆ Check for damaged fonts

If another application can use fonts that FrameMaker cannot use, the fonts may be damaged. Reinstall them using the original media.

◆ Remap unavailable fonts

You may want to permanently remap the unavailable fonts to available fonts. Deselect the Remember Missing Font Names option in the Preferences dialog box and then close, save, and reopen the file. The original font information will be lost.

◆ Switch printers (Windows only)

This is the most insidious and common cause of font problems on Windows! FrameMaker reads font information stored in the printer driver so that it can make fonts stored for the printer available for use within FrameMaker. In some cases, changing the default printer can change one or more fonts available in FrameMaker.

For more information on troubleshooting font problems, isolating damaged fonts or a damaged fonts folder, or reinstalling Type 1 fonts, see the Adobe Web site.

Troubleshooting text flow problems

You can troubleshoot text flow problems in documents with multiple flows by setting the zoom to 25% and setting page scrolling to Facing Pages (View > Options). Put your cursor in a flow and select all the text (Edit > Select All in Flow). You can easily see the text flowing from one text frame to the next (**Figure 16.28**). You can apply default or custom master pages in the Master Page Usage dialog box (**Figure 16.29**). You can also disconnect and connect text frames and keep selecting all of the text in the flow until you have diagnosed what's wrong and fixed it.

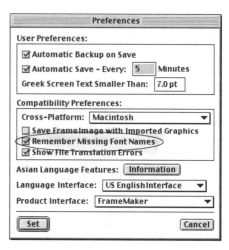

Figure 16.27 To preserve the names of unavailable fonts, select Remember Missing Font Names.

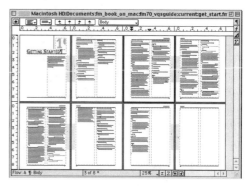

Figure 16.28 Zoom to 25% and select all of the text in a flow to troubleshoot flow problems in documents with multiple flows.

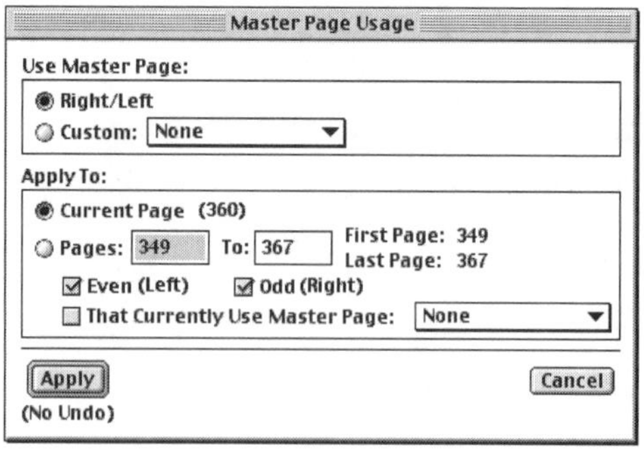

Figure 16.29 Apply default or custom master pages in the Master Page Usage dialog box.

Figure 16.30 Scroll down in the left frame of the Help page to find the Quick Reference links for both Windows and Mac OS.

Best Practices

Observe best practices whenever you are in a situation to do so, and promote them in your workgroup. For a small investment in learning the right way to do things in FrameMaker, you will reap the dividends of increased efficiency and productivity.

Shortcuts for new users

Bob Silva, Consultant, Stockton, CA: "One of the most powerful features in FrameMaker is its extensive set of shortcuts, which you can find in the platform-specific Quick Reference sections of the online help system (**Figure 16.30**)."

On Windows, you can open any menu by pressing Alt and the underlined letter at the top of each menu.

On Mac OS, the standard commands—Open, Close, Save, Quit, Undo/Redo, Cut, Copy, Paste—use the standard Command keyboard sequences.

If you're a new FrameMaker user, or if you're reluctant to learn shortcuts, start by commiting a few to memory, such as the following:

◆ When working with graphics, try learning graphics shortcuts, such as Select All, Group, Ungroup, Align, and Align Left.

◆ If you're importing graphics, use the shortcut to open the Import dialog box.

◆ Instead of using the mouse to open dialog boxes and windows, try using the keyboard shortcuts instead. Eventually, you'll rarely use the menus.

Maria Abrahms, Daly City, CA:
"Learn and use the keyboard shortcuts. The Esc key shortcuts are easy to remember (and are typically the same in both Windows and Mac OS)."

These keyboard shortcuts all start with the Esc key plus some combination of upper- and lowercase keys. The nice thing about the Esc shortcuts is that for the most part they follow the menus. For example: View > Borders is Esc V B, View > Text Symbols is Esc T S, and so on. *Be careful that Caps Lock is not on when you use the Esc shortcuts.*

Graphics

Lisa Kelly, Writers Plus, Cupertino, CA:
"If you import graphics by reference, you should periodically remove unused screen captures and other graphics files from your document directories. To determine which graphics to remove, use FrameMaker to list the imported graphics in your document or book."

To generate a list of imported graphics:

1. Choose Special > List of > References, and in the Set Up List of References dialog box, move Imported Graphics to the Include References list (**Figure 16.31**) and click Set.

   A list of imported graphics is generated for the file or book, with graphics listed page by page in the order in which they appear in the documents.

   or

   Choose Special > Index of > References, and in the Set Up Index of References dialog box, move Imported Graphics to the Include References list (**Figure 16.32**) and click Set.

   An alphabetical list of imported graphics is generated for the file or book.

2. Compare this list with the files listed alphabetically in a folder on your desktop, and relocate or delete unused files.

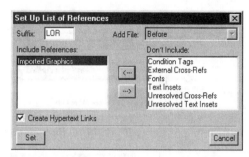

Figure 16.31 Move Imported Graphics to the Include References list.

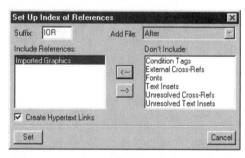

Figure 16.32 Use an index of references to view graphics listed alphabetically.

Formats you use most often appear at the top of the list in the Paragraph Catalog and on pop-up menus ...

```
                    ¶ Catalog
            aList Head
            aList Subtext
            Anchor
            Anchor In Text
            aNumber List
            Body
            Bullet List
            Callout Body
            Figure Caption
            Head 1
            Head 2
            Intro Figure Caption
            Introduction
            List 2 Subtext
            List Head
            List Subtext
            Table Caption
            Table Column Head
            Table Entry
            Table Title
            Tip
            Tip Head
            zAnchor Figure
            zAppendix Number
            zAppendix Title
            zBleedTab
            zChapter Number
            zChapter Title
            zDefinition
            zGlossary
            zGlossary Head

                    Delete...
```

... and formats you use less often appear at the bottom.

Figure 16.33 Add an "a" or a "z" at the beginning of format names to better organize the Catalogs.

Figure 16.34 Press F9 or Ctrl-9 or Control-9 to apply paragraph formats from the keyboard.

Figure 16.35 Press F8 or Ctrl-8 or Control-8 to apply character formats from the keyboard.

Formats

There are a number of best practices for naming paragraph and character formats. The two presented are representative.

Shelley Hoyt, San Jose, CA:
"Keep formats under control by thinking carefully when you design templates and create formats to avoid creating unnecessary formats. For example, following this advice, you could create an indented paragraph format for indented paragraphs to use under both bullets and numbered steps."

Begin paragraph tag names with an "a" if you use them frequently and want them to appear at the top of the list, and with a "z" if you want them to fall to the bottom of the list in the pop-up menu on the formatting bar, for example, or in the Paragraph Catalog (**Figure 16.33**).

Mike Hedblom, Burlingame, CA:
"Begin each paragraph and character tag name with a unique two- or three-letter abbreviation. This allows you to quickly type the name when using the F9 or Ctrl-9 or Control-9 tag assignment keys for paragraph formats; or the F8 or Ctrl-8 or Control-8 tag assignment keys for character formats."

Here are some examples:

◆ B.BulletList

◆ B1.BulletListIndent1

◆ P.Paragraph

◆ P1.ParagraphIndent1

To display the B1.BulletListindent1 paragraph format, for example, press B 1 (**Figure 16.34**); then press Enter or Return to apply the format to the current paragraphs. To display the CB.CalloutBold character format, press C B (**Figure 16.35**); then press Enter or Return to apply the format to selected text.

Using the Copy Special command

Mark Powell, www.wordscapes.com,
San Jose, CA:
"The one little tip that I use over and over in
Frame, and that I evangelize for other users
is the use of the items in the Edit > Copy
Special submenu (**Figure 16.36**)."

You can copy to the Clipboard not just text and
graphics, but also paragraph and character
formats, conditional text settings, and table
column widths.

Working in books

William Courington, ForWord
Communication, Palo Alto, CA:
"For best performance when working with a
book, especially if you are working remotely,
do the following."

To work efficiently in book files:

1. In the book window, hold down Shift and
   choose File > Open All Files in Book
   (**Figure 16.37**).

   Work on the files as usual; tasks such as
   book building, global search, and spell
   checking will go very quickly because the
   files are in memory.

2. Periodically, hold down Shift and choose
   File > Save All Files in Book.

3. When you're finished, hold down Shift
   and choose File > Close All Files in Book,
   and then close the book file.

Callouts and labels

Chris Klemmer, The Graphic Word, Inc.,
San Jose, CA:
"The ability to add text as callouts to
graphics in FrameMaker is a real time saver.
You can edit or reposition them without
having to go back to the application in which
the graphic was created. Also, FrameMaker
spell checks text in both text lines and text
frames (**Figure 16.38**)."

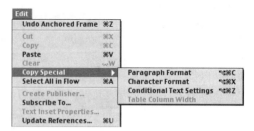

Figure 16.36 The Edit > Copy Special submenu.

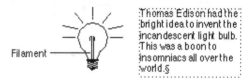

Figure 16.37 Hold down the Shift key
and in the book window, choose File >
Open All Files in Book.

Figure 16.38 FrameMaker spell checks text in both
text lines (left) and text frames (right).

Figure 16.39 Empty Paragraph Catalog and Character Catalog.

Figure 16.40 New format stored in the Paragraph Catalog.

Read-in templates

In workgroups, you often need to distribute a new paragraph, character, or table format to others in the group. Of course, you'll add it to the group's templates, but it's not always practical to ask people to import formats from the source templates once they get close to a deadline. A good approach is to use templates that contain only the format you want to distribute plus some instructions on how and where to use the new format.

To create a read-in template:

1. Open a blank FrameMaker document and delete all of the formats from the Paragraph, Character, or Table Catalog (**Figure 16.39**).

2. Copy and paste text with the new paragraph or character format or a table with the new table format.

3. Add the new format back to the Catalog. At this point, it will be the only format in the Catalog (**Figure 16.40**).

4. If you wish, add some text about the format and how to use it.

5. Save and name the file with the name of the new format.

   For example, you could name the read-in template `Para Indent3.fm` or `table_ReferenceWide.fm`.

6. Keep a record of new formats and when they were added by storing the read-in templates in the same location as the rest of your workgroup's templates.

To import a new format into a document:

1. Open the document or book file to which you want to add the new format and the read-in template.

2. From the File menu, choose Import > Formats.

(continues on next page)

BEST PRACTICES

3. In the Import Formats dialog box, from the Import from Document menu, choose the read-in template.

4. In the Import and Update area, select only the type of format you want to add (**Figure 16.41**).

5. Click Import.

The new format is added to the document or to documents in the book file and to the appropriate Catalog.

Using online resources

Here are two of the online resources for FrameMaker that were mentioned most often by FrameMaker users, both new and experienced.

◆ Adobe knowledgebase

http://www.adobe.com/support/products/framemaker.html

Several people who submitted tips and best practices called my attention to the Adobe FrameMaker knowledge base, freely available on the Adobe Web site (**Figure 16.42**). I've used it a number of times and find it invaluable, especially for issues involving fonts, page layout, and books.

You can also see what patches are available and download them from the Adobe download site.

◆ Frame Users group

http://www.frameusers.com

Frame started this group as the Frame User Network (FUN), and it's grown into a substantial international organization with a Web site full of good information (**Figure 16.43**).

The Frame Users group holds an annual national conference and regional meetings during the year. There might be a group in your area that holds regular meetings.

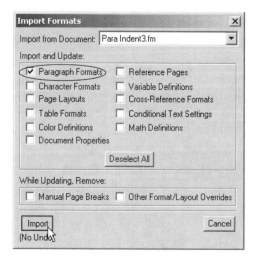

Figure 16.41 Import only the type of format in the read-in template.

Figure 16.42 Adobe's FrameMaker support page.

Figure 16.43 Frame Users group page.

KEYBOARD SHORTCUTS

FrameMaker's rich set of keyboard shortcuts can make you feel like the Liberace of the computer keyboard. Use of keyboard shortcuts increases productivity—to say nothing of the job satisfaction you experience as you watch your fingers fly across the keyboard—your work almost seems to do itself.

The FrameMaker 7.0 package includes a platform-specific *Quick Reference Card* in the box with your software and documentation. On the front is a complete set of commands accessible from the QuickAccess Bar (see page 15). Inside are keyboard shortcuts grouped under sections that reflect task areas, such as book commands, editing text, and entering special characters (see Appendix B).

✔ Tips

■ This appendix provides a subset of the complete set of FrameMaker 7.0 keyboard shortcuts, as does the *Quick Reference Card*. The keyboard shortcuts in online help are the most complete.

■ If you experience any problems using keyboard shortcuts, check to make sure that the Caps Lock key is off,

Typing Keyboard Shortcuts

In the sections that follow:

◆ A hyphen indicates that each key must be pressed simultaneously. For example, "Ctrl-C" means to press the Control and C keys at the same time.

◆ If the key sequence does not contain a hyphen, then press each key one after the other, for example, "Esc space T" means to press the Escape key, then the spacebar, then the T key.

◆ Keys are displayed as an uppercase letter to match what you see on the keyboard. If you need to actually type an uppercase letter, the Shift key is added to the combination. For example, "Esc F Shift-S" means to press the Escape key, then the F key, then an uppercase S.

◆ Where you can use either of two sequences, the sequences are separated by a comma.

Many of the keyboard shortcuts are intuitive. Others require a little more of a stretch, but figuring them out can be helpful.

For example, you can press Esc E S or Command-L to display the Spelling Checker window. What's the connection between the letters and the action? Esc E S is shorthand for Edit > Spelling Checker. In the Mac OS the letter "L" stands for "lexicon," another word for a dictionary.

Or consider Esc S C or Command-K, which display the Cross-Reference window. Esc S C is shorthand for Special > Cross-Reference. In the Mac OS shortcut, the "K" has the same sound as the "C" in "cross-reference."

Sometimes the shortcut represents a phrase. For example, Esc F I F, which you can use to import a graphics file into a FrameMaker document, is short for File > Import > File.

Windows

These are the abbreviations used for the keys in this section:

◆ Ctrl for the Control key

◆ Alt for the Alt key

Navigating through documents

The following table provides shortcuts for navigating through documents.

Navigation Shortcuts	
To display	**Press**
Previous page	Esc P P, Page Up
Next page	Esc P N, Page Down
First page	Esc P F, Alt-Page Up, Shift-Previous Page button
Last page	Esc P L, Alt-Page Down, Shift-Next Page button
Go To Page dialog box	Esc V P, Ctrl-G
To go to	**Do this**
Source of a cross-reference	Press Alt-Ctrl and click an active area
To move the insertion point in text to	**Press**
Start of word	Ctrl-Left arrow
End of word	Ctrl-Right arrow
Start of next word	Esc B W
Start of next paragraph	Esc B P
Start of flow	Alt-Shift-Page Up
End of flow	Alt-Shift-Page Down
Start of line	Ctrl-Page Up , Home
End of line	Ctrl-Page Down , End

Start of sentence   Ctrl-Home
End "   "   Ctrl-End

KEYBOARD SHORTCUTS

Working in book files

The following table provides shortcuts for working in FrameMaker book files.

Book Commands	
To	**Press**
Open New Book	Esc F Shift-N
Save Book	Esc F S, Ctrl-S
Update Book	Esc E Shift-U, Esc F G
Delete File from Book	Esc F X
Select All Files	Esc E A
Save All Files in Book	Esc F Shift-S
Close All Files in Book	Esc F Shift-C
Select a range of files	Shift-click
Select discontiguous files	Ctrl-click
Move a file up in book	Esc M U
Move a file down in book	Esc M D
Print Book	Esc F P
Print Selected Files in Book	Esc F Shift-F

Searching

The following table provides shortcuts for searching and finding and changing text.

Find and Change Shortcuts	
To	**Press**
Search forward	Esc F I N, Esc E Shift-F
Search backward	Esc F I P
Change current selection	Esc R O
Change all occurrences of Find text in document	Esc R G
Change and search again	Esc R A
Change settings to As Is in Find Character Format and Change To Character Format dialog boxes	Shift-F8
To find	**Type**
Tab symbol	\T
Forced return	\R
Nonbreaking space	\space
Thin space	\I, \ST
En space	\Shift-N, \SN
Em space	\Shift-M, \SM
End-of-flow symbol	\F
\ (backslash)	\\
Nonbreaking hyphen	\+
Suppress hyphenation symbol	_ (underscore)
Start of word	\<
End of word	\>
With Use Wildcards turned on, to find	**Type**
Any number of characters	*
Spaces or punctuation	I (bar)
Any one character	?
Beginning of a line	^
End of a line	$
Any one of the bracketed characters *ab*	[ab]
Any character except *ab*	[^ab]
Any character from *a* to *f*	[a-f]

Working in tables

The following table provides shortcuts for working in tables.

Table Shortcuts	
To select	**Press**
A cell	Ctrl-click cell
A row	Ctrl-double-click column border
A column	Ctrl-double-click row border
Current row	Esc T H R
Current column	Esc T H C
Current table	Esc T H T, Ctrl-triple-click cell
To move to	**Press**
Rightmost cell in current row	Esc T M E
Leftmost cell in current row	Esc T M A
Top cell in current column	Esc T M T
Bottom cell in current column	Esc T M B
To	**Press**
Type tab character in cell	Esc Tab
Add rows above selected row	Esc T Shift-R A
Add rows below selected rows	Esc T Shift-R B
Add columns to left	Esc T C L
Add columns to right	Esc T C R
Paste by replacing selected rows or columns	Esc T P R
Paste rows or columns before selection	Esc T P B
Paste rows or columns after selection	Esc T P A
Copy column width to Clipboard	Esc E Y W

handwritten annotation: Ctrl + Enter

Editing text

The following table provides shortcuts for editing text.

Editing Shortcuts	
To	**Press**
Cut	Esc E X, Shift-Delete, Ctrl-X
Copy	Esc E C, Ctrl-C, Ctrl-Insert
Paste	Esc E P, Ctrl-Y, Shift-Insert, Ctrl-V
Undo/Redo	Esc E U, Ctrl-Shift-Z, Ctrl-Z, Alt-Backspace
Transpose characters	Click between characters and press Ctrl-F9
Make selected text lowercase	Alt-Ctrl-L
Make selected text uppercase	Alt-Ctrl-U
Make selected text initial caps	Alt-Ctrl-C
Change current word to all lowercase	Alt-Ctrl-L, Alt-Ctrl-Shift-L
Change current word to all uppercase	Alt-Ctrl-U, Alt-Ctrl-Shift-U
Change current word to initial caps	Alt-Ctrl-C
Display the Capitalization dialog box	Esc E Shift-C
To select	**Do this**
A word	Double-click it
A word, then next words	Double-click it and drag, Double-click it and Shift-click
Current sentence, then next	Press Esc H S, Press Ctrl-Shift-End
Current sentence, then previous	Press Esc Shift-H Shift-S, Press Ctrl-Shift-Home
A paragraph	Triple-click it

KEYBOARD SHORTCUTS

Formatting text

The following table provides shortcuts for formatting one or more current paragraphs.

Paragraph Formatting Shortcuts

To	Use this shortcut
Start a paragraph anywhere	Esc J Shift-A
Start a paragraph at the top of a column	Esc J Shift-C
Start a paragraph at top of a page	Esc J Shift-P
Turn on hyphenation	Esc J H
Turn off hyphenation	Esc J N
Repeat last paragraph-related command	Esc J J
Display the Paragraph Catalog	Esc O P C
Display Update Paragraph Format dialog box	Esc O P U

The following table provides shortcuts to change the character format of selected text or of text you are about to type.

Character Formatting Shortcuts

To	Use this shortcut
Change text to default paragraph font; remove character tag from text in a text line	Esc O C P
Turn bold on or off	Esc C B, F4, Ctrl-B
Turn italic on or off	Esc C L, F5, Ctrl-I
Turn underline on or off	Esc C U, F3, Ctrl-U
Turn strikethrough on or off	Esc C S, Ctrl-/
Change text to plain	Esc C P, F2
Turn superscript on or off	Esc C + (plus)
Turn subscript on or off	Esc C - (minus)
Put text on baseline	Esc C = (equal)
Change text to small caps	Esc C M, Ctrl-E
Turn change bars on or off	Esc C H
Turn pair kerning on or off	Esc C K
Set font stretch to 100 percent	Esc [(left square bracket) N
Repeat the last font-related command	Esc C C
Display Character Catalog	Esc O C C

Menu commands

The following table provides shortcuts for commands on the File menu in a document window.

File Menu Commands (document)

Command	Press
New > Document	Esc F N, Ctrl-N
New > Book	Esc F Shift-N
Open	Esc F O, Ctrl-O
Close	Esc F C, Esc F Q
Close All	Esc F Shift-C, Esc F Shift-Q
Save	Esc F S, Ctrl-S
Save All	Esc F Shift-S
Save As	Esc F A
Revert to Saved	Esc F R
Import > File	Esc F I F
Import > Formats	Esc F I O
Print	Esc F P, Ctrl-P
Print Setup	Ctrl-Shift-P
Preferences	Esc F Shift-P
Exit	Alt-F4

The following table provides shortcuts for commands on the File menu in a book window.

File Menu Commands (book window)

Command	Press
New > Document	Esc F N, Ctrl-N
New > Book	Esc F Shift-N
Open All Files in Book	Esc F Shift-O
Close All Files in Book	Esc F Shift-C
Save Book	Esc F S, Ctrl-S
Save All Files in Book	Esc F Shift-S
Revert to Saved Book	Esc F R
Import > Formats	Esc F I O
Print Selected Files	Esc F Shift-F
Print Book	Esc F P, Ctrl-P
Print Setup	Ctrl-Shift-P
Preferences	Esc F Shift-P
Exit	Alt-F4

The following table provides shortcuts for commands on the Edit menu in a document window.

Edit Menu Commands (document)

Command	Press
Undo/Redo	Esc E U, Ctrl-Z
Cut	Esc E X, Ctrl-X
Copy	Esc E C, Ctrl-C
Paste	Esc E P, Ctrl-V
Paste Special	Ctrl-Shift-V
Clear	Esc E B
Copy Special > Paragraph Format	Esc E Y P
Copy Special > Character Format	Esc E Y C
Copy Special > Conditional Text Settings	Esc E Y D
Copy Special > Table Column Width	Esc E Y W
Select All in Flow	Esc E A, Ctrl-A
Find/Change	Esc E F, Ctrl-F
Find Next	Esc F I N, Esc E Shift-F
Spelling Checker	Esc E S
Thesaurus	Esc E T
Text Inset Properties	Esc E I
Update References	Esc E Shift-U

The following table provides shortcuts for commands on the Edit menu in a book window.

Edit Menu Commands (book window)

Command	Press
Undo/Redo	Esc E U, Ctrl-Z
Cut	Esc E X, Ctrl-X
Copy	Esc E C, Ctrl-C
Paste	Esc E P, Ctrl-V
Clear	Esc E B
Select All Files	Esc E A
Find/Change	Esc E F, Ctrl-F
Find Next	Esc F I N, Esc E Shift-F
Spelling Checker	Esc E S
Set Up Generated File	Esc F D
Delete File From Book	Esc F X
Update Book	Esc E Shift-U, Esc F G

The following table provides shortcuts for commands on the Add menu in a book window.

Add Menu Commands (book window)

Command	Press
Files	Esc F F
Table of Contents	Esc T O C
List of > Figures	Esc L O F
List of > Tables	Esc L O T
List of > Paragraphs	Esc L O P
List of > Paragraphs (Alphabetical)	Esc L O Shift-P
List of > Markers	Esc L O M
List of > Markers (Alphabetical)	Esc L O Shift-M
List of > References	Esc L O R
Standard Index	Esc I X

Working in windows and dialog boxes

The following table provides shortcuts to display a window or dialog box and make it active. If it is already open but is behind another window, these shortcuts bring it to the front.

Windows and Dialog Box Shortcuts

To display and make it active	Use this shortcut
Current document window	Esc Shift-F I D
Find/Change	Esc Shift-F I F
Hypertext	Esc Shift-F I H
Marker	Esc Shift-F I M
Spelling Checker	Esc Shift-F I S
Paragraph Designer	Esc Shift-F I P
Character Designer	Esc Shift-F I C
Conditional Text	Esc Shift-F I O
Custom Ruling and Shading	Esc Shift-F I R
Table Designer	Esc Shift-F I T

Documents

The following table provides shortcuts for opening, saving, and closing files.

Opening, Saving, and Closing Files

To open	Use this shortcut
A document in a book file	Double-click the filename in the book window
All files in an active book window	Esc F Shift-O, or press Shift and choose Open All Files in Book from the File menu
Display the Save Document dialog box	Esc F A
Save a document or book	Esc F S, Ctrl-S
Save all open files (also save all files in a book from an active book window)	Esc F Shift-S, or press Shift and choose File > Save All Open Files
Close all open files (also close all files in a book from an active book window)	Esc F Shift-C, or press Shift and choose File > Close All Open Files

The following table provides shortcuts for zooming.

Zooming Shortcuts

To	Use this shortcut
Zoom in one zoom setting	Esc Z I
Zoom out one zoom setting	Esc Z O
Fit page in window	Esc Z P
Fit window to page	Esc Z W
Fit window to text frame	Esc Z F
Zoom to 100 percent	Esc Z Z

Spell checking

The following table provides shortcuts to use while you're spell checking a document or book.

Spell Checking Shortcuts

To	Use this shortcut
Check selected text or a word containing the insertion point	Esc L S, or Ctrl-click Start Checking in Spelling Checker window
Check entire document	Esc L E
Check current page	Esc L P
Correct a word	Esc L C W
Add a word to your personal dictionary	Esc L A P
Add a word to the document dictionary	Esc L A D
Add a word to automatic corrections	Esc L A C
Delete a word from your personal dictionary	Esc L X P
Delete a word from the document dictionary	Esc L X D
Clear automatic corrections	Esc L C A
Create a file of unknown words	Esc L B
Mark all paragraphs for rechecking	Esc L R
Show a word's hyphenation	Esc L hyphen

Graphics tasks

The following table provides shortcuts for some common graphics tasks.

Graphics Shortcuts	
To	Press
Quick-copy a selected object	Alt-drag object
Rotate an object arbitrarily	Alt-drag a corner or reshape handle
Move an object along vertical or horizontal axis	Shift-drag object
Move object 1 point	Alt-arrow key
Move object 6 points	Alt-Shift-arrow key
Shrink wrap an anchored frame (shrink frame to an object and position at the insertion point)	Esc M P
Unwrap an anchored frame (enlarge the frame)	Esc M E
Turn text runaround off for a selected graphic	Esc G Q
To align object along	Use this shortcut
Tops	Esc J T, Ctrl-F1
Top/bottom centers	Esc J M, Ctrl-F2
Bottoms	Esc J B, Ctrl-F3
Left sides	Esc J L
Left/right centers	Esc J C
Right sides	Esc J R

Miscellaneous

The following table provides some miscellaneous shortcuts.

Miscellaneous Shortcuts	
To	Press
Display online help	Esc F H, F1
Redisplay a document or refresh screen display	Esc W R, Ctrl-L
Lock or unlock a document or book	Esc Shift-F L K
Display the Color Definitions dialog box	Press Esc V C D
Undo some FrameMaker commands	Esc E U, Ctrl-Z, Alt-Backspace
Turn display of graphics off or on	Esc V V
Insert a marker	Esc M K
Insert a hypertext marker	Esc M H
Open the Edit Custom Marker Type dialog box	Esc E M T
Display the Show/Hide Conditional Text dialog box	Esc V Shift-C
Turn condition indicators on or off	Esc V Shift-O
Select all the text around the insertion point with same condition tag settings	Esc H Shift-C
Make the selected text unconditional	Esc Q Shift-U, Ctrl-6

Mac OS

If you work with FrameMaker on both Windows and Mac OS, you'll find that the Esc shortcuts are the almost always the same on both platforms.

Navigating through documents

The following table provides shortcuts for navigating through documents.

Navigation Shortcuts	
To display	**Press**
Previous page	Esc P P, Option-Page Up
Next page	Esc P N, Option-Page Down
First page	Esc P F, Home, Shift-click Previous Page button
Last page	Esc P L, End, Shift-click Next Page button
To go to	**Do this**
Source of a cross-reference	Press Control-Option and click an active area
To move the insertion point in text to	**Press**
Start of word	Command-Left arrow
End of word	Command-Shift-Option-Right arrow
Start of next word	Esc B W, Command-Right arrow
Start of paragraph	Command-Up arrow
End of current paragraph	Command-Shift-Option-Down arrow
Start of next paragraph	Esc B P, Command-Down arrow
Start of flow	Command-Home

Working in book files

The following table provides shortcuts for working in FrameMaker book files.

Book Commands	
To	**Do this**
Open New Book	Esc F Shift-N
Save Book	Esc F S, Command-S
Update Book	Esc E Shift-U, Esc F G
Select All Files	Esc E A, Command-A
Save All Files in Book	Esc F Shift-S
Close All Files in Book	Esc F Shift-C
Select a range of files	Command-Shift-click
Select discontiguous files	Shift-click
Print Book	Esc F P, Command-P
Print Selected Files in Book	Esc F Shift-F

Searching

The following table provides shortcuts for searching and finding and changing text.

Find and Change Shortcuts

To	Press
Search forward	Esc F I N, Command-G
Search backward	Esc F I P, Command-Shift-G
Change current selection	Esc R O, Command-R
Change all occurrences of Find text in document	Esc R G
Change and search again	Esc R A, Command-Control-R
Change settings to As Is in Find Character Format and Change To Character Format dialog boxes	Shift-F15, Command-Shift-X

To find	Type
Tab symbol	\T
Forced return	\R
Nonbreaking space	\space
Thin space	\l, \ST
En space	\Shift-N, \SN
Em space	\Shift-M, \SM
End-of-flow symbol	\F
\ (backslash)	\\
Nonbreaking hyphen	\+
Suppress hyphenation symbol	_ (underscore)
Start of word	\<
End of word	\>

With Use Wildcards turned on, to find	Type
Any number of characters	*
Spaces or punctuation	I (bar)
Any one character	?
Beginning of a line	^
End of a line	$
Any one of the bracketed characters *ab*	[ab]
Any character except *ab*	[^ab]
Any character from *a* to *f*	[a-f]

Working in tables

The following table provides shortcuts for working in tables.

Table Shortcuts

To select	Press
A cell	Option-click cell
A row	Option-double-click column border
A column	Option-double-click row border
Current row	Esc T H R
Current column	Esc T H C
Current table	Esc T H T, Option-triple-click cell

To move to	Press
Rightmost cell in current row	Esc T M E
Leftmost cell in current row	Esc T M A
Top cell in current column	Esc T M T
Bottom cell in current column	Esc T M B
Next cell, select its text	Tab, Esc T M N
Previous cell, select its text	Shift-Tab, Esc T M P
Cell below, select its text	Control-Tab
Cell above, select its text	Control-Shift-Tab

To	Press
Type tab character in cell	Esc Tab, Control-I
Add rows above selected row	Esc T Shift-R A
Add rows below selected rows	Esc T Shift-R B, Control-Return
Add columns to left	Esc T C L
Add columns to right	Esc T C R
Paste by replacing selected rows or columns	Esc T P R
Paste rows or columns before selection	Esc T P B
Paste rows or columns after selection	Esc T P A
Copy column width to Clipboard	Esc E Y W

Editing text

The following table provides shortcuts for editing text.

Editing Shortcuts	
To	**Press**
Cut	Esc E X, Command-X
Copy	Esc E C, Command-C
Paste	Esc E P, Command-V
Undo/Redo	Esc E U, Command-Z
Quick-copy text	Click where you want to insert copied text, press Command-Control, and drag through text
Transpose characters	Click between characters and press Control-T
Make selected text lowercase	Control-Option-L
Make selected text uppercase	Control-Option-U
Make selected text initial caps	Control-Option-C
To select	**Do this**
A word	Double-click it
A word, then next words	Double-click it and drag, Double-click it and Shift-click
Current sentence, then next	Press Esc H S
Current sentence, then previous	Press Esc Shift-H Shift-S
A paragraph	Triple-click it
To delete	**Press**
Previous character	Delete, Control-H
Backward to start of previous word	Esc K B
Backward to start of a line	Control-U, Control-Delete
Backward to end of previous sentence	Esc K A
Next character	Control-D
Forward to end of a word	Esc K F
Forward to end of a line	Control-K
Forward to start of the next sentence	Esc K S

Formatting text

The following table provides shortcuts for formatting one or more current paragraphs.

Paragraph Formatting Shortcuts	
To	**Use this shortcut**
Start a paragraph anywhere	Esc J Shift-A
Start a paragraph at the top of a column	Esc J Shift-C
Start a paragraph at top of a page	Esc J Shift-P
Start a paragraph at the top of a left page	Esc J Shift-L
Start a paragraph at the top of a right page	Esc J Shift-R
Turn on hyphenation	Esc J H
Turn off hyphenation	Esc J N
Repeat last paragraph-related command	Esc J J
Display the Paragraph Catalog	Esc O P C
Display Update Paragraph Format dialog box	Esc O P U

The following table provides shortcuts to change the character format of selected text or of text you are about to type.

Character Formatting Shortcuts	
To	**Use this shortcut**
Change text to default paragraph font; remove character tag from text in a text line	Esc O C P
Turn bold on or off	Esc C B, Command-Shift-B
Turn italic on or off	Esc C L, Command-Shift-I
Turn underline on or off	Esc C U, Command-Shift-U
Turn strikethrough on or off	Esc C S, Command-Shift-\, Shift-F12
Change text to plain	Esc C P, Command-Shift-P, Shift-F9
Turn superscript on or off	Esc C + (plus)
Turn subscript on or off	Esc C - (minus)
Put text on baseline	Esc C = (equal)
Change text to small caps	Esc C M, Command-Shift-A

Character Formatting Shortcuts

To	Use this shortcut
Turn change bars on or off	Esc C H, Command-Shift-Y
Turn pair kerning on or off	Esc C K, Command-Shift-K
Set font stretch to 100 percent	Esc [(left square bracket) N
Repeat the last font-related command	Esc C C
Display Character Catalog	Esc O C C

Menu commands

The following table provides shortcuts for commands on the File menu in a document window.

File Menu Commands (document)

Command	Press
New > Document	Esc F N, Command-N
New > Book	Esc F Shift-N
Open	Esc F O, Command-O
Close	Esc F C, Command-W
Close All	Esc F Shift-C, Esc F Shift-Q
Save	Esc F S, Command-S F7
Save All	Esc F Shift-S
Save As	Esc F A, Shift-F7
Revert to Saved	Esc F R
Import > File	Esc F I F, Command-I
Import > Formats	Esc F I O, Command-Option-O
Page Setup	Shift-F8
Print	Esc F P, Command-P, F8
Preferences	Esc F Shift-P
Quit	Command-Q

The following table provides shortcuts for commands on the File menu in a book window.

File Menu Commands (book window)

Command	Press
New > Document	Esc F N, Command-N
New > Book	Esc F Shift-N, Command-Option-N
Open All Files in Book	Esc F Shift-O
Close All Files in Book	Esc F Shift-C
Save Book	Esc F S, Command-S
Save All Files in Book	Esc F Shift-S
Revert to Saved Book	Esc F R
Import > Formats	Esc F I O, Command-Option-O
Page Setup	Shift-F8
Print Selected Files	Esc F Shift-F
Print Book	Esc F P, Command-P
Preferences	Esc F Shift-P
Quit	Command-Q

The following table provides shortcuts for commands on the Edit menu in a document window.

Edit Menu Commands (document)

Command	Press
Undo/Redo	Esc E U, F1, Command-Z
Cut	Esc E X, Command-X, F2
Copy	Esc E C, Command-C, F3
Paste	Esc E P, Command-V, F4
Clear	Esc E B
Copy Special > Paragraph Format	Esc E Y P, Command-Option-C
Copy Special > Character Format	Esc E Y C, Command-Option-X
Copy Special > Conditional Text Settings	Esc E Y D, Command-Option-Z
Copy Special > Table Column Width	Esc E Y W
Select All	Esc E A, Command-A
Text Inset Properties	Esc E I
Update References	Esc F G, Command-U
Find/Change	Esc E F, Command-F

Edit Menu Commands (document)

Command	Press
Find Next	Esc F I N, Command-G
Spelling Checker	Esc E S, Command-L
Thesaurus	Esc E T, Command-Shift-T

The following table provides shortcuts for commands on the Edit menu in a book window.

Edit Menu Commands (book window)

Command	Press
Undo/Redo	Esc E U, F1, Command-Z
Cut	Esc E X, Command-X
Copy	Esc E C, Command-C
Paste	Esc E P, Command-V
Clear	Esc E B
Select All Files	Esc E A
Find/Change	Esc E F, Control-S, Command-F
Find Next	Esc F I N, Esc E Shift-F, Command-G
Spelling Checker	Esc E S, Command-L
Set Up Generated File	Esc F D
Delete File From Book	Esc F X
Update Book	Esc F G, Command-U

The following table provides shortcuts for commands on the Add menu in a book window.

Add Menu Commands (book window)

Command	Press
Files	Esc F F
Table of Contents	Esc T O C
List of > Figures	Esc L O F
List of > Tables	Esc L O T
List of > Paragraphs	Esc L O P
List of > Paragraphs (Alphabetical)	Esc L O Shift-P
List of > Markers	Esc L O M
List of > Markers (Alphabetical)	Esc L O Shift-M
List of > References	Esc L O R
Standard Index of Authors	Esc I X

The following table provides shortcuts for commands on the Format menu in a document window.

Format Menu Commands

Command	Press
Style > Plain	Esc C P, Command-Shift-P
Style > Bold	Esc C B, Command-Shift-B
Style > Italic	Esc C I, Command-Shift-I
Style > Underline	Esc C U, Command-Shift-U
Style > Strikethrough	Esc C S, Command-Shift-\
Style > Change Bar	Esc C H, Command-Shift-Y
Style > Superscript	Esc C + (plus,) Command-Shift-+
Style > Subscript	Esc C minus, Command-Shift-minus
Style > Small Caps	Esc C M, Command-Shift-A
Characters > Designer	Esc O C D, Command-D
Characters > Default Paragraph Font	Esc O C P, Command-Shift-space
Paragraphs > Designer	Esc O P D, Command-M
Page Layout > Master Page Usage	Esc O M U
Customize Layout > Connect Text Frames	Esc Shift-C Shift-C
Customize Layout > Disconnect Previous	Esc Shift-C Shift-P
Customize Layout > Disconnect Next	Esc Shift-C Shift-N
Customize Layout > Disconnect Both	Esc Shift-C Shift-B
Document > Text Options	Esc O T O, Command-F9
Headers & Footers > Insert Page #	Esc O H P
Headers & Footers > Insert Page Count	Esc O H C
Headers & Footers > Insert Current Date	Esc O H D

The following table provides shortcuts for commands on the View menu in a document window.

View Menu Commands

Command	Press
QuickAccess Bar	Esc V Q
Borders	Esc V B, Command-Option-H
Text Symbols	Esc V T, Command-Y
Rulers	Esc V R, Command-Option-U
Grid Lines	Esc V G, Command-Option-I
Options	Esc V O
Go to Page	Esc V P, Command-T
Body Pages	Esc V Shift-B, Command-Option-B
Master Pages	Esc V Shift-M, Command-Option-M
Reference Pages	Esc V Shift-R, Command-Option-R

The following table provides shortcuts for commands on the Special menu in a document window.

Special Menu Commands

Command	Press
Page Break	Esc S P B, Shift-Enter
Anchored Frame	Esc S A, Command-H
Footnote	Esc S F, Command-E
Cross-Reference	Esc S C, Command-K
Variable	Esc S V, Command-B
Marker	Esc S M, Command-J
Conditional Text	Esc S Shift-C, Command-5
Table of Contents	Esc T O C
Index	Esc I X
Add Disconnected Pages	Esc S P A, Command-Option-A
Delete Pages	Esc S P D, Command-Option-D

The following table provides shortcuts for commands on the Graphics menu in a document window.

Graphics Menu Commands

Command	Press
Group	Esc G G
Ungroup	Esc G U
Bring to Front	Esc G F
Send to Back	Esc G B
Align	Esc G A
Distribute	Esc G D
Reshape	Esc G R
Smooth	Esc G S
Unsmooth	Esc G M
Flip Up/Down	Esc G V
Flip Left/Right	Esc G H
Rotate	Esc G T
Scale	Esc G Z
Set # Sides	Esc G N
Join	Esc G J
Object Properties	Esc G O
Pick up Properties	Esc G Shift-O
Runaround Properties	Esc G Shift-R
Gravity	Esc G Y
Snap	Esc G P

The following table provides shortcuts for commands on the Table menu in a document window.

Table Menu Commands

Command	Press
Insert Table	Esc T I
Table Designer	Esc T D
Row Format	Esc T R
Custom Ruling & Shading	Esc T X
Add Rows or Columns	Esc T A
Resize Columns	Esc T Z
Straddle/Unstraddle	Esc T L
Convert to Table/ Convert to Paragraphs	Esc T V
Sort	Esc T S

Working in windows and dialog boxes

The following table provides shortcuts to display a window or dialog box and make it active. If it is already open but is behind another window, these shortcuts bring it to the front.

Windows and Dialog Box Shortcuts	
To display and make it active	Use this shortcut
Current document window	Esc Shift-F I D
Find/Change	Esc Shift-F I F
Hypertext	Esc Shift-F I H
Marker	Esc Shift-F I M
Spelling Checker	Esc Shift-F I S
Paragraph Designer	Esc Shift-F I P
Character Designer	Esc Shift-F I C
Conditional Text	Esc Shift-F I O
Custom Ruling and Shading	Esc Shift-F I R
Table Designer	Esc Shift-F I T

The following table provides shortcuts to use in the Paragraph and Character Designers.

Paragraph and Character Designer	
To	Use this shortcut
Change all settings to As Is	Command-Shift-X
Change all settings to match selected text	Command-Shift-V
Display the previous set of properties	Esc P P, Page Up
Display the next set of properties	Esc P N, Page Down
Apply only the current group of properties	Option-click Apply

Documents

The following table provides shortcuts for opening, saving, and closing files.

Opening, Saving, and Closing files	
To	Use this shortcut
Open a document in a book file	Double-click the filename in the book window
Open all files in an active book window	Esc F Shift-O, or press Shift and choose Open All Files in Book from the File menu
Display the Save Document dialog box	Esc F A
Save a document or book	Esc F S, Command-S
Save all open files (also save all files in a book from an active book window)	Esc F Shift-S, or press Shift and choose File > Save All Open Files
Close all open files (also close all files in a book from an active book window)	Esc F Shift-C, or press Shift and choose File > Close All Open Files

The following table provides shortcuts for zooming.

Zooming Shortcuts	
To	Use this shortcut
Zoom in one zoom setting	Esc Z I
Zoom out one zoom setting	Esc Z O
Fit page in window	Esc Z P
Fit window to page	Esc Z W
Fit window to text frame	Esc Z F
Zoom to 100 percent	Esc Z Z

Spell checking

The following table provides shortcuts to use while you're spell checking a document or book.

Spell Checking Shortcuts	
To	Use this shortcut
Check selected text or a word containing the insertion point	Esc L S, or Option-click Start Checking in the Spelling Checker window
Check entire document	Esc L E
Check current page	Esc L P
Correct a word	Esc L C W
Add a word to your personal dictionary	Esc L A P
Add a word to the document dictionary	Esc L A D
Add a word to automatic corrections	Esc L A C
Delete a word from your personal dictionary	Esc L X P
Delete a word from the document dictionary	Esc L X D
Clear automatic corrections	Esc L C A
Create a file of unknown words	Esc L B
Mark all paragraphs for rechecking	Esc L R
Show a word's hyphenation	Esc L hyphen

Graphics tasks

The following table provides shortcuts for some common graphics tasks.

Graphics Shortcuts	
To	Press
Quick-copy a selected object	Option-drag object
Rotate a selected object arbitrarily	Press Command and drag a corner or reshape handle
Move an object along vertical or horizontal axis	Shift-drag object
Move object 1 point	Option-arrow key
Move object 6 points	Option-Shift-arrow key
Shrink wrap an anchored frame (shrink frame to an object and position at the insertion point)	Esc M P
Unwrap an anchored frame (enlarge the frame)	Esc M E
Turn text runaround off for a selected graphic	Esc G Q
To align object along	Use this shortcut
Tops	Esc J T, Command-Option-Up arrow
Top/bottom centers	Esc J M
Bottoms	Esc J B, Command-Option-Down arrow
Left sides	Esc J L, Command-Option-Left arrow, Command-Shift-L
Left/right centers	Esc J C, Command-Shift-C
Right sides	Esc J R, Command-Option-Right arrow, Command-Shift-R

Miscellaneous

The following table provides some
miscellaneous shortcuts.

Miscellaneous Shortcuts	
To	Press
Display online help	Esc F H, F1
Redisplay a document or refresh screen display	Esc W R, Control-L
Lock or unlock a document or book	Esc Shift-F L K
Display the Color Definitions dialog box	Press Esc V C D
Turn side-head area on or off	Esc J P Shift-S
Undo some FrameMaker commands	Command-Z, F1
Turn display of graphics off or on	Esc V V
Insert a marker	Esc M K, Command-Option-K
Insert a hypertext marker	Esc M H
Open the Edit Custom Marker Type dialog box	Esc E M T
Display the Show/Hide Conditional Text dialog box	Esc V Shift-C, Command-Option-V
Turn condition indicators on or off	Esc V Shift-O
Select all the text around the insertion point with same condition tag settings	Esc H Shift-C

SPECIAL CHARACTERS

As you type text into a FrameMaker document, you'll eventually need to use special characters, such an en or em dash or nonbreaking space. Or you may need to type accented characters for a foreign language. You may also need to enter characters that don't appear on the keyboard into a text box in a dialog box.

You use combinations of keys to type bullets, dashes, fixed-width spaces, and accented characters such as ç, ñ, and ö.

If the Symbol font is installed on your system, you can type any of the symbols in that font. If Zapf Dingbats font (or any other "picture" font) is installed on your system, you can type any of the special symbols in that font.

You may also need to enter characters that don't appear on the keyboard into the text box in a dialog box.

✔ Tips

■ The Quick Reference sections in online help contains all the special characters listed in this appendix.

■ The online manual, *FrameMaker Character Sets*, lists the character sets used for FrameMaker 7.0 documents using Western fonts, and shows how to type each character in the set.

Typing Special Characters

In the sections that follow,:

◆ A hyphen indicates that each key must be pressed simultaneously. For example, "Ctrl-C" means to press the Control and C keys at the same time.

◆ If the key sequence does not contain a hyphen, then press each key one after the other, for example, "Esc space T" means to press the Escape key, then the spacebar, then the T key.

◆ Keys are expressed as uppercase letters to match what you see on the keyboard. If you need to actually type an uppercase letter, the key Shift is added to the sequence. For example, Esc F Shift-S means to press the Escape key, then the F key, then an uppercase S.

(Windows only) These are the abbreviations used for the keys in the sections that follow:

◆ Ctrl for the Control key

◆ Alt for the Alt key

Note that some of the characters in this appendix are shown larger than the font size of their surrounding text. For example, the trademark and registered trademark symbols are shown at 18 points.

✔ Tips

■ If you experience any problems using special characters, check to make sure that the Caps Lock key is off,

■ You do not need Symbol font or Zapf Dingbats installed to use these special characters.

■ Thin spaces are very useful for situations where you want just a little extra space as in the following example: (%). I added thin spaces around the percent sign to give it a little "breathing space" within its parentheses.

■ What's the difference between an en dash and an em dash?

▲ En dashes are used to describe a range, for example, "June 15–July 15."

▲ Em dashes express an interruption in thought or enclose a parenthetical expression, for example, "Just when you think it's safe to go back into the water—you see a shark circling!"

Windows

The following table includes keystrokes for typing special characters in the document window in Windows.

Special Characters (Window)	
Character	**Keystrokes**
• (bullet)	Ctrl-Q %
† (dagger)	Ctrl-Q space
‡ (double dagger)	Ctrl-Q '
™ (trademark)	Ctrl-Q *
© (copyright)	Ctrl-Q)
® (registered trademark)	Ctrl-Q (
¶ (paragraph symbol)	Ctrl-Q &
§ (section or end-of-flow symbol)	Ctrl-Q $
... (ellipsis)	Ctrl-Q Shift-I
— (em dash)	Ctrl-Q Shift-Q
– (en dash)	Ctrl-Q Shift-P
' (with Smart Quotes on)	Ctrl-'
" (with Smart Quotes on)	Esc "
' (with Smart Quotes off)	Ctrl-Q Shift-T
' (with Smart Quotes off)	Ctrl-Q Shift-U
" (with Smart Quotes off)	Ctrl-Q Shift-R
" (with Smart Quotes off)	Ctrl-Q Shift-S
Em space	Esc space M, Ctrl-Shift-space
En space	Esc space N, Alt-Ctrl-space
Nonbreaking space	Esc space H, Ctrl-space
Numeric space	Esc space 1 (one)
Thin space	Esc space T
Nonbreaking hyphen	Esc hyphen H
Forced (soft) return	Shift-Enter

Mac OS

The following table includes keystrokes for typing special characters in the document window in Mac OS.

Special Characters (Mac OS)	
Character	**Keystrokes**
• (bullet)	Control-Q %, Option-8
† (dagger)	Control-Q space, Option-T
‡ (double dagger)	Control-Q ', Shift-Option-7
™ (trademark)	Control-Q *, Option-2
© (copyright)	Control-Q), Option-G
® (registered trademark)	Control-Q (, Option-R
¶ (paragraph symbol)	Control-Q &, Option-7
§ (section or end-of-flow symbol)	Control-Q $, Option-6
... (ellipsis)	Control-Q Shift-I, Option-;
— (em dash)	Shift-Option-hyphen
– (en dash)	Option-hyphen
' (with Smart Quotes on)	Option-'
" (with Smart Quotes on)	Option-"
' (with Smart Quotes off)	Option-]
' (with Smart Quotes off)	Option-}
" (with Smart Quotes off)	Option-[
" (with Smart Quotes off)	Option-{
Em space	Esc space M, Command-Option-9
En space	Esc space N, Command-Option-8
Nonbreaking space	Esc space H, Option-space
Numeric space	Esc space 1 (one), Command-Option-o (zero)
Thin space	Esc space T, Command-Option-7
Nonbreaking hyphen	Esc hyphen H, Command-'
Forced (soft) return	Shift-Return, Option-Return, Enter

Typing Accented Characters

Even if you work mainly in English language documents, you may want to use a word from another language that uses accented characters. The relevant letters are shown below. Windows and Mac OS keystrokes are the same.

Accented Characters	
Accent	Keystroke
acute	Esc ' (apostrophe) then the letter: é, É
grave	Esc ' (left quote) then the letter: à, À
tilde	Esc ~ (tilde) then the letter: ñ, Ñ
diaeresis	Esc % (percent) then the letter: ü, Ü
circumflex	Esc ^ (caret) then the letter: ô, Ô
ring	Esc * (asterisk) then the letter: å, Å
cedilla	Esc , (comma) then the letter: ç, Ç

✔ Tip

- ■ Some of these keystrokes are mnemonic in nature, that is, what you type has some sort of cue to help you remember. Here are some that may help you:
  - ▲ The words "acute" and "apostrophe" both start with the letter "a."
  - ▲ A grave accent looks like the a left quote.
  - ▲ A percent sign has two "dots" like a diaeresis accent.
  - ▲ A caret looks exactly like a circumflex.
  - ▲ The words "cedilla" and "comma" both start with the letter "c."

Typing in Dialog Boxes

You can enter many characters in a dialog box by pressing the corresponding keys on the keyboard.

Windows

If a character doesn't appear on the keyboard, you can usually enter the character by using the character's key sequence beginning with a backslash (\ ). Although the backslash appears in the dialog box, it will not appear in the document itself.

The following table shows the sequences to type in a dialog box. In a few cases, you can choose between two backslash sequences for a character. In these cases, the sequences are separated by a comma.

Typing in Windows Dialog Boxes	
Character	Keystrokes
• (bullet)	\B
† (dagger)	\D
‡ (double dagger)	\Shift-D
... (ellipsis)	\E
— (em dash)	\M
– (en dash)	\N
‹ (with Smart Quotes off)	\"
" (with Smart Quotes off)	\'
" (with Smart Quotes off)	\'
Em space	\SM, Shift-M
En space	\SN, Shift-N
Nonbreaking space	\space
Numeric space	\S#, \#
Thin space	\ST, \I
Hyphen	\- (hyphen)
Nonbreaking hyphen	\+ (plus)
Suppress hyphenation	_ (underscore)
Forced (soft) return	\R
Tab character	\T
Trademark serif	\Shift-T Shift-M

Mac OS

You type characters in Mac OS dialog boxes in the same way as you type them in a document window. However, for the following characters, you can also type a backslash sequence.

Typing in Mac OS Dialog Boxes

Character	Keystrokes
– (en dash)	\N
— (em dash)	\M
Em space	\SM, Shift-M
En space	\SN, Shift-N
Numeric space	\S#, \#
Thin space	\ST, \l
Nonbreaking hyphen	\+
Forced (soft) return	\R
Tab character	\

✔ Tips

- For a literal backslash in a dialog box, type two backslashes in a row (\\).

- If you are using a cross-reference format with a page number of the format "page xx" type a nonbreaking space between the word "page" and the building block for the page number (**Figure B.1**).

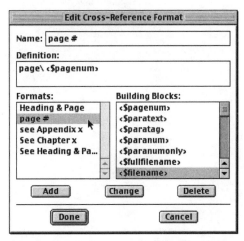

Figure B.1 Create a new cross-reference format or edit an existing one, choose Special > Cross-Reference > Edit Format.

GLOSSARY

This glossary contains both terms that are specific to FrameMaker and others that are general publishing and Web terms.

A

Adobe Acrobat
The program used to customize PDF files by editing them and adding PDF-specific features such as bookmarks.

Adobe Acrobat Distiller
The tool in Adobe Acrobat that converts PostScript files to PDF format. The latest version of Acrobat Distiller is included with FrameMaker 7.0. *See also* PDF.

Adobe Acrobat eBook Reader
A tool that allows you to read electronic books and annotate and search their pages.

Adobe Acrobat Reader
The tool in Adobe Acrobat that allows users to view and print PDF documents. The latest version of Acrobat Reader is included with FrameMaker 7.0. Both Acrobat Reader and eBook Reader are available free from the Adobe Web site: www.adobe.com. *See also* PDF; tagged Adobe PDF.

Adobe Online

Provides access to up-to-the-minute information about services, products, and tips for using Adobe products You can set up Adobe Online so that Adobe notifies you when new information is available. View and download new files whenever you wish using the Help > Updates command.

Adobe Type Manager (ATM)

A font utility that allows your computer to use PostScript fonts so you can view and print them.

altText

Text that describes graphical elements in a document so people with visual disabilities can make sense of the document's contents. For example, for a chart showing financial data, the altText could be a summary of the data, which could be read by a screen reader.

anchored frame

A frame for graphics anchored to text in a text column. When you edit the text, the frame and its contents move along with the text automatically. To add an anchored frame, choose Special > Anchored Frame. *See also* unanchored graphic frame.

As Is setting

Indicates that a text selection has mixed properties, for example, two paragraphs with different alignments. Also indicates that a property should be left unchanged when you apply settings.

attribute

In a structured document, provides optional information about an element that is not part of the element's content. For example, an attribute could describe the draft version of a Chapter element. *See also* element; structured document.

Autoconnect

A flow property that controls whether a new page is generated when you come to the end of the last text frame of a text flow. If Autoconnect isn't on and you keep typing, a solid line appears at the bottom of the last text frame of a flow.

B

bitmap

Defines a display space and the color for each pixel or "bit" in the display space. GIF and JPEG are examples of graphic image file types that contain bitmaps. Typically, an image is created using vector graphics and then is converted to (or saved as) a raster graphic file or bitmap. *See also* raster graphic file; vector graphic file.

BMP (Bitmap)

Windows native graphic bitmap file format that generally uses the file suffix `.bmp`. For Web use, you should convert to GIF, JPEG, or other Web-friendly format. *See also* GIF; JPEG.

body page

One of the three types of pages in a FrameMaker document and the place where you do most of your work. You enter text by typing in the document window. When you reach the end of a page, FrameMaker automatically creates a new page. To display body pages, choose View > Body Pages. *See also* master page; reference page.

book file

A file that contains the filenames of documents in a book, as well as specifications for how the files should be paginated and numbered. Book files contain both document files and generated files, such as TOCs and indexes. *See also* generated file.

book window

A window that appears when you open a book file, displaying all of the files that compose the book, including generated files.

C

Cascading Style Sheet (.css)

A file that contains formatting specifications that duplicate the font, style, size, indents, spacing, and margins of the original document. When you save a FrameMaker document as HTML, a `.css` file is automatically created in the same folder as the HTML file.

change bar
A vertical line in the page margin that indicates an addition, change, or deletion of text.

Character Catalog
Contains character formats that have been created and stored to ensure consistent formatting of characters, words, and phrases.

Character Designer
A window in which you create and change character formats and store them in the Character Catalog. *See also* Character Catalog; Paragraph Designer; Table Designer.

character format
The text format that affects only selected text in a paragraph—in other words, it overrides the paragraph format. When you use a character format to change selected text within a paragraph, you can change a number of font properties of the text without changing the rest of the paragraph. *See also* paragraph format.

CMYK
A model used to simulate the appearance of any color by using just four colors of ink or toner: cyan, magenta, yellow, and black. The term "four-color process printing" refers to the CMYK color model. *See also* RGB.

condition indicator
Changes to the appearance of conditional text that make it easy to identify, for example, red and underlined text. You can turn condition indicators on or off; when they are on, they are printable. To turn condition indicators on and off, choose Special > Conditional Text > Show/Hide.

condition tag
The name of a version of a conditional document.

conditional document
A document that contains the text for several versions; it includes both unconditional text, which appears in all versions, and conditional text, which appears in one or more versions.

conditional text
Content specific to a version of a document. You can make any unit of text conditional. You can also conditionalize anchored graphics, tables, cross-references, footnotes, markers, and table rows (but not columns). To apply condition tags or create new ones, choose Special > Conditional Text. *See also* condition indicator; unconditional text.

D

document dictionary
A list of acceptable words in a particular document for the purpose of spell checking; FrameMaker uses this dictionary regardless of who is working in the document. *See also* personal dictionary; site dictionary.

DTD (Document Type Definition)
A collection of structural and validity rules for an SGML or XML document. The DTD spells out which elements and attributes are allowed and in what order. An internal DTD can also be part of the XML document itself. *See also* EDD; schema; XML Schema.

E

EDD (Element Definition Document)
A file that contains element definitions for a a structured document. It includes both the structural rules for the document and the style rules. *See also* DTD.

element
There are two classes of elements: container elements, which can hold text, other elements, or both; and object elements, which are single objects, such as a marker, cross-reference, or anchored frame. In a structured document, an element's definition has content rules that determine what the element can be.

Element Catalog
In a structured document, lists the elements that you can use at the current location, provides commands for adding and editing elements, and may display other information about the current location, such as whether you can type text.

end-of-flow symbol

A nonprinting symbol (§) that appears at the end of the text in a text flow when text symbols are on. You can't put the insertion point after an end-of-flow symbol.

EPS (Encapsulated PostScript)

A graphic file format supported by many graphics applications, such as Adobe Illustrator. You can import EPS files into FrameMaker.

F

font subsetting

The action that Acrobat Distiller takes to embed only a subset of characters used in a document, as opposed to embedding an entire font when creating a PDF file.

format override

Difference between the format of text or tables in a document and the corresponding format in the Paragraph, Character, or Table Catalog.

FrameMaker dictionary

A collection of words and hyphenation information that FrameMaker uses to check spelling and hyphenate words. *See also* document dictionary; main dictionary; personal dictionary; site dictionary.

G

generated file

A file such as a TOC, list of procedures, or index, created by extracting paragraphs or marker text from one or more document files in a book.

GIF (Graphics Interchange Format)

A graphics file format. GIF, along with JPEG, is one of the two most common file formats for graphic images on the Web. It generally uses the file suffix .gif. GIF is a de facto standard image format on the Internet.

graphic frame

In FrameMaker a rectangular frame, which can be anchored or unanchored, that control the position of graphics. *See also* anchored frame; reference frame; unanchored graphic frame.

H

HTML (Hypertext Markup Language)

The set of markup symbols or codes inserted in a file intended for display on a Web browser page. The markup tells the Web browser how to display a Web page's words and images for the user. Each individual piece of markup code is referred to as an element or a tag.

hypertext

Refers to the linking and display of related information on different pages or in different documents. In FrameMaker you can add hypertext links to create online and Web-ready documents. FrameMaker can also add hypertext links automatically to generated files.

J

JPEG (Joint Photographic Experts Group)

A graphic image format commonly used to display photographs and other continuous-tone images on the Web. Together with GIF and PNG, JPEG is one of the image file formats supported on the Web. It generally uses the file suffix .jpg.

L

leading

The white space between lines in a paragraph, usually measured in points. *See also* line spacing.

line spacing

The space between lines in a paragraph, measured from the baseline of one line to the baseline of the next. *See also* leading.

logical structure

The organization of a document, such as title page, chapters, sections, and subsections.

LZW data compression

A good, all-purpose data compression technique that replaces strings of characters with single codes. TIFF file format supports LZW compression. *See also* TIFF.

M

main dictionary
Contains words found in a standard dictionary. You can't change the contents of this FrameMaker dictionary.

marker
In a FrameMaker document, a nonprinting character (T) that you insert to indicate an index entry, the source of a cross-reference, a hypertext command, or conditional text.

master page
A nonprinting FrameMaker page that contains the page design for body pages. A master page can include background text and graphics and template text frames. You can create custom master pages for special types of pages, such as the opening page of a chapter. To display master pages, choose View > Master Pages. *See also* body page.

metadata
Descriptive information about an individual document that can be searched and processed by a computer. Metadata can provide information about the contents of a document to other applications.

MIF (Maker Interchange Format)
A text file that contains a group of statements describing a FrameMaker document, used to exchange information between FrameMaker and other applications.

MML (Maker Markup Language)
A text file that contains statements that define a document's content and format. You can create an MML file using a text editor. When you open the MML file, FrameMaker interprets the statements and applies the correct formats.

O

OLE (Object Linking and Embedding)
(Windows only) OLE is Microsoft's framework for a compound document technology, something like a display desktop. In FrameMaker you can use OLE when importing graphics by reference.

orphan
A line of text that is "stranded" at the top or bottom of a page or column of text. You can set orphan control options for paragraphs in the Paragraph Designer and for table rows in the Table Designer. *See also* widow.

P

PANTONE® MATCHING SYSTEM (PMS)
A standard system for specifying ink or toner colors based on the CMYK color model. Used most extensively in the US. *See also* CMYK.

paragraph
In FrameMaker, anything that ends with a nonprinting end-of-paragraph symbol (¶) is treated as a paragraph. For example, in this glossary, the title "Glossary" is a paragraph, as are each letter heading, term, and definition.

Paragraph Catalog
Contains formats that have been created and stored to ensure consistent formatting of paragraphs.

Paragraph Designer
A window in which you create and choose paragraph formats and store them in the Paragraph Catalog. It includes the following groups of paragraph properties: Basic, Default Font, Pagination, Numbering, Advanced, and Table Cell. *See also* Character Designer; Paragraph Catalog; Table Designer.

paragraph format
The formatting information for a paragraph, including the typography, overall shape, tab settings, pagination, heading style, autonumbering, and special settings for paragraphs in table cells. *See also* character format; Paragraph Catalog; Paragraph Designer.

paragraph symbol
The symbol (¶) that appears at the end of a paragraph when text symbols are on. *See also* text symbols.

PDF (Portable Document Format)

The standard for electronic document distribution. Adobe PDF is a universal file format that preserves all of the fonts, formatting, graphics, and color of a source document regardless of the application and platform used to create it. PDF files can be viewed on virtually any platform using Acrobat Reader. *See also* Adobe Acrobat.

personal dictionary

A dictionary of words that you use often and that you can tell FrameMaker to use when you spell check a document (for example, your name). *See also* document dictionary; site dictionary.

PNG (Portable Network Graphic)

A graphics file format used as an alternative to GIF for displaying images on the Web. PNG format preserves all color information and uses lossless compression to reduce file size.

PostScript (PS)

A technology developed and trademarked by Adobe Systems that describes the appearance of text and graphics in a document.

R

raster graphics

Digital images created or captured as a set of samples of a given space. A raster is a grid of x and y coordinates on a display space. A raster image file identifies which of these coordinates to illuminate in monochrome or color values. A raster file is usually larger than a vector graphics image file. Examples of raster image file types are BMP, TIFF, GIF, and JPEG.

reference frame

An unanchored graphic frame on a reference page in a FrameMaker document. A graphic, such as a rule or icon, placed in a reference frame can be used in a paragraph format. *See also* reference page.

reference page

A non-printing page containing reference frames that can be used above and below paragraphs. Reference pages store frequently used graphics that you want to position consistently throughout a document, specifications for generated files such as TOCs and indexes, and mappings between FrameMaker formats and HTML tags. To display reference pages, choose View > Reference Pages. *See also* body page; master page.

reshape handles

Small, black, square handles on a curve that define the curve and control its location. *See also* selection handles.

runaround text

Text flowing around a graphic.

run-in head

A type of special heading that sits on the same line as the following normal body text, but is in its own separate paragraph, typically with a different font or weight for contrast. Because run-in heads are in their own paragraph, you can include them in TOCs, create cross-references to them, include them in headers and footers, and so on.

running header or footer

A header or footer, the text of which depends on the corresponding body page's contents. Running H/F system variables allow you to specify the contents of running headers and footers on a master page. *See also* master page; system variable.

S

schema

A set of rules that specify which elements and attributes are allowed or required in a complying document. A schema defines what elements the document(s) can contain and in what order, their content, and what attributes the elements can contain. *See also* DTD; XML schema.

selection handles

Eight small, black, square handles that appear around a selected object. *See also* reshape handles.

SGML (Standard Generalized Markup Language)
The international standard for all markup languages for data exchange and storage. SGML is a descriptive rather than a procedural language, meaning that the same document can be processed by different systems, each applying different processing instructions. You can transfer SGML documents from one system to another without loss of data.

site dictionary
A list of words that FrameMaker uses for spell checking; usually contains technical terms common to your site or workgroup, for example, the company name and product names. *See also* document dictionary; personal dictionary.

small caps
Capital letters that are not full height. A true small cap typeface retains the appropriate character weight but offers it at a smaller size.

Smart Quotes
A FrameMaker feature that automatically inserts the appropriate left or right single ('_') or double ("_") quotation marks as you type. To turn Smart Quotes on or off, choose Format > Document > Text Options.

Smart Spaces
A FrameMaker feature that prevents extra spaces when editing text. To turn Smart Spaces on or off, choose Format > Document > Text Options.

snap grid
The invisible grid that attracts objects to it as you draw, rotate, resize, or drag objects. Choose Graphics > Snap. *See also* visible grid.

spot color
A color that is printed with a single color ink or toner rather than as a process color. Spot color can be a very cost-effective means of adding color to a printed document.

spread
The horizontal space between individual pairs of letters and numbers. Font sets come with letter spacing information so that letters and numbers appear evenly spaced. In monospaced fonts, such as Courier, every character has the same width and letter spacing. Also known as letter spacing or kerning.

Structure View
In structured documents, a window that shows a hierarchy of elements for the current document or flow that contains the insertion point. It also identifies errors in the document's structure. The structured document window and the Structure View are both editable, and any change made in one is reflected in the other.

structured application
A collection of files that describes how to process a structured file; usually includes a DTD and other items, such as read/write rules and a template. *See also* DTD; EDD.

structured document
A document created in the Structured FrameMaker interface, including the Structure View and Element Catalog, which help you organize SGML and XML elements in a valid structure. FrameMaker can import and export structured documents in either SGML or XML format. *See also* SGML; XML.

Subscribe
(Mac OS only) An alternative to the File > Import > File command when importing graphics by reference.

SVG (Scalable Vector Graphics)
A graphics file format and Web development language based on XML. When you import SVG graphics into a document, FrameMaker automatically rasterizes them; when you create HTML, XML, and SGML files, you can output the raster version or the original SVG code.

system variable
A built-in variable used mainly in running headers and footers. For example, you can use a system variable to display the current date, current page number, or total number of pages in a document. To add a system variable, choose Special > Variable. *See also* user variable.

T

Table Catalog
Contains formats that have been created and stored to ensure consistent formatting of tables. Formats stored in the Table Catalog are accessible from the Insert Table dialog box and the Table Designer.

Table Designer
A window in which you can create and change table formats and store them in the Table Catalog. You can access the following groups of table properties: Basic, Ruling, and Shading. *See also* Character Designer; Paragraph Designer; Table Catalog.

table format
The formatting information for a table, including its indents, alignment, placement on the page, placement of the table title, and ruling and shading for table rows and columns. This information can be stored in the Table Catalog.

Tagged Adobe PDF
An enhancement to the PDF specification that allows PDF files to contain logical document structure, which refers to the organization of a document, such as the title page, chapters, sections, and subsections. Tagged Adobe PDF documents can be viewed on a broad range of devices, such as handheld devices and ultra-compact laptops, and thus offer better support for repurposing of content.

text flow
The text in a series of connected text frames. A text flow can also be contained in a single text frame, unconnected to any other.

text frame
A rectangular frame that controls placement of the document text. *See also* anchored frame; reference frame; unanchored graphic frame.

text insert
Text imported by reference into a FrameMaker document from another document, from a file created in another application, or from a text file. A text insert is linked to text in the source document; when the source text changes, FrameMaker automatically updates the insert.

text line
In FrameMaker, a graphic object created with the Text Line tool that contains a single line of text. A one-line callout is most often a text line; a longer callout might be multiple text lines or a text frame. *See also* text frame.

TIFF (Tagged-Image File Format)
A graphics file format used to exchange files between applications and computer platforms. It generally uses the file suffix `.tif`.

TrueType
A font format developed by Apple Systems, Inc., and licensed to Microsoft. TrueType fonts are natively supported by Windows and Mac OS. On Mac OS, both the printer and screen fonts are combined in a single TrueType font suitcase file.

U

unanchored graphic frame
Used to crop graphics that stay in the same place on the page. You can also use an unanchored graphic frame to hold reference art. Graphics placed in unanchored frames will not be exported to HTML, Microsoft Word, or RTF. *See also* anchored frame; reference frame.

unstructured document
In FrameMaker, a document created in the standard FrameMaker interface.

unwrap
In a structured document, describes the action of removing a parent element from its child elements—in effect, unwrapping them. *See also* wrap.

user variable
A variable that you can define to use in place of text that appears repeatedly, for example, a product name or book title. To add a user variable, choose Special > Variable. *See also* system variable.

V

variable
Text that is defined once but that can be used several times. Variables are updated automatically when their values change. *See also* system variable; user variable.

vector graphic
A graphic composed of mathematically defined lines and curves in a given two- or three-dimensional space. *See also* bitmap.

vector graphics file
The file that results from a graphic artist's work, created and saved as a sequence of vector statements. At some point, a vector image is converted into a raster graphics image. Most images created with tools such as Adobe Illustrator are in the form of vector image files. *See also* raster graphics file.

visible grid
In FrameMaker, the grid that appears as horizontal and vertical lines on screen but not on the printed page. To turn on the visible grid, choose View > Grid Lines. *See also* snap grid.

W

WebDAV (Web Distributed Authoring and Versioning)
A set of extensions to the Hypertext Transfer Protocol (HTTP) that facilitates collaborative editing and file management among users located remotely from each other on the Internet.

WebWorks Publisher Standard Edition
A tool for converting FrameMaker documents to multiple online formats, including HTML, dynamic HTML, eBook formats for Microsoft Reader and Palm Reader, and XML. It comes standard with FrameMaker 7.0. *See also* HTML.

widow
A short word or part of a word that breaks over to a new line of text, a situation to be avoided if possible. Widow control options are set in the Paragraph Designer's Pagination properties. *See also* orphan.

wrap
In a structured document, describes the action of adding a parent element to one or more child elements—in effect, "wrapping" them. *See also* unwrap.

X

XML (Extensible Markup Language)
A metalanguage, or a language for creating language; a flexible way to create common information formats and share both the format and the data over the Internet. XML describes document content in terms of the data that is being described. For example, the word "phonenum" placed within markup tags might indicate that the data that followed was a phone number. Depending on how the application on the receiving computer wants to handle the phone number, the number could be stored, displayed, or dialed. *See also* HTML.

XML schema
One of two principal systems (the other is DTD) for writing a schema for an XML document. An XML schema, written in XML itself, lets you define both global and local elements. See also DTD; schema; XML.

INDEX

Symbols

INDEX

INDEX